Imaging and Mapping Eastern Europe

Imaging and Mapping Eastern Europe puts images centre stage and argues for the agency of the visual in the construction of Europe's east as a socio-political and cultural entity. This book probes into the discontinuous processes of mapping the eastern European space and imaging the eastern European body. Beginning from the renaissance maps of Sarmatia Europea, it moves onto images of women in ethnic dress on the pages of travellers' reports from the Balkans, to cartoons of children bullied by dictators in the satirical press, to Cold War cartography, and it ends with photos of protesting crowds on contemporary dust jackets.

Studying the eastern European 'iconosphere' leads to engagement with issues central for image studies and visual culture: word and image relationship, overlaps between the codes of othering and self-fashioning, as well as interaction between the diverse modes of production specific to cartography, travel illustrations, caricature, and book cover design.

This book will be of interest to scholars in art history, visual culture, and central Asian, Russian and Eastern European studies.

Katarzyna Murawska-Muthesius teaches in the Department of History of Art at Birkbeck College, University of London. She was Deputy Director of the National Museum in Warsaw.

Cover image: Katarzyna Perlak, *Niolam Ja Se Kochaneczke* (I once had a lover), 2016. Film-still. ©Katarzyna Perlak.

Routledge Advances in Art and Visual Studies

This series is our home for innovative research in the fields of art and visual studies. It includes monographs and targeted edited collections that provide new insights into visual culture and art practice, theory, and research.

The Iconology of Abstraction
Non-Figurative Images and the Modern World
Edited by Krešimir Purgar

Liquid Ecologies in Latin American and Caribbean Art
Edited by Lisa Blackmore and Liliana Gómez

Contemporary Art, Photography, and the Politics of Citizenship
Vered Maimon

Contemporary Art and Capitalist Modernization
A Transregional Perspective
Edited by Octavian Esanu

Art and Merchandise in Keith Haring's Pop Shop
Amy Raffel

Art and Nature in the Anthropocene
Planetary Aesthetics
Susan Ballard

Imaging and Mapping Eastern Europe
Sarmatia Europea to Post-Communist Bloc
Katarzyna Murawska-Muthesius

Arts-Based Methods for Decolonising Participatory Research
Edited by Tiina Seppälä, Melanie Sarantou and Satu Miettinen

For a full list of titles in this series, please visit www.routledge.com/Routledge-Advances-in-Art-and-Visual-Studies/book-series/RAVS

Imaging and Mapping Eastern Europe

Sarmatia Europea to Post-Communist Bloc

Katarzyna Murawska-Muthesius

Routledge
Taylor & Francis Group

NEW YORK AND LONDON

First published 2021
by Routledge
605 Third Avenue, New York, NY 10158

and by Routledge
2 Park Square, Milton Park, Abingdon, Oxon, OX14 4RN

Routledge is an imprint of the Taylor & Francis Group, an informa business

Library of Congress Cataloging-in-Publication Data
A catalog record for this book has been requested

ISBN: 978-1-138-49085-7 (hbk)
ISBN: 978-1-032-00361-0 (pbk)
ISBN: 978-1-351-03442-5 (ebk)

Typeset in Sabon
by Apex CoVantage, LLC

To Michał and Stefan

Contents

Figures

Acknowledgements

During my work on this book, I have incurred many debts from scholars, friends, and institutions. I was lucky to obtain a Research Fellowship from The Leverhulme Trust for my research on cartography and cartoons of eastern Europe in 2003.

I would also like to thank those who generously gave me permissions to reproduce their own art works, maps, book covers, and other images: Steve Bell, Scott Clissold, Nicolas Grospierre, Zuzanna Lipińska, Katarzyna Perlak, Jonathan Pugh, and Valdis Šmits; Cambridge University Press, Central Library of Geography and Environmental Protection IGSO PAN in Warsaw, Geographical, London, Houghton Library Harvard University, Los Angeles County Museum of Art, Museum of Caricature in Warsaw, Oxford University Press, Palgrave, Prestel, Random House Group, Reaktion Books, JRP/RINGIER, Routledge, and SUNY Press.

I would like to acknowledge help and encouragement from my former teachers Lisa Tickner and Jon Bird at the earliest stages of working on this project. My special thanks go to my colleagues at Birkbeck College: Francis Ames Lewis, Tag Gronberg, Valerie Holman, Christine Lindey, Elizabeth McKellar, Robert Maniura, Simon Shaw-Miller, David Murray, and most of all, Leslie Topp. I had a privilege of spending two teaching semesters at the Institut für Kunst- und Bildgeschichte at Humboldt University in Berlin, and I owe gratitude for all kinds of intellectual stimuli and help to Adam Labuda, Hans Bredekamp, Charlotte Klonk, Katja Bernhardt, Constance Krüger, Paulina Ochman, and Barbara Lück.

The list of friends and colleagues who helped in a variety of ways is very long. Especially, I would like to send my thanks to Anu Allas, Edit Andras, Mathilde Arnoux, James Aulich, Lena Bader, Wojciech Bałus, Arnold Bartetzky, Djurdja Bartlett, Jérôme Bazin and Pascal Dubourg Glatigny, Timothy O. Benson, Elisabeth de Bièvre and John Onians, Wendy Bracewell, Ella Chmielewska, David Crowley, Marina Dmitrieva, Alex Drace-Francis, Norbert Götz, Elwira Grossman, Susan Haskins, George Hyde and Barbara Hyde, Agata Jakubowska, Irena Kossowska, Ludmilla Kostova, Lucia Kvočáková, Elżbieta Laskowska, Clément Layet, Paweł Leszkowicz and Tomek Kitliński, Joanna Kordjak, Zuzanna Lipińska, Amani Maihoub, Peter Martyn, Dóra Mérai, Sergiusz Michalski, John and Victoria Mitchell, Eszter Molnár, Magdalena Nieslony, Anca Oroveanu, the late Piotr Paszkiewicz, Bojana Pejić, György Péteri, Maria Piotrowska, Marija Podzorova, Carmen Popescu, Aneta Prasał-Wiśniewska, Karolina Prymlewicz, Magdalena Radomska, Susan Reid, Piotr Sikora, Marta Sylvestrová, Matylda Taszycka, Waldemar Tatarczuk, Sarah Wilson, Wojciech Tomasik, Ewa Toniak, Stefan Troebst, Dorota Tubielewicz Mattson, Nicholas Warr, Michael

Wintle, and Karolina Zychowicz. I am especially grateful to Isabella Vitti and Katie Armstrong at Routledge for their continuous patience and support.

I was very privileged to work closely with the late Piotr Piotrowski with whom I spent hours talking about eastern Europe. I am extremely lucky that my son Michał Murawski also explores the region as a social anthropologist. The most heartfelt thanks go to my husband Stefan Muthesius, who read and queered everything I have written on the topic. Without his patience, trust and love, this book would have never been finished.

Preface

This is a book about images of eastern Europe. Since 1989, a record number of publications have been devoted to the area in a massive attempt to fix its meaning and boundaries, to rewrite its history, and to reconceptualise its socio-political status as both the victim and locus of orientalist discourses. Hardly any of those studies include images. If so, they are few and far between, customarily treated as transparent vessels which simply 'illustrate' arguments expressed in words, and which do not seem to require any commentary.

Led by the belief that cognition is not solely linguistic, this book puts images centre stage and addresses them as the principal objects of inquiry. It claims that images, art and non-art alike, have played much underestimated roles as mediators in the construction of Europe's east as a political, spatial, and cultural entity. The entity is the keyword here, as the book focuses on the representations aiming to grasp the whole of the region, rather than on individual countries and ethnicities, customarily treated as *partes-pro-toto* of an otherwise nebulous idea of Eastern Europe. Not extending into the moving image, nor to the boundless sphere of mental mapping, the book focuses on static visual images which are graspable and reproducible. Looking at renaissance maps of Sarmatia Europea, at the images of women in ethnic costumes on the pages of travellers' reports from 'Turkey in Europe', at cartoons of children bullied by dictators in the satirical press, at the photos of protesting crowds on dust jackets designs, the book examines the ways of creating the region by mapping it and populating it with bodies. It is not a picture history of eastern Europe though, but an inquiry into the discontinuous ways of picturing the region, stretching over a long-time span, from the early modern era to the present.

This book would not have been written, had I not moved from Poland to Britain precisely at the time when eastern Europe emerged from behind the Berlin Wall and became the object of an immense scrutiny. It featured on the first pages of newspapers, in TV news and documentaries, and was the topic of articles in colour magazines, and of a plethora of books on the end of communism, of art projects, novels, and feature films. This was also the time when I was reinventing myself as an art historian who, brought up on iconology and trained as curator of Italian painting at the National Museum in Warsaw, had to face challenges posed by the New Art History. The production of visual knowledges about eastern Europe presented itself to me as an obvious subject of my new research, facilitated by new approaches offered by the then emerging discipline of Visual Culture. This project became my most long-standing research, stretching over two decades, from 1999 to 2020. There is no need to state that eastern Europe did not stand still during that time. Not only its name, its external and internal boundaries, its political alliances and economic status, kept shifting radically, but the sense of unity, so strong after the Fall of Wall, has been systematically disappearing. More disturbingly, the transformation of the socio-political ethos of some of the countries, the disavowal of democracy, hostility to immigrants, and the LGBTQ communities turned the otherised object of the 1990s into the othering subject of the 2010s, adding contradictory meanings to old images, and laying bare the contingency and temporality of my initial claims. This is what prompted me to finalise this book. The region was changing, while a study of its visual representation was missing.

Chapter 1, 'Welcome to Slaka', is a revised version of 'Welcome to Slaka, or, Does Eastern (Central) European Art Exist', published in *Third Text*, 18, no. 1, 2004: 25–40. Chapter 2, 'Mapping Eastern Europe' amalgamates articles 'Mapping the New Europe: Cartography, Cartoons and Regimes of Representation', *Centropa*, 4, no. 1, 2004: 4–18; and 'Mapping Eastern Europe: Cartography and Art History', *Artl@s Bulletin*, 2, no. 2 (Fall 2013): 14–25. Chapter 4, 'Mr Punch Draws Eastern Europe' is a rewritten version of 'On Small Nations and Bullied Children: Mr Punch Draws Eastern Europe', *The Slavonic and East European Review*, 84, no. 2 (2006): 279–305.

The book does not exclude Russia and the former republics of the Soviet Union, but my research focuses on the territory of the former 'satellites'. Most of the material presented in the book comes from Britain, but I have also used cartographic and travel-related sources from Italy, Germany and France, as well as North America, while the chapter on dust jackets, explores the Anglo-American world of academic publishing. I went for the lower key in the term eastern Europe, when applying it before the emergence of 'Eastern Europe' as a socio-political entity during the Cold War. I also use the term 'East Central Europe', much favoured after 2000.

Katarzyna Murawska-Muthesius
October 2020

1 Welcome to Slaka

Writing Slaka

Malcolm Bradbury's *Rates of Exchange*, shortlisted for the 1983 Booker Prize and proclaimed a 'penetrating satire' on east-west relations, describes the vicissitudes of a 'hapless Dr Petworth', teacher of linguistics at a lesser British university on his lecture tour around 'Eastern Europe's most rigidly controlled country', named Slaka.[1] Not to be found on any map, Slaka is a Cold War simulacrum of the other Europe behind the Iron Curtain. Its violent history and politics, unstable boundaries, and its hybrid heritage overridden by socialist realism have been constructed out of a plethora of primary features taken for the essence of the timeless 'eastern Europeanness'.

> Slaka is . . . the historic capital and quite the largest metropolis of that small dark nation of plain and marsh, mountain and factory known in all the history books as the bloody battlefield (*tulsto'ii uncard'ninu*) of central eastern Europe. Located by an at once kind and cruel geography at the confluence of many trade routes, going north and east, south and west, its high mountains not too high to cut it off, its broad rivers not too broad to obstruct passage, it is a land that has frequently flourished, prospered, been a centre of trade and barter, art and culture, but has yet more frequently been pummelled, fought over, raped, pillaged, conquered and opposed by the endless invaders through this all too accessible landscape. Swedes and Medes, Prussians and Russians, Asians and Thracians, Tartars and Cassocks, Mortars and Turds, indeed almost every tribe or race specialist in pillage and rape, have been there, as to some necessary destination, and left behind their imprint, their custom, their faiths, their architecture, their genes. This is a country that has been now big, now small, now virtually non-existent. Its inhabitants have seen its borders expand, contract and on occasion disappear from sight, and so confused is its past that the country could now be in a place quite different from that in which it started. And so its culture is a melting pot, its language a *potpourri*, its people a salad.[2]

Although the novel is set in the summer of the British Royal Wedding of 1981, and thus firmly anchored in British/western time, the Slakanian time unfolds in a different dimension. It is locked down at the heydays of communism, when the large portraits of the Party leaders surveyed the streets and the pictures of 'the happy workers and the clean tractors' monopolised museum rooms. By 1981, however, the communist Slaka had gone, the paraphernalia of Stalinism long demoted, destroyed, or shuffled away to the archives of eastern Europe's embarrassing past. Moreover, the summer of 1981 was marked by the workers' revolution in Poland, which made headlines both east and west, dismantling the status quo of the divided Europe. And yet, as testified by Bradbury's narrative, in the 1980s the end of the Cold War could not have been predicted, and the disjunction between the 'historic' western time and the frozen eastern European time could safely be posed as eternal, foreclosing any significant transfer between the two incompatible worlds. The last lines of the book assert the reader that Petworth's luggage with the smuggled manuscript of Katya Princip's dissenting novel, to be published in Paris, was destroyed by airport security.

The most ingenious of Bradbury's fabrications and the most pertinent vis-à-vis the professional expertise of Dr Petworth's is the Slakan language. This uncanny hybrid of Latin and Slavonic phonemes, morphemes, and syntax made comical by blending familiarity with incongruity, is elaborated into an explicit signifying code of what constitutes the essence of 'eastern Europeanness', the evidence of its impurity. During Petworth's visit to Slaka, it is indeed the language which becomes the terrain of 'a small revolution', prompted by some unspecified drive towards liberalisation and resulting in a short-lived displacement of doubled 'i' with doubled 'u' and back again. But in spite of its alterity, the Slakan language is not an obstacle for Dr Petworth. From the moment of crossing the border, his linguistic expertise allows him to mimic basic tenets of Slakan and to introduce himself to a Slakan airport officer with confidence: *Prif'sorii universitayii linguistici, hospitalito officiale*.[3] Even if Petworth's hosts, Slakan university lecturers, novelists, and ministry officials speak English fluently, they cannot match his skills. Their faults ('Do you surprise I like Hemingway?') are the markers of Slakanian otherness.[4] Petworth's lectures in Slaka on the 'transformation of English as a medium of international communication' discusses the inevitability of its distortion. And yet, behind the detached academic description of the process hides the implied binary of purity versus contamination, and the Self versus Other dichotomy.

The same focus on an inept English lies at the core of the novel's follow-up *Why Come to Slaka?* (Figure 1.3), a parody travel guide which grew out of the original introduction to *Rates of Exchange*, 'Visiting Slaka: a few brief hints'. Its major part is a phrase book which juxtaposes the comical phrases in faulty English to their ostensibly correct Slakan prototypes: 'Our artists love socialist realism/*No malori amico realismusim social'iskim*'.[5] The implied asymmetry between the incorrect English and the 'correct' Slakan makes clear that it is exclusively the Slakan 'I', attempting to represent itself in English, which is to be inferiorised and mocked, but not the other way round.[6] The Slakan speaker of English has been disempowered in advance and doomed to enunciate his/her difference – the English speaker of Slakan/Dr Petworth retains his authority, for his self-proclaimed correctness is unverifiable.

Concerned with the visual construction of eastern Europe, I began, somewhat perversely, from Bradbury's strategies of writing about Slaka, because they compressed the most pervasive tropes of eastern European discourse during the Cold War. At that time, the region was widely perceived as 'just one block',[7] as a uniform *terra socialistica*,[8] and the assumptions of its backwardness, instability, and propensity to subjugation gained the status of Jane Austen's 'truths universally acknowledged'. Bradbury's metaphors, including the emphasis on the region's 'cruel geography', comparing its culture to a '*pot-pourri*, its people to 'a salad', carrying the genes of 'endless invaders' were satirical versions of the regular tropes in western histories of eastern Europe, produced from the late 1950s onwards. Bearing metaphorical titles, such as 'lands between', those books would almost invariably include a paragraph on the absence of natural geographical boundaries, comparing the physical features of the territory to an organism 'with vertebrae and arteries but no external shell', open to penetration by 'marauders and interlopers' from all directions.[9] The notion of rape and conquest would indeed serve as the region's master narrative, turning into a key argument in major cultural disputes on the international scene. Among others, it was successfully adopted in Milan Kundera's claim of central Europe as 'kidnapped west' (1984).[10]

Eastern Europe as an imaginary land, however, is older than the Cold War. Bradbury was not the first to produce a satirical vision of a country invented from scratch, together with its name, history, and language. He followed the well-established rules of writing about unknown lands in general and about Europe's east in particular. Since Mozart's adoption of gibberish, Slavonic-sounding names for his entourage during his stay in Prague in 1786, or Anthony Hope's invention of Ruritania and Kravonia (1896),[11] an endless string of fictional kingdoms and dictatorial 'republics', located in this remote part of Europe and ruled by officials bearing names as bizarre as those of their countries, have been conjured up by twentieth-century novelists and satirists. They include Agatha Christie's Hertzoslovakia,[12] and more recently, a counter-guide to Molvania, 'the world's number one producer of beetroot', which was plainly modelled on Bradbury's Slaka, not to mention Slovetzia and Krakozhia, the autocratic countries invented for the sake of Hollywood.[13] As argued by Larry Wolff, 'the employment of nonsense in the rendering of Eastern Europe' constituted one of the ways of dealing with its disorienting geography and history, as well as with the incomprehensibility of its languages roundly perceived as hilarious.[14]

It was also Wolff who in his influential study of 1994 initiated the process of inquiry into the western invention of eastern Europe *tout court*. Examining eighteenth-century literature, travel diaries, and philosophical and socio-political pamphlets centred on Russia and Poland, he argued that the idea of a backward, barbarian, and underdeveloped eastern Europe was a cultural product of the Enlightenment, inseparable from the process of the invention of the modern western Self. Wolff's study was soon complemented by Maria Todorova's deconstruction of the derogatory discourse on the Balkans,[15] as well as by Vesna Goldsworthy's analysis of the literary perceptions of the Balkans in novels.[16] Those three books became the point of departure for an extensive transdisciplinary analysis of the rules of the discourse, representing eastern European societies and their culture in literature, the media and movies as well as in academe itself. Books, conferences, PhD dissertations, and articles followed in great numbers. Among the key topics examined were the notions of the 'east' and 'eastness' as the Other in identity formation, the Balkans as a metaphor, post-communist transition, gender politics, human rights and ethnic minorities, the rise of nationalist movements, as well as post-communist memory and nostalgia.[17] In the new millennium, the perception of eastern European migrants turned into the theme of TV documentaries, novels, and films, transgressing the boundaries of academic inquiry.[18] Although the terms 'image', 'imaging', and 'imagining' abound in the titles of those studies, the issue of visual representation of the region was raised just in a handful of texts.[19] As far as methods were concerned, the usability of postcolonial discourse analysis and its interpretive tools, as well as the question of the postcolonial status of the region dominated the debates.

Is 'Post' in Post-Communist the Same as 'Post' in Postcolonial?

So what kind of Other is the eastern European Other? The centuries of territorial conquest by the Habsburgs, Prussia, as well as by the Ottoman and Russian empires, experienced in different ways by individual states and regions, were followed by a political and economic submission to the Soviet Union, misleadingly seen as homogenous. Subsequently, at the post-communist stage, another form of surrender to western/global hegemony was underscored by the rhetoric of liberation and return to Europe. But how does the eastern European alterity compare to that invested in the postcolonial Other in Asia and Africa?

The image suggests an answer before the text. At the heyday of the Cold War confrontations, the colonial condition of eastern Europe and its affinity to that of the Third World was declared in almost purely visual terms, and with a surprising directness, by Leslie Illingworth's cartoon, published in *Punch* in April 1958 (Figure 1.1). Harold Macmillan and Nikita Khrushchev appear as boys with bunches of balloons in their hands, which stood for the Commonwealth and the Communist Bloc, respectively. By showing Macmillan, letting his balloons free and encouraging Khrushchev, who is holding his bunch tight, to do the same: '"Now let one of yours go – I dare you!"', the cartoon juxtaposed Britain's decolonisation policies to the unrelenting grip of Soviet Russia, which had just suppressed the Hungarian Revolution of 1956. Regardless of the standard Cold War emphasis on the moral superiority of capitalism over communism, this is one of the few western examples of a visual comparison between the Third World and the Second World, aligned on the basis of their subjection to foreign powers. By presenting communism as colonialism, Illingworth's cartoon formulated questions which would indeed be asked about communism for decades to come.[20]

At the same time, Illingworth's cartoon laid bare the ultra-conservative views of *Punch*, whose contribution to the construction of eastern Europe as an image will be the topic of Chapter 4. In communist visual rhetoric, the affinities between the Third World and the Second World would be expressed by the semi-utopian vision of the workers from all over the world, marching together in protest against the First World's capitalism and in defence of peace. For *Punch*, however, the idea of agency on the part of the colonised did not arise at all, eliminated as it was by the very choice of balloons as signifiers. Whether granted freedom or not, all the countries were represented as nothing more than toys in the hands of the rulers, as balloons which, when let free, would drift away with the wind, unable to steer a course. The disempowered do not speak. While the preferred reading of the cartoon reduces communism to colonialism, the oppositional reading prompts an inquiry into the neo-colonial regimes of truth disseminated by the western media. Those two contrasting interpretations of eastern Europe as the colonial subject, conveyed by Illingworth's cartoon, are traceable in different approaches to postcolonial theory in east European studies.

The aim of postcolonial discourse analysis, theorised in the writings of Indian and African intellectuals in diaspora, pointed to the epistemic violence which, wrought by western colonisation on all spheres of life and culture, kept reproducing its logic of subjugation long after regaining independence.[21] At the turn of the new millennium, the 'Other Europe' was acclaimed by some eastern European scholars as an almost paradigmatic case for studying the processes of cultural subordination.[22] There was no consensus, however, regarding the suitability of the postcolonial interpretive categories. Initially, only a narrow group adapted the concept of the orientalising discourse to analyse the western disparaging accounts of the region. This was in tune with Rasheed Araeen's suggestion that the term 'postcolonial' expands beyond the areas affected by the legacy of colonial exploitation and could serve as a key term of cultural analysis, which questions and deconstructs the cultural pre-eminence of the west. It was also

"Now let one of yours go—I dare you!"

Figure 1.1 Leslie G. Illingworth, '"Now Let One of Yours Go – I Dare You!"', *Punch*, 30 April 1958. By permission of Topfoto.

Araeen who invited articles examining orientalising discourses on eastern Europe into *Third Text*, the leading journal for postcolonial studies in Britain.[23]

The issue raised from the start was that eastern Europe never really made the colonial subject as defined by Edward Said, Gayatri Spivak, and Homi Bhabha. The fundamental incompatibilities, as was argued, included its proximity to the west, shared culture, white skin of its inhabitants, as well as the multiple identity of its colonisers.[24] The most significant obstacle, however, was the pronounced distrust towards the 'spectre of Marxism' among eastern European intellectuals, which was particularly strong at the time of the rise of postcolonial theory in the west in the 1980s. Significantly, east European studies, developed in the west within the framework of the Cold War, focused on the praxis of resistance to communism and Marxism, and situated themselves on the entirely opposite political pole to postcolonialism.[25] Even those who embraced feminist and queer approaches would often refuse to adopt a postcolonial perspective, pointing to the historical and spatial differences, and claiming that the east European Other does not make a 'real Other'. As a result, postcolonial theory has provided a possible point of departure for a new 'post-communist theory', which would produce other ways of problematising the truths about the world post-1989. This often distinctly conservative turn was particularly pronounced in the area of Polish studies, which derived its impetus from the demands to 'break the conspiracy of silence concerning Russia's colonial practices',[26] disregarding conquest and exploitation within the region of Europe's east itself.

On the other hand, postcolonial critique, confined almost exclusively to the relations between the First World and the Third World, espousing terms such as 'eurocentrism' and 'non-western' as its passwords, has silently ignored the blatant reductionism of the particle 'euro' in Eurocentrism, reducing Europe to western Europe and the non-western to the Third World exclusively.

The heated debates continued, differing substantially in reference to diverse areas of eastern Europe.[27] When in 2014, the Polish highbrow literary journal entitled, significantly in this context, *Second Texts* (*Teksty Drugie*), presented several diametrically opposing views on the use of postcolonial theory, it also proposed the critical departure from the precepts of colonial critique towards a new model of comparative studies, which would develop concepts of 'new cosmopolitanisms, alternative modernities, and peripheral modernities'.[28] A primary example of such a 'postcolonial transfer' is the 2013 book of the Romanian scholar Cristina Șandru, *Worlds Apart*, which reads post-communist literature of the whole region both through the prism, and against the grain, of postcolonial theory, advocating a creative compromise between the two.[29] In Șandru's words:

> there is an evident postcolonial sensibility in the way East Central Europe articulates both its recent past and its embattled present: how it places itself at the heart of the European project yet at the same time . . . seeks to articulate and manifest its separateness; how it struggles to rememorize, rewrite and reinterpret its history, both more distant and more recent; and how it negotiates its continued semi-peripheral status in the European Union. The advantages of imagining Eastern Europe and the former colonial world within the same intellectual paradigm would thus be reciprocal.[30]

I have to admit that for my research on imaging eastern Europe, postcolonial theory was inspirational. Said's critique of Orientalism and Bhabha's approach to hybridity lent me tools for reading Bradbury's construction of Slaka, while Spivak's inquiry into the voicelessness of the subaltern opened my eyes to the asymmetry of language skills between the Slakans and their western visitors. True, postcolonial theory did not pay much attention to images. Likewise, the debates on its use in east European studies have been conducted almost exclusively within the realm of literature and verbal discourses.[31] But, as will become clear in the following chapters of the book, postcolonial sensibilities accompanied my studies of visual representation of Europe's east, including its maps, travel imagery, cartoons, and book covers. Illingworth's cartoon itself testifies that the perception of eastern Europe as a quasi-colonised subject, explicitly, and as the passive object of history, implicitly, must have been strong enough to be articulated at the *Punch* Table. I have argued in the past, and I am still subscribing to the view that the ideological construction of the racialised colonial Other and the 'undeservingly white' eastern European br(Other) has revealed too many points in common to be ignored: signifying practices marginalising the peripheral and the migrant, recognised by another shade of white, dress, demeanour, and a foreign accent. Even further, east European and postcolonial studies have developed a shared vocabulary, both stressing the 'in-betweenness', the trauma of un-belonging, and both investing value in cultural hybridity. Even if eastern Europe cannot be neatly accommodated into race, class, gender, and sexuality binaries, it has attracted a wide range of othering procedures. Its culture was repeatedly class*ified* in western discourses as non-urban and backward, it was occasionally racialised along the pigmentocracy scale, as well as notoriously gendered and sexualised as a victim of imperialist or communist abuse. From the other position, it was also accused of xenophobia, masculinism, and homophobia, as well as of a 'pathological' heterosexuality.

Those latter charges acquired a frightening urgency during the last decade, under the rule of far-right parties in Poland and Hungary, which adopted socially conservative policies in relation to sexual orientation, immigration, and women's rights. This led to banning gender studies and academic freedom, as in Hungary, and to the rise of the 'LGBT-free zones' in Polish provinces before parliamentary and presidential elections in 2019 and 2020. But, as I want to argue, xenophobia and homophobia are not intrinsic properties of the region. The *pars-pro-toto* fallacy of treating governments' policies in selected countries as the features of the region as a whole is one of the manifestations of othering strategies underscoring the discourses on eastern Europe, repeatedly imagined as Slaka. A major exhibition of homoerotic themes and aesthetics in art, from antiquity to the present, was staged in a major museum institution in eastern Europe, Warsaw's National Museum, under the previous liberal government.[32] In spite of the radicalisation of the far-right at the level of government, there have been new examples of the attention to LGBTQ rights by the lawmakers of the area. Above all, however, there is a wide-scale resistance on the part of 'ordinary people', as well as a number of public bodies, including universities, publishers, a large sector of the art world, not to mention the social media.[33] And it is resistance, as both an attitude and skill which, practised widely across the region for centuries, could at least compete with social phobias as an 'essential' property of the 'eastern European' mentalities.

Imaging Slaka

The book focuses on images, but 'the potential shift from word to image' underscores all of the following chapters.[34] In maps and cartoons, images dictate the rules, but words are needed to complete the message, even if on the sliding scale of their indispensability, as far as cartoons are concerned. Macmillan's address to Khrushchev '"Now let one of yours go – I dare you!"' is hardly needed; the message is conveyed by the visual metaphor, substituting the colonial and communist countries by balloons, as well as by the gestures and body language of the rulers. By contrast, images in travel reports and on dust jackets are often just optional companions to the texts which dominate, letting the images complete their contents. But this, in turn, gives images a freehand to go their own way, providing their own outline of events, by amplifying the message, modifying it, or rising quietly against it, as in the cover of *Why Come to Slaka*, to be discussed below.

Paratextual components of books on eastern Europe will be the topic of my final chapter, focusing on the shifting stock of images on their dust jackets. Luck has it that the covers of Bradbury's books on Slaka offer a foretaste of such an inquiry. Both books were first published by Martin Secker & Warburg, known for its anti-Soviet stance, and within the first few years went through several editions with diverse publishers in London and New York.[35] Their covers, all by different designers, looked for the appropriate signifiers of Eastern Europe under communism. Imaginary maps and non-descript chaotic airports, with a figure of the perturbed Dr Petworth accompanied by his fateful suitcase, featured on many covers of *Rates of Exchange*. When making a point about communism however, designers tried to go beyond the much overused motifs of the red star, or hammer and sickle that had dominated books on the history and politics of the region since the 1950s. Secker & Warburg opted for a vision of a 'communist cityscape' as the dust jacket for *Rates of Exchange* (Figure 1.2) and a folk dance postcard for *Why Come to Slaka* (Figure 1.3).

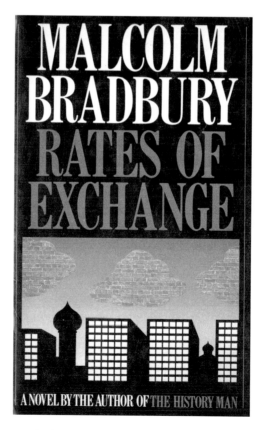

Figure 1.2 Dust jacket. Malcolm Bradbury, *Rates of Exchange*. London: Martin Secker & Warburg, 1983. By copyright Malcolm Bradbury 1986. Reproduced by permission of The Random House Group Ltd.

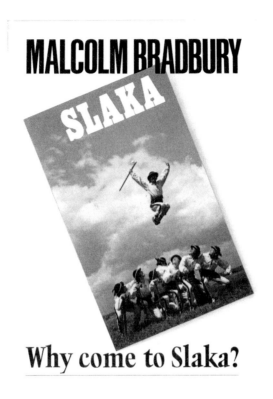

Figure 1.3 Front cover. Malcolm Bradbury, *Why Come to Slaka?* London: Martin Secker & Warburg, 1986. By copyright Malcolm Bradbury 1986. Reproduced by permission of The Random House Group Ltd.

A rectangular view of a city, framed by an ominously black background, was designed especially for *Rates of Exchange*. It juxtaposes a row of uniform blocks to the black silhouettes of churches crowned with onion domes, which point to the hybridity of Slaka as the 'melting pot' of cultures. The surreal serenity of the blue sky is disrupted by three clouds which open up to a brick wall, communicating the sense of political imprisonment. The dark mood of the cover reads like an anti-communist manifesto and does not sit well with the satirical vein of the book, and no later edition would borrow this design. A much lighter tone has been adopted for the cover of *Why Come to Slaka?* Parading as a tourist guide, it includes a reproduction of a postcard with a group of mountaineers in ethnic costumes, performing a dance in an open landscape. The dance culminates in a particularly high jump of one of them, soaring skywards above the heads of his companions, who are kneeling to the ground to marvel at his spectacular leap. The image invites the viewer to read it as a signifier of Slakan culture which, reduced to folklore, promotes competitive masculinity and phallic verticality as the criteria of excellence. Its position next to the somewhat clumsily formulated title of the book makes the dance hilarious, disempowering any claims to performative brilliance. The choice of the medium is equally significant. As argued by Malek Alloula, the postcard is an index of travel and a 'fertilizer of the colonial vision'.[36] In this case, however, the identity of the coloniser is more complex. The postcard was clearly made in Slaka, or, to be precise, in Poland, as it unmistakeably represents Polish mountaineers performing *Zbójnicki*, the 'bandit's' dance. However, the fantasy it satirises for the benefit of the 'western reader' is not that of the Slakan Self, but of the communist elevation of folklore to the epitome of the Self. It cannot be excluded that the image was capable of activating non-political fantasies on the part of the reader in the same way in which postcards of Algerian women, discussed by Alloula, triggered the 'sexual phantasm' of the harem. In any case, the image of the dance proved successful and was repeated in Penguin edition of the book.[37]

As a spoof guide, *Why Come to Slaka* includes also a handful of photographs of unknown origins, most likely reproduced from 'eastern European' tourist brochures or newspapers, all carefully chosen for their awkwardness.[38] If Slakan language is entirely of Bradbury's invention, the images belong to a different order of representation. The indexicality of the photography turns them into the records of reality which, however altered, must have been there. Thus, to attune them to the satirical mode of the counter-guide, they had to be manifestly parodic, erratic, and hardly decipherable, manifestly different from the 'celebratory' pictures that belong to the convention of the tourist guide. Ethnic topics with male performers dominate, interspersed with grainy photos of blocks of flats, a huge concrete university building with a large puddle in front of it, a film frame of a women brigade at work, and an illegible detail of a monument to an unknown battle, all accompanied by captions which emphasise the comical effect because they are grammatically incorrect and only loosely connected to the illustrations themselves. Not only the relationship between the captions and the images is problematic, but the latter have very little to do with Bradbury's text. Descriptions of the 'communist city' with blocks of flats and onion domes, or ethnic performances and monumental sculpture could hardly be found in Bradbury's books. The photographs, clearly, belong to a different realm of representation. They do not necessarily disrupt the text, but provide another dimension of Slaka, competing with, and completing Dr Petworth's encounters with Katya Princip and party officials, his elaborate descriptions of the airport and the fin-de-siècle interiors of his hotel. Detached from the text, the images form part of the already established repertory of visual signifiers of eastern Europe which, even if changing and discontinuous, has been accumulating for a long time, accommodating both ethnic imagery and blocks of flats, alongside maps of the ever-changing boundaries, bullied children, communist insignia, and protesting crowds.

The following chapters focus precisely on exploring the processes of the formation of this repertory. Looking at maps, travelogues, cartoons as well as book covers, all of them foregrounded in Bradbury's vision of Slaka, this book explores diverse strands of the visual construction of eastern Europe as an entity, stretching over a long-time span. It begins from the humanist image of Sarmatia Europea, followed by the early modern explorers' vision of the remote lands of Europe, the modern travellers' spectrum of the *Volksmuseum* of Europe, the politicians' New Europe, ending with the socio-cultural constructs of the Iron Curtain Europe and the post-communist Europe. It restricts the enormity of the visual evidence to cartography, travel imagery, satirical press, and book covers, leaving out the material provided by cinematic imagery, and the media, such as TV documentaries, the news as well as newspaper photographs.

The book borrows from many disciplines, and it follows a mixture of methods. By putting images centre stage, it subscribes to the belief that cognition is not 'dominantly and aggressively linguistic', and that images, including non-art images, have contributed substantially not only to the representation of eastern Europe, but also to the construction of the region as a geo-political and socio-cultural entity.[39] It examines the ways in which diverse visual technologies not only frame the visual representation of the eastern European space and the eastern European body, but also become the mechanisms for carving the space and fashioning the body, situating both of them within social hierarchies and relations of power, established by mapping and imaging. In embarking on the study of the visual representation of eastern Europe and embracing diverse kinds of visual imagery, as well as by drawing amply from postcolonial theory, semiotics, psychoanalysis, literary criticism, New Cartography, and Human Geography, the book positions itself within the interdisciplinary area of Visual Culture, and it uses the case of eastern Europe to follow the mechanisms of the social construction of the visual and the visual construction of the social.[40] But, apart from borrowing concepts from western scholars, from Sigmund Freud and Roland Barthes, to Hayden White, J.B. Harley, Gérard Genette, Ernst Gombrich, Thomas DaCosta Kaufmann, and W.J.T. Mitchell, the book testifies to my art historical training in Poland in iconology by my teacher Jan Białostocki.[41]

The very idea of examining the image of eastern Europe from the early modern period to the present implies assembling a massive range of iconographies of the region, across the continents, across the media, and across centuries, identifying their origins and affiliations, as well as 'chasing' diverse meanings invested in them by their makers and viewers alike. The procedure of 'motif-hunting', one of the universally condemned 'sins' of iconology,[42] was my staple diet in Poland, both at the university and in the museum, and this book has not entirely abandoned this strategy. On the contrary, considering the absence of a comprehensive research on visuality and the construction of eastern Europe, this was the only approach available for the task. Instead of opting for a site- and time-specific research path and narrowing my inquiry, say, to examining the renaissance cartographies of Sarmatia Europea, the Cold War visuality, or to LGBTQ visual strategies of resistance in the new millennium, the book criss-crosses the vast visual field in many directions, looking for connections, discontinuities, and absences. Indifference to social inequality has been identified as another shortcoming of Panofsky's iconology; however, this research, looking at the ways in which representations of the region communicate disdain, desire, or dissent, does require an investigation of the complex matrix of social and political relations. Risking a misinterpretation of Mitchell's words, the book does testify to the belief that an encounter of Panofsky's iconology with Althusserian ideological critique is not improbable, not only making iconology 'ideologically aware and self-critical', but also making 'ideological critique iconologically aware'.[43] To complete the list of debts to my eastern European upbringing, I also use the term 'iconosphere', coined by the Polish art historian Mieczysław Porębski, aiming to formulate the rules of 'iconics', and devised to study the ubiquity of images in a spatial context.[44]

Summary of Chapters

Each of the following four chapters is devoted to a specific visual medium, instrumental in the process of the visual construction of eastern Europe as a region. They are discussed in the order of their ascendancy: the map, providing its spatial dimensions and claiming scientific accuracy, the travel image, and a typical cartoon, both commenting on the eastern European body and dress, and, finally, the dust jackets of books about East Central Europe, a potent tool for resetting the fading iconography of region in the new millennium. As it happened, all of the chapters have their conceptual roots in Bradbury's construction of Slaka, a country 'that has been now big, now small, now virtually non-existent',[45] its culture explainable in a thin tourist guide which not only is entirely made up of jokes, but also provokes a range of conspicuous covers, some of them drawn as cartoons.

Chapters 2 and 3 reach far back into the past. Borrowing from the New Cartography and the writings by J.B. Harley, 'Mapping Eastern Europe' looks at the bewildering range of the cartographies of Europe's east, covering radically different territories. Beginning from the Ptolemy-inspired maps of Sarmatia Europea in the fifteenth century, it moves to the vastness of Šafařík's counter-hegemonic projection of Slavic Europe in the nineteenth century and to the arrival of the much maligned map of the post-WWI New Europe, squeezed between Germany and Russia, and drawn on the bodies of the collapsed empires under the aegis of Woodrow Wilson. After the discussion of the Iron Curtain maps, which literally framed the region for half a century, the chapter ends with the post-communist reorientations of Europe.

'The Lure of Ethnic Dress' assembles an even wider assortment of images of the region published by travellers from the seventeenth century onwards. The chapter follows the transformations of the image of a peasant woman in ethnic dress, which has risen to a timeless, omnipresent, and multivalent signifier of the region, fitting both the codes of representation and of self-fashioning. Recurring in drawings, prints, and photographs for over 400 years, it has been standing as much for backwardness, as for the national revivals in the interwar era, for an index of the communist redistribution of power, and a performative declaration of regional, as well as gender and sexual identity.

Chapter 4, 'Mr Punch Draws Eastern Europe', stays mostly within the twentieth century, examining the role of cartoons in creating the image of the 'eastern European group person'. Beginning from an inquiry into the operational mechanisms of 'cartoonwork', it argues that it was British *Punch* which, borrowing from both mapmakers and travellers, had arrived at an apt visual formula to conceptualise the region's spatial indeterminacy and its ethnic apparel, fused into one pregnant image. Since the 1930s and for many decades to come, a cartoon with a bunch of children in ethnic costumes, squeezed together in a narrow space of a classroom or a playground and disciplined by Dame Europa, Hitler, or Stalin, was to be instantly recognisable as a metaphorical 'group portrait' of the region. The chapter looks also at the ways in which eastern European cartoonists represented the 'warmongering' west, while claiming that the overproduction of warmonger cartoons was underscored by ironical resistance within the region.

Chapter 5 'The Battle of the Dust Jackets' revisits the range of master images again, while looking at the covers of academic books on eastern Europe produced in the new millennium. Identifying the visual themes which, negotiated by teams of authors, publishers, and designers, migrate freely between different disciplines, this chapter examines the continuity of the established tropes, but also the emergence of new bodies and spaces, new emphases, and new silences.

Notes

1. Malcolm Bradbury, *Rates of Exchange* (Harmondsworth: Penguin Books, 1985), blurb. Bradbury acknowledged that Slaka is an amalgam of his experiences of Bulgaria, Romania, Yugoslavia, and Hungary, 'with tiny little bits of Poland stuck in as well' – Malcolm Bradbury, 'New Rates of Exchange: British Fiction and Britain Today', in Ludmilla Kostova et al., eds, *Britain and Europe* (Sofia: Petrikov, 1994), 21.
2. Bradbury, *Rates of Exchange*, 1–2.
3. Bradbury, *Rates of Exchange*, 40.
4. Bradbury, *Rates of Exchange*, 76.
5. Malcolm Bradbury, *Why Come to Slaka?* (Harmondsworth: Penguin Books, 1991), 64. Slaka has made a subsequent appearance in Bradbury's television comedy-drama 'The Gravy Train Goes East' (Channel 4, 1990), discussed by Paul G. Nixon, 'A Never Closer Union? The Idea of the European Union in Selected Works of Malcolm Bradbury', in Susanne Fendler and Ruth Wittlinger, eds, *The Idea of Europe in Literature* (New York: St Martin's Press, 1999), 138–55.
6. Bradbury has often exercised his skills of parodying the misuse of English by foreigners, but the 'Slakan case' differs here precisely in the impossibility to verify his impersonating faculty.
7. As admitted by Bradbury in an interview with Istvan Rácz, '"A Writer Is Sceptical, Questioning, Dialogic" (and Interview with Malcolm Bradbury)', *Angol Filológiai Tanulmányok/Hungarian Studies in English* 21 (1990): 101.
8. Tatyana Stoicheva, 'Rates of Exchange: Rates of Constituting Eastern Europe', in Kostova et al., eds, *Britain and Europe*, 126.
9. Adam Palmer, *The Lands Between: A History of East-Central Europe Since the Congress of Vienna* (London: Weidenfeld and Nicolson, 1970), 1.
10. Milan Kundera, 'The Tragedy of Central Europe', *The New York Review of Books*, 26 April 1984: 33–38.
11. Larry Wolff, *Inventing Eastern Europe: The Map of Civilization on the Mind of the Enlightenment* (Stanford, CA: Stanford University Press, 1994), 106–11; Vesna Goldsworthy, *Inventing Ruritania: The Imperialism of the Imagination* (New Haven and London: Yale University Press, 1998), 42–50.
12. Agatha Christie, *The Secret of Chimneys* [1925] (London: HarperCollins, 2010).
13. Santo Cilauro, Tom Gleisner and Rob Sitch, *Molvania: A Land Untouched by Modern Dentistry*, Jetlag Travel Guide (London: Atlantic Books, 2004); Ken Kwapis, *The Beautician and the Beast* (Paramount, 1997) and Steven Spielberg, *The Terminal* (Amblin Entertainment, 2004).
14. Wolff, *Inventing Eastern Europe*, 106–11.
15. Maria Todorova, *Imagining the Balkans* (New York and Oxford: Oxford University Press, 1997).
16. Goldsworthy, *Inventing Ruritania*.
17. Among others, see Iver B. Neumann, *Uses of the Other: "The East" in European Identity Formation* (Manchester: Manchester University Press, 1999); Dubravka Ugrešić, *The Museum of Unconditional Surrender* (London: Phoenix, 1999); Milica Bakić-Hayden, 'Nesting Orientalisms: The Case of Former Yugoslavia', *Slavic Review* 54, no. 4 (1995): 917–31; Dušan I. Bjelić and Obrad Savić, eds, *Balkan as Metaphor: Between Globalization and Fragmentation* (Cambridge, MA: The MIT Press, 2002); Maria Todorova and Zsuzsa Gille, eds, *Post-Communist Nostalgia* (New York: Berghahn Books, 2010); Barbara Korte, Eva Ulrike Pirker and Sissy Helff, eds, *Facing the East in the West: Images of Eastern Europe in British Literature* (Amsterdam and New York: Rodopi, 2010); Tomasz Zarycki, *Ideologies of Eastness in Central and Eastern Europe* (New York and London: Routledge, 2014); Andaluna Borcila, *American Representations of Post-Communism: Television, Travel Sites, and Post-Cold War Narratives* (London and New York: Routledge, 2014); Ewa Mazierska, Lars Kristensen and Eva Naripea, eds, *Postcolonial Approaches to Eastern European Cinema: Portraying Neighbours on Screen* (London: I.B. Tauris, 2013); Anita Starosta, *Form and Instability: Eastern Europe, Literature, Postimperial Difference* (Evanston, IL: Northwestern University Press, 2016). See also Diana Mishkova and Balázs

Trencsényi, eds, *European Regions and Boundaries: A Conceptual History* (New York and Oxford: Berghahn, 2017); Irina Livezeanu and Árpád von Klimó, eds, *The Routledge History of East Central Europe Since 1700* (London: Routledge, 2017).

18. Among others, Vedrana Veličković, *Eastern Europeans in Contemporary Literature and Culture: Imagining New Europe* (London: Palgrave Macmillan/Springer Nature Ltd, 2019).
19. Andrew Hammond, 'Through Savage Europe: The Gothic Strain in British Balkanism', *Third Text* 21, no. 2 (March 2007): 117–27. See also Arnold Bartetzky, Marina Dmitrieva and Stefan Troebst, eds, *Neue Staaten – neue Bilder? Visuelle Kultur im Dienst staatlicher Selbstdarstellung in Zentral und Osteuropa seit 1918* (Cologne, Weimar and Vienna: Böhlau Verlag, 2005).
20. David Chioni Moore, 'Is the Post- in Postcolonial the Post- in Post-Soviet? Toward a Global Postcolonial Critique', *PMLA* 116, no. 1 (January 2001): 111–28; Cristina Șandru, *Worlds Apart: A Postcolonial Reading of Post-1945 East-Central European Culture* (Newcastle: Cambridge Scholars Publishing, 2012).
21. Leela Gandhi, *Postcolonial Theory: A Critical Introduction* (New York: Columbia University Press, 2019).
22. Ryszard Nycz, 'Forewod', in *Post-Colonial or Post-Dependence Studies*, special issue of *Teksty Drugie* 1 (2014), 5, http://tekstydrugie.pl/wp-content/uploads/2016/06/t2en_2014_1 webCOMB.pdf.
23. Rasheed Araeen, 'A New Beginning. Beyond Postcolonial Cultural Theory and Identity Politics', in Rasheed Araeen et al., eds, *The "Third Text" Reader* (London: Continuum, 2002), 333–45.
24. Anikó Imre, 'White Man, White Mask: Mephisto Meets Venus', *Screen* 40 (Winter 1999): 405–22.
25. Imre, 'White Man, White Mask'.
26. Ewa M. Thompson, *Imperial Knowledge: Russian Literature and Colonialism* (Westport, CT, and London: Greenwood Press, 2000).
27. Stanley Bill, 'Seeking the Authentic: Polish Culture and the Nature of Postcolonial Theory' and Jan Sowa, 'Forget Postcolonialism, There's a Class War Ahead', both *Nonsite.org* (Online Journal in the Humanities), no. 12 (August 2014), non-paginated.
28. Dorota Kołodziejczyk, 'Post-Colonial Transfer to Central-and-Eastern Europe', *Teksty Drugie* 1 (2014): 140, http://rcin.org.pl/Content/51837/WA248_71048_P-I-2524_kolodz-post-colon.pdf.
29. Șandru, *Worlds Apart*, followed by Dorota Kołodziejczyk and Cristina Șandru, eds, *Postcolonial Perspectives on Postcommunism in Central and Eastern Europe* (London: Routledge, 2016). A similar position of creative negotiation, an extension of the Third World experience of colonialism into the region of East Central Europe was articulated Ewa Mazierska et al., *Postcolonial Approaches to Eastern European Cinema*.
30. Șandru, *Worlds Apart*, 281.
31. See Piotr Piotrowski, 'East European Art Peripheries Facing Post-Colonial Theory', *Nonsite.org* (Online Journal in the Humanities), no. 12 (August 2014), non-paginated.
32. Maura Reilly, '*Ars Homoerotica* / The National Museum in Warsaw (Poland), curated by Paweł Leszkowicz', in *Curatorial Activism: Towards an Ethics of Curating* (London: Thames and Hudson, 2018), 196–201.
33. Roger D. Petersen, *Resistance and Rebellion: Lessons From Eastern Europe* (Cambridge and New York: Cambridge University Press, 2001); Radzhana Buyantueva and Maryna Shevtsova, eds, *LGBT+ Activism in Central and Eastern Europe: Resistance, Representation and Identity* (Cham: Palgrave Macmillan, 2019).
34. W.J.T. Mitchell, 'Word and Image', in Robert S. Nelson and Richard Shiff, eds, *Critical Terms for Art History* (Chicago and London: The University of Chicago Press, 1996), 47.
35. *Rates of Exchange* was published simultaneously by Alfred A. Knopf in New York (1983) and Arena in London (1984, 3 paperbacks with different covers), Penguin 1985, and New York's Picador, 2000. *Why Come to Slaka* after the Secker and Warburg edition of 1986, appeared with Arena 1987, Penguin 1991 and Picador, 2012.
36. Malek Alloula, *The Colonial Harem*, trans. Myrna Godzich and Vlad Godzich (Minneapolis and London: University of Minnesota Press, 1986), 4.

37. The 1994 Arena cover also adopted the motif of the dance but changed that into a crude caricature of a dance performed by an elderly peasant couple, with many random signifiers of the Eastern Bloc drawn from the popular lore, such as hammer and sickle, or the Dracula Castle, none of them featuring in Bradbury's texts.

38. The images in Bradbury's Slaka have never attracted attention, unlike those included by W.G. Sebald into his books from around 1990. Coincidentally, Sebald was Bradbury's colleague at the School of English and American Studies of University of East Anglia.

39. Barbara Stafford, *Good Looking: Essays on the Virtue of Images* (Cambridge, MA, and London: The MIT Press, 1996), 7.

40. W.J.T. Mitchell, 'Showing Seeing: A Critique of Visual Culture', *Journal of Visual Culture* 1, no. 2 (2002), 170; Peter Erickson and Clark Hulse, *Early Modern Visual Culture: Representation, Race, Empire in Renaissance England* (Philadelphia: University of Pennsylvania Press, 2000), 1–2.

41. For a posthumous selection of his publications, see Jan Białostocki, *The Messsage of Images: Studies in the History of Art* (Vienna: IRSA, 1988). The uses of iconology and its significance for art history in Eastern Europe, were discussed during a major international conference *Iconologies: Global Unity or/and Local Diversities in Art History*, organised by Wojciech Bałus at the Jagiellonian University in Cracow in May 2019, www.ahice.net/conferences-call-for-papers/detail/project/conference-iconologies-global-unity-orand-local-diversities-in-art-history-cracow-23-2505201/. Its proceedings are forthcoming with Routledge.

42. See, W.J.T. Mitchell, 'Four Fundamental Concepts of Image Science', in *Image Science: Iconology, Visual; Culture and Media Aesthetics* (Chicago and London: The University of Chicago Press, 2015), 14.

43. W.J.T. Mitchell, *Picture Theory* (Chicago and London: The University of Chicago Press, 1994), 30.

44. Mieczysław Porębski, *Ikonosfera* (Warsaw: PIW, 1972). See Ella Chmielewska, 'Logos or the Resonance of Branding: A Close Reading of the Iconosphere of Warsaw', *Space and Culture* 8, no. 4 (2005): 349–80; Wojciech Bałus, 'Mieczysław Porębski: Man and Architecture in the Iconosphere', in Ákos Moravánszky and Judith Hopfengärtner, eds, *Re-Humanizing Architecture: New Forms of Community, 1950–1970* in *East West Central Re-Building Europe 1950–1970*, vol. 1 (Basel: Birkhäuser, 2017), 85–98.

45. Bradbury, *Rates of Exchange*, 2.

2   Mapping Eastern Europe

In order to exist as a region, eastern Europe had to be entered on a map. It had to be allocated a space and given a name, both of them constituting a cartographic image. Diverse cartographies of the area, inspired by Ptolemy's *Geography*, labelled with different names, representing different lands linked together for different reasons, had been produced since the fifteenth century by humanists, cosmographers, travellers, mercenaries, philologists, and artists (Figure 2.1). Those maps constitute the oldest visual record of the region long before the term eastern Europe became current. They were followed by other maps, issued as broadsheets or entered into atlases, covering widely different territories. Either focusing on Hungary and Bohemia, or on Poland with Russia, or just on Russia, they extended southwards to the Balkans, or northwards to Scandinavia. The production of maps accelerated with the Crimean war, when the numerous projections named *l'Europe orientale* were drawn by military cartographers, but it really gained speed only with the radical reconfigurations of Europe by WWI and, subsequently, after WWII. Mapping the area now involved geographers, historians, and politicians, as well as journalists and cartoonists. Throughout the twentieth century, the region's boundaries both kept changing and kept being fixed, and its defining impermanence was reaffirmed by the equally unstable lexicon of exonyms, the names given to it by non-natives. Apart from the standard Eastern Europe, Central Europe, and East Central Europe, the region attracted an astonishing assortment of other names, such as Sarmatia Europea, Slavic Europe, New Europe, 'shatter zone', 'the belt of political change', *cordon sanitaire*, 'Other Europe', Communist Bloc, 'kidnapped west', and post-communist Europe. They kept testifying to the shifting political landscapes of the European continent as a whole and to the unceasing battle over the region's geopolitical and cultural bearings.[1]

Regardless, or perhaps, because of the condition of impermanence, it was the map which constituted an active tool in articulating the region's identity, capable both of projecting the notion of the region's instability and submissiveness, as well as serving as a script of resistance. Not only did it precede the territory, but it was also routinely chosen as the area's 'ur-metaphor'. The post-WWI launch of the first cartographic mandate of the region identified it with a bunch of the 'small states of Europe', drawn by 'the mapmakers of Versailles' on the bodies of the collapsed empires.[2] The subsequent arbitrary gesture of reshaping the map of Europe in Yalta stabilised the territory by confining it behind the Iron Curtain.[3] Even if not preceded by a specific map, the 'Fall of the Wall', an instant metaphor in its own right, was hastily followed by the influx of new maps and atlases, redefining the boundaries of the eastern periphery of Europe as it had emerged from behind the debris.[4] The map keeps reappearing as the

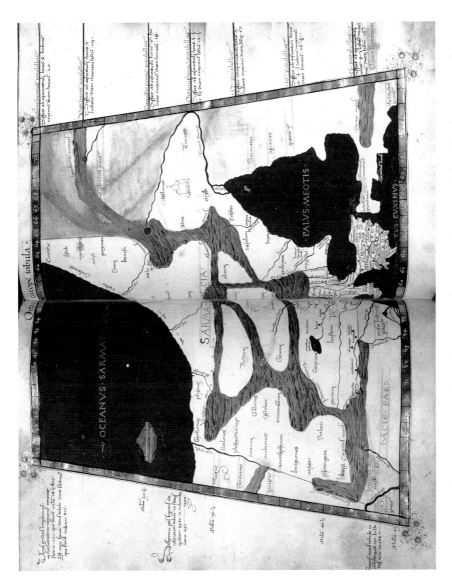

Figure 2.1 Nicolaus Germanus, 'The Eights Map of Europe (Sarmatia)', ink and colour on parchment, in *Cosmographia Claudii Ptolomaei Alexandrini*, ca. 1460. The New York Public Library, Manuscript and Archive Division. In the public domain.

central metaphor of recent books about the region, to include *Map Men* by Steve See-gel on Versailles cartographers, as well as Yuliya Komska's collection of texts, *Eastern Europe Unmapped: Beyond Borders and Peripheries*.[5] The title of a new collection of texts from a large area of East Central European studies entitled *Anti-Atlas* indicates a similar condition of inseparability.[6] Thus, regardless of the attempts to move beyond the map when rethinking the area, the map is here to stay, and it is in need of critical interrogation.

If the map precedes the territory, what does precede the map? Cartographies of eastern Europe have seldom provided material for a theoretical inquiry into the 'nature of maps' among geographers. They did attract historians though who, exam-ining 'collective concepts' associated with the region, investigated the shifting strate-gies of its mental mapping and its 'imagined identities', disseminated by texts, by the maps themselves, as well as by other visual material, such as book illustrations, or media photographs.[7] This chapter takes a similar approach, the major difference being the emphasis on the visual rather than the textual, or, to be more precise, on the strategy of deriving the conceptual from images rather than texts. Looking at maps of the region, I approach them as images that refer to other images, unpacking them in the process of visual analysis, searching for their visual sources, repetitions, and omissions, their affinity to landscapes or group portraits, as well as cartoons. Fol-lowing insights from the fields of critical cartography and visual culture, this chapter compares different maps of Sarmatia in Europe, of Slavic Europe, of Woodrow Wil-son's New Europe, and of communist as well as post-communist Europe, looking for unwritten affiliations and aspirations that are likely to escape other kinds of analyti-cal approaches.

Mapmaking as Image-Making

Is it then the image that precedes the map? The visual premises of geography and the visual nature of the map have been vigorously debated.[8] For Halford Mackinder, known for the use of hand-drawn images in his lectures and writings (Figures 2.8 and 2.11), the ability 'to visualise' constituted 'the very essence of geographical power'.[9] A theoretical inquiry into the map as image was developed much later by the pioneers of critical cartography, Brian Harley and David Woodward. Their ground-breaking texts of the 1980s and the 1990s challenged the map's time-honoured claims to scientific neutrality, revealing instead its inherent relationship with power and artifice.[10] Wood-ward's collection of essays on art and cartography, written by an interdisciplinary group of scholars, examined diverse aspects of the aesthetics of mapmaking, its use of figurative imagery, colour, and ornamentation, as well as links between the visual strategies of cartography and those of painting. If the latter, in its descriptiveness, is driven by the 'mapping impulse', cartographic representation testifies to the extent to which artifice constitutes an inseparable component of scientific imagery.[11]

This last issue constituted one of the major research questions for Harley, who pos-ited maps as social constructs through comparing them to images:

> The distinctions of class and power are engineered, reified and legitimated in the map by means of cartographic signs. The rule seems to be 'the more pow-erful, the more prominent'. To those who have strength in the worlds shall be added strength in the map. Using all the tricks of the cartographic trade – size of

symbol, thickness of line, height of lettering, hatching and shading, the addition of colour – we can trace this reinforcing tendency in innumerable European maps.[12]

Significantly, Harley's deconstruction of the cognitive claims of cartography had been inspired not just by poststructuralist thinkers, such as Barthes, Foucault and Derrida, but also by art historians. To advance his critique of the map, Harley had turned to Erwin Panofsky's iconology, adopting his tripartite method of image analysis in 1980.[13] Eight years later, in the opening chapter on theoretical perspectives in his 'Maps, Knowledge and Power', Harley openly declared: 'My aim here is to explore the discourse of maps in the context of political power, and my approach is broadly iconological'.[14] By that time, however, Harley drew also from a novel approach to the domain of the visual, which had just been proposed in W.J.T. Mitchell's *Iconology: Image, Text, Ideology* (1986), the founding text of Visual Culture.[15] Developed in parallel with critical cartography and sharing its attention to disempowerment, visual culture launched an inquiry into technologies of vision and, contesting the elitism of art history, Panofsky's iconology included, it embraced all kinds of images, mainstream, popular, and scientific.[16] Mitchell's thesis on the socially constructed nature of visual representation suited directly Harley's placement of maps within the 'broader family of value-laden images'.[17]

And yet, in spite of the obvious kinship with Mitchell's inquiry into the politics of the image, it was Panofsky's description of the progressive stages of image analysis, which had inspired Harley's thinking about 'the symbolic dimension' of the map as an image. Harley kept returning to Panofsky's method many times over the period of his most intense production of theoretical statements about maps, adapting it for the use of the New Cartography by displacing the contents, theme, and the intrinsic meaning of an artwork with the signifiers, the topography, and the ideology of space. Thus, the first level of Panofsky's ladder, the recognition of the 'primary or natural subject matter' would be translated by Harley into the primary task of the recognition of conventional cartographic signs; the second step, identifying the picture's 'secondary or conventional subject matter' would be aligned with the recognition of the topographical identity of the 'real place' represented on the map; and, finally, the last stage of Panofsky's image interpretation which aims to decipher its broad symbolical values as cultural symptoms – would decode maps as 'a visual metaphor for values enshrined in the places they represent', or, in Harley's parlance, as the 'ideologies of space'.[18]

Panofsky's method, widely criticised by New Art History for its adherence to the notion of intrinsic meaning and for its indifference to social relations,[19] might appear entirely out of tune with Harley's approach, unveiling the map as an instrument of power-knowledge. But it must have appealed to him precisely for its promise to identify the deeper meaning of an image and to link it to other cultural manifestations of the time. As he wrote in 1990:

> The question: "what did the map mean to the society that first made and used it?" is of crucial interpretive importance. Maps become a source to reveal the philosophical, political, or religious outlook of the period, or that which is sometimes called the spirit of the age.

But, even if obviously seduced by the interpretive powers of iconology, Harley would position the orthodoxies of iconology alongside other methods of cultural hermeneutics, such as discourse analysis and social theory, and filtering its approaches through the prism of his own radical alertness to the mechanisms of power and social discrimination. He continued:

> An iconographical interpretation can be used to complement the rules-of-society approach. While the latter reveals the tendencies of knowledge in maps – its hierarchies, inclusions and exclusions – the former examines how the social rules were translated into the cartographic idiom in terms of signs, styles and expressive vocabularies of cartography.[20]

Over the recent decades, however, the claims that maps are the instruments of power, and that space is not given but produced, have gained the status of established truths, to be supplemented by new approaches which redefine the map as a process rather than a product, stressing its contingency, corporeality, and performativity.[21] Woodward's and Harley's interests in mapping as imaging have been taken into entirely new directions, and research on the 'varied modalities taken by the visual in the discipline', their 'foci, zooms, their highlights, their blinkers, and blindnesses', has travelled far beyond the comparison of maps to images.[22] It adopted visual culture's concerns with technologies of vision and the problematic status of visual knowledge, launching new inquiries into the relationship between cartography and contemporary art and exploring a vast range of new visualities offered by the digital age.[23]

I want to round up this section with a brief overview of research on the seemingly preposterous affinities between maps and cartoons. The proximity of maps and caricatures was signalled briefly in the concluding paragraph of Jeremy Black's *Maps and Politics* and was developed by Sébastien Caquard and Claire Dormann, as well as by Peter Vujakovic.[24] Having reasserted the role of the iconographical aspect of maps, Black put forward an idea of an analogy of maps and caricatures, even if the first are 'commonly seen as objective by intention, content and technique of production', and the latter are 'commonly seen as subjective by all three criteria'. Both of them are political, he argued, both are made of images and texts, and both need titles to anchor their meaning, which may otherwise not be obvious. The latter is indeed crucial for maps of eastern Europe, and the affinity of cartography and caricature and cartoons was raised also in my earlier research on mapping the region.[25] I argued that both operate, not unlike like dreams, by mechanisms of distortion and selection, displacement, condensation, as well as metaphor. Both assert the primacy of drawing as well as the textuality of the image. By means of captions in small print, by elaborate speech balloons, or extensive legends invading the image, they are drawing attention to their 'icon-textuality' to the perpetual dialogue of word and image, turning their viewer into a reader. It is the line which is given predominance in both. Both maps and cartoons are super-persuasive in soliciting the trust of the viewer in their messages. While maps declare scientific objectivity, promising a direct correspondence between the three-dimensional reality and its cartographic rendering, cartoons, by contrast, proclaim subjectivity and pose subversion as a guarantee of a real insight into the hidden truth. Impropriety and distortion belong to the fundamental principles of the mode of caricature, and every dissent confirms the 'ironic episteme', in which the truth is best expressed by its reversal. Both cartoons and maps, ultimately, control the regimes of seeing, while obscuring the arbitrary mechanisms of representation.

Whether scientific or popular, maps and images are in constant dialogue, they borrow from each other, raise against each other, and correct and supplement their visual accents and blindnesses. The image activates the map, and the map activates the image. The territory seems to play a secondary role in this game, and the title, like the cartoon caption, is a constitutive part of the map. Looking at maps of eastern Europe, this chapter will approach them as images, using the methods of visual analysis and following insights from the field of cartography and visual culture.

Mapping Sarmatia

As argued by Katharina Piechocki, mapping of Europe's east was the process of both literary and visual translation of ancient geographical knowledge.[26] The major source was Ptolemy's description of the territory of the ancient Sarmatia Europea, a land in-between the Vistula and Don rivers, which he had included into Book Three of his illustrious *Geography*, a synthesis of what was known about the shape of the world written c. 150 CE. When a copy of Ptolemy's manuscript, long lost in Europe, was rediscovered in Byzantine hands and translated into Latin in 1406, it turned into a blueprint of the emerging discipline of renaissance cartography, not only detaching it from the realm of the religious, but also supplying the mapmakers with a theoretical exposé of how to project the spherical shape of the earth through the grid of longitudinal and latitudinal lines onto the plane surface of the map.[27] It electrified European humanists and instigated an avalanche of the text's new editions, as well as modern reconstructions of its maps.[28] And it was the loss of the original maps designed by Ptolemy, their actual existence vigorously debated by historians of cartography,[29] which provided the stimulus for European cartographers to reconstruct them, as well as to create new contemporary maps of those territories. It led to the advancing of the cartographic description of the modern *oikoumene* at the dawn of geographical discoveries.

Such was the case with the mapping of Ptolemy's Sarmatia Europea. His description of this ancient land paved the way for defining the geography of Europe's east of early modern times, activating the development of local cartographies, especially in the Polish Commonwealth.[30] Ptolemy's text had been based, in turn, on ancient accounts of the migration of the Iranian nomadic tribes of the Sarmatians from the Caspian plains of Asia to Europe and their settlement on the territories which were later to be taken over by Slavic peoples. The novelty was his division of Sarmatia into Asian and European parts (Sarmatia Europea and Sarmatia Asiatica) which, described by Ptolemy in different books of his treatise, could be seen on the same maps, separated by the Black Sea/Pontus Equinus.[31] European Sarmatia covered the territory between the rivers Vistula in the west and the Don/Tanais in the east, the latter seen by ancient historians as the border with Asia. Ptolemy's description of the region, listing its rivers and mountains accompanied by their coordinates, was rather technical and, relying on numerical data, could hardly be turned back into an image.

> European Sarmatia is terminated on the north by the Sarmatian ocean adjoining the Venedicus bay and by a part of the unknown land, a description of which is the following: mouth of the Chronus river 50*00 56°00; mouth of the Rubonis river 53*00 57°00 . . . .[32]

Its maps, preserved in Byzantine manuscripts of Ptolemy's *Geography* and drawn by unknown mapmakers, had served as the matrix for early fifteenth-century authors, including the illustrators of the Burney manuscript and the Harley codex in the British Library.[33] Even if different in size, the territory and the position of mountains and rivers, the maps of the ancient Sarmatia in Europe seem to have followed the same archetype, with an instantly recognisable dark blotch of the Black Sea at the lower right which, extended vertically, adopted the distinctive shape of an oversized lily. When the reconstructions of *Geography* were published as printed volumes, the German cartographer Nicolaus Germanus redrew all the maps using the trapezoidal projection, recommended by Ptolemy (Figure 2.1).[34] It created a paradigmatic vision of Ptolemy's Sarmatia Europea (1460), enclosed within a vertical frame, extending between Oceanus Sarmaticus/The Baltic Sea in the north and Pontus Euxinus in the south. Bordering with its Asian counterpart on the east, with Magna Germania on the west, and with Pannonia and Dacia in the south, it was criss-crossed by exaggerated mountain chains, most of them imaginary. This pattern was widely followed by late fifteenth-century mapmakers, including the painter Tadeo Crivelli in Bologna, the physician and book collector Hartmann Schedel in Nuremberg, and the German cartographer Martin Waldseemüller, active in Saint-Dié-des-Vosges and famous for producing the first world map which included the American continent.[35]

Ptolemy's ancient Sarmatias were to be re-created in historical atlases for centuries; however, it was the process of mapping the modern counterpart of Sarmatia Europea, of removing the fictitious mountains and correcting the flow of rivers, of populating the area with modern kingdoms, dukedoms, provinces, and cities, reshaping and renaming, which mark the beginning of a long ordeal of defining and redefining the territory of Europe's east. The incessant battles for power within the area, its relationship with Magna Germania, with Russia and Tartary, with 'Turkey in Europe', as well as with the rising ideology of Sarmatism were to live their latent lives in those *tabule moderne*, and, inadvertently, would cast a shadow on the region's historiography.

The most celebrated map that included Sarmatia's territory within a wider section of Europe, with Magna Germania in the west, was devised by the German humanist Nicolaus Cusanus around mid-fifteenth century, and is known in two printed editions.[36] Composed of parts borrowed from Ptolemy, it proposed a breath-taking panoramic view over the northern part of the continent extending between the rivers Rhine and Don. It abandoned the term Sarmatia, replacing it with names of contemporary countries and provinces, including Polonia, Ungaria, Transylvania *sive Septem Castrum*, Valachia, as well as Moscovia Ducatus, Russia Alba, and on the western side, Holandia, Danis Marchia, and Boemia. The placement of the Sarmatia territory next to the powerful Magna Germania on the same cartographic sheet was not without consequences though. The map's printed edition of 1491 by the same Nicolaus Germanus who had provided the model of Sarmatia Europea, renamed the same territory as *parva Germania tota tabella* (small map of the whole Germany). Cusanus's innovative cartographic project has entered the history of cartography as the first modern map of central Europe, occasionally named as a map of *Mitteleuropa*. Those early 'geopolitical' tensions specific to this territory were to be replicated in cartographies of modernity.[37] Nonetheless, the Cusanus-nominated territory of central and eastern Europe as a new cartographic topos inspired the makers of modern maps/*tabule moderne*, such as Marco Beneventano. His map of 1507, depicting much the same territory but entitled, more informatively, *Tabula moderna Polonie, Ungarie, Boemie, Germanie, Russie, Lithuanie*, introduced more topographical details of princedoms, regions, and smaller towns, due to the collaboration with a Polish cartographer Bernard Wapowski.[38]

Somewhat surprisingly, this new cartographic frame of central Europe, stretching from Germany to Russia, would also have been used at that time to represent solely the Ptolemaic Sarmatia Europea. This is how it was done by the already-mentioned Martin Waldseemüller in his '*Tabula Moderna Sarmatie Eur. sive Hungarie, Polonie, Russie, Prussie*', of 1513, which formed part of a particularly large contingent of modern *tabulae* in yet another edition of Ptolemy's *Geography* (Figure 2.2).[39] As if to avoid any additional clashes in this already contested space, the map left both the Russian and German lands entirely blank, with no cities or topographical details, apart from the mountains surrounding Bohemia, between Germany and Austria. Such an unusual configuration gives the impression that Waldseemüller had taken part in an imaginary dialogue between the mapmakers of early modern Europe, Cusanus, Nicolaus Germanus, Schedel, and Beneventano. As if he tried to reconcile among the diverse cartographic claims to this conflict-ridden territory, silencing the eastwards pressure, inflicted by both Magna Germania and Sarmatia, in order to erase any tensions from his image. By reverting to Ptolemy's terms Sarmatia and Mare Sarmaticum and adopting the name 'Modern Map of the European Sarmatia, that is of Hungary, Poland, Russia, Prussia', Waldseemüller demonstratively took a position in this dialogue, devising an image of modern 'transnational' Sarmatia as a distinct part of central and eastern Europe. However, he also extended the mapped area considerably southwards to include not just Hungary, Wallachia, and Transylvania, but also the lands of the southern neighbours, Bulgaria, Serbia, and Bosnia, as well as Sclavonia (Slovenia), which he clearly marked as occupied by Turchia. Only Dalmatia is missing from what could be seen as an early modern archetype of the Versailles eastern Europe. The map might not have got rid of the fictitious mountains, but it captured the precarious position of this multinational, multilingual, as well as multiconfessional region of Europe's east, stretched and squeezed between Germany and Muscovy, as well as Tartaria and Turchia.

At the time when Waldseemüller was preparing his map, the term Sarmatia was already being used as a synonym of Poland, and further claims to the Polish kingdom's identification with Sarmatia's large territory were made by Polish humanists, including Maciej Miechowita and Marcin Kromer, to justify Polands' territorial expansion eastwards both in the name of geographical discoveries, as well as a defence against the Teutonic order.[40] Polish claims to Sarmatia and the rising ideology of Sarmatism which was to define Polish culture throughout the later sixteenth and seventeenth centuries does not belong to this book as it focuses on the multinational image of eastern Europe.

I want to return here to the relationship between text and image in the conceptualisation of Europe's east, for which maps provide a strong stimulus. While Ptolemy's description of Sarmatia, excessively laconic, made of a dry gazetteer of names of places and their coordinates, was a key to reading his lost maps, none of the maps discussed earlier derived solely from this ur-text. All of them must have been based on the pre-existing cartographical visualisations, repeating and revising the chorographical details of the depicted landscapes, correcting and translating the toponymes,

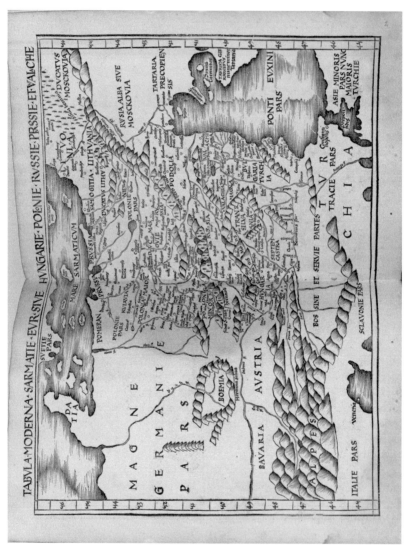

Figure 2.2   Martin Waldseemüller, 'Tabula Moderna Sarmatie Eur. sive Hungarie Polonie Russie Prussie et Valachie', woodcut, in Claudii Ptolemei viri Alexandrini mathematice discipline philosophi doctissimi Geographie opus nouissima traductione e Grecorum archetypis castigatissime pressum, ceteris ante lucubratorum multo prestantius. Strassburg; Ioannis Schotti, 1513. Washington, DC, Library of Congress. In the public domain.

reconfiguring the imaginary boundaries, and redrawing them in the complex process of translation. As commented by Piechocki:

> Maps call our attention to the oblique relationship between words and images. They serve as a reminder that words do not "illustrate" images or vice versa, but are subject to a complex hermeneutics that requires a skilful interpretive navigation between these two types of figuration.[41]

The map of Sarmatia could not have been made up just of words and numbers, and even if migrating from one cartographic frame to another, if still hesitant about its borders, its neighbours, and its allies, if still accompanied by supplemental spaces and legendary mountains, it was becoming settled into its image.

Queens and Folk

The trajectory from text to map included an image, and image-making dominated the process of mapmaking now and then. This was particularly prominent in allegorical maps, a very special form of cartographic translation, in which either the whole continent of Europe was represented as a human body, or its regions were fitted into contours of animals or plants, such as *Leo Belgicus* or *Bohemiae Rosa*.[42] This distinctive genre of maps, which willingly subordinated the cartographic mode of representation to that of allegory, was initiated by the anthropomorphic representation of Europe as a Queen. It shaped the continent into the form of a human body and, turning it by 90°, made it look like a full-length standing portrait (Figure 2.3).

The claim to cartographic objectivity succumbed to the trust in the illuminating distortion and displacement. The analogy between the body and the territory, investing the latter with meaning, betrays a similarity to the modus operandi of physiognomy, as well as that of caricature. All of them share the belief in the existence of the relationship between the external and the internal, which can be 'uncovered' by metaphorical distortion. *Uncovering* what had already been there was tantamount however to the process of *covering* the meaningless with the meaningful, of inventing the presumed essence. Physiognomy claimed the possibility of telling a character of a person from the features of human face and body, but that was possible only by imposing on it the resemblance to an animal, its character already fixed by classical lore. In analogy, allegorical maps were proclaiming the ability of determining the political role of a country from its position on the continent, however, the defining principle was their presumed analogy to the hierarchical body parts as well as the queen's costume. The 'hidden truth' could only be reached by the metaphorical substitution of the imperceptible and vague with the definite and fixed. The meaningful affinity between the body and the territory was to become instrumental for early twentieth-century science of anthropogeography and geopolitics, arguing for the supremacy of *Mitteleuropa* over eastern Europe. It also underscored the nineteenth-century satirical maps of Europe, as well as cartoon representations of eastern Europe as a disorderly assembly of bodies in folk costumes, to be discussed in Chapter 4.

Known under their metaphorical names, such as *Europa Regina* or *Europa Triumphans*, the allegorical maps originated from the image created by Johannes Putsch in 1537, the poet and mathematician. He dedicated it to Ferdinand I, the ruler of the hereditary lands of the Habsburg, which included Bohemia and Hungary, and the

Figure 2.3 Allegorical map of Europe as Queen, woodcut, in Sebastian Münster, *Cosmographey, das ist Beschreibung aller Länder, herzschaften und für nemesten Stetten des gantzen Erdbodens sampt ihren elegenheiten, Eygenschaften, Religion, Gebräuchen, Geschichten und Handtierungen.* Basel: Sebastianum Henricpetri, 1614. Warsaw, Central Library of Geography and Environmental Protection. Institute of Geography and Spatial Organization of the Polish Academy. In the public domain.

future Holy Roman Emperor. Diverse variations of this cartographic allegory were produced in German lands for another hundred years.[43] As with Putsch's prototype, the major claim was the European superiority and unity under the Habsburg rule, with Spain as the head of the Queen. The calls for peace within Europe were premised on the idea of the Christian unity of the continent, which had to be defended against the Turks and Tartars.[44] The detachment of the body of the Queen from the Asian continent, achieved by the drastically distorted shape of the Black Sea extending almost to the Baltic Sea, with the land of Tartaria shown as the only bridge between Europe and Asia, indicated that the sovereignty and power of the first were predicated on its separation from the latter.[45]

The image was followed by others, such as *Europa Prima Pars Terrae in Forma Virginis*, published by Heinrich Bunting in *Itinerarium sacrae Scriptura* in 1581,[46] and the allegorical map added in 1588 to Sebastian Münster's *Cosmography* (Figure 2.3).[47] This magnanimous description of the world, with hundreds of woodcuts by major German artists, edited several times since its first edition in 1544, was translated into many languages and was constantly augmented and republished.[48] The map follows the pattern, representing Spain as the Queen's head, Portugal as the crown, France her chest, Italy her right arm holding Sicily represented as the orb. Denmark, her left arm, holds a sceptre with a flag standing for the British Isles. Germany forms the core of the body, and Bohemia surrounded by the Bohemian forest is shown as a precious jewel in her belt, the seat of the emperor. Other kingdoms in the east, however, deprived of boundaries and hence functionless, are blended together in the image of the Queens long robe. Although the map as such is roughly based on Ptolemaic Europe, the term Sarmatia is left out; instead, Polonia, Lithuania, Livonia, Moscovia, and Scythia are entered on the right, and Ungaria, Sclavonia, Macedonia, Grecia, and Bulgaria on the left. The principal rivers with the reigning Danube and the Tanais at the bottom, the Carpathian Mountains and the Lithuanian forests are all clearly marked. Tartaria, sliding away at the lower right corner, as well as Asia and Africa, belong to different political realms. While glorifying the House of Habsburg, the map is silent about the expansion of its threatening rival, Turkey which, by the time the map was published, had already made very substantial inroads into the Queen's robe, reaching as far as Buda. The knowledge, as well as the fear, of the Turkish conquest is censored in the map by the Habsburgian power and repressed by condensing it into an image of a mighty city of Constantinopolis at the lower edge of the Queen's skirt.

The concept of the map of Europe as a body was followed by maps of the continent which were framed by plans of the major cities, as well bodies of its inhabitants, to augment their geographical data and the relations of power. If the selection of these 'cartographic bodies' has been examined by Valerie Traub in reference to race and gender,[49] the absences of the cities and bodies in Europe's south-east have not attracted much attention. Those elaborate maps of the continent by Willem Blaeu in the Netherlands (Figure 2.4), or John Speed in England, as a rule did include the Hungarian, Bohemian, Polish, and Greek couples into the family of Europe.[50] By contrast, the inhabitants of Wallachia, or Bulgaria, which had been conquered by the Turks in the middle ages, were notoriously excluded from the cartographic bodies rank. With the reconfiguration of the relations of power in Europe after the Thirty Years' War, the rise of Bourbon France and the Dutch Republic in Europe's west, the kingdoms of the south-east were being knocked out of the map of the continent, either swallowed by Turkey or absorbed by the Republic of Venice.

Figure 2.4 Willem Janszoon Blaeu, *Europa recens descripta*, engraving, Amsterdam, 1640. Warsaw, Central Archive of Historical Records. In the public domain.

In the north, the last sovereign kingdom, the Polish and Lithuanian Commonwealth was devastated by wars with its neighbours, Sweden, Russia, Moldavia, Tartary, and Turkey. While the position of the old Sarmatia kept diminishing in its role within the continent, Russia was rising steadily, accelerating with the conquests as well as reforms of Peter the Great and Catherine the Great. At the same time, as argued by Wolff, the eighteenth-century philosophers kept downgrading the east of Europe altogether, valorising the secular, the civilised, and the modern, which were now seen as the unique property of the west.[51] In cartographic terms, however, the changes in the radical repositioning of European geography alongside the west-east rather than the south-north axis had already been underway in the late seventeenth century. The rarely discussed double map of Europe of c. 1689, commissioned by the Venetian Senator Giovanni da Mula and made by the famous cosmographer Vincenzo Coronelli, the author of the gigantic terrestrial and celestial globes for Louis XIV, was composed of two separate sheets, '*Parte Occidentale dell'Europa*' and '*Parte Orientale dell' Europa*' (Figure 2.5).[52] Arguably, this is the earliest map which represented the whole area of Europe's east on a separate sheet, naming it accordingly, even if its territory was marked solely by the abstract geographical coordinates, regardless of physical features or political borders. It cut the boundary between east and west, arbitrarily, along the longitude 50° east which, extending from the North Pole across the Arctic Ocean, crossed through Finland, Volhynia, Moldavia, and Bulgaria. Significantly, the

Figure 2.5 Vincenzo Coronelli, '*Parte Orientale Dell' Europa, Descritta, e Dedicata Dal P. Cosmografo Coronelli All Illustrissimo, et Eccellentissimo Signore Giovanni da Mula, Senatore amplissimo Nella Serenissima Republica de Venetia*'. Venice [1689], engraving, in V. Coronelli, *Atlante Veneto*. Venice, Vol. 1, 1691. Vilnius, University Library. In the public domain.

map identified Europe's east almost solely with Russia, and hence the border with Asia had to be stretched further east, until the longitude 140° east, far beyond the Ural Mountains, reaching the River Ob.

If Coronelli's attention to the cartographic definition of eastern Europe seems to be an exception, the emerging hierarchy of civilised versus non-civilised was to be visualised throughout the eighteenth century on the patterns borrowed from cartographic imagery.[53] A striking example is provided by yet another allegorical print, chosen as a frontispiece in the report of the French astronomer Jean-Baptiste Chappe d'Auteroche, who travelled through the whole Europe, from Tours to Tobolsk, to observe the transit of Venus in Siberia in 1761 (Figure 2.6).[54] The print was indeed selected by Wolff as cover image for his seminal book.[55] The engraving, entitled '*Carte Générale: La France et l'Empire, la Pologne et la Russie*', was made by French artist Jean-Baptiste Le Prince, who accompanied the astronomer on his journey, producing also several portfolios of orientalising prints of everyday life in European and Asiatic Russia. The cartographic component of the image consists of the journey's graphic itinerary, complete with cities and major rivers, is inscribed prominently on the curtain at the background. It leads from Tours and Paris to Strasbourg, Mainz, and Vienna, and further to Warsaw, St Petersburg, and Moscow, ending in the most remote town of Tobolsk in Siberia. If the itinerary serves as an index to confirm the empirical status of this scientific escapade, the message of the map is conveyed by its figurative part, through the allegorical juxtaposition of the 'cartographic bodies' of France and the Holy Roman Empire to the humble figures of Poland and Russia. In stark contrast to the two imperial figures, brightly lit, draped in sumptuous classical attire and displaying the royal insignia – the figures of Poland and Russia, pushed to the back and cast in shadow, are marked as folkish, almost peasant-like, diffident, insecure, and powerless. Stripped of any identification which could testify to their actual royal status as the representatives of the ancient Kingdom of Poland and the powerful Russian Tsardom of Catherine the Great, they are dressed in quasi-ethnic costumes and hold military weapons, suitable for low-ranking soldiers, such as a bow and a halberd. One is sitting directly on the ground, and both of them look up to the western sovereigns, who seem entirely oblivious of their presence. It is not difficult to see that the spatial configuration of the personifications of France, the Holy Roman Empire, Poland, and Russia is heavily indebted to the common theme of the cartouche iconography in seventeenth-century maps, in which allegorical figures standing for Asia, Africa, and Americas bow to the authority of Europe.[56] By juxtaposing the disempowered monarchies of Poland and Russia to the enthroned figures of France and Germany, the print adopted the established cartographic code of the geopolitical hierarchy of the world onto the internal hierarchy of Europe. If the Ptolemaic maps positioned Europe's east on the cartographic image of the continent, from the seventeenth century onwards the cartography-derived imagery translating the hierarchy of space into the hierarchy of bodies, relegated the bodies of Europe's east to the realm of peasants, and status-less folk, prompting the discourse of eastern European civilisational backwardness. The nineteenth-century ethnographic turn would seal the image of the region as the land of folk.

Slavic Europe

With the end of the eighteenth century the Polish and Lithuanian Commonwealth was swallowed by the expanding empires of Prussia, Russia, and Austria, completing

Figure 2.6 Jean-Baptiste Le Prince, etched by Jean Baptiste Tilliard, '*Carte Générale: La France et l'Empire, la Pologne et la Russie*', in Jean-Baptiste Chappe d'Auteroche, *Voyage en Sibérie*. Paris: chez Debure Père, 1768. Frontispiece to Volume IV (with maps). Houghton Library, Harvard University. FC7.C3683.768v (A). In the public domain.

the process of the erasure of this region from the map.[57] Up to the Austro-Hungarian compromise of 1867, the European east was uniformly submerged under the overflowing bodies of the four Great Empires. The disappearance of the old eastern European kingdoms and principalities was followed by an increased attention to the region by historians, geographers, and ethnologists. The nineteenth century was the period of the systematic post-Enlightenment effort to assemble an encyclopaedic body of knowledge about the world and its inhabitants, to describe, measure, and classify all the aspects of nature and culture, including languages, ethnicities, and races.[58] Even if the underlying principle was the justification of the occidocentric hierarchy of civilisations and imperial conquest, this reintroduced the subjugated nations of Europe's east to the ethnographic maps and atlases. A part of this forceful ethnographic exercise was the rediscovery of a Slavic Europe, inspired to a large measure by Johann Gottfried Herder's eulogy of Slavic people in his *Ideas upon Philosophy and the History of Mankind*, pronounced in 1791.[59] This required, of course, the invention of a new set of representational regimes, suitable for putting the Slavs on the map of mankind in spatial and bodily terms. By mid-1850, in the early historical and ethnographic atlases, maps of Slavs were classified as belonging to northern Europe, which included Scandinavia, Poland, and Russia.[60] They were accompanied by explanations of the physical, intellectual, and moral character of a distinct 'Sclavonian variety' of people, of 'skull and face more square than oval . . . stature stout and broad . . . when subjected, cunning, deceitful and revengeful . . . in consequence of national misfortunes, a great leaning towards paternal and despotic authority . . . the love of country without a spirit for adventure'.[61]

But the emergence of the Slavic myth in its inescapable ethnographic veil was not just the product of western scholarship, but to a large extent it was created by the Slavs themselves. One of the most powerful visual manifestations of this myth was a map, an ethnographic map of the world of Panslavism (Figure 2.7). Covering a much larger territory than Sarmatia Europea and Coronelli's '*Parte Orientale dell' Europa*', and spreading widely between the rivers Oder and Volga, the Baltic, the Adriatic, and the Black Sea, the map offered the first image of an imagined community, now defined on the basis of the shared Slavonic language.[62] Named '*Slowanský zeměvid*' (survey of Slavic lands) and published in 1842, the map was painstakingly compiled by Pawel Josef Šafařík, a Slavonic philologist, who spent many years collecting regional cartographies, establishing original Slavic names of towns and villages and fitting them into his taxonomy of Slavdom. Born in Slovakia (then part of the Kingdom of Hungary), educated in the University of Jena in Germany, while active in Novi Sad in Serbia and then in Prague, Šafařík was one of the first modern scholars who significantly contributed to the establishment of Slavic studies, and whose work, to borrow from R.W. Seton-Watson, 'had a very direct political hearing upon the whole development of the Slav world'.[63] His pioneering map of Slavic people, engraved by the graphic artist and cartographer Věnceslav Merklas, hand coloured, and published initially in 600 copies, was attached to *Slowanský Národopis* (Slav Ethnography), Šafařík's survey of Slavic languages, and folk songs.[64] Covering a vast area of Europe, the map presents the Slavs as a unified 'single body', defined by the uniformity of green which overpowers the image. It clearly distinguishes Slavs from non-Slavs, marking the territories of the latter by contrasting colours, yellow and blue. Colour is clearly loaded with significance and, as discovered by Josef Hůrský in Šafařík's papers, the philologist has chosen green for its association with hope.[65] The Slav enclave of Lusatia within

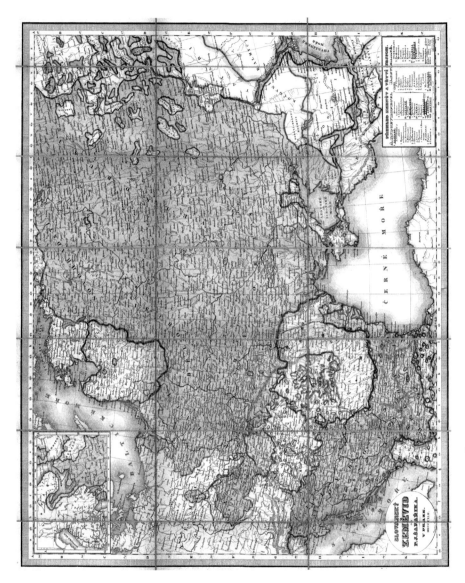

Figure 2.7 Pawel Josef Šafařík, engraved by Věnceslav Merklas, 'Slowanský zeměvid', in *Slowanský Národopis, s mappau*. Prague: Wydawatele, 1842. In the public domain.

Saxony is clearly shown, and the map makes obvious that many Slavs are at home in parts of Germany and of course within the Austrian Crownlands. What counts is the unity and the vastness of the territory occupied by the Slavs, as well as their sheer number, 80 million in total, as summed up in the book.[66] The name of the map, rendered in strikingly ornate lettering, using several fonts of different scale, attempts to evoke Slavic ornaments. Its elaborate legend lists all the ethnic groups classified by their languages, reasserting Slavs's domination over the region, both within the group of Indo-European peoples (Lithuanians, Romanians, Germans, Bulgarians, Greeks, Armenians, and Ossetians) and 'the Northerners' (the Uralic people, Tatar, Turkish, Kalmykian, and Caucasians).[67]

Šafařík's map proved immensely successful. It was used by many subsequent ethnographic surveys, such as the one by Karl Sprunner or Heinrich Berghaus,[68] thus establishing the cartographic codes for mapping Slavic Europe on the terms of the Slavic mapmaker and reinscribing the west's Other as the Slavic Self. The book to which the map was attached went through at least two editions in the first year and was translated into Polish and Russian; in the latter case, it included the map.[69] The map was indeed its main attraction. Neatly folded in an inconspicuously Baedeker manner, it made a huge impact on its Slavic readers. Stanko Vraz, one of the leaders of the Illyrian movement, wrote from Zagreb to Prague: 'When I brought a copy of this map, the local patriots and even the non-patriots almost tore it out of my hands. All of them cannot get over the fact that the Slav nation is spread so far. The map arouses more patriots here than a whole literature could do'.[70] Arguably, even if Šafařík's map had come about before the establishment of art history faculties in universities, it introduced a 'spatial turn' which affected the whole discipline of Slavic studies, helping to change it from an almost 'exclusively linguistic and philological enterprise', into a much broader Slavic antiquarianism, including archaeology and, later on, art history as well.[71]

And indeed, vested in the Herderian glorification of the language and folk culture, *Slowanský zeměvid* was a powerful script of cultural emancipation, and a rallying call for Panslavism.[72] The map was, both literarily and metaphorically, superimposed on that of *Mitteleuropa*, produced in multiple separate sheets for the use of the Prussian army by Daniel Gottlob Reymann, greatly respected for its accuracy.[73] By moving the point of view towards the east and by translating all the German names into their Slavic versions (mostly into Czech), thus laying bare the Slavic roots of the territories it covered, the map turned into a counter-map, participating in the battle for signification to subvert the emerging cartographic power of *Mitteleuropa*, perceived by the Slavs as directly linked with a threat of a Germanic hegemony. It bred an imagined community of the Slavs, instigating the wave of ethnic pilgrimages across Slavic countries. Furthermore, by visualising the omnipresence of the Slavic language, the map demonstrated that the history and culture of the Slavs, even if deprived of their own archival records, has been preserved in language. To borrow a term from Gayatri Spivak, this map constituted the first 'strategically essentialist' attempt to forge a Slavonic collective identity, united by language, folk-culture, and by the aim of spiritual regeneration of the whole of Europe.[74] As claimed by Hans Kohn, Šafařík 'wished not only to be a scholar but the prophet of the national awakening of his race, which he glorified, stressing apologetically its unique character and mission'.[75] His map was an act of cultural resistance against the denigration of the Slavs as barbarians by western philosophers and historians.

The effectiveness of the map, I want to argue, stemmed to a large extent from its visual rhetoric, sanctioned by the authority of cartography. As testified by Vraz's enthusiastic account, the map provided an image of an inhabitable Slavic collective identity, of the desirable Slavonic Self, but also a visible record of Slavic power. The act of unfolding the map was tantamount to the discovery of the legitimacy of Slavic Europe, spreading from Berlin to the Urals. The physical features of the territory were largely de-emphasised, but much of the rhetorical power of the map came from its association with landscape, wide-spread, uniformly green, agrarian, and welcoming. The Czech term '*zeměvid*', which means 'map', is a compound of '*země*', land, and '*vid*', aspect, thus connoting the act of viewing a land. The affinity between map and landscape is one of the much discussed topics of cultural cartography and visual culture, both pointing to the tension between the aesthetic values of landscape as an artistic genre and the claims to ownership of the land it represents, whether on the part of a landed gentry or the communities which defend their shared territory, and their ethno-cultural links to the soil.[76] But, it is from this perspective that *Slowanský zeměvid* reveals its double nature, emancipatory and discriminatory at the same time. The cartographic gaze, the mapmaker's commanding view from above, so clearly implied here, is a particular instance of the disembodied gaze, controlling access to knowledge and power.[77] The vastness of the Slavic lands is enhanced by the use of colour, and the same shade of green stands for all Slavic people, without any divisions into northern, western, or southern. While the linguistic boundaries between the Slavs are marked by the dainty lines made of dots, the thick state borders of the occupiers, highlighted in red, resemble instead scars on the Slavic body. At the same time, the isolated areas inhabited by non-Slavs, such as Hungarians and Romanians, as well as the Germans, are rendered in contrasting tones of yellow and blue. The use of Slavic names restored and confirmed the Slavic rights to the land in much the same way in which German names on the maps of *Mitteleuropa* were giving authority to Teutonic expansion. Jews and Roma, customarily ignored by nineteenth-century ethnographic maps, had not been entered on Šafařík's map either. Inclusion is always, and inevitably, related to exclusion. The counter-map is always already a map of domination.

The nineteenth century left also a number of non-ethnographic maps focused on, and labelled, 'eastern Europe', made by both amateurs and professional cartographers. The region's borders were fluid, established arbitrarily by their makers. An intrepid mercenary soldier and a military engineer, involved in independence movements in Poland, Hungary, Nicaragua, and the United States, Charles Frederic Henningsen added a hand-drawn map of the Slavic Europe area to the frontispiece of the book on the russification policies of Tsar Nicholas I in Poland.[78] The Crimean war prompted a whole series cartographies of *L'Europe Orientale* as the theatre of war, and by the late 1860s, *Ost-Europa* became the topic of six detailed maps by the cartographer Adolf Stieler in his *Hand-Atlas* of the world. It began from the north, with a sheet with Norway and Sweden and, moving southwards through Russia and Russian Poland, ended in the Caucasus. Maps of a variously defined eastern Europe were entered into a range of historical atlases, as in the Balkan-centred 'Eastern Europe as regulated by the Treaty of Berlin 1878' in Labberton's *Historical Atlas* of 1884.[79]

The nineteenth century revived also the allegorical maps, of which the most widely known were the series called *Nouvelle Carte d'Europe*, or, *Serio-Comic Map of Europe*, both composed of caricatural personifications of nation states, produced from 1870 to the outbreak of WWI. Published cheaply in many variations and languages, they were designed, unsurprisingly, by cartoonists, such as the Frenchman Paul Hadol and the Briton Frederic W. Rose.[80] They filled Europe with caricatures of its nation states, all of them fighting and plotting against each other, while dominated by aggressive expansionisms of Prussia and Russia. Every caricature was drawn in such a way as to fill in exactly the shape of a state's boundaries, so as to 'caricaturise' them in the same way in which the whole continent had been 'allegorised' earlier, when compared to a body of the queen. The series, although retaining the physiognomic principles of cartographical allegories which aimed to uncover the truth by covering the meaningless with the meaningful, constitutes however a radically different kind of representation – the parodic mood, where aggression and exaggeration, typical for the language of caricature, sets the order. A courteous renaissance allegory has been displaced by an irreverent political cartoon.

The maps, designed in response to the changing political scene, were reproduced by printing houses of Europe, from Dublin to Moscow, their lengthy captions translated into many languages. It is difficult to establish a particular political allegiance of the cartoonist-mapmaker as, seemingly, no nation-state was spared the mockery. The source of power, however, can manifest itself also in the legitimised silences. Clearly, ethnographic knowledge was of no concern to the wider audiences, and the non-sovereign nations of Europe's east, numerous in the image of Europe the Queen, could hardly been given room in the late nineteenth-century metaphorical visualisations of the continent. The occupied nationalities, deprived of statehood and frontiers, were by and large excluded from the picture. The fate of Poland was occasionally commented upon by an image of a crushed body in the tentacles of the octopus. The latter was, alongside the steam-roller and a rag-collector, one of the recurring signifiers of Russia.[81] The humorous maps produced across Germany and Austria paid more attention to the subjugated territories, and in the lesser known *Humoristische Karte des Deutschen Reiches und von Oesterreich-Ungarn*, of 1887, among the whole range of shoddy personifications of various lands of Germany and Austria-Hungary, a group of street musicians stand for Bohemia, a shoemaker for Moravia and an image of a dandy, who strikes the sleeping Austrian with his walking stick across the border – for Hungary.[82] When Bulgaria, Romania, Serbia, Montenegro, and later, Albania regained their sovereignty from the Ottoman Empire in 1878, they would often be entered into the variants of the comic map, first as babies, then children, to grow into soldiers just in time for the Balkan Wars of 1912–1913, fighting both 'the Turk' and Austria, without any attempt to invest their unfamiliar boundaries with any meaning other than military.[83]

Geopolitical Diagrams and the Versailles New Europe

At the turn of the century, the meaning of geography as the mapping of the unknown was displaced by a new concept of geography as a theoretical science, striving to an all-embracing causal analysis of the known.[84] Both anthropogeography and geopolitics, motivated by Friedrich Ratzel's redefining states and regions as 'earthbound organisms',[85] aimed to reveal the relationship between the primary geographical factors, such as location and global relations of power.[86] The physical properties of the soil and climate were elevated to the rank of the most potent factors, breeding specific racial types, different classes of citizens, as well as political systems. Importantly, geopolitics often reverted to the help of diagrams, unveiling 'a formula . . . of geographical causation in universal history', as explained by the aforementioned Halford

Mackinder in his article 'Geographical Pivot of History', of 1904.[87] One might argue that by professing the capability to reveal the natural grounds for the unequal disposition of power in Europe, geopolitical analysis was based on similar premises to those of physiognomy and allegorical cartography. The by now familiar mechanism of uncovering the truth by explaining the unknown in terms of the known has not been abandoned. The difference was that the truths about Europe were no longer inferred with the help of arbitrary metaphorical substitutions, provided by an image of a queen's body or a figure of a soldier, but were now sought in situ, in and under the ground, in the natural environment. Yet, in spite of professed scientific objectivity, the truths were as arbitrary as, say, linking courage to the sea.

The belief that seas and mountains generate different people from those growing among as steppes and marches generated the argument of 'Geographical Pivot of History', which presented European civilisation as 'the outcome of the secular struggle against the Asiatic invasion'.[88] The seas versus steppes binary formed the kernel of Mackinder's explanation of the whole history of Europe as determined by a physical inequality between 'the unbroken lowland of the east and the rich complex of mountains and valleys, islands and peninsulas [of the west]'. The peninsular western Europe, inhabited by the naturally courageous and entrepreneurial seamen, was under the constant threat from nomadic hordes of the land-men pouring westwards from the continental mass of the Eurasian steppes, extending from the easternmost edges of Russia to the frontiers of German lands. The article was an explicit warning that the threat of the Asiatic invasion increased infinitely in the era of the trans-Siberian railway which accelerated the land-power mobility, diminishing the resistance of the peninsular Europe. He named the Eurasian landmass as the 'geographical pivot of history' and, convinced of the power of the visual, supported his argument with five cartographic diagrams.[89]

Apart from the much discussed and reproduced diagram 'The Natural Seats of Power', showing the Euroasiatic land mass as the pivot of the global power struggles, the very first image in Mackinder's article is that of 'Eastern Europe before the 19th Century' (Figure 2.8). Shown as defined exclusively by forests, marches, and steppes, and extending from the Carpathian to the Ural Mountains, just like Šafařík's *Slowanský zeměvid*, it was described as a gateway, through which 'a remarkable succession of . . . nomadic peoples . . . established themselves . . . and . . . dealt blows northward, westward, and southward against the settled peoples of Europe'.[90] As all other diagrams, Mackinder's image of preindustrial eastern Europe, was a meta-map, using pre-existing cartography to generate synthetic propositions on the relationship between the territory and human agency. Based on the physiographic analysis of the Eurasian continent in the *Berghaus Atlas*, schematic and breathtakingly arbitrary,[91] it took advantage of the bird's eye viewpoint to de-emphasise features which did not fit his argument, while exaggerating the Ural Mountains to mark the boundary with Asia. It expressed in visual terms one of the emergent regimes of truth about the region, associating eastern Europe with plains, forests, marches, steppes and, to quote Bradbury again, with the 'endless invaders who, from every direction, have swept and jostled through this all too accessible landscapes'.[92] Mackinder's map looks like the first anthropogeographical portrayal of whole of Europe's east which passes a verdict on its 'timeless' *geophysique*. Not only is it named 'Eastern Europe', but it is also framed by double lines. This prominent frame turns its contents into a visual manifesto of geographical determinism, a synthetic portrait of Europe's east, indicating

Figure 2.8 Halford Mackinder, 'Eastern Europe before the 19th Century' (after Drude in
   Berghaus' *Physical Atlas*), in H. Mackinder, 'The Geographical Pivot of History',
   Geographical Journal 23, no. 4 (1904).

explicitly what this region is made of. Moreover, it presents its territory as not just
being sliced out from the double spread of the Eurasian landmass as in the *Berghaus
Atlas*, but also as detached from the 'western peninsula'. A similar formula of ramifi-
cation and separation will soon return in countless cartographic diagrams of this part
of Europe, produced during and after the calamities of WWI.

   Few would dispute that, precisely, it was the Great War and the collapse of the Great
Empires which constituted the truly 'pivotal' moment in the history of mapping, making, and imaging eastern Europe. Drawn in the process of painstaking negotiations at
the Peace Conference in Versailles (1919–1920), Woodrow Wilson's map of the New
Europe which created a new region of 'small states' in the middle of the continent,
carved out from the territories of Austria-Hungary, Russia, and Prussia, was one the
most decisive and, at the same time, one of the most heavily condemned acts of cartographic projections of the twentieth century. The 'spectacular failure' of the Wilso-
nian principle of national self-determination, which had aimed to secure the justness
and durability of the new boundaries by correlating them with ethnic divisions, has
been widely debated by historians. In tune with the geopolitical interests of the Allies,

the principle was rewarding the victors and punishing the losers. The latter included also Hungary, which lost two-thirds of its territory to Romania, Czechoslovakia, and Yugoslavia. Not all the minorities were granted their sovereign statehood, and the entirely new federal states of Yugoslavia and Czechoslovakia were devised as multi-ethnic republics. As a corollary, the redrawn map of 1920, the conference's outcome and signifier, has been notoriously accused for setting free the dormant nationalisms and for provoking the disasters of the twentieth century which reverberate until today. Recent publications by Steven Seegel and Larry Wolff documented in detail the process of the negotiations and controversies among the international team of the 'map men' and politicians led by the American President who had never visited eastern Europe and relied on the maps supplied by international delegates and the Supreme Council and the Territorial Commissions.[93] Both books are remarkable for focusing on people, on their public and private worlds, friendships and enmities, professional careers, and tragedies. Both are illustrated with photographs of the 'map men' or of monuments to Wilson in eastern Europe, while the reproductions of maps, even if most carefully annotated, as in Seegel's book, are relegated to a supplement at the end.

As noted by Guntram Henrik Herb, it was indeed the maps, and in particular ethnographic maps, which played an unprecedented role during the proceedings, used as arguments by ministers, academic experts, and delegates, both to judge and to support the validity of territorial claims.[94] There was a marked difference, however, in the status ascribed to the maps: while those employed by the experts, in particular by the professedly neutral American House Inquiry, carried the 'aura of scientific documents, of being accurate and objective', those appended by representatives of the 'small states' were viewed with suspicion, as if inevitably perverted by nationalist fervour, as untrustworthy as the folkloric dress worn for an effect by some delegates.[95] The metaphorical relationship, or rather an umbilical cord, between the map and the ethnic body was performed there to a great effect. The most striking comment on the deliberate distortion of maps presented by the delegates was made by Isaiah Bowman, Director of the American Geographical Society and the Chief Territorial Specialist of the House Inquiry, who wrote in his evaluation of the Parisian conference:

> Each one of the central European nationalities had its own bagful of statistical and cartographical tricks. When statistics failed, use was made of maps in colour. It would take a huge monograph to contain an analysis of all the types of map forgeries that the war and the peace conference called forth. A new instrument was discovered – the map language. A map was as good as a brilliant poster, and just being a map made its respectable, authentic. A perverted map was a life-belt to many a foundering argument. It was in the Balkans that the use of this process reached its most brilliant climax.[96]

A 'huge monograph' on the maps' forgeries committed by the small nations at the Peace Conference, examining those distrusted maps as 'brilliant posters' and as means of self-representation, is still to be completed.[97] Of course, the embarkation on such a project is problematic from the start because *all* maps are inherently rhetorical. The partiality of the western cartographers involved in the Conference, such as the pro-Romanian Emmanuel de Martonne, was documented by Gilles Palsky.[98]

As stated by Seegel, 1,200 maps of the region were collected by the House Inquiry[99] and many more of them had been drawn both before and long after the conference.

The Geographical Society of America and the major cartographic publishers, such as Rand McNally,[100] Caleb S. Hammond, and John George Bartholomew, were producing detailed maps of the New Europe, showing the old and new boundaries, with copious information on the Conference treaties on the margins. An avalanche of thematic maps, often staged as a narrative which visualised in two or more cartographic diagrams the unprecedented transformation of the body of Europe, were disseminated by school atlases and books, as in Walter Consuelo Langsam's documentary histories of Europe *The World since 1914*, followed by *The World since 1919* (Figure 2.9).[101] In Germany and Hungary, a great number of the maps, propelled by loss, were drawn in an angry response to the Paris treaties. Apart from Pát Teleki's famous *Carte Rouge*, 1919, which had been prepared for the Conference to overshadow the Romanian claims by the sheer force of the vibrant red,[102] the most polemical and the most widely reproduced was Albrecht Penck's *Karte des deutschen Volks- und Kulturbodens*, 1925, which, clinging to Ratzel's anthropogeography, was campaigning for Germany's economic, linguistic and cultural rights to *Lebensraum* in the east.[103]

The disputes about the boundaries of the particular states were developing in parallel to a search for a new formula suitable for the representation of the whole cluster of emancipated nations as a distinct political region. A new common denominator for these diverse European states was needed, a new image which would abandon the rhetoric of vastness and cultural commonality, or even that of territorial uniformity, claimed by Šafařík's map and Mackinder's diagram. The process began during WWI, when a number of prominent historians, intellectuals, and politicians campaigned for the dismemberment of the Habsburg Empire

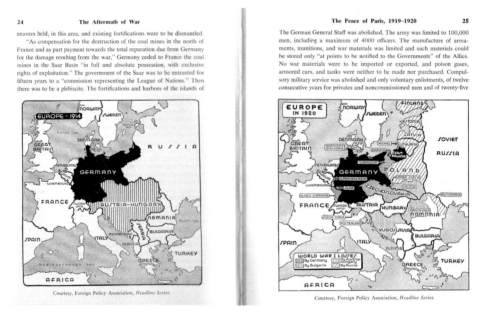

Figure 2.9 The map of 'Europe 1914' juxtaposed to 'Europe 1920' in Walter Consuelo Langsam, *The World Since 1919*. New York: The Macmillan Company, 1933.

and for granting the sovereignty rights to the oppressed nations. Among the most persuasive were the British historian Robert W. Seton-Watson, described as the 'maker of a New Europe', and his close friend, the Czech philosopher and politician Tomáš G. Masarýk, the future President of Czechoslovakia. Both Seton-Watson and Masarýk lectured at the School of Eastern European and Slavonic Studies which, newly established in 1915, was the first university department in Britain devoted to the research on the newly invented part of Europe, its politics, history, languages, and cultures. Both of them published influential books, to include Masarýk's *The Problems of Small Nations in the European Crisis* (1916) and *The New Europe* (1918), as well as Seton-Watson's *German, Slav, and Magyar: A Study in the Origins of the Great War* (1916).[104] Their titles provided the key terms around which the political discourses of the era were hinged. And for both of them maps were the tools of expressing their political ideas. Together, they launched a new periodical called *The New Europe*, which vehemently opposed the refreshed spectre of *Mitteleuropa*, proposed by Friedrich Naumann in 1915.[105] It promoted the alternative vision for central Europe, purified not only of Teutonic domination, but also of Germany itself. Echoing Šafařík and Panslavist ideology, it was meant to embrace predominantly Slavic states and nations, ideally consolidated into a powerful multiethnic federation, for which Czechoslovakia and Yugoslavia were designed as templates. Their *New Europe* was kind to maps. Its first issue, published in October 1916, opened from a vivid cartographic analysis of the hidden agenda of Germany's call to armistice, demystifying it as a smoke-screen for further expansion into Asia achieved through the completion of the Berlin-Baghdad railway.[106] A large foldout map, followed by the leading article 'Pangermanism and the Eastern Question' by Thomas Masarýk, acted as a manifesto, laying bare the aim of the periodical, dedicated to the emancipation of central and south-eastern Europe from German and Magyar control.[107] Suggestively coloured in pink and blue, entitled 'Why Germany Wants Peace Now' and anchored by extensive legends supporting the main argument, the map positioned itself in the role of an editorial cartoon. Even if it constituted a major discursive accent of the issue, the map was focused on the threat of German expansionism rather than presenting a coherent image of the not yet fully invented region, labelled in the caption as central Europe.

A more regular cartographic vision of the New Europe-in-the making was included in Seton-Watson's book on the origins of the Great War, published in the same year. The map was entitled 'The New Europe on a Basis of Nationality' (Figure 2.10). The signature of The Mappa Company revealed that Seton-Watson's vision, made of lines and dots, was based, like Mackinder's diagrams, on the ready-made map, to which he added the proposed boundaries of the new states.[108] While disregarding cartographic accuracy, the map would not give up on its rhetorical potential. The small legend at the bottom, indicating the 'existing' and 'new' frontiers, plus 'Free Ports', and especially its overblown title, clearly vying for attention, formed an important part of the image, emphasising its manifesto-like message, a project of a 'regenerated' Europe. Reflecting the author's sympathies, it turned to be generous to Bohemia, Romania, and Yugoslavia, but less so to Hungary and Poland, denying the latter an access to the sea.[109]

The map constitutes an early example of the novel cartographic regime in imaging the New Europe. Unlike Waldseemüller's Sarmatia Europea and Šafařík's *Slowanský zeměvid* both extended horizontally, it now represents the region in a vertical format

Figure 2.10 Robert W. Seton-Watson, 'The New Europe on a Basis of Nationality', in *German, Slav, and Magyar – A Study in the Origins of the Great War*. London: Williams & Norgate, 1916.

of a 'single portrait', as a separate unit which, within the narrow stretch of land dividing Germany from Russia, incorporates a whole cluster of those not fully formed political bodies, including both Slavic and non-Slavic ones. The Sarmatian opulence and Slavic vastness shrivelled to a narrow belt of *Zwischeneuropa*.[110] This new way of portraying eastern Europe as the 'lands between', has since been repeated so many times that today it is taken for granted. It stresses both the distinctiveness of the newly invented region, as well as communicating its separateness, the removability from western Europe.

   There is no doubt that Seton-Watson's *New Europe* was intended as a counter-map, restoring sovereignty to the oppressed nations, and its vertical format simply corresponded with their position on the map of Europe. However, as with Šafařík's map, it was the rhetorical power of the image itself which invested the map with additional layers of meaning and activated its socio-political status in the twentieth century. The landscape frame was displaced by the portrait frame. The genre of portrait, as much as landscape, is essentially celebratory and makes extra-aesthetic claims pertaining to the social status and power of the sitter. Its subspecies, the group portrait, comments on the relationship between individuals, emphasising marks of shared identity based on legal contracts, blood ties or social affiliation.[111] Unlike the single portrait which usually opts for vertical size, the group portrait uses the horizontal format suitable for multifigure compositions. The most evocative feature of Seton-Watson's *New Europe*, however, is the disparity between the conventions of a group portrait and a single portrait format. In contrast to its celebratory caption, it shows an anxiety-ridden image of a chaotic array of new states, small and insecure within their unfixed boundaries, and crowded uncomfortably one on top of another. What they share, the image seems to say, is their 'newness', smallness, instability, and propensity to discord.

Another issue is separateness. The new states are portrayed as occupying an isolated region which, in order to be represented, had to be excised from the map of the continent and framed as an independent territory, that of the 'New Europe', positioned between western Europe and Russia. If *Slowanský zeměvid* prompted the long-standing regime of representing eastern Europe as bound to Russia, Seton-Watson's map established another enduring cartographic trope that naturalised the understanding of the region in terms of inherent political instability and separateness. Both were intended as maps of resistance, and both were liable to be also read as visual documents of domination and subjugation. Their affinities to the landscape and portrait formats contributed to opacity and ambiguity, generating oppositional readings.

Mackinder had to have the last word. After WWI, his revised pivot theory was published in his new book *Democratic Ideals and Reality* (1919).[112] Illustrated with 31 maps and diagrams, and re-edited several times both during and after WWII, the book proposed new terms, such as Heartland (the pivot area extended eastwards), World-Island ('the joint continent of Europe, Asia and Africa'),[113] as well as identified a new geopolitical threat, now coming from a potential alliance between Bolshevik Russia and Germany. To prevent that, Mackinder argued, the so-called 'Middle Tier' of states, set up within the Heartland should function as a territorial buffer between democracy and despotism.[114] This new geopolitical role given to the region, that of a *cordon sanitaire* between Germany and Russia, was visualised by Mackinder in yet another sketch map (Figure 2.11).[115] Dropping the name 'Eastern Europe' and disregarding its alleged physical features, it filled the territory with the new nation states, as they were discussed in Paris. Unframed, drawn from memory, with no concern for exact boundaries, Mackinder's hand-drawn map displayed both the lightness of *disegno* and the heaviness of a loaded caricature. Its off-hand style suited the idea of the region's newness and an intrinsic insecurity: 'The peoples of the Middle Tier – Poles, Bohemians, Hungarians, Rumanians, Serbians, Bulgarians, and Greeks – are much too unlike to federate for any purpose except defence', Mackinder advised.[116] The notion of discord and instability were anchored further in by the caption, stressing that 'many boundary questions have still to be determined'. Mackinder's diagnosis would be reproduced with slight variations by other maps of the region, accompanied by increasingly metaphorical captions, such as 'shatter zone' or 'belt of political change', well until the 1940s and beyond.[117] If Mackinder's first map portrayed eastern Europe as a terrain enabling an unobstructed transfer for invaders from the east, his second map reinvented it as the zone of containment. In Mackinder's rhetoric: 'Who rules East Europe commands the Heartland: Who rules the Heartland commands the World-Island: Who rules the World-Island commands the World'.[118]

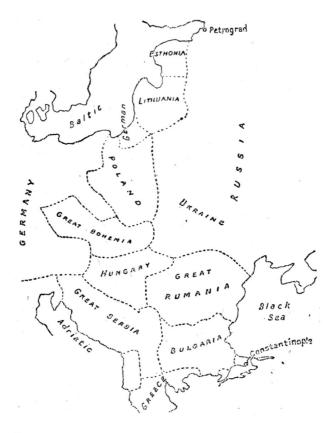

Figure 2.11 Halford Mackinder, 'The Middle Tier of States between Germany and Russia. Many boundary questions have still to be determined', in H. Mackinder, *Democratic Ideals and Reality: A Study in the Politics of Reconstruction*. London: Constable and Co, 1919.

Eastern Europe Equals Communist Bloc

As if in fulfilment of Mackinder's prophecy, the space of eastern Europe became one of the most the contested trophies of the Cold War.[119] The conflict over the command of eastern Europe post-1945 brought the first unbridgeable rift within the Grand Alliance, instigating the Cold War.[120] If in the interwar era, eastern Europe had emerged on the map as a distinct region, the Cold War locked it behind the Iron Curtain. The new discourse of containment and its institutional formations produced Eastern Europe as we knew it, turning it from a raw product of Versailles mapmakers into a distinct full-blown entity, political, military, economic as well as cultural. Spelled with two capital 'E's, framed by the Churchillian Iron Curtain, consolidated internally by the Cold War institutions, such as Comecon and the Warsaw Pact, Eastern Europe came to be identified with the lands and minds captured by Soviet communism.[121] Separated from the West and attached to the vast territory of the Soviet Union, not only did it acquire the shape of Šafařík's map, but it also extended a long way westwards, reaching beyond Berlin. Its brand new maps entered classroom atlases and were widely disseminated by the press, especially in the aftermath of Churchill's Fulton speech, which constituted the decisive moment for the rise of the specific Cold War cartography.

Delivered in March 1946 and entitled 'Sinews of Peace', Churchill's Fulton address went down in history as the 'Iron Curtain speech' and has been widely studied as a masterpiece of political rhetoric.

> A shadow has fallen across the scenes so lately lighted by the Allied victory. Nobody knows what Soviet Russia and its communist international organisation intends to do in the immediate future, or what are the limits, if any, to their expansive and proselytizing tendencies . . . From Stettin on the Baltic to Trieste on the Adriatic an iron curtain has descended across the Continent. Behind that line lie all the capitals of the ancient states of Central and Eastern Europe – Warsaw, Berlin, Prague, Vienna, Budapest, Belgrade, Bucharest and Sofia. . . . This is certainly not the liberated Europe which we fought to build up.[122]

The speech skilfully explored the 'fearful vividness' of the Iron Curtain phrase which, as argued by Max Lerner, 'rolle[d] up into a single image all the fears that the Soviet State has invoked since the Russian Revolution'.[123] Although the metaphor of the iron safety curtain was by no means new, having been used in the context of Bolshevik Russia since the 1920s, it was Churchill who introduced the term to the language of politics and everyday discourse.[124] A familiar phrase in newspaper headlines and parliamentary debates, as well as in atlases and history books, the Iron Curtain turned into a performative boundary, a diacritical marker of the Self/Other nexus. It acted both as the master signifier and as a potent instrument to naturalise all the former tropes of eastern European difference. It generated an Iron Curtain visuality, pervading all spheres of culture.

The Cold War cartography thrived in newspapers.[125] As in the case of the geopolitical diagrams, the point of the newspaper maps was to make a claim rather than survey the territory. The ways in which those countless maps were openly charged with meaning, transcending the standard repertory of the cartographic sign system, brought them close to the strategies of newspaper cartoons. As I have signalled earlier, both operated by simplification and distortion to emphasise the essence of the argument, often strengthened by caption (Figure 2.14). And since many cartoons themselves had a strong cartographic component, the boundaries between those two media became indistinguishable. The maps of the Cold War did not hide but emphasised their belongingness to the family of images. The major theme of both maps and cartoons, published in newspapers right or left, was the split of the world into the two mutually hostile blocks West and East.

The torn-apart map is the topic of George Whitelaw's "Opeless" in the *Daily Herald*, known as the 'working class' newspaper.[126] It shows Churchill at a rally of the United Europe Committee in the Albert Hall in London in May 1947, campaigning for the federal organisation of western European states. Standing on a stage in front of a huge wall-map of Europe, he has just ripped out its eastern part, throwing it on the floor. The cartoon, positioned next to the editorial entitled 'The Mapmakers' in an obvious reference to the arbitrariness of the mapmaking in Versailles, accuses Churchill of excluding Russia and 'her Slavonic fraternities' from any idea of a trans-European alliance.[127] The caption suggests, cleverly, the ways in which it should be read: while

Churchill points out to the large letters 'EUR', while the missing 'OPE', in bold, from the torn-off section of the map, is turned into the caption "OPEless' in working class slang, as if coming from the mouth of the reader. One week later, the cartoon was reproduced by the German weekly *Der Spiegel*, which had just been launched in Hanover under the sponsorship of the British administration (Figure 2.12). A short commentary repeated the views of the *Daily Herald*, pointing out that Churchill's real goal was the division of Europe and the exclusion of Russia together with the countries it occupied.[128]

The Soviet occupation of Eastern Europe dominated the media, whether in cartoons or maps. It also led to a plethora of aggressive cartographic diagrams in history books, which, alongside films and novels, almost obsessively emphasised the separateness of the Iron Curtain countries, repeatedly evoking the notion of emptiness, a sense of loss and of utter horror associated with the space trapped behind the Iron Curtain. Long before the Berlin Wall was built, countless cartographic cartoons kept conjuring up a wall running through Germany and Europe.[129] Many are still reproduced today on slide share sites and blogs, as visual evidence of the 'reality' of the Cold War.[130] Cold War gave also a new lease life to the genre of caricature maps, particularly appealing to cartoonists, including David Low and Leslie Illingworth in Britain, who were

Figure 2.12 George Whitelow, "Opeless', *Der Spiegel*, 24 May 1947 after *Daily Herald*, 16 May 1947. By permission of Reach Publishing Services.

outdoing each other in finding fitting signifiers for the European state of affairs at the time of post-war reconstruction, remilitarisation and austerity.[131]

A novel cartographic iconography of the Cold War came from America. As argued by Susan Schulten and Jeffrey Stone, the tone was set by American journals, such as *Fortune* or *Time*, which led the field in terms of printing technology, and employed trained cartographers.[132] Richard Edes Harrison's perspectival maps published in *Fortune* in the 1940s, both stylistically innovative and politically charged, treated the viewer to spectacular panoramic visions of whole continents in full colour, with mountain chains, rivers and cities, as if observed from a very high-flying plane.[133] Equally memorable were the maps produced by Robert M. Chapin Jr, Harrison's student and *Time* magazine's Chief Cartographer during the early Cold War era, who was supplying countless visions of the divided world. Playing directly into the propaganda of McCarthyism, Chapin's maps seamlessly combined the strategies of mapmaking with those of cartoon-making. His 'Europe from Moscow', published in *Time* in 1952 (Figure 2.13), constituted an archetypal anti-communist cartographic cartoon. Borrowing the concept from Harrison's map 'Europe from the East' (1944), it showed the European continent oriented northwards, as if following Europe as

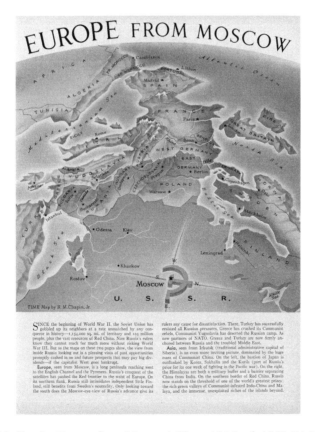

Figure 2.13 R.M. Chapin, 'Europe from Moscow', *Time*, 10 March 1952. Division of Rare and Manuscript Collections, Cornell University Library. Persuasive Maps: PJ Mode Collection.

Queen in Münster's *Cosmography*. The threat of the invasion coming from the East, which had been silenced in the sixteenth-century map, was emphasised by Chapin who, like Mackinder, invested the physical features of the territory with meaning and manipulated them to achieve a desired effect. He represented the Soviet lands as if encountered in a terrifying dream, as the uniformly flattened plateau of the Evil Empire in which all signs of life and environmental diversity had been eliminated. Overpainted in red, it resembled a monstrously overblown Red Square, ruled by hammer and sickle. The occupied countries of Eastern Europe, squeezed to a narrow space in the middle, were also coloured red, albeit some faint contours of mountains signalled life and hence resistance. By contrast, the western peninsula was almost covered by the overemphasised mountains, and rendered in the contrasting hues of green and orange. The reddish patches of the ground, however, pointed, in an unmistakably McCarthy's manner, to the communist threat and the need for staying alert.

Standard maps produced at that time were not entirely free of political persuasion either. The dominating rhetoric of division and containment could be communicated in different ways, such as the identification of Europe with western Europe, or by manipulating the names of maps. Joshua Hagen brought attention to 'the geopolitics of naming', to 'the importance of language and naming in shaping, contesting, and redrawing the imagined political geography of Europe'.[134] The term Eastern Europe might have entered the language of politics, academe, and the everyday, but it was not uniformly considered 'politically correct'. Significantly, the American *National Geographic Magazine*, one of the major producers of maps of the world which arrived as supplements into the mailboxes of five million subscribers by the mid-1950s,[135] banned the term. While announcing in December 1950, on the occasion of issuing the map of Western Europe, the forthcoming publication of the map of Eastern Europe 'which will cover the Balkan countries',[136] the editors changed its name in the last moment. The map, issued in February 1951, which covered the territory corresponding roughly with Seton-Watson's New Europe, was presented in a 'portrait format', and named 'Central Europe Including the Balkan States'. This was consistent with the magazine's unstated preference for the term central Europe since the beginning of WWI.[137]

Half-way between the sharp claims of newspaper maps and the presumed neutrality of standard maps came the cartographic visions of Eastern Europe in numerous atlases, historical, economic, or cultural. The latter were a German specialty, in which Ratzel's and Penck's theories would be rehearsed long after they were discredited by their links to Nazi propaganda. Hans Zeissig's *Neuer Geschichts- und Kulturatlas*, published in 1950 and reprinted many times well until the end of the millennium, mapped the spread of culture from west to east, stressing in particular the role of the Germans 'as settlers and pioneers of culture in European east', between the eleventh and nineteenth centuries.[138] The atlas associated culture almost exclusively with Roman influence, the spread of the gothic style, the rise of universities and with the translation of the Bible into vernacular languages. It excluded Orthodox churches, coffin portraits, wooden synagogues, and, curiously, even the imports of the Italian renaissance into Hungary and Poland. Accordingly, the lands of Europe's east, with just a few markers on their territory, were mapped as uncultured.[139] Historical atlases developed their own ways of pointing to the deficiencies of Eastern Europe. *The Oxford Atlas of European History*, 1957, for instance, systematically presented its territories throughout the whole of the twentieth century, whether sovereign or not, as colourless, that is as the essentially colonisable, deprived of their own identities, and in need to be framed and 'completed' by successive occupiers.[140]

I could multiply those examples, examining wall-maps for schools and economic atlases, in which Eastern Europe is left out,[141] as if following Whitelaw's cartoon. Correspondingly, I could point to similar exclusions in Communist Bloc atlases, analysed by Jeremy Black.[142] But, if the Cold War 'made' post-1945 Eastern Europe, then the changes in Eastern Europe of 1989, unexpectedly for the great majority of policymakers and mapmakers, unmade the Cold War. Although the latter was a global conflict, the first victorious rebellion of the 'satellites' against communism was proclaimed as the end of the Cold War, even before the collapse of the Soviet Union.[143] And, subsequently, the strategies of containment were displaced by those of enlargement. This process of transition was accompanied by the radical decentring of Eastern Europe, on the one hand, and its hasty reconstruction on the other hand, in both textual and visual terms.

Cartographies of Post-Communist Europe

The Fall of the Wall might have destroyed the material substance of the Cold War boundaries but, at the same time, it accelerated and intensified the production of the 'eastern European' difference.[144] The urgency of this project might be linked to the post-Wall lack of discernible 'primary' features of racial difference between western and eastern Europeans, such as the colour of the skin. One might even say that it was the Wall and its attributed chromatism, evoking the monotonous greyishness, routinely associated with the lands imprisoned behind the Iron Curtain, which had acted before 1989 as the displacement of Eastern Europe's 'coloured skin'. The abolition of the Wall, as the guarantee of the tangible division between deservingly and 'undeservingly white', to use the term of *The Guardian* columnist,[145] brought a growing anxiety over the absence of immediately perceivable markers of difference. The disappearance of the Wall as the othering device had to be compensated for by articulating the difference through other easily recognisable codes, such as dress, foreign accent, winter coldness, as well as through the use of maps. One of the after-effects was the intensified production of new cartographies of eastern Europe. New encyclopaedias and history books, and especially new atlases of all kinds, were now mobilised in the attempt to fix the meaning of the Other Europe, and to learn more about the notoriously confusing shape of the region before allowing its gradual access to major European security and economic organisations.[146] The liberation of the Baltic States, Belarus and Ukraine and the Republic of Moldova, as well as the breakup of Czechoslovakia, followed by the dramatic collapse of Yugoslavia, all required new maps, as well as new plausible geopolitical scenarios. In spite of the rhetoric of enlargement, the well-established principle of separation of Europe's east from the west still reigned supreme.

The maps of 'Europe redrawn' and the debates on the pros and cons of enlargement was the staple diet of the media, newspapers as well as television. In his analysis of the newspaper maps in Britain of the 1990s, proliferating especially in Sunday magazines, Peter Vujakovic pointed to the change of the cartographic rhetoric espoused by those maps which, by and large, were premised on the trope of Fortress Europe, and moved from optimism to a cautious pessimism, from the rhetoric of enlargement to that of anxiety, which was to be particularly prominent on the eve of the accession of Poland, Czechoslovakia and Hungary to the European Union.[147] The 'death of Eastern Europe' might have been announced by the media and academe, but its ghost would often be resurrected on maps of the globe in tabloid pages and websites published from the beginning of the new millennium, warning against global dangers to humankind, such as the epidemic of HIV, environmental pollution, women's rights and political instability. Eastern Europe would almost invariably be classified not only as separate from western Europe and attached to Asia, but also marked as a space of 'impurity and danger'. As argued by James Aulich and Marta Sylvestrová, the region was turned into an imagined site of latent horror, the 'threat of internecine war, uncontrollable immigration, nuclear terrorism, drugs, AIDS, the far-right, environmental disaster, and political and financial gangsterism'.[148]

Paul Magocsi's *Historical Atlas of Central Europe* was one of the most carefully prepared publications of this period, appearing in several editions since 1993 (Figure 2.14).[149] Two brightly coloured maps on the cover of its 2002 edition, which represent the eastern Europe of 1910 and of 2000, follow the now hegemonic format of the vertical portrait of the region. Positioned side by side, they visualise the epochal shift from the Europe of empires to the post-communist Europe which, over the span of 90 years, changed the political boundaries within the region so drastically that these two maps look as if they were representing two entirely different worlds. If the first used only a limited colour scale, the second required all colours of the rainbow to distinguish between the multitudes of new countries, settled within the same space. Significantly, both maps were named as 'central Europe', even if they covered roughly the same space as that selected by Mackinder in 1904 for his 'Eastern Europe before the 19th century', and came even closer to Seton-Watson's vertical portrait of 'New Europe on the basis of nationality' of 1916.

It is worth noticing that Magocsi's atlas was first published in 1993 as *Historical Atlas of East Central Europe*.[150] The change of its title was explained in the foreword to the 2002 edition as having been suggested by the publisher keen to avoid negative connotations carried by the names 'eastern or even east-central', and claiming that the choice of the term 'Central Europe' was 'based simply on geographical criteria'.[151] It indicated nonetheless the geopolitics of naming as one of the main concerns of the time. The major debate, initiated already by prominent eastern European dissidents during the 1980s, was about abandoning the term 'Eastern Europe' altogether, roundly perceived as derogatory and as a testament to the submission to the ideology of communism. It was argued that the region, or in fact, its 'central' areas with Czechoslovakia, Hungary and Poland had always been, historically and culturally, part of central Europe and should be renamed accordingly.[152] As argued by Hagen, even if motivated by the idea of getting away from the hegemonic east-west matrix, the debate was ultimately marked by the identification of central Europe with the west, turning into a tool of securing the leading positions in negotiating membership of western institutions. However, there are few doubts that, despite the end of the Cold War, the east-west divide has remained deeply ingrained in geographical imaginations across the continent.[153]

In the process of forming new formulas of self-representation, the region generated a new cartographic regime, employed directly in the aftermath of the 1989 revolutions by virtually all of the former countries of the Communist Bloc. Its core principle was detachment from Russia, or, more precisely, the removal of Russia from Europe, as if echoing the gesture of Churchill in Whitelow's cartoon. As argued by Donald J.

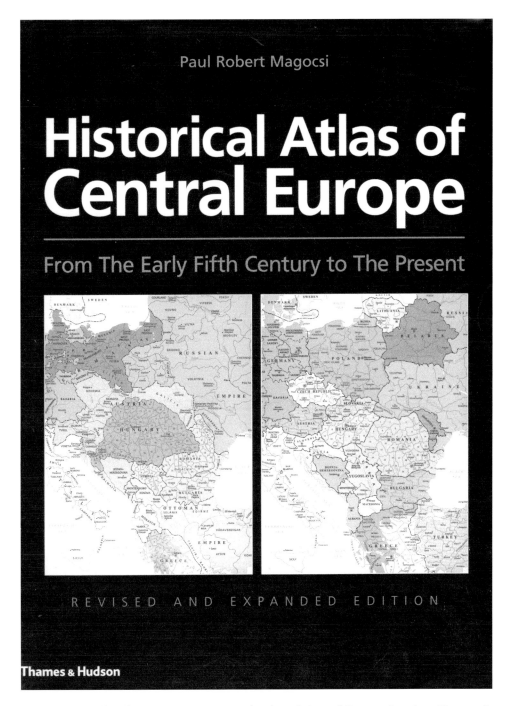

Figure 2.14 Paul Robert Magocsi, *Historical Atlas of Central Europe*. London: Thames & Hudson, 2002. By permission of Thames & Hudson.

Zeigler in his article 'Cartographies of independence', which analysed maps that had been sent by those countries to their embassies in Washington, the common denominator of all of them was the removal of Russia from the territory covered. None of them would extend 'farther east than the 40th meridian'. 'In a geopolitical sense', he wrote, '"Eastern Europe" as a region died suddenly at the end of the Cold War. None of the former communist states continued to show themselves in the neighbourhood where the world was used to finding them – behind the Iron Curtain, walled off from the West'.[154]

While it is debatable whether eastern Europe still constitutes a distinct topic for contemporary mapmakers, I want to close this survey of the shifting cartographies of the region with two maps produced in 2015. A tourist map of the eastern Europe and a refugee map of Europe[155] paint two contradictory images of the area: celebratory and critical. Rather surprisingly, when submitted to visual analysis, both of them revert to the old cartographic regimes of spatial instability, with the second one redefining the notion of separability as non-involvement in the major European projects of the present.

Almost immediately after the fall of the Berlin Wall, eastern Europe as a region developed an entirely new identity, that of tourists' and travellers' destination. Initially, the umbrella term 'Eastern Europe' prevailed, both in the production of tourist guides and maps, inviting foreign visitors to the entire area.[156] Soon came new guides and new maps, focused on specific countries and tourist spots. The cover of one of the very few maps of 'Eastern Europe' available in map shops today, issued by the Latvian Jāņa sēta Map Publishers, is particularly interesting in the context of the reshaping of the territory discussed in this chapter (Figure 2.15).[157] It shows a large swathe of Europe's east, which excludes its east central area and the Balkans almost entirely, while extending far into Russia, comparable in this respect to Coronelli's *Europa Orientale* from the end of the seventeenth century. Moreover, it sequesters the space of Europe's east into smaller sections. Apart from the area covering former Soviet Republics, with the Baltic states, Belarus, Ukraine, and Moldova, as well as Russia itself as far as St Petersburg and Moscow; there are further sections with the Volga district of Russia, the small Caucasus area, as well as a northern outpost around the White Sea, the latter appealing to travellers rather than tourists. By including the Russian partition of Poland, while cutting off practically all the countries which had not formed part of imperial Russia and the Soviet Union, such as Czechia, large parts of Slovakia and Hungary, as well as the Balkans, the map redefines eastern Europe yet again, pushing it radically eastwards. It could not have been more explicit in confirming the notion of spatial indeterminacy as the defining feature of the region, and most of all, its inescapable affinity with Russia.

But the tourists paying hard currency have not been the only incomers to the area during the last decade. Since 2015, Europe witnessed the steady influx of refugees from Syria and Africa, escaping war, hunger, and prosecution. The emerging cartography of the refugees routes through Europe since 2015 seems to merge the old formula of imaging eastern Europe as the region on the margin with a new emphasis on the yet again redefined notion of separateness and non-cooperation.[158] In 'Europe's Refugee Crisis' map, produced by Reuters' in 2015 (www.businessinsider.com/map-of-europe-refugee-crisis-2015-9?r=US&IR=T), the northern parts of the region lie conspicuously outside the network of the new migrants' routes.[159] As indicated by the multitude of red arrows, south-eastern Europe constitutes a

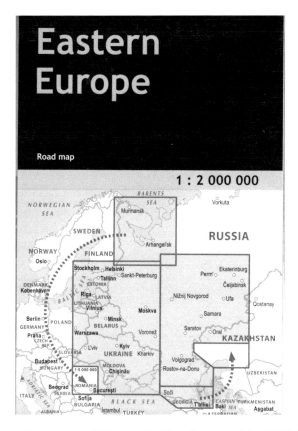

Figure 2.15 Eastern Europe. Road Map, 2015. Riga: Jāņa sēta Map Publishers.

transfer area, which includes the Balkans, Romania, as well as Hungary as the last stop before embarking on the trains heading west and north. The black line of the strengthened border between Croatia and Hungary, set up by the Hungarian nationalist government, which secured it with barbed wire and armed guards, testifies to the re-emerging principle of closed borders. As widely reported by the media, not just Hungary, but also Poland and Czech Republic (Czechia) have repeatedly refused to host the immigrants on their soil.[160] Strangely, however, the map shows the lack of hospitality as tantamount to self-marginalisation. Slovakia, Czechia, Poland, the Baltic countries, as well as Belarus and Ukraine yet again lie off the beaten track. Neither do they invite the refugees, the map seems to say, nor are they wanted by them.

The dynamics of migration has always been the major historical force in making Europe and its regions. After all, the first name given to Europe's east by ancient historians, that of Sarmatia Europea, acknowledged its creation by migrants from the Middle East. Few would doubt that the cartographies of refuge and migration will continue to play a significant role in redefining the hierarchies of the continent. It remains to be seen what position in this process will be adopted by Europe's east, regardless of what its boundaries will be.

Notes

1. On the issue of naming the region, see Gordon East, 'The Concept and Political Status of the Shatter Zone', in Norman J.G. Pounds, ed., *Geographical Essays on Eastern Europe* (Bloomington, IN: Indiana University Press, 1963), 1–27; recently, Frithjof Benjamin Schenk, 'Eastern Europe', in Diana Mishkova and Balázs Trencsényi, eds, *European Regions and Boundaries: A Conceptual History* (New York and Oxford: Berghahn, 2017), 188–89.

2. Geoffrey J. Martin, 'Paris Peace Conference', in Mark Monmonier, ed., *The History of Cartography, Volume 6: Cartography of the Twentieth Century* (Chicago: University of Chicago Press, 2015), 1049–53.

3. The first act of the WWII squabbling about the territory of Europe took place in Tehran, where during the final plenary session in December 1943 'the British and Russians were working on a map of Poland torn from *The Times* of London' – Charles E. Bohlen, *Witness to History, 1929–1969* (New York: Norton, 1973), 152–53.

4. R.J. Richard and Benjamin Crampton, *Atlas of Eastern Europe in the Twentieth Century* (London: Routledge, 1996); Paul Robert Magocsi *Historical Atlas of Central Europe: From the Early Fifth Century to the Present* (London: Thames and Hudson, 2002).

5. Steven Seegel, *Map Men: Transnational Lives and Deaths of Geographers in the Making of East Central Europe* (Chicago and London: University of Chicago Press, 2018); Yuliya Komska, 'Introduction: A Discontigious Eastern Europe', in Irene Kacandes and Yuliya Komska, eds, *Eastern Europe Unmapped: Beyond Borders and Peripheries* (New York and Oxford: Berghahn Books, 2018), 1–28. See also Jörn Happel and Christophe von Werdt, with assistance of Mira Jovanović, *Osteuropa kartiert – Mapping Eastern Europe* (Berlin: LIT Verlag, 2010).

6. Wendy Bracewell, Tim Beasley-Murray and Michal Murawski, eds, *Anti-Atlas: Towards a Critical Area Studies* (London: UCL Press, forthcoming).

7. Frithjof Benjamin Schenk, 'Mental Maps: The Cognitive Mapping of the Continent as an Object of Research of European History', *European History Online (EGO)*, 2013, http://ieg-ego.eu/en/threads/theories-and-methods/mental-maps/frithjof-benjamin-schenk-mental-maps-the-cognitive-mapping-of-the-continent-as-an-object-of-research-of-european-history; Larry Wolff, *Mental Mapping and Eastern Europe*. 12th Södertörn Lectures (Huddinge, Sweden: Södertörn University, 2016); Norbert Götz and Janne Holmén, eds, 'Mental Maps: Geographical and Historical Perspectives', special issue of *Journal of Cultural Geography* 35, no. 2 (2018).

8. Gillian Rose, 'On the Need to Ask How, Exactly, Is Geography "Visual"?', *Antipode* 35, no. 2 (March 2003); Mike Crang, 'Visual Methods and Methodologies', in Dydia DeLyser et al., eds, *The SAGE Handbook of Qualitative Geography* (London: Sage, 2009), 208–25; F. MacDonald, 'Visuality', and S. Hoelscher, 'Landscape Iconography', both in Rob Kitchin and Nigel Thrift, eds, *International Encyclopedia of Human Geography* (Chicago and London: Elsevier, 2009), vol. 12, 151–56; vol. 6, 132–39.

9. Halford Mackinder, 'The Teaching of Geography from an Imperial Point of View, and the Use Which Could and Should be Made of Visual Instruction', *The Geographical Teacher* 6, no. 2 (1911): 79–86; James R. Ryan, 'Visualizing Imperial Geography: Halford Mackinder and the Colonial Office Visual Instruction Committee, 1902–1911', *Ecumene* 1, no. 2 (1994): 157–76.

10. J.B. Harley, *The New Nature of Maps: Essays in the History of Cartography*, ed. Paul Laxton, introduction by J.H. Andrews (Baltimore, MD: The John Hopkins University Press, 2001); David Woodward, ed., *Art and Cartography: Six Historical Essays* (Chicago and London: University of Chicago Press, 1987).

11. David Woodward, 'Introduction', in D. Woodward, *Art and Cartography*, 1–9.

12. J.B. Harley, 'Deconstructing the Map', *Cartographica* 26, no. 2 (1989): 7.

13. J.B. Harley, 'Introduction: Texts and Contexts in the Interpretation of Early Maps', in David Buisseret, ed., *From Sea Charts to Satellite Images: Interpreting North American History through Maps* (Chicago and London: University of Chicago Press, 1990), 11–12. This text is reprinted in Harley, *The New Nature of Maps*, 33–50, and the same volume includes J.H. Andrews's critical assessment of Harley's adaptation of Panofsky:

J.H. Andrews, 'Introduction: Meaning, Knowledge and Power in the Map Philosophy of J.B. Harley', in Harley, *The New Nature of Maps*, 1–32. On Harley's use of Panofsky's method, see Matthew H. Edney, *The Origins and Development of J.B. Harley's Cartographic Theories* (Toronto: Toronto University Press, 2005).

14. J.B. Harley, 'Maps, Knowledge and Power', in D. Cosgrove and S. Daniels, eds, *The Iconography of Landscape* (Cambridge: Cambridge University Press, 1988), 277–312, in particular 278–79. Harley has developed his thoughts on suitability of Panofsky's three levels of iconological interpretation for critical cartography over the years, see Michael J. Blakemore and J.B. Harley, 'Concepts in the History of Cartography: A Review and Perspective', ed., Edward H. Dahl, *Cartographica* 17, no. 4 (1980): 76–86; J.B. Harley, 'The Iconology of Early Maps', in Carla C. Marzoli, ed., *Imago et Mensura Mundi: Atti del IX Congresso Internazionale di Storia della Cartografia* (Rome: Istituto della Enciclopedia Italiana, 1985), 2 vols, 1, 29–38.

15. Harley, 'Deconstructing the Map'; W.J.T. Mitchell, *Iconology: Image, Text, Ideology* (Chicago and London: University of Chicago Press, 1986).

16. See W.J.T. Mitchell, *Picture Theory: Essays on Verbal and Visual Representation* (Chicago and London: University of Chicago Press, 1994); James Elkins, *The Domain of Images* (Ithaca and London: Cornell University Press, 1999), 223–35.

17. Harley, 'Maps, Knowledge and Power', 278.

18. Harley, 'Introduction: Text and Contexts in the Interpretation of Early Maps', 11–12.

19. See, among others, Eric Fernie, *Art History and Its Methods* (London: Phaidon, 1995), 18–83.

20. Harley, 'Introduction: Text and Contexts in the Interpretation of Early Maps', 11–12.

21. Martin Dodge et al., eds, *The Map Reader: Theories of Mapping Practice and Cartographic Representation* (London: John Willey & Sons, Ltd, 2011).

22. Rose, 'On the Need to Ask', 213.

23. Crang, 'Visual Methods and Methodologies'; Denis Cosgrove, 'Maps, Mapping, Modernity: Art and Cartography in the Twentieth Century', *Imago Mundi* 57, no. 1 (2005): 35–54.

24. Jeremy Black, *Maps and Politics* (London: Reaktion, 2000), 164–65; Sébastien Caquard and Claire Dormann, 'Humorous Maps: Explorations of an Alternative Cartography', *Cartography and Geographic Information Science* 35, no. 1 (2008): 57–59; Peter Vujakovic, 'Maps as Political Cartoons', in Mark Monmonier, ed., *The History of Cartography, Volume 6: Cartography in the Twentieth Century* (Chicago and London: University of Chicago Press, 2015), 1162–65.

25. Katarzyna Murawska-Muthesius, 'Mapping the New Europe: Cartography, Cartoons and Regimes of Representation', *Centropa* 4, no. 1 (2004): 4–18.

26. Katharina N. Piechocki, 'Erroneous Mappings: Ptolemy and the Visualization of Europe's East', in Jane Tylus and Karen Newman, eds, *Early Modern Cultures of Translation* (Philadelphia: University of Pennsylvania Press, 2015), 76–96; Katharina N. Piechocki, *Cartographic Humanism: The Making of Modern Europe* (Chicago and London: The University of Chicago Press, 2019).

27. Ptolemy, *Cosmographia*, trans. Jacopo Angeli da Scaprpia (Rome: Arnoldus Buckink, 1478).

28. See Patrick Gautier Dalché, 'The Reception of Ptolemy's *Geography* (End of the Fourteenth to Beginning of the Sixteenth Century)', in David Woodward, ed., *The History of Cartography, Volume 3, Cartography in the European Renaissance* (Chicago and London: University of Chicago Press, 2007), 285–364.

29. Ptolemy himself warned that maps 'are often spoilt and distorted in the hands of the copyists, and that the form he has chosen – i.e., a list – warrants a greater durability to his work.' – Lauri O. Th. Tudeer, 'On the Origins of the Maps Attached to Ptolemy's Geography', *The Journal of Hellenic Studies* 27 (1917): 65.

30. Jarosław Łuczyński, 'Ziemie Rzeczypospolitej w kartografii europejskiej XVI wieku', *Polski Przegląd Kartograficzny* 41, no. 2 (2009): 128–44.

31. Piechocki, *Cartographic Humanism*, 84.

32. Ptolemy, *Geography*, trans. Edward Luther Stevenson (New York: Dover Publications, 1991), Book III, vii.

33. Marica Milanesi, 'A Forgotten Ptolemy: Harley Codex 3686 in the British Library', *Imago Mundi* 48 (1996): 43–64.
34. Nicolaus Germanus, 'The Eights Map of Europe (Sarmatia)', in *Cosmographia Claudii Ptolomaei Alexandrini, ca. 1460*, The New York Public Library, Manuscript and Archive Division, http://digitalcollections.nypl.org/items/510d47da-e68a-a3d9-e040-e00a 18064a99. Peter H. Meurer, 'Cartography in the German Lands, 1450–1650', in David Woodward, ed., *The History of Cartography, Volume 3: Cartography in the European Renaissance* (Chicago and London: University of Chicago Press, 2007), 1183.
35. Meurer, 'Cartography in the German Lands', 1182–83; 1204–07.
36. By Nicolaus Germanus (1491) and by Henricus Martellus Germanus, of ca 1480 – Meurer, 'Cartography in the German Lands', 1183–88.
37. Meurer, 'Cartography in the German Lands', 1184. In Martellus version of the map Ptolemy's *Oceanus Sarmaticus* was renamed as *Mare Germanicum*, a continuation of *Oceanus Germanicus*, the early modern name for the North Sea. Inserted into an elegant cartouche on top of the map, the name *Mare Germanicum* functions as an ethnically defining toponym, a declaration of the relations of power north of the Alps.
38. Czesław Chowaniec, 'The First Geographical Map of Bernard Wapowski', *Imago Mundi* 12 (1955): 59–64.
39. Martin Waldseemüller, 'Tabula Moderna Sarmatie Eur[opea] sive Hungarie Polonie Russie Prussie et Valachie', in *Geographia* (Strasbourg: Johann Schott, 1513), Washington: Library of Congress, www.loc.gov/item/48041351/. Meurer, 'Cartography in the German Lands', 1207.
40. Piechocki, *Cartographic Humanism*, 68–106.
41. Piechocki, 'Erroneous Mappings', 78.
42. Peter Meurer, 'Europa Regina. 16th Century Maps of Europe in the Form of a Queen', *Belgeo: Revue belge de géographie* 3–4 (2008): 1–12, http://journals.openedition.org/belgeo/7711; Elke Anna Werner, 'Anthropomorphic Maps: On the Aesthetic Form and Political Function of Body Metaphors in the Early Modern Discourse', in W.S. Melion, B. Rothstein and M. Weemans, eds, *The Anthropomorphic Lens. Anthropomorphism, Microcosmism and Analogy in Early Modern Thought and Visual Arts* (Leiden: Brill, 2015), 251–72.
43. Meurer, 'Europa Regina', 3–4.
44. Werner, 'Anthropomorphic Maps', 270.
45. Piechocki, *Cartographic Humanism*, 2–4.
46. Meurer, 'Europa Regina', 7–9.
47. Sebastian Münster, *Cosmographey* (Basel: Heinrich Petri, [1588] 1614); Meurer, 'Europa Regina', 7–9.
48. Matthew McLean, *The 'Cosmographia' of Sebastian Münster: Describing the World in the Reformation* (Aldershot: Ashgate, 2007).
49. Valerie Traub, 'Mapping the Global Body', in Peter Erickson and Clark Hulse, eds, *Early Modern Visual Culture: Representation, Race and Empire in Renaissance England* (Philadelphia: Pennsylvania University Press, 2000), 45.
50. Cf. Willem Janszoon Blaeu, *Europa recens descripta*, Amsterdam, 1640. In the collection of the Archiwum Akt Dawnych, Warsaw.
51. Larry Wolff, *Inventing Eastern Europe: The Map of Civilization on the Mind of the Enlightenment* (Stanford, CA: Stanford University Press, 1994).
52. Vincenzo Coronelli, '*Parte Orientale Dell' Europa, Descritta, e Dedicata Dal P. Cosmografo Coronelli All Illustrissimo, et Eccellentissimo Signore Giovanni da Mula, Senatore amplissimo Nella Serenissima Republica de Venetia*'. Published in Venice [1689]. In the collection of Vilnius University Library, https://kolekcijos.biblioteka.vu.lt/en/islandora/object/atmintis%3AVUB01_000359788. The map was included into Coronelli's multivolume atlas of the world, called *Atlante Veneto* (Venice: Girolamo Albrizzi, 1690–1701). See Marica Milanesi, Vincenzo Coronelli, Cosmographer (1650–1718) (Turnhout: Brepols, 2016). This clear-cut division of Europe into separated mesoregions will be followed Conrad Malte-Brun (1816) and Adriano Balbi (1833), but their books did not include maps. See Ezequiel Adamovsky, *Liberal Ideology and the Image of Russia in France (c.1740–1880)* (Bern: Peter Lang, 2006), 599–600 and Schenk, 'Eastern Europe', 190–91.

53. Larry Wolff, 'The Global Perspective of Enlightened Travellers: Philosophic Geography from Siberia to the Pacific Ocean', *European Review of History – Revue européene d'histoire* 13, no. 3 (2006): 437–53.

54. The image was published as '*Carte Générale: La France et l'Empire, la Pologne et la Russie*', in Jean-Baptiste Chappe d'Auteroche, *Voyage en Sibérie* (Paris, 1768), and it was republished on the cover of Wolff's *Inventing Eastern Europe*. See also Madeleine Pinault Sørenesen, 'Étude sur Le Prince et les dessinateurs et graveurs du *Voyage en Sibérie*', in Michel Mervaud, ed., *Voyage en Sibérie*, 2 vols (Oxford: Voltaire Foundation, 2004), vol. 1, 192–93.

55. Wolff, *Inventing Eastern Europe*.

56. See, for instance Michael Wintle, *The Image of Europe: Visualizing Europe in Cartography and Iconography Throughout the Ages* (Cambridge: Cambridge University Press, 2009).

57. Remarks about this rapid territorial change were a commonplace among historians c. 1900. See Ramsay Muir, *A New School Atlas of Modern History* (London: George Philip & Son, 1911, many later editions), xix.

58. Walter Goffart, *Historical Atlases: The First Three Hundred Years 1570–1870* (Chicago and London: The University of Chicago Press, 2003); Tomasz Kamusella, 'School Historical Atlases and Ethnolinguistic Nationalism', in Happel and von Werdt, *Osteuropa kartiert*, 215–33.

59. Johann Gottfried Herder, 'Slawische Völker', in *Ideen zur Philosophie der Geschichte der Menschheit (1774–1791)* (Riga and Leipzig: Johann Friedrich Hartnoch, 1792), vol. 4, 37–43. For English translation, see 'On Slav Nations: Johann Gottfried Herder (1774–1803)', trans. Ernest A. Menze with Michael Palma, in Jan Bažant, Nina Bažantová and Frances Starn, eds, *The Czech Reader: History, Culture, Politics* (Durham, NC: Duke University Press, 2010), 123–25. See also H. Barry Nisbet, 'Herder's Conception of Nationhood and Its Influence in Eastern Europe', in Roger Bartlett and Karen Schönwälder, eds, *The German Lands and Eastern Europe: Essays on the History of Their Social, Cultural and Political Relations* (Basingstoke: Macmillan, 1999), 115–35.

60. Karl Spruner, 'Die Völker und Reiche der Slaven zwischen Elben und Don bis 1125', in Karl Spruner's *Historisch-Geographischen Hand-Atlas zur Geschichte der Staaten Europa's von Anfang des Mittelalters bis auf die neueste Zeit* (Gotha: J. Peters, 1846). Note that this map is visibly pointing northwards, breaking its upper frame in a prominent way.

61. Gustaf Kombst, explanation to 'Ethnographic map of Europe, or the Different Nations of Europe, Traced according to Race, Language, Religion, and Form of Government', in Alexander Keith Johnston, ed., *National Atlas of Historical, Commercial and Political Geography* (Edinburgh [1843] 1856), B IV. See also 'Survey map of Europe with ethnographic borders of individual states' in Heinrich Berghaus, *Physikalischer Atlas* (Gotha: J. Peters, 1848). There are separate maps of Slavic Europe in 19th–century historical atlases, such as 'Karte der Slavischen Länder nach der Mitte des XVten Jahrhundert', in John Valerius Kutscheit, *Hand Atlas zur Geographie und Geschichte des Mittelalters* (Berlin: E.H. Schröder, 1843) and Spruner's 'Die Völker und Reiche der Slaven'. On the 19th–century discovery of Slavic Europe, see Adamovsky, *Liberal Ideology and the Image of Russia in France*.

62. On Šafařík's map, see Josef Hůrský, 'Vznik a poslání Šafaříkova Slovanského Zeměvidu', in Hana Hynková, with Josef Hůrský and Luboš Reháček, eds, *Slovanský Národopis* (Prague: Československé Akademie Věd, 1955), 218–88. I am following the spelling used in the title of the first edition of his book. See also, K. Murawska-Muthesius, 'Mapping Eastern Europe: Cartography and Art History', Artl@s Bulletin 2, no. 2 (Fall 2013), 19–21.

63. R.W. Seton-Watson, *History of the Czechs and Slovaks* (London: Hutchinson and Co, 1943), 176. On Šafařík, see Ján Tibenský, *Pavol Jozef Šafárik: život a dielo: hviezda prvej veľkosti v slovanskej vede* (Bratislava: Osvetový ústav, 1975).

64. Pawel Josef Šafařík, *Slovanský Národopis, s mappau* (Prague: Wydawatele, 1842). Hůrský, 'Vznik a poslání Šafaříkova Slovanského Zeměvidu, 218–88.

65. Hůrský, 'Vznik a poslání Šafaříkova Slovanského Zeměvidu', 220–21.

66. Šafařík, *Slovanský Národopis*, 148–51.

67. On the representation of Lithuania on the map, see Vytautas Petronis, *Constructing Lithuania: Ethnic Mapping in Tsarist Russia, ca. 1800–1914* (Stockholm: Acta Universitatis Stockholmiensis, 2007), 1/6–84.

68. Hůrský, 'Vznik a poslání Šafaříkova Slovanského Zeměvidu', 219.
69. P.J. Szafarzyk, *Słowiański Narodopis*, trans. Piotr Dahlman (Wrocław: P. Schletter, 1843), and P.J. Szafarik, *Slavianskoe narodopisan'e, z kartou*, trans. O. Bodianski (Moscow: Universitetskaia Tipografia, 1843).
70. Hans Kohn, *Panslavism, Its History and Ideology* (Notre Dame: Notre Dame University Press, 1956), 14. See also Wendy Bracewell, 'Travels Through the Slav World', in Wendy Bracewell and Alex Drace-Francis, eds, *Under Eastern Eyes: A Comparative Introduction to East European Travel Writing on Europe* (Budapest and New York: Central European University Press, 2008), 147.
71. On the linguistic origins of Slavic studies, see, among others, Florin Curta, *The Making of the Slavs: History and Archaeology of the Lower Danube Region, C. 500–700* (Cambridge and New York: Cambridge University Press, 2007).
72. The First Slavic Congress in Prague in 1848 opened with Šafařík's speech – Stanislav J. Kirschbaum, *Historical Dictionary of Slovakia* (Lanham, MD, Toronto and Plymouth: The Scarecrow Press, 2007), 253.
73. Daniel Gottlob Reymann, *Topographische Special-Karte von Mitteleuropa*, published successively in small sheets, between 1806–1908, http://maps4u.lt/en/maps.php?cat=38; Hůrský, 'Vznik a poslání Šafaříkova Slovanského Zeměvidu', 224.
74. Gayatri Chakravorty Spivak, *Outside in the Teaching Machine* (New York: Routledge, 1993), ix–26. Herder, 'Slawische Völker'.
75. Kohn, *Panslavism*, 13.
76. Denis Cosgrove, 'Introduction: Landscape, Map and Vision', in D. Cosgrove, ed., *Geography and Vision: Seeing, Imagining and Representing the World* (London: I.B. Tauris, 2008), 1–12.
77. On the cartographic gaze, see Gillian Rose, *Feminism and Geography: The Limits of Geographical Knowledge* (Cambridge: Polity, 1993), 108; John Pickles, *A History of Spaces: Cartographic Reason, Mapping and the Geo-coded World* (London and New York: Routledge, 2004), 75–91.
78. Charles Frederic Henningsen, *Eastern Europe and the Emperor Nicholas* (London: T.C. Newby, 1846).
79. Mikołaj Ambroży Kubalski, *Tableau de l'Europe Orientale, ou Recherches historiques et statistiques sur les Peuples d'origine Slave, Magyare et Roumaine* (Paris: Delarue, 1854); *Europe orientale indiquant les pays riverains de la Baltique et de la Mer Noire, La Russie, l'Empire Ottoman et les etats voisins pour server à intelligence de la guerre en Orient* (Paris: Fatout, 1854). Adolf Stieler, *Hand-Atlas über alle Theile der Erde und über das Weltgebäude* (Gotha: Justus Perthes, 1882, other editions), 50–55. Robert Henlopen Labberton, *An Historical Atlas: A Chronological Series of One Hundred and Twelve Maps at Successive Periods* (New York: T. Mac Coun, 1884), XLII.
80. Gillian Hill, *Cartographical Curiosities* (London: British Library, 1978); Heinrich Dormeier, 'Humoristisch-satirische Europakarten von 1848 bis zum ersten Weltkrieg. Bestand und Besonderheiten', in Thomas Stamm-Kuhlmann, Jürgen Elvert, Birgit Aschmann and Jens Hohensee, eds, *Geschichtsbilder. Festschrift für Michael Salewski* (Wiesbaden: Franz Steiner Verlag, 2003), 525–42; Roderick M. Barron, 'Bringing the Map to Life: European Satirical Maps 1845–1945', *Belgeo: Revue belge de géographie* 3–4 (2008): 445–64. https://doi.org/10.4000/belgeo.11935.
81. *Carte drôlatique d'Europe pour 1870. Dressée pour Hadol*, published by H.C. Panzer in London in 1870. A copy at the British Library.
82. *Humoristische Karte des Deutschen Reiches und von Oesterreich-Ungarn* (Stuttgart: Levy & Müller, 1887). A copy in the British Library.
83. Cf. J.H. Amschewitz, *European Revue: Kill That Eagle* (London: 'Geographia', 1914); or *Hark! Hark! The Dogs Do Bark!*, with note by Walter Emanuel, . . . designed by Johnson, Riddle & Co., [London:] G.W. Bacon & Co. [1914]. Both at the British Library.
84. Mike Heffernan, 'Fin de siècle? Fin du monde? On the Origins of European Geopolitics, 1890–1920', in Klaus Dodds and David Atkinson, eds, *Geopolitical Traditions* (London: Routledge, 2000), 27–51.
85. Mark Bassin, 'Imperialism and the Nation State in Friedrich Ratzel's Political Geography', *Progress in Human Geography* 11 (1987): 473–95.

86. Gearóid Ó Tuathail, *Critical Geopolitics: The Politics of Writing Global Space* (London: Routledge, 1996).
87. Halford Mackinder, 'The Geographical Pivot of History', *The Geographical Journal* 23, no. 4 (1904): 421–37.
88. Mackinder, 'The Geographical Pivot of History', 423.
89. Mackinder, 'The Teaching of Geography from an Imperial Point of View'.
90. Mackinder, 'The Geographical Pivot of History', 425–26.
91. It was published by the cartographic company Oxford Geographical Institute which, set up by the cartographer Bernhard Vernon Darbishire and the map-seller William Stanford, was sponsored by Mackinder himself. See Francis Herbert, 'The Royal Geographical Society's Membership, the Map Trade, and Geographical Publishing in Britain 1830 to ca. 1930: An Introductory Essay with Listing of Some 250 Fellows in Related Professions', *Imago Mundi* 35 (1983): 78. The Berghaus map was most likely a double page plate of Europe and Asia in Herman Berghaus, *Berghaus' Physikalischer Atlas: 75 Karten in sieben Abteilungen* (Gotha: Justus Perthes, 1892), pl. XI.
92. Malcolm Bradbury, *Rates of Exchange* (Harmondsworth: Penguin Books, 1983), 1.
93. Seegel, *Map Men*; Larry Wolff, *Woodrow Wilson and the Reimagining of Eastern Europe* (Stanford, CA: Stanford University Press, 2020).
94. Guntram Henrik Herb, *Under the Map of Germany: Nationalism and Propaganda 1918–1945* (London: Routledge, 1997), 13–33; Martin, 'Paris Peace Conference'.
95. Charles Seymour, 'The End of an Empire: Remnants of Austria-Hungary', in Edward Mandell House and Charles Seymour, eds, *What Really Happened at Paris: The Story of the Peace Conference, 1918–1919. By American Delegates* (London: Hodder & Stoughton, 1921), 93.
96. Isaiah Bowman, 'Constantinople and the Balkans', in House and Seymour, eds, *What Really Happened at Paris*, 142.
97. To a large extent a gap is fulfilled by the excellent book by the Polish historian Maciej Górny, *Kreślarze Ojczyzn: Geografowie i granice międzywojennej Europy* (Warsaw: Instytut Historii PAN, 2017) which, focused on the whole of the interwar era, provides an engaging discussion of mapping the New Europe.
98. Harley, 'Introduction: Texts and Contexts in the Interpretation of Early Maps', 5; Gilles Palsky, 'Emmanuel de Martonne and the Ethnographical Cartography of Central Europe (1917–1920)', *Imago Mundi* 54, no. 1 (2002): 111–19.
99. Steven Seegel, *Mapping Europe's Borderlands: Russian Cartography* in the Age of Empire (Chicago and London: University of Chicago Press, 2012), 267.
100. *The World Today and Yesterday: Europe as It Looks Today, Maps of the New Countries, What the New Treaties Mean* (Chicago: Rand McNally & Co., c. 1919).
101. Walter Consuelo Langsam, *The World Since 1919* (New York: Macmillan, 1933), republished until 1971.
102. The famous *Ethnographical Map of Hungary According to Population Density*, 1919–20, by the Hungarian geographer and the future Hungarian Prime Minister Count Pál *Teleki*, produced for the talks in Trianon, is known as *Carte Rouge* because of its use of the red, marking the Hungarian population, to overshadow the claims by the Romanians, represented by pink, difficult to distinguish from the more visible red. See Seegel, *Map Men*, 64–69, pl. 5.
103. Seegel, *Map Men*, 121–25.
104. Thomas G. Masarýk, *The Problems of Small Nations in the European Crisis*; inaugural lecture at the University of London, King's College ([London]: Council of International Relations, [1916]); Thomas G. Masarýk, *The New Europe* (The Slav Standpoint) (London: Eyre & Spottiswoode, 1918); Robert William Seton-Watson, *German, Slav, and Magyar: A Study in the Origins of the Great War* (London: Williams & Norgate, 1916). Hugh and Christopher Seton-Watson, *The Making of a New Europe: R. W. Seton-Watson and the Last Years of Austria-Hungary* (London: Methuen, 1981).
105. Friedrich Naumann, *Mitteleuropa* (Berlin: Georg Reimer, 1915). Seton-Watson's book includes one more map which warns against the 'Pan-German Plan' of conquering the East, in historical stages: Seton-Watson, *German, Slav and Magyar*, 175. See also Peter Bugge, '"Shatter Zones": The Creation and Recreation of Europe's East', in Menno

Spiering and Michael Wintle, eds, *Ideas of Europe Since 1914: The Legacy of the First World War* (Basingstoke and New York: Palgrave Macmillan, 2002), 48–49.

106. Nicolas Ginsburger, 'André Chéradame et l'émergence d'une cartographie géopolitique de guerre en 1916', *Cartes & géomatique*, *Comité français de cartographie*, no. 223 (March 2015): 79–90.

107. Thomas G. Masarýk, 'Why Germany Wants Peace Now', *The New Europe* 1 (1916).

108. The Mappa Company was owned by the London cartographer Arthur Henry Webb, see Herbert, 'The Royal Geographical Society's Membership', 94.

109. Seton-Watson, *German, Slav, and Magyar*, 146.

110. The term *Zwischeneuropa* initiated by Albrecht Penck as one of the descriptions of Central Europe (Robert Sieger and Albrecht Penck, 'Zwischeneuropa?', *Zeitschrift der Gesellschaft für Erdkunde zu Berlin* (1916): 177–80), was adopted as a pejorative name of the new states. See David Thomas Murphy, *The Heroic Earth: Geopolitical Thought in Weimar Germany, 1918–1933* (Kent, OH and London: The Kent State University Press, 1997), 144, 148–49; Bugge, '"Shatter Zones"', 58.

111. Shearer West, *Portraiture* (Oxford and New York: Oxford University Press, 2004), 105–31.

112. Halford Mackinder, *Democratic Ideals and Reality* (London: Constable & Co., 1919).

113. Mackinder, *Democratic Ideals and Reality*, 79.

114. Mackinder, *Democratic Ideals and Reality*, 212–13.

115. Mackinder, *Democratic Ideals and Reality*, Fig. 31, 198.

116. Mackinder, *Democratic Ideals and Reality*, 213.

117. Cf. J.F. Unstead, 'The Belt of Political Change in Europe', *The Scottish Geographical Magazine* 39 (1923): 183–92; Gordon East, 'The Concept and Political Status of the Shatter Zone', in Norman J.G. Pounds, ed., *Geographical Essays on Eastern Europe* (Bloomington, IN: Indiana University Press, 1963), 1–27. For Mackinder' failed project of a federation of Eastern Europe, see Simone Pelizza, 'The Geopolitics of International Reconstruction: Halford Mackinder and Eastern Europe, 1919–20', *The International History Review* 38, no. 1 (2016): 174–95.

118. Mackinder, *Democratic Ideals and Reality*, 186.

119. On Mackinder as a prophet, see Stephen Jones, 'Global Strategic Views', in *Military Aspects of World Political Geography* (Air University, Maxwell Air Force Base, Alabama: Air Force Reserve Training Corps, 1959), 39–67.

120. On Eastern Europe as a constituting factor of the Cold War, see Lynn Etheridge Davis, *The Cold War Begins: Soviet-American Conflict Over Eastern Europe* (Princeton, NJ: Princeton University Press, 1974); Stephen Fisher-Galati, *Eastern Europe and the Cold War: Perceptions and Perspectives* (New York: Boulder, 1994).

121. '. . . that part of Europe militarily controlled by the Soviet Union', as said by Timothy Garton Ash, 'Does Central Europe Exist?' [1986], in *The Uses of Adversity: Essays on the Fate of Central Europe* (Cambridge: Granta Books in association with Penguin Books, 1991), 188.

122. Winston Churchill, 'The Sinews of Peace' [1946], in Robert Rhodes James, ed., *Winston S. Churchill: His Complete Speeches, 1897–1963* (New York and London: Chelsea House, 1974), vol. VII, 7285–93. See, Fraser J. Harbutt, *The Iron Curtain: Churchill, America and the Origins of the Cold War* (Oxford and New York: Oxford University Press, 1986); Michael J. Hostetler, 'The Enigmatic Ends of Rhetoric: Churchill's Fulton Address as Great Art and Failed Persuasion', *Quarterly Journal of Speech* 83 (1997): 426–28.

123. Max Lerner, quoted in Lynn Boyd Hinds and Theodore Otto Windt, Jr, *The Cold War as Rhetoric: The Beginnings* (New York: Praeger, 1991), 107.

124. R.W. Burchfield, *A Supplement to the Oxford English Dictionary* (Oxford: Clarendon Press, vol. 2, 1976), 368–69.

125. On newspaper maps, see Mark Monmonier, *Maps With the News* (Chicago and London: University of Chicago Press, 1989); Susan Schulten, *The Geographical Imagination in America, 1880–1950* (Chicago and London: University of Chicago Press, 2001). On the Cold War maps, see Alan K. Henrikson, 'Maps, Globes and the "Cold War"', *Special Libraries* 65 (1974): 445–54; Jeremy Black, *Maps and History: Constructing the Image of the Past* (New Haven and London: Yale University Press, 1999), 149–72; Timothy Barnley,

Mapping The Cold War: Cartography and the Framing of America's International Power (Chapel Hill: The University of North Carolina Press, 2015); Jeffrey P. Stone, *British and American News Maps in the Early Cold War Period, 1945–1955* (Cham, Switzerland: Palgrave Macmillan, 2019).

126. George Whitelaw, "Opeless', *Daily Herald*, 16 May 1947: 2.
127. 'The Mapmakers', *Daily Herald*, 16 May 1947: 2.
128. A short comment outlined the Daily Herald position that Churchill does not envision the united Europe, but the divided one and that he wants to redraw the map of Europe, to exclude Russia together with the lands of Eastern Europe, attached to Russia. *Der Spiegel* 1, no. 21 (24 May 1947), 'Panorama' column.
129. See Chapter 4, 146–50.
130. Cary Schlager, *Cold War*, blog https://thecoldwarexperience.weebly.com/the-iron-curtain.html.
131. Leslie G. Illingworth, *Daily Mail*, 16 June 1947; David Low, *Picture Post*, 24 May 1952.
132. Schulten, *The Geographical Imagination in America*; Stone, *British and American News Maps*, 18.
133. Susan Schulten, 'Richard Edes Harrison and the Challenge to American Cartography', *Imago Mundi* 50 (1998): 174–88.
134. Joshua Hagen, 'Redrawing the Imagined Map of Europe: The Rise and Fall of the "Center"', *Political Geography* 22 (2003): 490–92.
135. Stephanie L. Hawkins, *American Iconographic: National Geographic, Global Culture, and the Visual Imagination* (Charlottesville: University of Virginia Press, 2010), 48.
136. 'Large-scale Western Europe Map First in New National Geographic Series', *National Geographic* 98, no. 6 (1950): 811–12.
137. 'Central Europe Including the Balkan States', published as a supplement to the *National Geographic* 99, no. 2 (1951), not discussed inside. *National Geographic*'s representation of the region will be discussed in Chapter 3.
138. Hans Zeissig, ed., *Neuer Geschichts- und Kulturatlas von der Urzeit zur Gegenwart* (Hamburg, Frankfurt and Munich: Atlantik Verlag, 1950), 80.
139. Zeissig, *Neue Geschichts- und Kulturatlas*, 47, 73.
140. 'Europe 1914–1950', in Edward Whiting Fox, ed., with the assistance of S. Deighton, *Atlas of European History* (New York: Oxford University Press, 1957), 60–61. Katarzyna Murawska-Muthesius, 'Iconotext of Eastern Europe: The "Iron Curtain" Cartography', in Katja Bernhardt and Piotr Piotrowski, eds, *Grenzen überwindend: Festschrift für Adam S. Labuda zum 60. Geburtstag* (Berlin: Lukas Verlag, 2006), 60–62.
141. Western Europe, *Oxford Regional Economic Atlas* (Oxford: Clarendon Press, 1971).
142. Black, *Maps and History*, 149–72.
143. For a variety of opinions on the end of the Cold War in the context of Eastern Europe, see Fisher-Galati, *Eastern Europe and the Cold War*.
144. Adam Burgess, *Divided Europe: The New Domination of the East* (London and Chicago: Pluto Press, 1997).
145. Julie Burchill, 'After the Flood', *The Guardian Weekend*, 28 July 2001: 7.
146. To name just a few: Robert Bideleux and Ian Jeffries, *A History of Eastern Europe: Crisis and Change* (London and New York Routledge, 1998); Richard Frucht, ed., *Encyclopedia of Eastern Europe: From the Congress of Vienna to the Fall of Communism* (New York and London: Garland, 2000); Richard and Ben Crampton, *Atlas of Eastern Europe*. A cartoon history of the region promised a 'fast-moving, easy-to-follow guided tour through . . . this explosive, crucial part of the world' - Paul Beck, Edward Mast Perry Tapper, *The History of Eastern Europe for Beginners* (New York and London: Writers and Readers Publishing, 1997).
147. Peter Vujakovic, '"A New Map Is Unrolling Before us": Cartography in News Media Representations of Post-Cold War Europe', *The Cartogrcophic Journal* 36, no. 1 (June 1999): 43–57. The front cover of *Newsweek*, of 3 May 2004, showed the map of Europe with a large text announcing 'The End of Europe: The Next Big Bang, and How the EU Will Never Be the Same Again'.
148. James Aulich and Marta Sylvestrová, *Political Posters in Central and Eastern Europe 1945–95* (Manchester and New York: Manchester University Press, 1999), 3; Murawska-Muthesius, 'Iconotext of Eastern Europe', 69–70.

149. Paul Robert Magocsi *Historical Atlas of Central Europe*.
150. Paul Robert Magocsi, cartographic design by Geoffrey J. Matthews, *Historical Atlas of East Central Europe* (Seattle and London: University of Washington Press, 1993).
151. Magocsi, *Historical Atlas of Central Europe*, xiii.
152. The debated was initiated by Milan Kundera, 'The Tragedy of Central Europe', *The New York Review of Books*, 26 April 1984: 33–38. See also Garton Ash, 'Does Central Europe Exist?'.
153. Hagen, 'Redrawing the Imagined Map of Europe'.
154. Donald J. Zeigler, 'Post-Communist Eastern Europe and the Cartography of Independence', *Political Geography* 21, no. 5 (2002): 671–86.
155. Mike Nudelman and Barbara Tasch, 'Europe's Refugee Crisis', *Business Insider*, 15 September 2015, www.businessinsider.com/map-of-europe-refugee-crisis-2015-9?r=US&IR=T.
156. Krzysztof Widawski and Jerzy Widakowski, eds, *The Geography of Tourism of Central and Eastern European Countries*, 2nd ed. (Cham, Switzerland: Springer, 2017).
157. *Eastern Europe* (Riga: Jāņa sēta Map Publishers, 2015).
158. On refugees' maps, see Maribel Casas-Cortes, Sebastian Cobarrubias and John Pickles, 'Riding Routes and Itinerant Borders: Autonomy of Migration and Border Externalization', *Antipode* 47, no. 4 (2015): 894–914. On Eastern Europe and the refugee crisis in Europe, see Dace Dzenovska, 'Eastern Europe, the Moral Subject of the Migration/Refugee Crisis and Political Futures', *Near Futures Online*, www.academia.edu/22938312/Eastern_Europe_the_Moral_Subject_of_the_Migration_Refugee_Crisis_and_Political_Futures.
159. Nudelman and Tasch, 'Europe's Refugee Crisis'.
160. Neli Esipova and Julie Ray, 'Syrian Refugees Not Welcome in Eastern Europe', *World*, 5 May 2017, https://news.gallup.com/poll/209828/syrian-refugees-not-welcome-eastern-europe.aspx.

3 The Lure of Ethnic Dress

Eastern Europe in the Traveller's Gaze

If maps conjure up political entities, travel writing contributes to the formation of cultural identities, generated in an unequal encounter between the traveller and the 'travellee', to use the term introduced by Mary Louise Pratt.[1] Accordingly, eastern Europe as a region would owe its construction as much to mapmakers as to travellers, and both Larry Wolff and Maria Todorova drew their arguments about derogatory representations of eastern Europe and the Balkans from travel writing.[2] The majority of studies on travel reports from the region focus almost exclusively on *writing*, while marginalising images included in the same books.[3] Even if occasionally reproduced, they are rarely given attention, let alone becoming the subject of a contextualised visual analysis. Reduced to 'mere illustrations' of texts, images are regularly denied their own cognitive functions and are approached as surrogate bearers of truths, decipherable first and foremost in textual analyses.[4]

Diving into the barely trodden topic of eastern Europe and travel *imaging*, this chapter focuses on images rather than texts, reversing the usual hierarchy. In order to examine the iconosphere of those 'remote lands of Europe', labelled as such by the seventeenth-century scientist-traveller Edward Brown, it has to take a long time span. It begins with prints in early modern travel literature, ending with photographs in twentieth-century geographical magazines.[5] As it will become evident below, analysis of images tends to lead to different conclusions than those established by scrutinising the text. The disapproving adjectives of verbal narratives do not always lend themselves to translation in visual terms. When encountering the Other, delight and aversion tend to be closely related and the visual opts for the celebratory rather than the critical. Subject to their own operational mechanisms, the images respond to other images, following the major aesthetic shifts brought up by modernity. Otherness is neutralised by aestheticised visions of ethnic dress, quaint villages, and impassable mountains and has to be expressed in different ways – by juxtaposition, avoidance, reduction, and repetition – rather than by obvious disapproval. And the boundaries between representation and self-fashioning blur and fade.

Another issue is the term. The concept of eastern Europe as represented by travelogues is hardly a straightforward one. Different parts of the region might have been named as such by a handful of nineteenth-century authors,[6] but as a travel destination in its own right eastern Europe was a latecomer. The lands that were to form the region post-WWII had been traversed for centuries by missionaries, diplomats, traders, scientists, itinerant artists, and adventurers, travelling either north to Moscow or south to Constantinople. But its open plains and high mountains, its towns and villages, not to mention the diverse languages of the travellees, were too dispersed, geographically and culturally, to be assembled into one distinctive area. Even their remoteness, by no means applicable evenly to all those territories at all times, was not enough to be a common denominator. The unquestionable centrality of Prague and Budapest refuted any attempts of standardisation and exempted them from the 'remote lands' labelling. Divided between different empires, the lands of the east of Europe belonged to diverse itineraries, guiding tourists southwards, through Southern Germany, Bohemia, and Austria, down to 'Turkey in Europe', or eastwards, via Northern Germany and Poland, to Russia. Neither Baedeker nor Murray would produce a guide to 'eastern Europe', or even classify it as a separate region. *Slowanský zeměvid's* appeal to travellers from Slavic lands was an exception.[7] As a tourist destination, eastern Europe is the product of the Cold War. The site of tourism within people's democracies, it was fully 'discovered' as a space for holidays and leisure with the fall of the Berlin Wall. The mushrooming tourist guides to eastern Europe *per se* sealed its status.[8]

Bearing in mind both the intrinsic opacity of the image and the late arrival of the term 'eastern Europe', this chapter looks at the ways in which a set of visual truths about those 'remote' lands and their inhabitants were produced by travellers. It begins from travel accounts to south-eastern territories, to the 'Turkey in Europe', which attracted more explorers and adventurers than the central and northern parts of the region (Figure 3.1). The 'primitive cultures' of the Morlacks, palikars, and the Wallacks were discovered among the mountains of the Balkans and the south-eastern provinces of the Habsburg Empire, and this is where, as I want to claim, the core visual regimes originated. Hinged around ethnicity and provinciality, accumulating over a long time, focused on the body and fed by the ethnic-oriented self-imagery of the liberated states of the New Europe, they were to shape the idea of eastern Europe from the early twentieth century onwards.[9]

Travel Writing and Travel Imaging

Over the last three decades, travel writing has attracted a considerable critical attention: it has been analysed as a hybrid literary genre, theorised as a tool of colonialism, as well as cross-examined from all kinds of perspectives: historical, geographical, political and anthropological, with major texts assembled in a number of handbooks and companions.[10] Recently, a significant turn in travel studies recognised the travellees as active producers of travel narratives, beginning with the eastern Europeans.[11] But, while travel texts are being discussed in relation to an increasing set of categories, it is *writing* which has remained the primary target of investigation.[12] Clare Farago brought attention to the hierarchies of art history, which privileged mainstream fine art over ethnographic imagery, as well as to the logocentric premises of anthropology, which praised the text but ignored the illustrations.[13] Exclusion both from art history as well as from travel writing studies is one of the features shared by several ethnographic images reproduced in this chapter. The critical attention to non-textual elements of travel reports is on the rise,[14] yet, within the circle of travel writing theorists, the agency of images has not been posed yet as a major topic of inquiry. Or, more correctly, travel imagery is being analysed in books written by visual rather than literary scholars.[15] W.J.T. Mitchell's comparison of the domains of word and image to 'two countries that speak different languages but . . . have a long history of mutual migration' seems particularly apt in this context.[16] This comparison was indeed quoted by Giorgia Alù and Sarah Patricia Hills, who went as far as to rephrase the hierarchy

Figure 3.1 'I entred in Moldavia; where for my welcome in the midst of a border-wood, I was beset with six murderers', woodcut, in William Lithgow, *The Totall Discourse of the Rare Adventures & Painefull Peregrinations of Long Nineteen Yeares Travayles from Scotland to the Most Famous Kingdomes in Europe, Asia and Africa.* London, 1640.

between word and image in terms of that between traveller and travellee.[17] Studies of eastern European travel writing are no exception to this rule. Kinship between visual representation and travel writing lies at the centre of my approach; it is the images that offer the clues which prompt an inquiry into the messages conveyed by the text, and not the other way round.

The major input into the analysis of the visual apparatus of travel books comes from early modern studies. Stephanie Leitch, focusing on sixteenth-century travel books reporting on the encounter with the New World, emphasised the agency of images vis-a-vis the fabric of the text. Not only did they enhance 'the authors' credibility' but, as she argued

> the authoritative nature of these images, in turn, reshaped narrative strategies. In sixteenth- and seventeenth-century accounts, images became central to certifying the author's witness claims. . . . As travel images increasingly posited the traveller as a first-hand observer, they helped establish empirical inquiry as a method and even stabilised subjects for investigation.[18]

Regardless of their epistemological status as the guarantors of truth, however, the early modern woodcuts representing people encountered in faraway lands were usually not the product of the artist's first-hand observation. Recycled from other books or borrowed from the margins of maps and costume books, they followed the ready-made formulas how to record cultural differences through the representation of body, dress and surrounding vegetation, stressing nakedness, facial piercing and feathered costumes.[19] Does this apply to images of eastern Europe?

The earliest illustrated accounts of travels to the lands of the east of Europe go back to the early seventeenth century, and Leitch's observations offer a set of methodological tools. Above all, a parallel between the discovery of the lands and people of the New World and those of the eastern and southern peripheries of Europe has been repeated at least since Edward Gibbon's remark comparing Albania to 'the wilds of America (1778)'.[20] But, even if eastern European peripheries were perceived as unknown as the faraway provinces of the New World, Africa, and India, they were still within a reasonable distance from the major European centres, such as Venice and Vienna. Travel might have been arduous but did not require crossing the ocean. Significantly, the authors of the earliest travel accounts from the region supplied their own illustrations, and hence the mechanism of the repurposing of the old wood blocks that had been used for the books described by Leitch, cannot be applied here to the same extent. What is pertinent for this inquiry is her stress on the sheer significance of the images, as well as on the close relationship between travel illustrations, cartographic imagery, and costume books, all pointing to dress as the major marker of cultural difference.

'In Some Remote Parts of Europe'

Among the first travellers who illustrated their reports from the east of Europe were the Scottish adventurer William Lithgow and the aforementioned scientist Edward Brown. Given the opposing temperaments of these authors, their images differ considerably, but they share the sense of entering the unfamiliar territories of Europe which meant danger and required primary description. William Lithgow, known in no other capacity than that of a traveller, went on several journeys around Europe, Africa, and the Near East between 1609 until the 1620s, describing his exploits in florid language in *The Total Discourse of the Rare Adventures and Painefull Peregrinations . . . to the Most Famous Kingdomes in Europe, Asia and Africa*.[21] Various editions of this book were published after his returns to Scotland, the most complete volumes appearing in 1632 and 1640.[22] For Lithgow, as noted by Peter Womack, travel served as a tool for the 'presentation of himself',[23] and the politics of self-display was extended also to the anonymous woodcuts in the book. The majority of them depict Lithgow almost in a selfie-like manner: dressed in fancy costumes and posing 'in the ruins of Troy', or, facing death when tortured by the Inquisition in Malaga. In 1616, returning from his African journey through Vienna, Lithgow took an unusual route, planning to explore the land of Tartary, which he eventually did not reach. Crossing the Turkish-occupied Hungary, Transylvania, and Moldavia, to Poland, he visited Belgrade, Budapest, Esztergom, Pressburg (Bratislava), and a number of smaller places, to continue later through Podolia to Lublin, Warsaw, and Dantzig (Gdańsk), where he met his compatriots from Scotland and sailed back home.[24] The detailed descriptions of people and the lands, opinionated and not particularly sympathetic, constitute a topic in itself. Remarkably, Lithgow's misadventure in a Moldavian forest was both narrated and illustrated. As he reports,

> I entred Moldavia; where for my welcome in the midst of a border wood, I was beset with six murderers; Hungarians and Moldavians; where having with many prayers saved my life, they robbed me of threescore Hungar duckets of gold, and all my Turkish clothes, leaving me stark naked . . . they carried me a little out of the way and bound my naked body fast to an oaken tree with wooden ropes.[25]

The accompanying woodcut shows a large figure of Lithgow in his underdress, being tied to a big tree by two men, while four smallish robbers at a distance point their guns at him (Figure 3.1). Haphazardly marked trees and hills at the background must stand for the 'high and unpassable mountains' he complained about when crossing from Transylvania to Moldavia.[26] This unusual depiction of robbery constitutes one of the earliest representations of the land and people of eastern Europe, even if in Lithgow parlance Moldavia would still be classified as 'Southern World'. While the image itself evokes associations with the iconography of martyrdom, it recalls the acts of violence encountered by travellers in the unknown lands of America, such as those depicted by Theodor de Bry, marking those peripheries of Europe as uncharted territory.[27] The theme of robbery, otherwise a standard trope in travel writing, will appear regularly in many textual dispatches from the region. However, as far as I can ascertain, it would not enter the standard iconography of travels to eastern Europe.[28] It is its equivalent, the 'unpassable mountains', even if barely outlined in Lithgow's woodcut, which are going to play a significant role.

An entirely different selection of images assembled on a journey through Hungary and 'Turkey in Europe' in 1669 were supplied by Edward Brown of Norwich, son of Sir Thomas Brown, and published as *A Brief Account of Some Travels in Hungaria, Servia, Bulgaria, Macedonia . . .* in 1673.[29] Member of the Royal Society and physician of Charles II, Edward Brown was considered one of the best educated people in Britain.[30] His extensive travels on the continent were motivated by his rich programme of scientific explorations of natural resources, including salt, copper, silver, and gold mines, about which he kept sending detailed reports to the Royal Society.[31] His travel to Hungary and the 'European Turkie' was prompted by his scientific interest in 'baths, mineral waters, and mines', but it expanded into local antiquities, history, and habits. Brown's itinerary followed what would become a standard route from Vienna to Athens, down the Danube to Bratislava and to Buda, still in Turkish hands at that time, and then through Croatia to Belgrade. It continued south through the country of Serbia towards the Balkan Mountains on the border with

Albania, and with some inroads into smaller places in the principality of Bulgaria, it proceeded through Macedonia and ended in Larissa in Thessaly.

In the introduction to the book, as if justifying the eccentricity of his route, away from the beaten track, Brown linked his account of what happened to him 'in some remote parts of Europe' to the specific spirit of curiosity characterising his times, but also to his own broad interests extending eastwards.[32] Primary description was his principal aim. The book is divided into several essays, providing plenty of enthusiastic comments on the territory he crossed by carriage, on horseback as well as by boat, on the beauty of great Hungarian plains, on rivers full of fish, on agriculture, mineral wealth, and natural curiosities, such as the disappearing lake of Zirchnitz (Cerknica, Slovenia), as well as on towns, and houses. Brown admires the 'rarities' in King Mathias Corvinus's library in Buda and, when complaining about the inaccessibility of Hungarian language, he expresses his admiration for the widespread command of Latin, even among coachmen. Brown also gives an account of the history of the region, and its conquest by the Ottomans, stressing the country's role in stopping the Turkish 'intrusion into the western parts of Europe'. While pointing to the difference in 'habits and manners' in the occupied lands, he often expresses his sympathy for the enslaved Christians. This has not stop him, however, from admiring the engineering skills of the famous Suleiman Bridge in Esseck (Osijek, Croatia), the splendours of the Turkish baths in Buda, and the Sultan's court in Larissa, the latter illustrated on a large foldout.[33]

Illustrations form an important part of Brown's travel account. The ten engravings, made from Brown's own sketches, are just a selection from a much larger portfolio, as he informs the reader in the introduction.

> I was unwilling to charge this work with numerous cuts, and prints; and therefore have inserted but a few, although I was not unprovided of many more, to the number of an hundred; proper to this work, of habits, postures, hills, castles, forts, monasteries, sepulchres, fountains, ruines, medals, coyns, bridges, columnes, statua's, &c. rarely or not at all to be met with.[34]

He did not forget to add that his own 'rude draughts and directions' were redrawn 'in their proper colours since [his] return'. The images, highly unconventional for the lack of established criteria of what 'ought to be seen' in this part of Europe, are the products of the scientist's gaze. Not aspiring to any aesthetic adornments, they refer directly to matters discussed in the text. Although some of them imitate images of the well-known sites, such as the ruins of a Roman Triumphal Arch in Petronell (Austria), others record what Brown considered 'rarely or not at all to be met with'. The most striking among those is an austere, proto-ethnographic record of the underground dwellings in Simonovitz (Šimanovci, Serbia), which reminded Brown of Herodotus's and Strabo's description of ancient troglodytes. 'In this country, many families, and the inhabitants of divers little towns, live all underground. . . . As we travelled by them, the poor Christians would betake themselves to their holes, like Conies'. Upon entering the houses, Brown assured the reader that they 'were better than we expected . . . divided into partitions . . . and all things neatly disposed as in other poor houses'.[35] His drawing, attached as a double-page foldout, does not try to add any cosy feature to the composition. An exercise in primary visualisation, it registers dispassionately a colony of those houses with their pitched roofs above a uniformly flat grassland, with an entrance and a window 'at the farther end, just above the ground'. Apart from a dog which 'came upon strangers' and a man drawing a bucket of water from a well, the place is empty, deprived of any trees, or vegetation, and only the puffs of smoke coming out of the chimneys add a sense of domesticity to the scene.[36]

The Ethnic Dress

Brown's documentary drawing of the underground dwellings did not follow any recognisable visual convention. A more complex affair are his drawings of people and their clothing. 'An Hungarian' and 'A Bulgarian Woman' in her ethnic dress (Figures 3.2 and 3.3) constitute a blend of empirical observation and conventions of costume imagery. The Hungarian nobleman is represented in a graceful pose, wearing a short dolman with an outer garment draped around his arm, tight trousers, and high leather boots. A *bulawa* (a ceremonial mace) in his hand signifies the highest ranks of nobility. He looks as one of the 'cartographic bodies' in national costumes on the margins of the maps of Europe, such as those produced at the time by Willem Blaeu or John Speed, discussed in Chapter 2 (Figure 2.4). But, even if this figure was lifted from

Figure 3.2 William Sherwin after William Brown, 'An Hungarian', engraving, in William Brown, *A Brief Account of Some Travels in Divers Parts of Europe*. London, 1673.

Figure 3.3 William Sherwin after William Brown, 'A Bulgarian Woman', engraving, in William Brown, *A Brief Account of Some Travels in Divers Parts of Europe*. London, 1673.

another source, a detailed explanation of the function of this dress testifies to Brown's full attention to this matter:

> This is the habit of an Hungarian, which is found to be so fit and convenient for all sort of exercise, especially on horse-back, and in war, that is made use of also by the Croatians, Schlavonians, and other nations, and by the Turks themselves who live near the frontiers, although otherwise they seldome change their own habit. The Hungarians delight most in colours, wearing blew, yellow, green and purple cloth; and it is rare to see any one in black.[37]

Surprisingly, the lower background of this image, usually corresponding with the milieu of the figure, geographical and social, shows the same underground dwellings which are described as the habitations of the poor just a few pages later. Those poor houses clash evidently with the figure's noble status. Brown's text does not comment on the gap between the rich and the abject conditions of the lower classes (this would come only in eighteenth-century travel reports), so the reason for turning the underground dwellings into a landscape frame of the nobleman is puzzling as the houses of the poorest poor unsettle the Hungarian's position as the representative of the European nobility.[38]

The figure of a woman presents further ambiguities. She holds a large fruit, a pumpkin grown in this area, demonstrating the fertility of the land in Serbia, as noted by Brown.[39] Although Brown described her as Bulgarian, he had met her in Baditzna (Batočina), south of Belgrade, in Serbia. Equally ambiguous are her social class and dress. Her simple garment, a long linen chemise, stiffly-starched and embroidered in a Slavic fashion, was a regular element of the peasant dress across the Balkans.[40] A bunch of keys hanging from her belt suggests however that she is a person of authority, though unlikely of a higher social status, given the obliteration of the Bulgarian nobility under the 'Turkish yoke'.[41] What attracted Brown's attention was her high headgear. Presumably, he had expected a headscarf instead. As he wrote,

> [In] Baditzna . . . the womens dress began to change, and was somewhat odd unto me. They wear a kind of canopye on their heads; which is set about, as also their foreheads, with all sorts of mony, which they can get of strangers. We left some small pieces among them, to add unto that curiosity: in this kind of ornament I have seen some Grecian women very rich, and somewhat after this fashion, but their head-dress not raised so high, having their foreheads covered with ducats of gold, and pearle.[42]

For Brown, her clothing was 'odd', because it was hybrid, mingling her dress of a Slavic peasant with a Greek headgear worn by well-off women. Her identity, both ethnic and social, could not be easily categorised, neither could her figure have been lifted from the margin of a map or a costume book, as in the case of the Hungarian nobleman.[43] In this part of Europe, where the names of places were rendered in German, Hungarian, Greek, Latin, and Turkish, as well as in a variety of Slavic languages, and where people's customs were fluid, crossing ethnic and political borders – to draw distinctions between nations, and even between high and low culture was particularly difficult.

And yet, in spite of his confusion about her identity, the image of the Bulgarian woman did enter Brown's book, and this inclusion, as I want to argue, marks the beginning of a long-lasting convention of visual reports from Europe's east which would not be complete without a representation of an 'ethnic body', that is a body which, regardless of its social status, is clothed in an ethnic dress. In later re-editions and translations of Brown's book, the nobleman and the woman would continue to appear together, sometimes even placed next to each other in one plate, with the same underground dwellings at the background, as in Alain Manesson-Mallet's *Description de l'univers* of 1683.[44] The nobleman's presence, however, already destabilised, would soon become almost redundant. The woman in her ethnic dress would suffice, metamorphosing into a personification of the whole region. Le Prince's allegorical print *Carte Generale* of 1768, discussed in the previous chapter (Figure 2.6), which opposed the courtly figures of France and the Holy Roman Empire to the humble folk signifying Poland and Russia, has already signalled that the most fitting visualisation of eastern Europe was a woman in her ethnic dress.[45]

One hundred years later, a similar image of a female in her ethnic costume, 'A Country Woman of the Canal of Zara' (Figure 3.4), opened another travel account from eastern Europe. *Travels into Dalmatia*, published in Venice by the palaeontologist and geologist Abbe Alberto Fortis in 1774, displayed significant similarities to Brown's *Brief Account*. Not only did it report on the results of a scientific expedition to the territories not far from those traversed by Brown, but it also widened its focus from the essentially empiricist observation of nature to history, culture, and popular customs. And in this case, it was precisely the transgression of the limit of the science-motivated survey which turned *Travels into Dalmatia* into a European bestseller.[46]

Figure 3.4 Giaccomo Leonardis after Angelo Donati (?), 'A Country Woman of the Canal of Zara', engraving, in Alberto Fortis, *Viaggio in Dalmazia*, Venice, 1774, Vol. 1.

Fortis's scholarly survey of fossils and geological formations of the Dalmatian coast would have been of interest to other scientists as well as to the Venetian Republic which controlled Dalmatia at that time. However, it was his comments on the manners of the Morlacks, a group of 'primitive' Slavic people inhabiting the inland territories of Dalmatia, which excited the readers. This was a truly modern discovery, in tune with the latest trends and interests of the enlightened Europeans. By supplying Europe's own incarnation of the 'noble savage', the book stirred the imagination of poets and playwrights, angered contemporary historians of Dalmatian extraction and activated publishers across Europe.[47] It has also attracted a sizeable secondary literature, which examined the book in the context of travel writing, posed it as the colonial project of the Venetian Republic, as well as reclaiming it as an important contribution to the geology of Dalmatia. *Travels into Dalmatia* has also been discussed by Larry Wolff as another proof in his longstanding argument about the invention of the primitive Slavic eastern Europe at the age of the Enlightenment.[48] While taking clues from Wolff's analysis, I will focus on the illustrations which set up the ethnic dress and the mountains as the two major components of the image of south-eastern Europe, to be followed by travellers up to the present.

Even if reproduced occasionally in the secondary literature, illustrations in *Travels into Dalmatia* have rarely attracted attention to themselves. Unlike Brown, Fortis did not try his skills as a draftsman, but he commissioned an artist to accompany him and produce sketches according to his exact instructions, so as not to leave out any important details of his specimens, often identified by letters, and explained at length in the text. Fortis never mentioned the artist's name, but he noted several times that a particular topic merited attention of his *disegnatore*.[49] Out of the 13 engravings, most of them attached as foldouts, the majority record the geological strata of the coast and fossils, one provides a map, two show ancient ruins, and three prints illustrate Morlack people from various sites of Dalmatia. The draftsman's identity was established on the basis of archival documents by Žarko Muljačić as Angelo Donati, most likely an amateur, as he is not listed as an artist in standard art historical dictionaries. His sketches were subsequently turned into prints by the professional graphic artist Giaccomo Leonardis of Padua.[50] The latter signed all the plates bottom right '*Jac Leonardis scul*', leaving empty the space on the left normally reserved for the draftsman, which might mean that Donati's work required too many corrections to acknowledge his authorship. Clearly, the scientist himself played a decisive role in the contents of the images.

Unexpectedly, given the book's scientific profile, its very first illustration shows a country woman from one of the islands near Zara (Figure 3.4). The label *scogliana* identifies her further as an inhabitant of one the rocky promontories typical for the Dalmatian coast. Fortis's commentary is premised on the sense of difference and geographical ambiguity, mirroring the ethnic ambivalence of Brown's description of the 'Bulgarian Woman'. Its first line emphasises the dissimilarity between the clothing of the Italian and Dalmatian peasants, by associating the latter with a 'neighbouring continent', by which he presumably meant Asia: 'The dress of the islanders, under the jurisdictions of Zara, is very unlike that of our peasants, resembling rather that which is used by the common people (*coltivatori delle terre*) on the neighbouring continent'. He softens this puzzling remark by saying: 'The women however, and particularly the young ones, have a kind of dress, with ornaments very prettily embroidered. I thought they merited the attention of my draftsman'.[51] Obviously, gender and age, as well as decorum applied to dress, mattered for Fortis. The image of the '*Scogliana del Canal di Zara*' could not be more approving. The statuesque pose of the figure, the regular features of her face, and above all, the carefully defined details of her dress: a woollen garment worn over the embroidered chemise, the head kerchief exposing her pendant earrings, an apron hanging from the belt, and a basket with figs gracefully supported on her arm – all of those add up to an iconic quality of the image. As in the case of Brown's couple, the traveller's image turned into an encyclopaedic illustration in a costume book, used as the prototype of a peasant woman of the islands of Zara in the later publication on Dalmatia, locally produced, with 48 miniatures representing the regional dress.[52] Composed, earnest, neat, and assiduous, the *scogliana* makes an ideal peasant, as if ready-made to enter the pages of Herder's *Slawische Völker*, eulogising the virtues of the Slavic folk, yet to be published. It is significant that Herder's much quoted chapter made the peasant status, as well as obedience and submissiveness, the defining features of the Slavic nations. Moreover, Herder made a call for the documentation of their 'domestic arts' (*häusliche Künste*), as well as 'customs, songs and legends . . . so that a comprehensive history of the Slavic peoples may at last be written, as called for in the panorama of humankind'.[53]

The *scogliana* drawing makes yet another claim. The young country woman is presented next to a branch of a fig tree, covered with pest which, according to Fortis, produces a red pigment, but also damages the tree and the fruit. The branch is labelled as 'A', and the pest, labelled 'B', is magnified below. If Fortis devoted just a few lines to the *scogliana* and her dress, the 'curious species of kermes' attracted his undivided attention, and a detailed description of the pest's behaviour, with ample references to scholarly literature, spreads over a good four pages.[54] Plate I acquires thus a totally new dimension: it can no longer be seen as a quasi-spontaneous record of Fortis's encounter with a young *scogliana* in her neat dress. It works, clearly, as an introduction, devised in visual terms, to the two major strands of Fortis's study in Dalmatia: nature and its phenomena as the main target, and the discovery of the culture of the Morlacks as a by-product. Both had to be identified, described, and illustrated, and the image of the ideal peasant turned into just another another specimen in the enlightened collector's portfolio. To the contemporary viewer, however, the juxtaposition of the young Morlacca to the tree damaged by a parasite strikes as something incompatible and disparaging, bringing into mind Brown's underground dwellings next to the Hungarian nobleman. The damaged fig tree as the context for the *scogliana*, unsettles the integrity of her persona, undermining the assumption of her horticultural skills, as well as, by implication, her purity.

Fortis's clearly declared aim was to restore the Morlacks' reputation, but the opening image of the book problematised his efforts from the start. A similar resistance underscores the text. As argued by Wolff, the scientist's enthusiasm towards the Morlacks was ambivalent and his remarks about the 'prodigious length of the breasts of the Morlacchian women', which outraged the Croatian writer Ivan Lovrich,[55] the intimations of uncleanliness and 'bad husbandry' and altogether the charge of barbarism, the latter to be observed even in the ornaments of their dress, underpinned his narrative.[56] Brown's image of the Bulgarian woman was an enigma because of her hybrid costume, but it commended her agricultural skills; in *Travels into Dalmatia* it is the other way round: *scogliana*'s dress ostensibly testifies now to her ethnic identity, while the image raises doubts about her horticultural experience, implying incompetence and backwardness, and the need of an external expertise.

Among the six figures of the Morlacks presented in the engravings, five of them are women. The absence of an image of a young male was most likely a strategic choice for Fortis, who described a typical Morlack's attire as consisting of 'one or two pistols . . . and a very large knife'. After concluding that 'No Morlack ever goes out of doors without his gun upon his shoulder', he directed the reader to the illustration of the Voievod Pervan, 'my good landlord of Coccorich', who, as a figure of authority, is 'better dressed'.[57] Clearly, Fortis wanted to steer his readers away from the image which would bear any similarities to that of a ferocious Morlack bandit Stanislavo Soçivizca, already famous both for his resistance against the Turkish terror as well as for his robberies. It is tempting to think that it is precisely the absence of the image of the typical Morlack male among Fortis's illustrations which provoked Lovrich not only to add a biography of Soçivizca to his book written in response to *Travels into Dalmatia*, but even to publish a print representing the famous bandit as a frontispiece.[58] This highly staged and de-masculinised set of images of the Morlacks was widely reproduced and often redrawn in the book's diverse editions all over Europe. Importantly, the 'noble savage', when discovered in south-eastern Europe, in visual terms was identified by Fortis with a peasant woman in her ethnic dress.

Mountains and Palikars

By excluding the image of an agile Morlack, Fortis might have tried to supress the aggressive masculinity of the Dalmatian folk, but the plate '*Cascata di Velika Gubaviza*', which records a huge waterfall of the Cettina river in the midst of 500-foot high rocky crevices (Figure 3.5) merits attention for that very reason. For centuries, the mountains had been identified as a space of danger, particularly for travellers. Lithgow was robbed in the Transylvanian mountains, while Brown, even if he explored the Carniola mountains for their mineral resources, did not hide his preference for 'open and clear plains', which provided unobstructed views and 'a handsome way of travelling in open chariots'.[59] Hundred years later, 'Waterfall Velika Gubaviza' is already a testimony to the discovery of the mountains as the source of the sublime. Not only does it respond almost directly to Edmund Burke's inquiry into a new kind of aesthetic pleasure, in which the sense of threat and horror evoke heightened emotions (1757),[60] but it locates the sublime mountains among the Morlacks. The topic of the rugged mountains is the least commented upon aspect of *Travels into Dalmatia*, yet it is significant for the iconography of eastern Europe emerging from travel books. If for the later historians, as discussed in Chapter 1, eastern Europe was uniformly flat and defenceless, travellers described it as predominantly mountainous and challenging.[61]

'Waterfall Velika Gubaviza' is also the only image in the book which breaks free from Fortis's way of looking at Dalmatian landscapes as agglomerations of geological strata, focusing instead on the sublime scenery, the dark rocks, crumbled stones, vegetation, and falling waters. Overwhelmed by the enormous height of the cascade and torn by the sensations of threat and wonder, Fortis echoed Burke in trying to restrain his emotions: 'In the noisy horror of the Cettina, buried between immense rocks, no man could live, but the one abandoned to despair, and enemy to light, to society, and to himself'.[62] Giving it a long dramatic description nonetheless and having ordered

Figure 3.5 Giaccomo Leonardis after Angelo Donati (?), 'Waterfall Velika Gubaviza', engraving,
in Alberto Fortis, *Viaggio in Dalmazia*, Venice, 1774, Vol. 2.

his *disegnatore* to draw 'this magnificent piece', the scientist did not miss the opportunity to continue his search for stones. Importantly, the visit to Velika Gubaviza was
the only occasion when Fortis identified himself with the Morlacks, 'those men born,
and hardened in fatigue'. The waterfall activated his 'agility in climbing and descend-
ing the rocks', and he was very pleased on hearing a compliment from the Morlacks:
'*Gospodine, ti nissi Lanzmanin, tissi Vlah!*' Sir, you are not an Italian poltron, you are
a Morlacco'.[63] He also found his companions 'more curious and observing than any
[Morlacks he] had before met with', following with 'great attention' the 'progress of
the drawing'.[64] The fury of the waterfall must have also liberated the *disegnatore*, who
included in the drawing a figure of himself. It is tempting to identify this figure as an
equivalent of his missing signature, as if confirming that this image, free from Fortis's
instructions, came directly from the draftsman's hand.

The *disegnatore* is the only human figure visible in this print but, in many ways,
'Waterfall Velika Gubaviza' acts in the book as a potent signifier of the Morlacks'
suppressed masculinity. The vastness, verticality, and the roughness of the cliffs, as well
as the untameable waterfall in their midst, lend themselves directly to be read as a
compensation for the missing image of a young Morlack with a gun on his shoulder.
Those tensions between absence and presence, innocence and corruption, and aver-
sions and affections, which underscore both Fortis's and Lovrich's book illustrations,
set up the two major tropes that will foreground and dominate the travellers' ways
of looking not only at the Morlacks, Dalmatia and the Balkans, but increasingly at
the lands of Europe's east as a whole. The female body in ethnic dress as well as the

masculinised terrain of the rugged mountains will act as the prisms, focussing their gaze, and attracting a diversity of meanings throughout the turbulences of the next two centuries.

Leonardi's print of the *Cascata* developed an international career of its own. Very close to the British eighteenth-century topographic watercolours of the rocks in the Lake District, and indeed, preceding William Gilpin's travels in search of the picturesque of the 1790s,[65] it was selected for the reproduction in the issue of *The Gentleman's Magazine* in April 1778, which announced the English translation of *Viaggio in Dalmazia*.[66] It also inspired other images and descriptions of the 'Dalmatian Alps', as well as other mountains and waterfalls throughout the nineteenth century.[67] 'Waterfall Velika Gubaviza' might have also signposted in visual terms another trendsetting discovery in Europe, the British Romantics' encounter with Albania.

The primary role in the discovery of 'the wilds' of Albania was played with brio by Lord George Gordon Byron. If Fortis owes his fame to the Morlacks, Byron's poetic success dates from his encounter with the Albanian warriors and mountains. This is where he acquired his Albanian costume and wrote his first verses of *Childe Harold's Pilgrimage*. The first edition of the poem, accompanied by Byron's copious notes and published in 1812, sold out just in three days. 'I awoke one morning and found myself famous', wrote Byron.[68] Canto II is largely devoted to his unrestrained eulogy of the 'sublime virtues' of the country. 'Land of Albania!' exclaims Byron, 'let me bend mine eyes/ On thee, thou rugged nurse of the savage men'.[69]

It is interesting to note here that, keen to position himself as the discoverer of the savage beauty of Albania, Byron called on the authority of Gibbon and his references to the ancient history of the territories shared by Albania and Greece in *The History of the Rise and Decline of the Roman Empire*. Byron went into trouble to dig out Gibbon's marginal note on the uncertainty of the location of Dodona, the place of the ancient Greek oracle in Epirus. Gibbon ended this note with a complaint: 'A country within sight of Italy is less known than the wilds of America', but he did not mention Albania by name.[70] Even if this remark might have indeed implied the unmapped territories of Albania, Byron misquoted the historian's actual phrase, by saying 'Of Albania Gibbon remarks, that a country "within sight of Italy is less known than the interior of America"'. He replaced the historian's term 'wilds' with a neutral term 'interior'. It appears that by both evoking Gibbon's authority and by 'doctoring' his words, Byron wanted to stress the pioneering nature of his own escapade into the terrain, 'where no other Englishmen have ever advanced', and, at the same time, to appropriate the rights to comment on the country's wilderness just to himself.[71] He succeeded in both. By recalling the statement about Albania as an uncharted territory, Byron triggered a string of the same misquotes of Gibbon, repeated until today.[72] Moreover, he appropriated Gibbon's rhetoric of wilderness, crucial for his own self-fashioning.

Byron's verses on the 'wilds' of Albania and the savage men inspired also a whole series of iconic images of Albania's mountains, peopled by the invincible palikars, the inhabitants of the impassable Suli summits, famous for holding up against any invaders onto their territory, a trope also already present in Gibbon's. They made their way to a number of the early nineteenth-century travelogues, including the one written by John Cam Hobhouse, Byron's companion on his journey.[73] One of the most striking images was produced by the architect Charles Robert Cockerell who met Byron in Greece and visited Albania in 1814 to sketch its antiquities and landscape. Cockerell's travel diary was published posthumously without any illustrations, but

Figure 3.6 Frederick Christian Lewis, after Charles Robert Cockerell, 'View of Albanian
          Palikars in Pursuit of an Enemy', engraving, in The Rev. Thomas Smart Hughes,
          Travels in Sicily, Greece and Albania. London, 1820, Vol. 2.

his watercolour of the Albanian palikars gained popularity when engraved in the
Reverend Thomas Smart Hughes's *Travels in Sicily, Greece and Albania*, published in
1820 (Figure 3.6).[74] It shows a group of troopers in their sheepskin coats and pleated
frocks in the midst of a wild landscape, made of rocks and forests. Armed to the teeth,
with pistols attached to their waists, rapiers hanging by their knees and a gun upon
their shoulders, they are moving in a single line, negotiating effortlessly the narrow
path among the crevices, just like the Morlacks described by Fortis. Their heads are
shaved in a Turkish manner, with a tuft of hair on top, covered by a small hat; their
eyes, wide open, cast a fiery gaze. The title given to the image in Hughes's book, 'View
of Albanian Palikars in Pursuit of an Enemy', clearly echoes Byron's verse:

> Fierce are Albania's children, yet they lack
> Not virtues, were those virtues more mature.
> Where is the foe that ever saw their back?[75]

The image sums up the agility, belligerence, and an almost animal-like alertness of the
warriors, born and bred in the heart of the mountains. Its Byronic title enhances the
scene, turning it into a narrative, a representation of a military excursion, or a vendetta,
requiring blood for offending the family's honour, the latter theme soon becoming

part and parcel of any travelogue account from Albania. Cockerell's palikars proved hugely popular in Europe throughout the nineteenth century, reprinted in books and periodicals, turned into paintings, inspiring photographs, attracting ever more travellers.[76] No doubt, the image supplied an irresistible formula for an orientalised group portrait of the Balkan's tribesmen, turning the words of romantic poetry into an icon, a perfect embodiment of savage Others and freedom fighters at the same time, threatening and heroic, immature and virtuous. 'Their wrath how deadly! But their friendship sure', Byron was eager to vouch for.[77]

Among the nineteenth-century travellers following into the footsteps of Byron was Edward Lear who, apart from nonsense poetry, practised all kinds of arts, including watercolours of landscapes, produced on his multiple journeys overseas.[78] He used them to illustrate his travel accounts, employing the newly invented technique of chromolithographs. During his travel to Albania in 1848, Lear visited Janina and embarked on an arduous escapade through the 'blood-stained Suli' to Ali Pasha's castle.[79] The image chosen to accompany this passage, depicting the mountain pass over the rocky summit, provides an equivalent to Cockerell's watercolour, but it removes the palikars and turns the mountains themselves into the protagonists (Figure 3.7).[80] The very high point of view, of eagles and clouds, reduces the barely discernible human figures to dots, and it is the rocks, towering above the bottomless abyss, their tops deprived of vegetation, which are now imbued with the Byronic drama, heroism, solemnity, and invincibility. The vertical format of the image enhances the sensation of ascendancy, as if addressing the viewer, challenging, or perhaps inviting him or her, to follow the path. If Cockerell's image of palikars confronted its viewers, almost face to face, with the violent romantic Other, 30 years later, Lear's 'Suli' was offering them a detached, panoramic view of an imaginary itinerary through the mountains, thrilling as much as beautiful, promising a different travel experience. The 1840s was already the time when Karl Baedeker and John Murray were publishing their first tourist guides, turning travelling into a business and travel destinations into commodities.[81] Those volumes were not illustrated, but Lear's prints, echoing the aesthetic pleasures of the '*Cascata*' print, aligned the regimes of looking at the east of Europe with those promoted by the rising tourism industry. They were turning away from natural sciences, history, and contemporary politics, focusing now on the lure of the mountains.

The Danube

The nineteenth century came out as an age in which travel and travel publishing were reinvented by the new modes of transport: steamboat, rail networks, and the motor car by the end of it. As pointed out by Brian H. Murray, throughout the nineteenth century the new technologies of transport were intertwined with new techniques of reproductions, such as the aforementioned lithography and chromolithography, as well as steel engraving and wood engraving.[82] This led to a considerable expansion of illustrations in travel books, as well as to the diversification of the repertory of images standing for Europe's east.

When Edward Brown was travelling across Hungary and Serbia, parts of his journey were made by boat and barge down the Danube River. The Danube has always been used by travellers and merchants as the most important waterway crossing central and eastern parts of Europe. The river's strategic and economic potential in connecting Habsburg and Ottoman empires had risen after the treaty of Adrianople in 1828, and the introduction of the steamboat service by an Austrian Company in the 1830s radically

Figure 3.7 Edward Lear, 'Suli', chromolithograph, in *Journals of a Landscape Painter in Albania*. London, 1851.

changed the accessibility and comfort of travel both down and up the river. The annual number or travellers rose dramatically from 17,000 to 200,000 in just a few years.[83] As suggested by Luminita Gatejel, this transformed the perception of the dangerous narrow gorge on the Danube at the Austrian-Ottoman border, flanked by high cliffs on both sides and known as the Iron Gates. It changed from an unbridgeable mental boundary between the west and the Orient to a romantic tourist experience, which was memorialised in countless descriptions of the Danube journeys (Figure 3.8).[84]

One of the most stylish among them, *The Danube, Its History, Scenery and Topography* (1842), was produced by yet another British physician, but also writer and poet, William Beattie.[85] He went down the river, accompanied by the foremost illustrator William Bartlett, who specialised in travel images. Both Beattie and Bartlett had already worked together on a number of similar publications in Scotland, Switzerland and the British coast, all resulting in luxurious publications in quarto, in which carefully executed illustrations played the major role. *The Danube* featured 79 separate plates with stupendous steel engravings of major sites and landscapes and, apart from that, sketches of people, costumes, interiors, and views as smaller wood engravings

The Kazan Pass.
(with the modern and Roman Roads)

LE PAS DE KAZAN, (AVEC LA ROUTE MODERNE ET LA ROUTE ROMAINE.)

Figure 3.8 James Charles Armytage after William Henry Bartlett, 'The Kazan Pass (with the modern and Roman Roads)', steel engraving, in William Beattie, *The Danube: Its History, Scenery, and Topography*. London, 1842.

embedded into the text. The plethora of details and the distinctive atmospheric effects of the plates invested the images with a high narrative quality, capable of turning the reader into an attentive viewer in search for the extra-textual. The lion's share of the text and illustrations were devoted to the relatively short part of the journey through the Habsburg lands, represented by romantic castles on high cliffs, gothic cathedrals, imperial tombs, town-halls, as well as large cities, including Vienna, with elegant town folk on its promenades (Figure 3.9). If Upper Hungary was still seen mostly through the prism of castles, the longest stretch of the whole journey, across Serbia, Wallachia, and Bessarabia, was shown as the flat land inhabited by peasants. The text shrunk to just over one chapter, in contrast to the three devoted to the Habsburg lands, while the views of historic towns and their grandiose buildings were displaced by a handful of plates of small villages, boatmen, or peasant gatherings.

'A Wedding at Orsova' shows a modest peasant fest with a few musicians and dancing couples, the Hungarian shepherds in their long sheepskin coats, a group of people who climbed a stack of hay for a better view, and a handful of Wallachian women with children who happily joined the dancers. The unrepaired roofs of the vernacular buildings in the foreground testify to neglect and poverty (Figure 3.10). The social

Figure 3.9 Robert Wallis after William Henry Bartlett, 'Vienna (From the Belvedere Gardens.)', steel engraving, in William Beattie, *The Danube: Its History, Scenery, and Topography*. London, 1842.

Figure 3.10 William Mossman after William Henry Bartlett, 'A Wedding at Orsova', steel engraving, in William Beattie, *The Danube: Its History, Scenery, and Topography*. London, 1842.

as well as cultural contrast with entertainment offered by German and Austrian cities, towns, and castles, cannot be more explicit. History, civilisation and strict social rules, created by kings and princes, give way to disorderly peasant rituals, the wedding becoming one of the most keenly followed rites to be studied by the nineteenth-century ethnographers cum travellers. After reaching the mountainous cliffs of the Iron Gates near the village, there are just a few Turkish settlements with large bath buildings, wooden Turkish cafes, but mostly pastures with mosques on the horizon. The Danube confirms its role as the intermediary between the Upper Danube in the west and the Lower Danube in the east under the Turkish rule, linking them just in order to expose their differences. Apart from emphasising the Turkish presence, the nineteenth-century travel imagery of the east of Europe expanded the range of its signifiers beyond the mountains and peasants to quaint villages and wedding ceremonies, weakening the historian's eye for the sake of the anthropologist's gaze.

Quaint villages, picturesque scenery with mountains and rivers, as well as plenty of ethnic dress dominated travel reports towards the end of the century, when many of them were conducted by train. In contrast to the modernisation of the Danube waterways, the network of railways in the east of Europe was developing with an uneven speed. In the 1840s, the first trains from Vienna went to Prague, Budapest, and Cracow, following onto Warsaw by 1848, from where, after the change of carriages, they could continue to Russia. In the 1870s, Budapest was connected by rail with Belgrade and Bucharest, and, after the establishment of the Orient Express in the 1880s, with Athens and Constantinople. The 1870s and the 1880s saw further investments in local railway connections, especially within Hungary and Romania, and many towns, such as the Transylvanian Klausenburg (Hungarian Kolozsvár; Romanian Cluj-Napoca) and Moldavian Iaşi joined the railway network by the 1870s. The improved comfort and speed of travel brought a growing number of travel reports, especially from places away from the beaten track.

Surrounded by mountains and forest on all sides, as reported already by Lithgow, Transylvania had been particularly difficult to reach.[86] An outpost of the Teutonic Knights and Saxon Germans since the middle ages, inhabited by Hungarians and Romanians (exonym name Wallachians), as well as Jews and Roma, it became the topic of many travel books, even before the improvement of travel conditions. The diversity of its names, derived from Latin (Transsylvania, meaning 'beyond the forest'), German (Siebenbürgen, seven castles), and Hungarian (Erdélyi, mountains), point to the mythical appeal of the land, arising both from its medieval past and its mountainous territory. In contrast to the luxury travel albums associated with the modern Danube cruises, books on Transylvania tend to be smaller, illustrated with modest wood engravings and occasional lithographic plates.

One of the most well-read was John Paget's *Hungary and Transylvania*, brought out by John Murray in 1839. Very well received in Hungary and republished several times in Britain, it attracted tourists and even investors.[87] Paget was a British medical doctor, who moved to Transylvania on marrying Baroness Polyxena Wesselenyi Banffy, and settled with her in a country house near Kolozsvár. He took an active part in the political life of the country, participating in the 1848 revolution against Habsburg dominance.[88] He was also a keen supporter of the Hungarian politician and reformer István Széchenyi, who stood behind the navigation of the Danube. When embarking on his journey through the country, Paget commissioned the landscape painter George Edward Hering to illustrate his book, explaining in the introduction that 'written description of the physical characteristics of a country and people convey . . . imperfect notions of them'.[89] His travel account aimed to extend the knowledge about Hungary 'in the west of Europe, and more especially in England',[90] and gave detailed descriptions of many aspects of life, politics, and industry, in both Upper Hungary and Transylvania. Hering's illustrations, however, did not match Paget's modernising concerns, most of them focusing on the country side, the mountains, the plains of the Hungarian *Puszta* (with the same type of wells as those recorded by Brown), quaint villages, as well as peasants of diverse ethnicity, Jews and Roma included.

It is the image selected as a frontispiece to Paget's book, however, which merits special attention, as it both broke away with the country-side imagery, while pointing to England as the model for Hungary's modernisation (Figure 3.11). Before the arrival of the dustjacket, nineteenth-century books used the space of frontispiece to declare in visual terms the arguments made inside. The first of Murray's volumes of *Hungary and Transylvania* featured the portrait of Széchenyi as the patron of Hungarian modernity, while the second volume provided a compelling vision of the modern makeover of Buda.[91] Distancing itself from Hering's image of Hungary as composed of mountains and peasants, it confronted the reader with a full-page print of the new suspension bridge linking Buda and Pest. The bridge, considered an engineering wonder of the time due to its unprecedented scale, was commissioned by Széchenyi and designed by the British engineer William Tierney Clark, the author of several, much smaller, suspension bridges in Britain. Its construction, supervised by the Scottish engineer Adam Clark, was completed in 1849.[92] The drawing in the book was submitted by Arthur Mee, an architect and a close collaborator of Tierney Clark's, and turned into an experimental print on zinc by Louis Hague and William Day. The book was published ten years before the bridge's completion and its frontispiece was based on the engineer's design, with added carriages, horsemen, and pedestrians.[93] The fact that the frontispiece was still a vision rather than reality strengthened Paget's forward-looking plans for Buda and Hungary. Adopting Hungarian identity, Paget openly declared, in a utopian vein: 'I cannot, like many of my countrymen, please myself with contemplating what is past. I must look forward. . . . The past is beyond our control; the future is still within our grasp'.[94] And a few pages later, when outlining a vision of a 'brilliant future for Buda-Pest', he asserted firmly the political agenda of this project as closely associated with the sovereignty of Hungary, 'and perhaps too the independence of the east of Europe'.[95] This is one of the early instances of a political project of seeking cooperation between the countries of the 'east of Europe' to overturn their foreign occupiers, whether Habsburg, Tsarist, or Ottoman, which would manifest itself even more strongly after 1848 among the exiled Romanian revolutionaries in Paris.[96] In Paget's terms, the way to political freedom was tantamount with the industrial revolution as embodied by the Széchenyi Bridge.

The symbolic value of the Széchenyi Bridge was appreciated by further travellers and authors, but it was to be substantially modified, turning from the quasi-redemptory signifier of modernity into yet another marker of the east-west boundary with the Ottoman Empire. By the end of the century, it appeared on the first page of Bram Stoker's *Dracula* (1897) in his much quoted enthusiastic description of Buda: 'The impression I had that we were leaving the West and entering the East; the most western of splendid bridges over the Danube, which is here of noble width and depths, took us among the traditions of Turkish rule'.[97] The harbinger of modernity and political liberation metamorphosed, at least on the level of verbal imaging, into a gatepost

Figure 3.11 Louis Haghe after Arthur Mee, 'The New Bridge, Between Pest & Buda. From a design by W. Tierney Clark', zincography, in John Paget, *Hungary and Transylvania*. London, 1839, Vol. 2.

'Turkey in Europe'.[98] Furthermore, frontispieces of further editions of Paget's *Hungary and Transylvania* advertised Hungary as the country of the mountains, picturesque villages and the romantic gorges on the Danube.[99]

Peasant Woman With a Distaff

In spite of Paget's attempt to associate the east of Europe with modernity, illustrations of mountains, villages, and women in ethnic dresses prevailed. Since the early nineteenth century, costume books included images of graceful peasant women in embroidered dresses from south-eastern Europe, carrying their weaving utensils, the distaff, and a frame loom, such as 'Women from the Mehadia Region', in the collection of folk costumes assembled by the Austrian author and etcher Karl Timlich in 1816. His prints, including the image of the two Mehadia women, were republished in turn in 1820 in an album devoted to the 'inhabitants of Pannonia with ethnographic explanation', assembled by the former officer of the Austrian Army Joseph Heinbucher Edlen von Bikkessy.[100] This particular motif, repeated in travel reports and travel images from this region, confirms not only the interaction between travel writing and costume books, but also the affinity of both of those genres with a wide-spread interest in folk culture and folk dress cultivated by amateurs.

By the second half of the nineteenth century, the image of a woman with a distaff in her hand, busy spindling to produce wool or linen for clothes for the whole family, rose to a veritable icon of textile craft. A colour lithograph of a 'Wallack Woman' appeared on the frontispiece of Charles Boner's *Transylvania; Its Products and Its People*, published in 1865 (Figure 3.12).[101] A British traveller and a poet, Boner lived in Germany at the time, employed as a teacher in upper class families. His book, discussing the history and culture of diverse nations inhabiting the country, including Jews and Roma, favoured opinions of a 'civilising mission' of the Saxons in Transylvania and was particularly critical about the Wallacks, the poorest and ethnically most complicated inhabitants of the land, sharing their ancestry with the Dalmatian Morlacks. He presented them as the descendants of barbarians, indolent and guilty of unspeakable atrocities against their Hungarian landlords during the 1848 revolution.[102] Most of the illustrations in Boner's book that show buildings and towns were based on prints and photographs, the latter redrawn in the book as wood engravings,[103] coming from the collections of the members of the German Antiquarian Society, the *Verein für siebenbürgische Landeskunde*, and to a considerable extent promulgated the ethnic prejudices of the Society.

Boner gave no hint as to the source of the anonymous print of the 'Wallack Woman', different from all other images in his book, neither did he provide a reason for selecting it for the frontispiece. It bears a mark of the French publisher Lemercier, and it must have been snatched from one of the numerous French prints and publications on Wallachia and Transylvania, which were circulating around the mid-century.[104] A mature woman stands barefoot in bright sunlight, a small thatched building at the background confirming the poverty of her surroundings. In Boner's words in the first chapter of the book, her dress is 'bright with colour'. The *obrescha*, a broad girdle with red fringe, gives her 'a wild witch-like air'.[105] A large distaff held under her arm with a thin wool floss thread spun onto a spindle are her defining attributes. The choice of this image for the frontispiece is puzzling, considering Boner's condescending attitude towards the Wallacks who, as he wrote in another section of his book, were made to

Figure 3.12 'A Wallack Woman', colour lithograph, in Charles Boner, *Transylvania: Its Products and Its People*. London, 1865.

be slaves, their building skills alone indicating 'a low grade of civilisation'.[106] But, not unlike Paget before him, quoting Homer on encountering the spinning woman,[107] Boner too, once having asserted his reader that 'nothing that art has produced is to be found here', burst into a sudden praise of the astonishing range of crafts mastered by the Wallack woman. Apart from spinning, her skills comprise weaving and dying wool, tailoring, sewing, embroidery, carpet-making, as well as basketry. 'How she manages it is more than I can tell; but she does it. She is an industrious creature, busy always'.[108] Her garments, Boner continued, 'are not well cut . . . and the sewing, I dare say, is not very regular; but with such uncouth needle and thread who would do better?' Neither did he spare her his compliments: 'And that bright *kratinza* . . . soft as it is and of fine texture, and with well-sorted brilliant colours – was made by her in that incomprehensibly primitive machine, of their own wool, and the broad girdle with its pretty pattern is her make and design too'.[109] And, after the description of the natural dyes, Boner gave the Wallack woman the most articulate appreciation of her craft by measuring her skills by western standards: 'The carpets woven in some parts of the country by the more skilful among the women are so handsome that they would be prized as an ornament in any London or Paris drawing-room. The taste with which they choose and arrange colours is admirable, and the designs, always *eastern* in character, are also entirely of their own'. He also warned against adoption of patterns 'of western Europe'.[110]

Thus, regardless of the widespread contempt towards her people, the appearance of the Wallack woman in her hand-made dress in the frontispiece of the book elevated the least 'civilised' ethnic minority of Transylvania to its emblem. She arrived there as a perfect image of the 'eastern' Other, endlessly seductive and 'incomprehensibly primitive' at the same time; so 'admirable' precisely because so 'uncouth'; so different from the western standards of beauty, because so 'eastern in character'.[111] At first sight, Boner's Wallack woman seems no different from Brown's Bulgarian woman and from Fortis's Morlacca – all three of them were depicted in their embroidered dresses, presenting diverse attributes of their occupational identities. And all three of them signified, in a variety of ways, the 'eastern European' Other. The markers of 'otherness' invested in those images, however, changed considerably from the seventeenth to the nineteenth century. An ethnic enigma for Brown, a pretty but unskilled peasant for Fortis, she has now been recognised by Boner as a craftswoman, identified by her portable distaff, and capable of producing objects which could easily compete on the international art market.

When Boner declared his fascination with the products made by hand out of the raw materials by Wallack peasants, the 'primitive' crafts were just being included into discussions about the source of art making in general, as well as about the origins of national cultures and national identities in many countries both west and east.[112] Boner's use of the Wallack craftwoman as the frontispiece of his book of 1865 was a bold gesture at the early stages of this process and was most likely facilitated by his exposure to the debates within the German cultural milieu. His blatant acknowledgment of Wallack craft has to be seen as an early response to the emerging cultural trends, initiated by Gottfried Semper who, in his book *Der Stil in den technischen and tektonischen Künsten* of 1860, traced the very origins of art-making to the elementary crafts, and especially textiles.[113] Semper's influential theories were adopted as the founding principle of the Museum of Applied Art in Vienna, which opened in 1864, the year before Boner's book was published. The museum's policies, in turn, especially the activities of its head curator Jacob von Falke, promoting women's needlework and folk art, paved the way for the major re-evaluation of peasant craft at international exhibitions, especially in Vienna in 1873, and to the wholesale vernacular revival movement in Europe towards the end of the nineteenth century.[114]

As has been well documented, vernacular revival movements were particularly strong in the east of Europe. In Russia, where the discussion between *slavophiles* and *zapadniki* dominated the second half of the nineteenth century; in partitioned Poland; in Bohemia and in Hungary struggling to dis-identify themselves from Germany and the Habsburgs; in Romania and in the lands of 'Turkey in Europe', the rediscovery of the Indigenous cultures by armies of antiquarians and artists went hand in hand with the struggle for cultural and political sovereignty.[115] In the 1830s, Paget identified the prospect of the political autonomy of Hungary, and even of the whole of the east of Europe, with the ultra-modern technology of the Széchenyi Bridge. By the end of the century, the products of peasant craftsmanship, showcased at international fairs, would take over as a meta-narrative of modernity, testifying to the strength of 'primitive' cultures, and their redemptive power, capable of preserving the essence of national identities.[116] The Széchenyi Bridge seemed to have lost out to the Wallack woman. Indeed, by 1900, and even more so after the restoration of the sovereignty to the countries of eastern Europe at Versailles, the Indigenous techniques and styles, which had been deemed as 'barbarian' by Fortis, would become the source of inspiration for the producers of high culture, revitalising modern art, and satisfying the demands for national distinctiveness.

From the end of the nineteenth century, the peasant woman in her ethnic dress would turn into the most widely recognisable signifier of the east of Europe, not only encountered by foreign travellers, but, most importantly, rediscovered by her middle-class compatriots as the epitome of the national Self all across the region. Her dress and her unending range of skills would now be described in detail by local ethnographers, emulated by local artists, and used by politicians for all kinds of goals. The details of her clothing and her socio-cultural identity might be changing, but she would keep returning in diverse roles and publications with an astonishing tenacity. By the twentieth century, she would virtually monopolise the image of the 'eastern European body' as seen by western travellers, and to a significant degree, by eastern Europeans themselves. Todorova's comment on the Balkan Peninsula perceived as the *Volksmuseum* of Europe becomes applicable to the whole of the eastern peripheries of the continent.[117]

Photographing 'Savage Europe'

For the publisher of Boner's book of 1865, the process of reproducing photographs from the collections of the members of the Transylvanian society required turning them first into wood engravings. By the end of the nineteenth century, the introduction of a mass-produced camera, as well as the improvement of the technology of photogravure, registering tones as well as lines, made photography the preferred medium of both the traveller and the publisher, the tool of production as well as the reproduction of images. More importantly, the ensuing rise of photographic studios all across Europe provided an opportunity to transform the hierarchy between the traveller and the travellee, by giving the latter a chance for self-fashioning. This did not mean, however, that the existing representational regimes were instantly challenged by the novel counter-hegemonic ways of seeing. In spite of the inherent indexicality of photography and its undeniable documentary potential, the travellers' gaze was slow to change, and the conventions of the photo-reportage from the 'remote parts' of Europe, whether undertaken by foreign or local photographers, tend to follow the old pre-photographic formulas.

One of the first travelogues of the region illustrated entirely with photographs, entitled *Through Savage Europe*, recorded hardly any other female bodies, apart from those of peasants and queens, many of them supplied by local agencies. It was commissioned from the professional travel writer Harry De Windt by the *Westminster Gazette,* and published in 1907 in the series devoted to the Balkans and Russia.[118] De Windt's journey covered an unusually large territory, stretching from Montenegro to the Russian Caucasus, with a stop in Warsaw on the way back, where he witnessed one of the bloody revolts against the Tsarist rule, to end in Budapest, 'within the commonplace but comfortable realms of civilisation'.[119] This was the time when Serbia, Romania, Bosnia and Herzegovina, as well as Bulgaria, liberated from the Ottoman Empire, functioned as sovereign kingdoms and principalities, though many boundary questions were still unresolved, to paraphrase Mackinder's 1919 phrase. The term eastern Europe not being common yet, De Windt opted for the phrase 'savage Europe' which, as he explained, could stand as an accurate description of 'the wild and lawless countries between the Adriatic and the Black Seas'.[120] Of Byronic origins, but hardly Byronic in its tenor, such a harsh rhetoric reflected the lack of sympathy in Britain at the time towards the national liberation movements.[121] As commented by *The Spectator*'s contemporary reviewer, 'there is savagery everywhere in Europe, but "savage Europe", *par excellence*, is to be found in South East'.[122] Among the 100 photographs in the book, many were taken by the professional photographer John Mackenzie who accompanied De Windt, while a good number of diverse images came from local agencies. Seen together, however, the illustrations do not expand the standard repertory of topics. Images of peasant women, rugged mountains, and quaint villages, including Mostar with its now famous bridge, are interspersed with photographs of royalty and political leaders. Although De Windt acknowledged in the text the presence of the middle class and a vibrant city life, naming Bucharest 'The City of Pleasure', there are no photographs of restaurants, cafes, or lively streets with cars, let alone people in non-ethnic clothes.[123] A visual code for urban pleasures and the modern body was not yet available for this part of Europe. A town view, such as that of Serbian Nisch (Niš), showing a street with a tool shop sign *Strugarska Radnja* (lathe shop) in the foreground, could only serve as a backdrop to the figures of two women peasants in their thickly woven hand-made dresses, walking briskly with baskets on their arms (Figure 3.13). It is they who caught the attention of the photographer. His camera registered also other peasants in the street, as well as the body of a man in a modern coat and a hat, barely visible in a distance, who must have entered the picture accidentally.

Apart from the photograph of the graves of the victims of the Tsarist police massacre in Warsaw, there are no images of savagery either. A clue to what 'savagery' meant for De Windt is provided however by the unusual cover of the book with a silhouette of a bearded Don Cossack, armed to his teeth, just like an Albanian palikar. Embossed in gold, it acts as an emblem of the 'wild' Europe to be described inside. Thus, in visual terms, savagery was identified with ethnic bodies armed with guns, and with the exclusion of any signifier of modernity, either in architectural or in sartorial

Figure 3.13 John Mackenzie/ Harry De Windt, 'Peasant Women at Nisch', photograph, in Harry De Windt, *Through Savage Europe*. London, 1907.

terms. And yet, the boundaries between the ethnic and modern body were not imper-meable. Paradoxically, the iconic savage body on the cover lends itself also to be read as an alter ego of De Windt himself, who – not unlike Lithgow whose itinerary he followed unknowingly – presents himself as a 'dashing explorer', travelling 'with a revolver in his pocket', to face warriors and robbers in the Caucasus.[124] The juxta-position of the image of the Don Cossack with De Windt's photograph as a perfect bourgeois (taken in a Belgrade atelier), shown in the frontispiece and presenting the author in an elegant hat, a dark coat, and a glaringly white collar – not unlike the man in the street in Nisch – suggests the ambiguity on the Self/Other axis, which will pervades many of the twentieth-century travel images of the region.

A significant change in travel publishing at the dawn of the twentieth century was the emergence of an entirely novel kind of travelogue – a periodical, devoted almost exclusively to travel reportage. Its chief value was continuity. To satisfy the increas-ing demand for illustrated reports about faraway spaces, it would appear regularly throughout the year, delivered conveniently through the letter box. The model was provided by the American journal, *National Geographic Magazine*. Set up in 1888 and distributed to members of the National Geographic Society, it was developed into 'the world's most widely recognised distributor of images' by successive members of the Grosvenor family, occupying positions of chief editors throughout the twentieth century.[125] While the readership of travel books counted in thousands, *National Geo-graphic* reached one million of households by the mid-1920s, and this number sky-rocketed to ten million by the end of the millennium.[126] Remarkably, in the world increasingly saturated with images, the magazine proved capable of holding its hege-monic position of 'a window to the world' in the field of travel reportage through more than a hundred years. As widely commented on, the key to the magazine's suc-cess was its strict editorial policy introduced by Gilbert H. Grosvenor as early as 1915, which included a number of stringent rules, such as the avoidance of anything of a 'trivial . . . partisan or controversial character', and the imperative of seducing its subscribers with the 'abundance of beautiful, instructive and artistic illustrations'.[127] If eastern Europe was indeed invented by travelogues, *National Geographic* must have played a substantial role in this process.

The rest of this chapter examines some aspects of eastern Europe's visual presence in twentieth-century geographical magazines. Did their photographs expand the exist-ing repertory of images in response to the reforms and calamities of the twentieth century taking place in the lands of the region? And how did they visualise what has already come to the fore in De Windt's book, the emergence of modernity and the changing relationship between the ethnic dress, the city, and the modern body? Not limiting itself just to *National Geographic*, this chapter extends the survey by looking at its British counterpart, *Geographical Magazine*. Established by Michael Huxley in London in 1935, it never matched the popularity of the American journal, neither did it attract a comparable critical attention. Nonetheless, those magazines share a number of features. Both of them are closely related to leading geographical societies in their countries, and both are still running, adapting their strategies to the requirements of the age of the World Wide Web. Significantly, both have devoted a substantial space to the countries of eastern Europe, putting the region into the global context. Finally, both of them have been classified as popular magazines that pay little regard to the 'serious pursuit' of geography as the academic discipline practised at universities, 'which managed to extricate itself from the imperial mind-set of racist foreign adventures'.[128] It is precisely this charge of popularity, often provoked by the emphasis on images, which makes those magazines particularly suitable for the argument of this chapter.

National Geographic has attracted a substantial literature, both celebratory and critical.[129] Its powers of seduction, including its visual strategies, were unravelled from the perspective of class, race, and gender by a number of authors. The anthropologists Catherine A. Lutz and Jane L. Collins read the American magazine through the postcolonial prism and, focusing on the post-WWII years, examined its glossy images of non-western peoples and spaces, adopting the Lacanian concept of the objectifying gaze.[130] More recently, Tamar T. Rothenberg and Stephanie L. Hawkins, reaching back to the magazine's early years, exposed its programmatic celebration of diversity and progress as the America-centred vision of the world, founded on imperialism, masculinism, and racism.[131] The vast majority of critical studies have focused on *National Geographic*'s coverage of the Third World, otherwise the prime territory of the magazine's travel correspondence. Its treatment of selected European countries was also scrutinised, but not much critical attention has been paid to its approach to eastern Europe.[132] An exception is a recent article by the Serbian historian Nemanja Radonjić, providing a comprehensive analysis of *National Geographic*'s stereotypical images of the Balkans.[133] This in itself reflects the attitude of the magazine which, from the early decades of the twentieth century considered 'the Balkans' as a geocultural entity, making it the theme of both its articles and maps.[134] Importantly, it also brings attention to its lack of recognition of 'eastern Europe' as a distinctive region, the ruling policy of the magazine up to 1990.

Chapter 2 already raised the issue of the lack of enthusiasm on the part of *National Geographic* to acknowledge the existence of eastern Europe in cartographic terms, either post-Versailles or post-WWII. The absence of the map went hand in hand with the absence of the term, which entered the magazine, paradoxically, only with the end of the Cold War, when the term 'Eastern Europe' began appearing in articles' titles as well as maps.[135] Most likely, the explicit absence of the term was linked directly to the magazine's editorial policy and its particular modes of self-fashioning, reliant on the most traditional principles of classical aesthetics, rejecting the ugly and controversial.[136] In the interwar period, the relatively novel term 'eastern Europe' did not match the requirements of the beautiful and the uncontroversial, and the reports from individual countries of the region were titled seductively as 'Transylvania and its Seven Castles' (1926) or 'Czechoslovakia – Key-Land to Central Europe' (1921), opting, wherever possible for 'central Europe' instead. With the escalation of conflicts after WWII, the term 'Eastern Europe' acquired even more negative connotations, associated with Stalin's conquest of the region. Commenting on 'some strange lacunae' during the Cold War era, Lutz and Collins claimed that 'favourable portrayals of eastern bloc nations would be unpatriotic; yet to dwell on their evils would violate editorial policy'.[137] Likewise, across the ocean, *Geographical Magazine* was also slow to introduce the term 'eastern Europe' to its vocabulary, but its editorial strategy differed substantially from that of *National Geographic*, being far more open towards the region, and even appreciative of the grand projects of its post-WWII modernisation.

Importantly, the articles on the lands of eastern Europe in both of the journals generated thousands of photographs and maps over the course of the twentieth century. During the whole period of its running, between 1888 and 2019, *National Geographic* made the individual countries of eastern Europe the topic of over 120 articles and photo supplements, illustrated in total with a whopping number of circa 2600 photographs. Even more attentive to the region, *Geographical Magazine* produced roughly the same number of 120 texts illustrated with 1200 photographs over a shorter period of 85 years, since 1935. If the British magazine (renamed *Geographical* in 1988) devoted more space to texts, the American journal was far more generous with images, and therefore in what follows, I will pay more attention to the photographs published by the latter.

National Geographic covered the whole of the twentieth century. Its first articles on eastern peripheries of Europe reported from Russia, which attracted incomparably more attention over the years, especially its faraway territories, such as Siberia.[138] The early 1900s, however, brought the first texts devoted exclusively to other countries of the region. At that time, the vast majority of them focused on the Balkans. Although their authors referred to the Balkan wars, the assassination of the Archduke Franz Ferdinand in Sarajevo, or the remapping of the region in Versailles,[139] *National Geographic*'s explicit rule was not to report on current events directly, focusing rather on issues that have 'permanent value', giving a balanced, 'timeless' view of life in the region. Thus, leaving politics aside and following closely the patterns established by nineteenth-century travel writing, the correspondents kept discovering anew the beauty of the landscape,[140] quaint villages,[141] as well as the customs of the locals. At the centre of attention was, once again, the folk dress, generating long descriptions of its homespun fabrics, natural pigments, and embroidery patterns. Folk dress was duly held up as the tool of resistance against centuries of oppression, and, from a different perspective, it was in demand as a commodity to be purchased cheaply.[142] Otherwise, the texts were rehearsing the old stereotypes of the 'wild Albanians, martial Serbians, and proud brave Montenegrins',[143] as well as the old tropes, such as Albania 'the most romantic country in Europe . . . parts of [which] are as forbidding to the foreigner as darkest Africa'.[144] Following Grosvenor's principle of matching the expectations of the American reader while disguising critique as a beautiful image, the commentary on the Kingdom of Serbia by magazine's staff writer William Joseph Showalter summed up the tenor of reporting on the Balkans: 'The country is rugged and mountainous, and the people fit perfectly with the landscape. They have all the virtues of the mountaineer: their wants are as few as their sorrows: they live largely under that communal system that produces a morally clean race, and eat those foods that produce strong bodies'.[145] Needless to say, the familiar images of the mountains, folk dress, or women spinning on the way to the market, photographed now all across the Balkan peninsula, as well as those of intrepid warriors, resembling the Albanian palikars, or the Cossack from the cover of De Windt's book, dominated the magazine's pages.[146] The mountains and quaint villages did feature strongly in the magazine's iconographies of the Balkans. Even if similar images would also appear in its reports from other parts of the world, it was the peasant body in ethnic dress which prevailed in Europe's east. The rest of this chapter will follow its elevation to an instantly recognisable image of the region.

The photograph of two Wallachians, in their sheepskin coats and massive belts to carry pistols and knives, by the American journalist Frederic Moore (Figure 3.14), was first reproduced in his book *The Balkan Trail* which had been published eight years before, in 1905.[147] The magazine's editors, in an attempt to contextualise the confusing term, expanded its original laconic caption 'Vlachs', into 'Wallachians (or Kutso-Vlachs, as They are Known in Macedonia), one of the seven distinct races

Figure 3.14 Frederic Moore, 'Wallachians', photograph, in 'The Changing Map of the Balkans', *National Geographic*, 24, no. 2, 1913. By permission of Nat Geo Image Collection.

of Macedonia'. The accompanying text 'The people whose blood affinity with the Rumanians gives Rumanians excuse for claiming territorial compensation for their annexation by Bulgaria' might not have clarified the ethnic complexities for the reader, but it did not fail to invest the image with the notion that 'fighting is the breath of their nostrils', to use the phrase of another *National Geographic* correspondent from the Balkans.[148] According to Barthes, examining the role of captions under the photographic image, 'the text constitutes a parasitic message designed to connote the image'.[149] The 'anchorage' role of captions which are capable of directing the reader 'towards some meanings and away from others', had been fully recognised by the *National Geographic* editors.[150]

Not all the texts would come with their own photographs, and a usual practice of the editors was to select relevant images from the archives of the National Geographic Society.[151] Over the years, its growing eastern European section incorporated large portfolios of pictures by freelance photographers and journalists, such as Felix J. Koch, operating in Croatia, Bosnia, Bulgaria, and Macedonia in the early 1900s, or A.W. Cutler. The latter, known from his photographs of rural England, Ireland, and Italy, went also on a tour through Hungary before 1914. His detailed documentation of the elaborate embroidery culture in the village of Mezőkövesd near Eger, was inserted into a long feature on Hungary by C. Townley-Fullam.[152] A caption under Cutler's photo 'Cottage Scene at a Little Village in Hungary', showing a group of peasant women in front of the ivy-clad porch, which announces: 'Where, I was told, no photos had ever been taken before by an Englishman or an American for publication', reminiscent of Byron's insistence on his virginal visit to Albania, testifies that the region was at that time a veritable shooting ground for photographers coming from afar, and that the images of peasant life were much in demand by publishers and journals.[153] Importantly, the pictures in *National Geographic*'s image archives were not only submitted by western photographers, but acquired from various photographic studios across Europe. Their captions were always meticulously acknowledging the source. A considerable number of illustrations in the magazine are credited to 'Photo Erdelyi', the studio which was run by the eminent Hungarian photographer Mór Erdéleyi in Budapest, since the 1890s. Among his many commissions were the photographs of the whole of the territory of Greater Hungary, which were displayed at the 1900 World Exhibition in Paris, and subsequently published in a luxury photographic album about Hungary in 1909/1910.[154] Some of them sold also as postcards and entered various photographic collections, including the Alinari, as well as those of the National Geographic Society in Washington. The Erdélyi pictures were often reproduced in the magazine alongside those taken by Cutler, sharing their iconographies and ethnic rhetoric: women with their distaffs, barnyards, and peasant interiors, occasionally juxtaposing the Saxonian Siebenbürgener outfit to a Romanian folk dress, as in the photo 'The Fair and the Frivolous' by Mór Erdélyi.[155] The patterns of representation of the peripheral regions of Austria-Hungary seemed almost indistinguishable from those disseminated by ethnographers and historians based in Vienna, often underscored by ethnic prejudice against the Romanian (Wallachian) peasantry, revealed also in the nineteenth-century travel reports by John Paget and Charles Boner.[156]

The multiethnic pictures signal furthermore the transformation of the meanings of the ethnic costume at the time of the radical remapping of the centre of Europe after the collapse of the Great Empires. Transcending the connotations of peasantry and craftsmanship, the ethnic dress turned into the signifier of national identities, as effective as language. The recognition of the centrality of folk culture in eastern Europe for the preservation of national values and revitalisation of cultural expression had been brewing since the late nineteenth century. The wholesale discovery of its potential came at the time of the establishment of new sovereign states in the middle of the continent and the urgent need to assert their distinctiveness. As said earlier, the power of ethnic dress was discovered not just by travel writers, ethnographers, curators, artists, and authors, but was also promptly instrumentalised by politicians. According to Woodrow Wilson's adviser Isaiah Bowman, reporting from the Peace Conference in Paris, the ethnic dress, on a par with language and ethnographic maps, was used as an irrefutable evidence, an index of ethnicity, as in the case of a 'delegation from Orawa in the foothill region of the Carpathians [which] came to Paris in native peasant costumes to argue union with Poland'.[157]

National Geographic responded by multiplying ethnic photographs in virtually every single article about the countries of eastern Europe, including the newly formed state of Czechoslovakia, as well as Poland. Both of them had been associated by the magazine with central Europe and were represented mostly by historical towns and gothic cathedrals, even if accompanied by images of poverty, too. The case in point are the illustrations in the article 'The Races of Europe', written by Edwin A. Grosvenor, professor of history at Amherst College, and the father of the editor Gilbert H. Grosvenor. Published just after the armistice and filling the whole issue of December 1918, the text served as a misplaced introduction to the ethnic conundrum emerging in Europe after the end of WWI. While using the term race as a synonym of linguistic communities of Europe, Grosvenor aimed to justify the supremacy of the Anglo-Saxons by juxtaposing photographs of uncouth shepherds of Yugoslavia and Hungary to a reproduction of a portrait of an American woman with long curly hair, 'The Daughter of a Race of Empire-Builders', by an otherwise unknown artist Abel Boyle.[158] Grosvenor's article testified also to the distinction between the Balkans and central Europe, most clearly expressed through the choice of images, all of them from the collection of the National Geographic Society, including photos by A.W. Cutler and Mór Erdélyi. While the Balkan 'races' were represented by the photographs of peasants, the 'Czechoslovakian race' was visualised by a panorama of Prague and the activities of the Sokol gymnastics society. The 'Polish race', in turn, was identified with the photo of Ignacy Paderewski, the pianist turned politician involved in the restoration Poland's sovereignty, but also with a number of evocative images of Jewish communities.

Rainbow Costumes and Colour Supplements

From the 1920 onwards, however, large doses of photographs of peasants in their national costumes would dominate visually over any other pictures, also in the texts about Poland and Czechoslovakia. The key role in this transformation was played by the German photographer Hans Hildenbrand, who had made his name with colour photographs of the WWI battle sites.[159] From the late 1920s to mid-1930s, he almost monopolised the field, submitting countless, colour-post-card-like, images of peasants, posing in their elaborated costumes. Hildenbrand's autochromes of Slovak, Polish, Croatian, as well as Hungarian peasants were published as colour supplements, inserted into the middle of articles on related topics. His two sequels *In the Land of the White Eagle* and *Rainbow Costumes of Poland's Peasants* (Figure 3.15), accompanied articles by prominent staff writers, the future chief editor Melville Bell Grosvenor and Maynard Owen Williams, extolling Poland's struggle for independence and its post-WWI development, respectively.[160]

Figure 3.15 Hans Hildenbrand, 'Gold-Crowned Peasant Girls of Łowicz', colour photograph, in *Rainbow Costumes of Poland Peasants*, *National Geographic*, 63, no. 3, 1933. By permission of Nat Geo Image Collection.

From the 1920s, colour supplements played a special role in *National Geographic*, reporting from all parts of the world and composed solely of a dozen or more photos with captions. Before the arrival of the magazine's iconic cover images and the whole-sale adoption of colour at the end of the 1950s, its colour supplements offered dis-traction and alternative modes to engage with the contents, adding a special value to the pictures included in them.[161] In many ways, colour supplements functioned as an equivalent of a cover image, or a frontispiece in a book. Apart from the use of colour, their significance resided in their autonomy from the text and the ways in which they built the argument primarily in visual terms. Hildenbrand's supplements are particu-larly instructive in this respect. They are invested with the sense of timelessness to pro-vide a 'balanced view' of life in this part of Europe, obliterating however any Jewish or Roma presence. Significantly, Hildenbrand's photos are borrowing heavily from the regimes of self-representation, set up in those very countries.

The photo entitled 'Gold-Crowned Peasant Girls from Łowicz', published in Hilden-brand's *Rainbow Costumes of Poland's Peasants* sequence of 1933, provided a pretty picture of two young women posing in front of a cottage, and displaying proudly their characteristic striped homespun skirts from the region of Łowicz (Figure 3.15). Their dress, known for its particularly vivid use of colour, has often been singled out as a shortcut to the essence of Polishness. The thatched roof behind them no longer signifies poverty, as in Wallack's woman print in Boner' book, already elevated to the emblem of the vernacular décor. The bulky multicoloured skirts and apron, supported by many layers of petticoats, the embroidered and beaded vests over white chemises, the red coral-bead necklaces, and yellow kerchiefs on their heads are no longer valued just for their craft, but also for the ways in which they convey national sentiment. The liaison between the national and folk cultures was strongly encouraged in Poland at that time, supported by the rise of institutions preserving the Indigenous techniques of weaving, carpentry, and paper-cutting, and constructed by the growing number of artists and architects building their successful careers on the incorporation of folk-art motifs, styles, and techniques. The vernacular was also the most successful idiom of Poland's self-representation on the international scene, as proven by the success of the Polish Pavilion at the Exhibition of Decorative Arts and Industrial Design in Paris in 1925.[162] Its frescoes of folk festivals by Zofia Stryjeńska, with many figures of peasant women in ethnic dress, provide a high-culture background for Hildenbrand's commercial photographs. The awareness of the high-culture credentials of the peas-ant figure in Poland is also evident in the caption which begins with a quote from the Polish author Władysław Reymont's celebrated novel *The Peasants* that won him the Nobel Prize in 1924 and was soon translated into English.[163] Considering that the action of his book is located in a village from the Łowicz region, the choice of the quotation is very appropriate. The last line of the caption, however, 'Low slippers are displacing the high-laced boots, even in rural districts', all of a sudden breaks the celebratory mode. By trying to justify the presence of the black shoes on heels, clearly acquired in a town rather than manufactured by the village shoemaker, the caption brings attention to the disparities within the image and even raises doubts whether the photograph constitutes a record of life in a Polish village or that of a performance for the sake of the camera.

Clearly, Hildenbrand's image of Polish peasant women appears so emblem-like because it has been carefully staged. And yet, its artificiality is significant in itself. It serves as an index of a number of processes surrounding the revival of folk-culture with a special emphasis on folk dress in Poland, as well in other parts of eastern Europe.[164] The presence of city shoes in the illustrative image of the peasant dress testifies to the process of its disappearance from the Polish countryside. The celebration of the traditional peasant costume was parallel to its imminent displacement by much cheaper, mass-produced town clothes, including modern shoes.[165] Peasant culture, and especially the folk dress, was already being documented, and reanimated by state-supported workshops, schools, cooperatives, and shops specialising in folk-products for town-dwellers, as well as for tourists. The black heel shoes, as I want to argue, point also to the radical changes in the folk dress's status, its imminent detachment from the social class, and, subsequently, its 180° shift on the Self/Other nexus. If the pre-WWI representations of the barefoot 'Wallack woman', analysed earlier, were invariably the images of the essentialised Other, formed either in the gaze of the traveller, ethnographer, or photographer, and marginalised because of her social class, Hildenbrand's photo, informed by the official celebration of the peasant culture in Poland, mimics the essentialised vision of the Polish Self, inhabitable regardless of social status.

There are more issues which have to be raised apropos Hildenbrand's photographs. The vernacular was the idiom of national identity in the new states of eastern Europe. But, in the eyes of the external observer, the folk costumes of particular regions and countries differed only in details and appeared very much alike when seen by the readers of *National Geographic* from across the Atlantic. The majority of Hildenbrand's supplements followed the same memorable formula which could be traced back to the frontispiece in Boner's *Transylvania*, to the opening image in *Travels into Dalmatia*, and even further back to Edward Brown's image of the Bulgarian woman. Hildenbrand's photographs confirm yet again that eastern Europe was identified with the image of woman in her ethnic dress. Significantly, the image of the 'Gold-Crowned Peasant Girls from Łowicz' shows again a pair of women. Unlike Erdélyi's 'The Fair and the Frivolous', which was based on the principle of the meaningful opposition, the structure of Hildenbrand's image is that of equality, agreement, and sameness, suggesting sisterhood, a 'synecdoche for all relationships between women'.[166] Twinning the women and their costumes acts like a double statement, strengthening the argument.

As regards the term 'eastern Europe', there could not be a mistake, its absence did not obstruct the formation of the image. Or, rather, the image was already there, it had originated before the term was coined and had been used before the term was approved. When seen in their 'rainbow costumes' against other colour supplements of the magazine, the eastern European women's geographic affiliation was instantly recognisable in much the same way, in which the black bare-breasted women, the African mother or a Polynesian dancer, functioned as signifiers of the non-European world, while a white lady in a modern dress was inseparably connected with the west.

Would such a master formula of recognising the faraway lands on the basis of the body image be applicable also to British *Geographical Magazine*? With its first issue in May 1935, *Geographical Magazine* adopted the cover image, almost a quarter of a century before *National Geographic*; it also used photographic supplements, in black and white, or sepia rather than in colour. While subscribing to the same principle of delivering messages by means of images, the British magazine avoided however 'ethnographic erotica', at least as far as black female bodies were concerned. Neither was it keen on the overexposure of the 'western body'. But what it did share with *National Geographic* was the identification of eastern Europe with ethnic dress.

The British periodical was launched at the time when the new states of Europe created in Versailles were already established, pursuing the tasks of modernisation and industrialisation, even if retaining their agricultural profiles. As said earlier, *Geographical Magazine* devoted a considerable attention to the region, presenting it both from the ethnographic angle as well as paying close attention to the changes brought to it by modernity. Among the notable authors dealing with eastern Europe were writers like Sacheverell Sitwell, and eminent ethnographers, such as Christoph von Fürer-Haimendorf, an Austrian ethnologist and professor at the School of Oriental and African Studies in London, both reporting on wedding rituals in Romania and Bulgaria. There were also scientists and poets, such as John Lehmann, who submitted a series of articles on Hungary, Slovakia, and the Balkans.[167] The British magazine invited also authors from the region. The Polish journalist and translator Aleksander Tadeusz Lutosławski contributed an article on the rise of the new city, the modern seaport of Gdynia, built from scratch on a narrow strip of the Baltic coast, the Czech linguist and folklorist Naděžda Melniková-Papoušková presented the modern architecture of Prague, while the Polish botanist and the pioneer in nature conservation Professor Władysław Szafer wrote about the policy of national parks in Poland. A number of eastern European-born writers submitted their texts as well, including Judith, Countess of Listowell, Hungarian by birth, married to William Hare, 5th Earl of Listowell, who wrote a passionate text on the sovereign nature of the Hungarian nation, while the American journalist (and an opera singer) of Polish origins, Louise Llewelyn Jarecka, submitted a well-researched text on Polish folk art, commenting also on its state-sponsored revival.[168]

The modern transformation of eastern Europe might have been a topic for *Geographical Magazine* articles and photographs inside them, but it never made it onto its covers. Not only the images of modern bodies, but also any potential icons of modernity 'belonged' to the west: a picture of a busy harbour on the magazine's May 1938 cover would stand for Britain, while a modern city skyscraper in July 1939 would be an immediately recognisable reference to New York. Among the five 'eastern European' covers published by *Geographical Magazine* before the war, four confirmed the folk-dress formula as a sure signifier of the region. The first appeared in March 1937, connected to an article by Lehmann which praised the economic reforms brought to Slovakia after its incorporation into the Republic of Czechoslovakia.[169] His article comprised a good number of modern buildings and industry, but the picture chosen for the cover showed two young Slovakian women in embroidered costumes. It was selected from a photo-supplement following Lehmann's text which, entitled 'Among the Slovakian Mountains', included masterful studies of peasants by the well-known Slovak photographer Karel Plicka (Figure 3.16).[170] Plicka, who was also an experimental film-maker and ethnomusicologist, was preparing at that time a monumental publication of his photographs of Slovakian people, landscape, cities, and culture, and the image of the two young women in elaborate wedding dresses, taken in the village of Čičmany, was connected to this project.[171] The codes of self-fashioning proved as seamlessly adaptable as the formulas of representation.

This Slovakian cover deserves attention also for other reasons. It bears a set of stamps which declare the magazine's destination as 'U.C.L./ Professors' Smoking Room', with an instruction 'Not To Be Taken Away'. The same stamps feature on almost every issue of *Geographical Magazine* until 1940, held in the University College London library. On the one hand, the stamps confirm that in its early decades

Figure 3.16 Karol Plicka, 'Among Slovakian Mountains', photograph, *Geographical Magazine*, 4, no. 5, March 1937. By permission of *Geographical*.

the magazine was read by university professors of diverse disciplines, but, on the other hand, they also make perfectly clear that it was intended for their smoking room rather than the library. Altogether, the stamps and the label, which confirm the magazine's current location in the library storage, function as indexes of its readership cultures, pointing to the exchange between the smoking room, the lecture theatre, and the library. This story of the magazine's readership not only problematises the thesis on the unbridgeable gap between the academic and popular geography but, as it happens, it also tells the story of the circulation and reception of the image of the eastern European body in ethnic dress. The stereotype belongs to the smoking room, but it also filters through to the world of academia. Three other eastern European covers of *Geographical Magazine* in the 1930s, all of them bearing the same set of stamps, followed the well-tested iconographies: a mountainous landscape in the Balkans, the Hungarian shepherd in his sheepskin coat, and the image of the peasant wedding in Romania. The only non-ethnic cover presented a Rodchenko-like picture of a quasi-military youth camp in Romania, from the article by the Balkan correspondent Derek Patmore.[172]

By the early 1930s, *National Geographic* also elaborated on the changes brought by rapid industrialisation and urban development in eastern Europe, focusing, likewise, on its central and northern areas: Czechoslovakia and Poland. In 1933, Maynard Owen Williams included a reportage from Gdynia in his article 'Poland of the Present', while another reputed contributor to the magazine, John Patric, published a long account of his tour round Czechoslovakia in August of 1938, labelling the Czechoslovaks as the 'Yankees of Europe'.[173] Patric began his article from reporting on the American management methods introduced by Thomas Bata to his shoe factory in Zlín in Moravia, submitting also a good photo of its modern premises. This was followed by a number of other photographs of modernity and modern life, including wide angle panoramas of the large industrial conglomerate of the Škoda Works in Plzeň and of the gymnastic performance of Sokol, as well as an image of modern Prague with a group of people watching Václavské Náměstí, leaning over the balustrade above the square (Figure 3.17).[174] This particular scene is one of the first *National Geographic* photos to acknowledge the presence of the modern city in eastern Europe which is not reduced to buildings in empty streets. It was shot by the photographer W. Robert Moore, the future chief of Foreign Staff in the magazine, who must have accompanied Patric on this journey. Unlike the picture in De Windt's *Through Savage Europe*, in which a modest street in Nisch served just as a background for the display of the two women peasants, in Moore's image it is the square itself which constitutes the topic. This is emphasised by the group of male figures in the foreground, including a soldier and two men in suits accompanied by two boys who are seen from behind, being caught in the act of looking. As contemporary *flâneurs*, they are watching modern life, the traffic, a tramway stop and pedestrians crossing the square. The first words of the photograph's long title 'Gaiety and Business in Praha Centre' summarises the experience of modernity conveyed by the image. This is further strengthened by the caption that confirms that the square is 'a favoured location for hotels, automat cafeterias, coffeeshops and stores'. The caption does not miss the opportunity to comment on Prague's links with the west, by explaining that the 'statue of Good King Wenceslaus' is the character 'of whom English carollers sing at Christmas'. This view of Václavské Náměstí, taken from the top of the stairs leading to Prague's National Museum, functions today as an iconic sight of Prague, repeated in thousands of postcards (see also Figure 5.3).[175]

GAIETY AND BUSINESS IN PRAHA CENTER ABOUT WENCESLAUS SQUARE, NAMED FOR THE PATRON SAINT OF BOHEMIA

Photograph by W. Robert Moore

A statue of Good King Wenceslaus of whom English carolers sing at Christmas, page 177, faces down the square. Less than half a mile long, the street, called Vaclavské naměstí is the finest in the Republic. It is a favored location for hotels, automat cafeterias, coffeeshops and stores. Movie theaters are usually built in basements.

Figure 3.17 W. Robert Moore, 'Gaiety and Business in Praha Center about Wenceslaus Square, Named for the Patron Saint of Bohemia', photograph, in John Patric, 'Czechoslovaks, Yankees of Europe', *National Geographic*, 74, no. 2, 1938. By permission of Nat Geo Image Collection.

But, in spite of those glimpses of modernity, there was no way of steering away from the ethnic body. Alongside the black and white photos, Patric's article was accompanied by a hefty colour supplement *The Czechoslovakian Cyclorama*, with 30 pictures by Moore.[176] It included the obligatory images of Old Prague, with the Charles Bridge and the Bell Tower, as well another panoramic view, this time of a modern café in Barandov outside Prague, with an 'urbane clientele', enjoying themselves on the rose-fringed terrace overlooking the river. The overwhelming majority of the *Cyclorama* photos, however, focused on peasants in their colourful costumes. They made an impact not just by numbers, but also through the proportions of bodies within the picture plane. The peasants were photographed in close-ups to give a full visibility to the details of their dress, but the bourgeois café crowd was minimalised to the barely visible figurines round the tables, reduced to a human staffage.

The absence of the modern eastern European body in travelogues before WWII is perfectly understandable. For the traveller, interesting is that which is different and not that which is the same. Accordingly, the regimes of looking are not configured to focus on modern bodies in faraway places. With no suitable visual code to represent a modern city dweller in a non-western country, the modern body and the modern dress belonged exclusively to the maker of the image, in this case the photographer. This has been a steady principle in *National Geographic* images of the Third World countries, whereby the photographer inserts himself or herself into the picture,[177] but it was applied also to eastern Europe. An opening photo in a reportage on cycling through Romania, published by a young American journalist Dorothy Hosmer in November 1938, presented herself as 'the author in blouse and divided skirt', standing by her bike, and talking to 'the best-dressed girl in the village of Răşinari, in Transylvania'.[178] The binary opposition structure of the photo was stressed by its condescending title, 'A Study in Skirts – And Centuries Lie Between'. The description of the Romanian dress provided by the caption was just another attempt to steer away from the ethnic prejudice underscoring the image, which has now moved onto a higher register, claiming a 'civilisational' hierarchy between the western dress and the ethnic costume. Another example of the inseparability of the modern dress and the western body is provided by a striking juxtaposition of two photos in *The Czechoslovakian Cyclorama* supplement, discussed earlier, both showing a pair of girls in the street. On the left, a couple of young ladies in urban clothes are examining souvenirs in a china shop (Figure 3.18), and on the right, two girls in traditional costumes sell vegetables. The young ladies outside the shop look like foreign tourists, and the girls in ethnic dress belong obviously to the local community. Their titles do not give any clues: 'Pottery reflects a nation's love of colour' and 'Watch the cauliflower, sis, I'm going to mass', respectively. Only the caption under the pottery shop image reveals that the 'tourists' are in fact 'two city girls [who] dress more simply than their country cousins': the mistake seems unavoidable.[179] As argued before, the modern dress could not have been anything other than the signifier of the west. By the 1930s, the magazine might have acknowledged the presence of the modern city in eastern European space, but the eastern European body, by and large, has remained confined within the ethnic dress.

Headscarves and Cities: Welcome to Eastern Europe

The second World War, neither narrated nor photographed in either of the magazines, constituted a major break. And, from the mid-1940s onwards, a new generation of

Figure 3.18 W. Robert Moore, 'A Pottery Reflects a Nation's Love of Colour', colour photograph, in *The Czechoslovakian Cyclorama*, *National Geographic*, 74, no. 2, 1938. By permission of Nat Geo Image Collection.

authors and photographers traversed the region, producing hundreds of new images. From 1950 until today, *National Geographic* has published 50 articles on eastern European countries, illustrated with almost 1,000 photographs, while *Geographical Magazine*, as before more productive with words than images, has produced over 70 articles and 500 pictures. An inquiry into the ways in which the unprecedented tragedies and accomplishments of this era were portrayed by the correspondents of the geographical magazines deserves a separate research project. This final part of my survey continues instead on what has emerged as its major theme, the ubiquity of the eastern European woman in ethnic dress, and her return after the end of WWII.

What also has to be acknowledged, however, is the topic of the modern eastern European city, which did receive considerable attention on the pages of *Geographical Magazine* from the 1940s until the late 1980s. Behind that was a group of British university lecturers who travelled behind the Iron Curtain, gathering material for their books and lectures, and publishing the first drafts in the magazine. A recent article, written collectively by David Matless, Jonathan Oldfield, and Adam Swain, entitled 'Geographically Touring the Eastern Bloc', provides an account of those texts, arguing for the significance of the cultures of travel for the development of an academic geography of Eastern Europe, disproving the earlier critique of those magazines.[180] Many of those contributions commented on the post-war reconstruction of Yugoslavia, Albania, Bulgaria and Poland, investigating dispassionately, without a political bias, the scale of transformation of those countries, rebuilding their economies, cities, societies, and everyday life. The articles tackled also the Hungarian uprising of 1956 and the effects of rapid urbanisation.[181] In a special issue of 1978, devoted to the contemporary city, F.E. Ian Hamilton included a subchapter 'The East European and the Soviet City', next to texts on the North American City, the Third World City, and the city of the future.[182] This was the first time when the term 'Eastern Europe' was used in the magazine. Almost all of the articles about the region were illustrated with the authors' own photographs. They featured a vast range of topics, from communist festivities and collective farms, to sport stadiums, industrial complexes, oil refineries and hydro-electric power stations, but also plenty of pictures of mountains (*pace* Barthes), forests with bisons, wooden horse carts in villages and towns, architectural monuments and folk art, and, increasingly, city streets and city centres, shops, cafes, sea resorts, mountain climbing, as well as many images of pedestrians in their town, non-ethnic, outfits.

Between 1945 and 1989, *Geographical Magazine* issued six eastern European covers. Surprisingly, in spite of the attention to cities and the economy, the rules on how to select a representative image did not change at all. All of the covers, whether referring to Albania, Czechoslovakia, Bulgaria, Poland or Romania, featured women in their ethnic costumes. Such a choice, a residue of the magazine's pre-WWII ethnographic gaze, by the 1950s acquired new political tones. At that time, folk culture was already fully instrumentalised by the official visual propaganda of people's democracies, which elevated the image of a female peasant in her ethnic dress to the icon of the communist transformation. By subscribing to that formula, too, *Geographic Magazine* emulated, if not endorsed, the same visual policy. Significantly, if most of the covers utilised photographs, one of them, announcing an article about popular art in Poland and its sponsorship by the communist state on an unprecedented scale, written by the British graphic artist Pearl Binder, featured a papercut, showing a Łowicz costume-clad woman, riding a bicycle (Figure 3.19).[183] By departing from the usual

The

JULY 1960   2/6

GEOGRAPHICAL
MAGAZINE

ALL CLASSES OF INSURANCE TRANSACTED

CAR & GENERAL INSURANCE CORPORATION, **L**^TD.

83 PALL MALL, LONDON, S.W.1

Figure 3.19 'Papercut from a Polish Village', *Geographical Magazine*, 33, no. 3, 1960. By permission of *Geographical*.

magazine's routine of selecting a photograph, the cover turned, inadvertently, into a sign of the artificiality of folk art and its commodification.[184]

Five years later, the August 1965 cover featuring 'Country Visitors to Sofia' (Figure 3.20), broke with the usual celebratory presentation of folk dress.[185] It shows two women in the city centre, with blocks of flats neighbouring older buildings, who are viewing an invisible structure in front of them. Most likely, the women's gaze is focused at a monument, since a group of Asian tourists in the background looks in the same direction. The photo provides a commentary on social changes in Bulgaria, the migration from the country to the city, as discussed by F.E. Ian Hamilton in his article 'Bulgaria: Land of Change'.[186] But it also records the disappearance of the ethnic dress, as well as the sense of uneasiness of the peasant women, observed both by the camera and by foreign tourists. One of the women is holding an expanding carrier bag, an indispensable item in the Communist Bloc, where one had to be prepared for commodity hunting. Their everyday clothes, somewhat scruffy, are almost entirely deprived of the folk costume elements, the white headscarves being the only remainders of the traditional outfit, and the signifiers of their peasant status. On the earlier *Geographical Magazine* cover, published in August

Figure 3.20 'Country Visitors to Sofia', colour photograph, *Geographical Magazine*, 38, no. 4, 1965. By permission of *Geographical*.

1949, which also showed a group of Bulgarian women whose dress retained more traditional parts, including white chemises, black vests, and aprons over woollen skirts, while the white headscarves were wrapped around their heads, the sign of their Muslim identity.[187] As pointed out by Mary Neuburger, the communist authorities in Bulgaria attempted to eradicate the residues of Turkish culture by prohibiting Muslim garments, including veils.[188] On the 1965 cover, the scarves are tied under the women's chins, in the manner of non-Muslim peasants. There is no way of checking whether the 'Country visitors to Sofia' photo bears any message which could be linked to the anti-veiling campaign, but what it does communicate is the significance of the headscarf which, in the absence of the ethnic dress in the post-WWII era, turned into a marker of the Eastern European woman.[189] The next and the last appearance of women in their ethnic dress, pretty much reduced to headscarves, on the *Geographical Magazine* cover of February 1989, was just a small inlet, one of four visual announcements of the contents, but the huge letters underneath 'Romania Demolished' emphasised its significance. The photo was made by the author of the article critiquing Ceaușescu's plan to extinguish private agriculture and the independent peasantry, and was entitled in a brash journalistic manner, 'Return of the Vampire'.[190] It was published a few months before the fall of the Berlin Wall and the 'Vampire's' execution marked the end of Eastern Europe. How was all this going to affect the image of the woman in ethnic dress?

If the dominant stance of *Geographical Magazine* in the post-WWII years was that of an inquiry, often sympathetic, into the socio-economic and cultural changes within people's democracies, *National Geographic*, unhesitatingly, adopted the anti-communist approach, in line with the US federal policy of containment. Accordingly, ethnic dress fell out of favour as not suited to the accounts of modernisation and, above all, as discredited by having been hijacked by communist propaganda. The first post-war report was a photo essay 'Airlift to Berlin' in May 1949, followed by 'Berlin Island in the Soviet Sea' in November 1951, with plenty of despatches from the divided city appearing systematically until 1989. Yugoslavia, as the country expelled by Stalin from the Communist Bloc, also attracted attention. The first feature, published in 1951, was accompanied by a fabulous colour supplement by Volkmar Ventzel. Gilbert Melville Grosvenor, grandson of Gilbert H. Grosvenor and the future chief editor, travelled to Belgrade in person in 1962 to produce a long article 'Yugoslavia's Window on the Adriatic', which included a photograph of himself interviewing Josip Broz Tito in his villa on the island of Brioni. The Hungarian Revolution of October 1956 did not bring an article on Stalin's atrocities, but the fate of those Hungarian refugees who, having been granted asylum were flown to the United States, was presented in detail in Robert Sisson's photo essay of March 1957, complete with images of a Hungarian family celebrating Christmas in Rhode Island. Poland was chosen for the first long report from inside the Communist Bloc in 1958 which, lavishly illustrated with Erich Lessing's photos from Magnum, set the tone of the discourse, both verbal and visual: it recorded the ruins of Warsaw and the post-war reconstruction, framing the photo of 'Stalin's gift' of the Palace of Culture in Warsaw with a sarcastic commentary, and it lightened the account with images of hiking in the Tatra Mountains. Evocative shots of Catholic rituals initiated a new trope of mass religious pilgrimages, to be identified with Poland's resistance against communism until the end of the millennium.[191]

From the later 1950s, images of eastern Europe in *National Geographic* diversified enormously, becoming less predictable than before the war. Instead of the ethnic body, it was the modern body which became now more and more prominent. No longer belonging just to an anonymous pedestrian seen from afar, the modern body turned into one of the central themes, whether that of the worker, the Škoda director, a Polish Jewish artist, or a Hungarian pop-singer. One of the very few of *National Geographic*'s covers related to eastern Europe, published in April 1982, displayed the face of the Polish miner against a black background.[192] It referred directly to the killing of nine striking miners in Katowice by the police after the declaration of martial law in December 1981, and was put on display as an expression of support for Solidarity, the mass resistance movement in Poland. This was one of the few occasions when the policy of non-involvement in current politics was bypassed by the editors 'in salute to the tormented Polish people'. And although the April 1982 issue did not comment on the martial law, a supplement *The Face and Faith of Poland* was published as a separate leaflet, announced in the contents on the cover.[193] More portraits came throughout the 1980s, including those of the members of the Jewish community in Poland, as well as dissidents, composers, journalists, and film directors, photographed for *National Geographic*'s centenary issue of 1988, which was another gesture of solidarity with the struggle for political autonomy in the region. The same issue included also the first feature in which the Polish journalist Małgorzata Niez-abitowska who, working in tandem with the photographer Tomasz Tomaszewski, 'returned the gaze', publishing pictures of America's own underprivileged inhabitants. Increasingly, the texts on the region were submitted by Priit L. Vessilind, of Estonian origins, as well as by a number of free-lance authors with eastern European roots, such as Tad Szulc and Yva Momatiuk.[194]

Disappointingly, *National Geographic* did not publish any commentary on the fall of the Berlin Wall, the event which shook up the map of the continent, redefining the eastern European space and the eastern European subject. Even if dictated by the magazine's strict editorial policy, this created an acute gap in the magazine's 'window' onto Europe. The 'classic' photographs of the event, subscribing to the iconography of the male warriors, strangely reminiscent of Cockerell's palikars, were distributed instead by press agencies, newspapers, and television. A short note appeared in the magazine only four months later, in the March 1990 statement by the President of the National Geographic Society, Gilbert Melville Grosvenor, the same who had inter-viewed Tito in 1962. His address focused on the events in the Soviet Union and on its new map; it began from a reference to his grandfather's pioneering article on Russia of 1914 and included a paragraph on 'the breath-taking speed with which the U.S.S.R. and the nations of Eastern Europe have been moving from the shadows into the light – clamouring to be heard and understood'. This was the first time when the term 'Eastern Europe' was used by *National Geographic*. As if in denial of his own and the maga-zine's long-standing engagement with the region, Grosvenor added, 'As we come to know the people and regions concealed so long by the Iron Curtain, I think we may be experiencing one of the most incredible geography lessons of our time'.[195]

Paradoxical as it appeared, this act of naming the region exactly at the time when it was on the verge of dissolution, intensified for a while *National Geographic*'s reports from eastern Europe, which became the topic of four major feature articles published within the span of 12 months. The issue of August 1990 brought a report on the ethnic conflicts in the Balkans, followed in November by a text on the breakout of the Baltic nations from the Soviet Union. The term 'Eastern Europe', spelled with two upper key 'E's, entered titles and captions. A comprehensive reportage 'Dispatches from Eastern Europe' by Tad Szulc, accompanied by the bravura photographs by Tomasz Tomaszewski (Figure 3.21),[196] was published in April 1991 and, in June, an article on pollution in Romania, under the telling title 'East Europe's Dark Dawn'. Most remarkably, some of the photos made it to the magazine's covers.[197] The strik-ing photo by Larry Price 'Debased and Decommissioned, Joseph Stalin Gets the Brush-off in Vilnius, Capital of Lithuania', which shows reportedly a worker (alas, his fashionable beard and a black turtle neck pullover suggests a different social sta-tus), sweeping an overturned and paint-stained statue of Stalin, formed part of the iconography of the fallen statues of communism. Tomaszewski's double-spread pic-ture showing three members of the staff of the newly established Museum of Socialist Realism, in the remote Polish village of Kozłówka, who are carrying the disgraced busts of Stalin past a cherry orchard, makes an equally salient contribution to that group. Both images confirm that the victory over communism could only have been represented as men's work. Interestingly, the two other featured images, a peasant woman in a headscarf by Steve McCurry on the Yugoslavia cover, and the image

Figure 3.21 Tomasz Tomaszewski, 'Spring Cleaning', doublespread colour photograph, in Tad Szulc, 'Dispatches from Eastern Europe', *National Geographic*, 179, no. 3, 1991. By permission of Nat Geo Image Collection.

of Romanian children by James Nachtwey, look back to the old codes associated with the region. The long captions, listed on the Contents pages: 'An ethnic Albanian farm woman wears the dimitë, or *culotte*, that distinguishes Muslims in Macedonia, the southernmost republic of Yugoslavia. Her granddaughter chooses nontraditional dress', and 'Carbon-blackened boys play near a factory in Copşa Mică, Romania, in the heart of polluted Eastern Europe', are reminiscent of the old captions in the same magazine, pointing to ethnic tensions while covering prejudice and condescension. The Kosovo war provided an ideal candidate for the generic image of the suffering body, the female victim, as in Alexandra Boulat's photo 'Kosovo-Macedonia Border, March 30, 1999. Breakdown in a Field', published in her photo reportage *Eyewitness Kosovo*.[198] The novelty was the pars pro toto approach, whereby anyone, or any site within the territory of eastern Europe was now being seen as bearing the defining characteristics of the whole region.

The major change was the ultimate invention of eastern Europe as a tourist destination. In many ways, both *National Geographic* and *Geographical* had already participated in the process of presenting the region for potential tourists, but the opening of the borders changed the scale dramatically, legitimising the region, reinventing its boundaries, geographical features and cultural treasures, in order to open it for mass tourism. *Geographical* was quick to comment on its tourist potential with a text 'Eastern Europe Opens its Doors', published in April 1990. Apart from the analysis of the tourism industry in the region so far, it outlined its economic advantages, but also provided practical information for visitors about visas and tourist agencies.[199] The agency in representing Eastern Europe was now taken over by tourist guide books, and tourism-oriented reports, invariably adorned with lavish photographs multiplied in both magazines. They promoted Croatia's 'hidden gems', 'wonders of nature' in Poland with bisons and wild boars, as well as advocating the experience of tracking the wolf in the Carpathian Mountains, or exploring the Saxon legacy in Romania. While historical monuments were included in the list of tourist sites, the 'impassable mountains' have proven the best-selling points, promising remote locations, forgotten villages, and skiing opportunities. *National Geographic*'s presentation of the rediscovered lands of eastern Europe also swung into that direction, especially after the end of the Balkan conflicts. They tempted the travellers to Romania with atmospheric pictures of Dracula's castle, the nomadic community of Csángó people, as well as the forgotten villages in Transylvania which preserved intact their crafts and customs from pre-industrial times. Ethnic body and dress have returned now with a vengeance, coinciding with folk revival movements in many parts of the region.

Among Rena Effendi's photographs in an article on the ancient methods of producing hay in Transylvania, published in 2013, ethnic dress features prominently (Figure 3.22).[200] The double spread of the opening pages presents two girls, young and slim, in a modern version of folk costumes, walking through a village in the Maramureş region on an early evening. The sisterhood rhetoric returns, confirmed by the caption which also provides the reasons for which the girls have chosen the traditional dress. 'Cousins Anuţa and Magdalena Mesaroş, 17, Are on Their Way to a Wedding in Sat Şugatag, Maramureş'. The girls' identical outfit is an elaborate imitation of the local folk dress, complete with floral skirts on petticoats, white and stiffly-starched chemises with the traditional Wallachian wide sleeves and lace finish (see Figure 3.12), embroidered and beaded vests, and floral headscarves wrapped under their chins. The only differences are that aprons are absent, that the fabric of their

Figure 3.22 Rena Effendi, 'Cousins 'Anuţa and Magdalena Mesaroş, 17, Are on Their Way to a Wedding in Sat Şugatag, Maramureş', colour photograph, in Adam Nicolson, 'Hay Beautiful', in *National Geographic*, 224, no. 1, 2013. By permission of Nat Geo Image Collection.

skirts is no longer home-made, and that the length of the skirts is radically shortened. An accompanying image showing an older woman 'spinning raw wool at home' who, like other mothers and grandmothers, 'devote[s] hundreds of hours a year to making traditional embroidered clothes for [her family]' assures the reader of the authenticity of the local craft traditions. The girls' fashionable boots which, as in the case of the Łowicz women photographed by Hildenbrand, must have been bought in a shop, strengthen the overall performative nature of the dress. Again, the regimes of representation borrow heavily from the codes of self-fashioning. The Maramureş region is widely promoted in tourist guides and the media as a part of Romania which, due to its remoteness, has been 'protected from the influence of modern ways'.[201]

For the *National Geographic* correspondent, the girls are the travellees and hence they should be pictured according to the prescribed patterns. Effendi's photograph, a masterful amalgam of diverse codes of representation, conforms to almost all of the old travelogue formulas discussed in this chapter. It obeys the principle of imaging a sisterhood, staying in tune with Hildenbrand's peasants. It pays tribute to the ethnic traditions as well as to the craftsmanship that Charles Boner raved about, and it positions itself safely within the category of wedding rituals, studied by ethnographers travelling down the Danube. It even conforms to Alberto Fortis's preference for young women.

Is there anything new? Does the photo lend itself to alternative readings, which would transgress the travelogue formulas? Rena Effendi, the successful female artist based in Istanbul, and nominated for the Prix Pictet Award 2019 precisely on the basis of her *National Geographic* photo-reportage on haymaking in Transylvania, was born in Kazakhstan and therefore does not belong to the category of the western traveller. The former 'civilisational boundary' between the traveller and the travellee, named 'the battle of skirts' by Dorothy Hosmer in 1938, has lost its sharpness or has disappeared altogether. Identities are no longer firmly juxtaposed and are bound to be crossed, performed, and exchanged. But one thing has remained the same. Whether for a foreigner, or an insider, just one look should suffice to identify the girls dressed in ethnic outfits as eastern Europeans.

To summarise: this chapter looked at the shifts within the set of images associated with eastern Europe, appearing over a period of almost 350 years on the pages of early modern and modern travelogues, followed by glossy photographs of geographical magazines. The primary role in assembling the iconosphere of the region was played by travellers, followed by ethnographers and photo-reporters. The absence of the term 'eastern Europe' did not obstruct the formation of the image, or, rather, the key image of the female peasant in her ethnic dress had originated before the term was coined and had been used before the term became current. It was extended over the expanding territory of the east of Europe. The peasant woman dominated over the peasant man as the most recognisable and adaptable signifier of the region, beginning with the prints in early modern travel books and finishing with the return of the folk imagery in contemporary geographical magazines. Meanings attached to ethnic dress over the course of time varied considerably. In the early modern era, the folk dress served as the identification of eastern European otherness with peasantness. Modernity upgraded the ethnic dress to the signifier of craftsmanship and challenged the boundary between its designation as the eastern European Other and the eastern European Self. Elevated to the icon of national identity in the interwar era and then hijacked as an index of the communist redistribution of power and the logo of the Communist Bloc, it has been reidentified as a tool of a performative declaration of the regional identity.

The formula of two girls presenting their peasant dress in an idyllic setting is being redeployed and subverted in the recent counter-folk movement which originated in a number of Eastern European countries in the post-communist era.[202] The Polish artist Katarzyna Perlak, based in London, whose art centres around the issue of eastern Europeanness and sexuality, repeated this formula in her video, based on a folk song *Niolam Ja Se Kochaneczke* (I once had a lover), 2016 (Figure 3.23).[203] It is being sung by young women dressed in folk dresses who, apart from the balaclavas, look uncannily similar to the Transylvanian cousins, Slovakian bridesmaids, and the Łowicz girls.

Figure 3.23 Katarzyna Perlak, *Niolam Ja Se Kochaneczke* (I once had a lover), 2016. Film-still. By permission of Katarzyna Perlak.

The difference, signalled by the masks, is that the sex of the lovers has been altered and, instead of the usual celebration of heteronormativity, the song tells the story of love between two women, playing on and subverting the sisterhood rhetoric, as well as radically opening up the range of identities communicated by the ethnic dress. The masks in Perlak's film are a sign of resistance, queering the values invested in folk culture, whether nationalist or heteronormative. The standard closeness of two folk women could now mean the rights to love which is regulated by administrative rules.

The ethnic body has confirmed its seductive appeal as the identity marker, and there is no end to the shifts of its meanings. The second decade of the twenty-first century brought not only the revival of ethnic dress, but also the rising hostility to immigrants, as well as new iconographies of the barbed wire on the eastern European borders, of groups of refugees surrounded by police, as well as those of far-right marches in eastern European cities which now cast a long shadow on ethnic dress as the signifier. As yet, belonging to the category of media imagery, they are slow in solidifying into the visual codes disseminated by travelogues. I will return to them, however, discussing the images chosen for covers of recent books on politics, society, and cultures of eastern Europe, in the chapter 'The Battle of the Dust Jackets'. The following chapter will pay attention to a different type of images, now opting for the critical rather than the celebratory, looking for faults rather than beauty, for the topical rather than the timeless. It will examine the ways in which the collective identity of eastern Europe was visualised throughout the twentieth century by cartoonists of the major satirical magazines, focusing on the British magazine *Punch*.

Notes

1. Mary Louise Pratt, *Imperial Eyes: Travel Writings and Transculturation* (New York and London: Routledge, 2008), 133. For the reversal of the traveller/travellee relationship, see Wendy Bracewell and Alex Drace-Francis, eds, *Under Eastern Eyes: A Comparative Introduction to East European Travel Writing on Europe* (Budapest: CEU Press, 2008) and Wendy Bracewell and Alex Drace-Francis, eds, *A Bibliography of East European Travel Writing in Europe* (Budapest: CEU Press, 2007).
2. Larry Wolf, *Inventing Eastern Europe: The Map of Civilization on the Mind of the Enlightenment* (Stanford, CA: Stanford University Press, 1994); Maria Todorova, *Imagining the Balkans* (New York and Oxford: Oxford University Press, 1997).
3. Exceptions are Božidar Jezernik, *Wild Europe: The Balkans in the Gaze of Western Travellers* (London: SAQI/ The Bosnian Institute, 2004); Bracewell and Drace-Francis, *Under Eastern Eyes*; Andrew Hammond, 'Through Savage Europe: The Gothic Strain in British Balkanism', *Third Text*, 21, no. 2 (March 2007): 117–27; Katarina Gephardt, 'The Mirror Image: British Travel Writing and Bram Stoker's Eastern Europe', in *The Idea of Europe in British Travel Narratives, 1789–1914* (Farnham: Ashgate, 2014), 141–91.
4. As observed by Hayden White many years ago in relation to history writing in 'Historiography and Historiophoty', *The American Historical Review* 93, no. 5 (1988): 1193–99. See also Peter Burke, *Eyewitnessing: The Uses of Images as Historical Evidence* (London: Reaktion, 2001).
5. Edward Brown, 'To the Reader', in *A Brief Account of Some Travels in Divers Parts of Europe: viz. Hungaria, Servia, Bulgaria, Macedonia, Thessaly, Austria, Styria, Carinthia, Carniola, and Friuli: as Also Some Observations on the Gold, Silver, Copper, Quick-Silver Mines, Baths and Mineral Waters in Those Parts: With the Figures of Some Habits and Remarkable Places* (London: Printed for Benj. Tooke, 1763), unpaginated.
6. Ezequiel Adamovsky, *Euro-Orientalism: Liberal Ideology and the Image of Russia in France* (Oxford: Peter Lang, 2006), 247–60.
7. On the itineraries within Europe, see Wendy Bracewell, 'Europe', in Carl Thompson, ed., *The Routledge Companion to Travel Writing* (London and New York: Routledge,

2015), 341–50. For tourist guidebooks, Rudy Koshar, '"What Ought to be Seen": Tourists' Guidebooks and National Identities in Modern Germany and Europe', *Journal of Contemporary History* 33, no. 4 (July 1998): 323–40.

8. Patryk Babiracki and Kenyon Zimmer, eds, *Cold War Crossings: International Travel and Exchange Across the Soviet Bloc, 1940s–1960s* (College Station: Texas A&M University Press, 2014); Anne E. Gorsuch and Diane P. Koenker, eds, *Turism: The Russian and East European Tourist under Capitalism and Socialism* (Ithaca: Cornell University Press, 2006); Sune Bechmann Pedersen and Christian Noack, eds, *Tourism and Travel During the Cold War: Negotiating Tourist Experiences across the Iron Curtain* (New York and London: Routledge, 2019). The numerous tourist guides to Eastern Europe published after 1989, which rapidly change images on their covers, moving attention from the travellee to monuments and sites, require a separate inquiry.

9. Alex Drace-Francis, 'The Traditions of Invention. Representations of the Romanian Peasant from Ancient Stereotype to Modern Symbol', in *The Traditions of Invention: Romanian Ethnic and Social Stereotypes in Historical Context* (Leiden and Boston: Brill, 2018), 1–59.

10. Among others, Pratt, *Imperial Eyes*; Peter Hulme and Tim Youngs, eds, *The Cambridge Companion to Travel Writing* (Cambridge: Cambridge University Press, 2002); Tim Youngs, ed., *The Cambridge Introduction to Travel Writing* (Cambridge: Cambridge University Press, 2013); Thompson, *The Routledge Companion to Travel Writing*; Nandi Das and Tim Youngs, eds, *The Cambridge History of Travel Writing* (Cambridge: Cambridge University Press, 2019).

11. See note 1, also Alex Drace-Francis, 'Travel Writing from Eastern Europe', in Das and Youngs, *The Cambridge History of Travel Writing*, 191–205.

12. 'In order to prepare the dish "travel writing", the essential ingredient is writing, not travel'. Alex Drace-Francis, 'Towards a Natural History of East European Travel writing', in Bracewell and Drace-Francis, *Under Eastern Eyes*, 7.

13. Clare Farago, 'Silent Moves: On Excluding the Ethnographic Subject from the Discourse of Art History', in Donald Preziosi, ed., *Art of Art History: A Critical Anthology* (Oxford and New York: Oxford University Press, 2009), 195–214.

14. Margaret Topping, 'Travel Writing and Visual Culture', in Thompson, *The Routledge Companion to Travel Writing*, 78–88; Mary Henes and Brian H. Murray, eds, *Travel Writing, Visual Culture and Form, 1760–1900* (Basingstoke and New York: Palgrave MacMillan, 2016); Giorgia Alù and Sarah Patricia Hill, eds, 'Travel Writing and the Visual', special issue of *Studies in Travel Writing* 22, no. 1 (2018); Stephanie Leitch, 'Visual Images in Travel Writing', in Das and Youngs, *The Cambridge History of Travel Writing*, 456–73.

15. See, for instance, Barbara Maria Stafford, *Voyage Into Substance: Art, Science, Nature, and the Illustrated Travel Account, 1760–1840* (Cambridge, MA: MIT Press, 1984).

16. W.J.T. Mitchell, 'Word and Image', in Robert S. Nelson and Richard Shiff, eds, *Critical Terms for Art History* (Chicago and London: Chicago University Press, 1996), 49.

17. Giorgia Alù and Sarah Patricia Hills, 'The Travelling Eye: Reading the Visual in Travel Narratives', *Studies in Travel Writing* 22, no. 1 (2018): 1–15; 2.

18. Leitch, 'Visual Images in Travel Writing', 456.

19. Leitch, 'Visual Images in Travel Writing', 458.

20. Edward Gibbon, *The History of the Decline and Fall of the Roman Empire*, vol. 4 (London: A. Strahan and T. Cadell, 1788), 296, note 25.

21. William Lithgow, *The Total Discourse of the Rare Adventures and Painefull Peregrinations of Long Nineteene Yeares Travailes From Scotland, to the Most Famous Kingdomes in Europe, Asia and Africa* (London: I. Okes, 1640).

22. C. Edmund Bosworth, *An Intrepid Scot: William Lithgow of Lanark's Travels in the Ottoman Lands, North Africa, and Central Europe, 1609–21* (Aldershot: Ashgate, 2006), 136–50. The book is described by Bosworth as a 'long detour home though Central and Eastern Europe'.

23. Peter Womack, 'The Writing of Travel', in Michael Hathaway, ed., *A Companion to English Renaissance and Culture* (Malden: Blackwell, 2000), 156–58.

24. Lithgow, *The Total Discourse*, 412–26.

25. Lithgow, *The Total Discourse*, 417–19.

26. Lithgow, *The Total Discourse*, 416.

27. Michiel van Grossen, *The Representations of the Overseas World in the De Bry Collection of Voyages (1590–1634)* (Leiden and Boston: Brill, 2008).

28. A Dutch translation of the book, in which Lithgow's woodcuts were replaced by splendid engravings, preserved the scene of the robbery in a Moldavian forest, but redrawing it substantially: *Willem Lithgouws 19 jaarige lant-reyse, uyt Schotlant nae de vermaerde deelen des werelts Europa, Asia en Africa* (Amsterdam: Jacob Benjamin, 1653), part 2, 47.

29. Brown, *A Brief Account*.

30. Norman Moore, 'Edward Browne (1644–1708)', in Stephen Leslie, ed., *Dictionary of National Biography* (London: Smith, Elder & Co, 1886), vol. 7, 42–43.

31. The Philosophical Transactions of the Royal Society in London, 1669–1774, accessible online on The Royal Society website, royalsocietypublishing.org/action/doSearch?AllField=edward+brown.

32. Brown, 'To the Reader', in *A Brief Account*.

33. Brown, *A Brief Account*.

34. Brown, 'To the Reader'. Some of the prints are signed by William Sherwin, an English engraver and publisher.

35. Brown, *A Brief Account*, 38. On the underground dwellings of the poor, described also by other travellers, see László Kósa, *A Cultural History of Hungary: From the Beginnings to the Eighteenth Century* (Budapest: Corvina, 1999), 162.

36. Brown, *A Brief Account*, 38.

37. Brown, *A Brief Account*, 22.

38. Alain Manesson-Mallet, *Description de l'univers* (Paris: Denys Thierry, 1683), 142–43. In Dutch and German translations of Brown's book, the figures of Hungarian man and the Bulgarian women were presented in one plate: *Naauwkeurige en Gedenkwaardige Reysen van Edward Brown . . . Door Nederland, Duytsland, Hongaryen, Serbien, Bulgarien, Macedonien, Thessalien, Oostenr., Stierm., Carinthien, Carniole en Friuli, enz* (Amsterdam: Jan ten Hoorn, 1696), fol. 95; Edward Brown, M. D. auf *genehmgehaltenes Gutachten und Veranlassung der Kön. Engell. Medicinischen Gesellschaft in Londen durch Niederland, Teutschland, Hungarn, Servien, Bulgarien, Macedonien, Thessalien, Oesterreich, Steurmarck, Kärnthen, Carniolen, Friaul, etc gethane gantz sonderbare Reisen* (Nürnberg: Johann Ziege, 1711), 100.

39. Brown, *A Brief Account*, 40.

40. On Bulgarian ethnic dress, see Liz Mellish, 'Bulgarian Ethnic Dress', and Linda Welters, 'Differences and Similarities in Ethnic Dress in East Europe, Russia, and the Caucasus', both in Djurdja Bartlett and Pamela Smith, eds, *The Berg Encyclopedia of World Dress and Fashion, Volume 9 East Europe, Russia, and the Caucasus* (Oxford: Berg, 2010), 412–18; 37–71.

41. R.J. Crampton, *Bulgaria* (Oxford: Oxford University Press, 2009).

42. Brown, *A Brief Account*, 41–42.

43. The volume 9 of Vecelio's compendium of the world's costume, devoted to Hungary does not include any comparable dress. In fact, Hungarian males dress in Vecellio's, including 'Ungaro nello suo proprio, e vero habito' could not have been the model for Brown either. Cesare Vecellio, *Habiti antichi et moderni di tutto il mondo; di nuovo accresciuti di molte figure. Vestitus antiquorum recentiorumque totius orbis* (Venice: Gio. Bernardo Sessa, 1598), 410.

44. See note 38.

45. For the relevance of ethnic dress as a signifier of the region, see Djurdja Bartlett, 'Introduction to Dress and Fashion in East Europe, and the Caucasus', in Bartlett and Smith, *The Berg Encyclopedia of World Dress and Fashion, Volume 9*, 3. See also, Irena Turnau, *History of Dress in Central and Eastern Europe From the Sixteenth to the Eighteenth Century* (Warsaw: Institute of the History of Material Cultures, Polish Academy of Sciences, 1991), 130.

46. Alberto Fortis, *Viaggio in Dalmazia* (Venice: Alvise Milocco, 1774).

47. Alberto Fortis, *Travels into Dalmatia* (London: J. Robson, 1778), all citations from Fortis refer to the English translation of his book. Among other translations, are *Die Sitten der Morlacken* (Bern: Typographische Gesellschaft, 1775); Alberto Fortis, *Reisen in Dalmatien* (Bern: Typographische Gesellschaft, 1776). For the contemporary response,

see Giovanni Lovrich, *Osservazioni di Giovanni Lovrich: sopra diversi pezzi del Viaggio in Dalmazia del Signor Abate Alberto Fortis: coll'aggiunta della vita di Sociviza* (Venice: Francesco Sansoni, 1776).

48. Larry Wolff, *Venice and the Slavs: The Discovery of Dalmatia in the Age of the Enlightenment* (Stanford: Stanford University Press, 2001); Maša Surić et al., 'Geological Issues in Alberto Fortis' *Viaggio in Dalmazia* (1774)', *C.R. Geoscience* 339 (2007): 640–50; Wendy Bracewell, 'Lovrich's Joke: Authority, Laughter and Savage Breasts in an 18th-C. Travel Polemic', *Études Balkaniques* 2, no. 3 (2011): 224–49; David McCallam, '(Ac)claiming Illyria: Eighteenth-Century Istria and Dalmatia in Fortis, Cassas, and Lavallée', *Central Europe* 9, no. 2 (November 2011): 125–41.

49. Fortis, *Travels into Dalmatia*, vol. 1, 21.

50. Žarko Muljačić, *Putovanja Alberta Fortisa po Hrvatskoj i Sloveniji (1765–1791)* (Split: Književni krug, 1996) 57. See also Žarko Muljačić, *Fortisološke studije* (Split: Književni krug, 2011), 92–93.

51. I am modifying the original translation to English, in which the term *disegnatore* was systematically displaced with 'drawing'. Fortis, *Viaggio in Dalmazia*, vol. 1, 8; Fortis, *Travels into Dalmatia*, 1778, vol. 1, 7.

52. Francesco Carrara, *La Dalmazia Descritta . . . con 48 tavole minate rappresentanti i principali costumi nazionali* (Zara: Fratelli Battara, 1846–48), nonpaginated.

53. Johann Gottfried Herder, *Ideen zur Philosophie der Geschichte der Menschheit (1774–1791)*, IV: 16, 4. For English translation, see 'On Slav Nations: Johann Gottfried Herder (1774–1803)', trans. Ernest A. Menze with Michael Palma, in Jan Bažant, Nina Bažantová and Frances Starn, eds, *The Czech Reader: History, Culture, Politics* (Durham, NC: Duke University Press, 2010), 123–25.

54. Fortis, *Travels into Dalmatia*, vol. 1, 10–14.

55. Fortis, *Travels into Dalmatia*, vol. 1, 77. Bracewell, 'Lovrich's Joke'.

56. Fortis, *Travels into Dalmatia*, vol. 1, 200, 270, 293.

57. Fortis, *Travels into Dalmatia*, vol. 1, 1778, 82.

58. Lovrich, *Osservazioni*. For a different analysis, see Wolff, *Venice and the Slavs*, 250–53, Fig. 12.

59. Brown, *A Brief Account*, 9.

60. Edmund Burke, *A Philosophical Enquiry Into the Origin of Our Ideas of the Sublime and Beautiful* (London: R. and J. Dodsley, 1757), 41–72.

61. Barthes' comments on the indispensability of 'mountains, gorges, defiles and torrents' as prerequisite in twentieth-century travel guides, could be applied directly to eastern Europe: Roland Barthes, 'The *Blue* Guide', in *Mythologies* (London: Vintage, 1993), 74–77.

62. Fortis, *Travels into Dalmatia*, vol. 1, 246.

63. Fortis, *Travels into Dalmatia*, vol. 1, 247. The transcription from the original Morlack language confirms that the Morlacks identified themselves as Vlachs, meaning shepherds which, in turn, points to the relationship between the Morlacks in Dalmatia and Wallacks (Vlachs) in Romania. For the relationship between Morlacks and Italians, see See, Wolff, *Venice and the Slavs*, 248–49.

64. Fortis, *Travels into Dalmatia*, vol. 1, 246–47.

65. William Gilpin, *Three Essays on Picturesque Beauty; on Picturesque Travel; and on Sketching Landscape: to Which Is Added a Poem, on Landscape Painting* (London: R. Blamire, 1792). The *Cascata* image bears an uncannily resemblance to Thomas Hearne's watercolour, *Sir George Beaumont and Joseph Farington sketching a waterfall*, 1777, The Wordsworth Trust, Grasmere.

66. 'Travels into Dalmatia. In a Series of Letters from Abbé Alberto Fortis, &c.', *Gentleman's Magazine* 43 (April 1778): 181.

67. F.L. Cassas, 'Vue de la Grad Cascade de la Cettina, appellée Velika Gubowiza', in Joseph Lavallée, ed., *Voyage Pittoresque et Historique de L'Istrie et la Dalmatie* (Paris: Louis François Cassas, 1802), pl. 38; Joseph Wilson, *A History of Mountains, Geographical and Mineralogical . . . to Accompany a Picturesque View of the Principal Mountains of the World . . . Painted and Published by Robert Andrew Riddell* (London: T. Bensley, 1809), vol. 2, 708.

68. Aidan Chalk, 'Childe Harold's Pilgrimage: A Romaunt and the Influence of Local Attachment', *Texas Studies in Literature and Language* 40, no. 1 (Spring 1998): 48.

69. Lord Byron, *Child Harold's Pilgrimage*, Canto II: XXXVII, in Lord [George George] Byron, *Romaunt and Other Poems* (London: John Murray, 1812, 3rd ed.).

70. Gibbon, *The Rise and Decline of the Roman Empire*, vol. 4, 296, note 25. Byron, *Child Harold's Pilgrimage: Romaunt*, 137.

71. Byron, *Child Harold's Pilgrimage: Romaunt*, 137.

72. Byron's wording of Gibbon's has been repeated by virtually all authors who write about Albania's past, from travel writers to historians, see Norman Davies, *Europe: A History* (Oxford: Oxford University Press, 1996), 645.

73. J.C. Hobhouse, *A Journey Through Albania and Other Provinces of Turkey in Europe and Asia to Constantinople During the Years 1809 and 1810* (London: James Cawthorn, 1813).

74. Rev. Thomas Smart Hughes, *Travels in Sicily, Greece and Albania*, 2 vols (London: J. Mawman, 1820), vol. 2, 99. Cockerell's watercolour is in the collection of the British Museum, inv. 1923,0113.30.

75. Byron, *Childe Harold's Pilgrimage*, Canto II, LXIV.

76. See a colour lithograph *Albaneser* in *Karlsruher Unterhaltungsblatt* (Karlsruhe: C.F. Müller, 1828), Pl. XVII, 211; *Albanesen in Verfolgung des Feindes*, reproduced in Jezernik, *Wild Europe*, 113; a colour photogravure dated to 1830 (photo in Hulton Archive/ Getty Images www.gettyimages.co.uk/detail/news-photo/albanian-palikars-in-pursuit-of-an-enemy-wear-long-haired-news-photo/3063125.

77. Byron, *Childe Harold's Pilgrimage*, Canto II, LXIV.

78. Bejtullah D. Destani and Robert Elsie, eds, *Edward Lear in Albania: Journals of a Landscape Painter in the Balkans* (London: I.B. Tauris, 2008).

79. Edward Lear, *Journals of a Landscape Painter in Albania, &c* (London: Richard Bentley, 1851), 362.

80. Lear, *Journals of a Landscape Painter*, 364.

81. Koshar, '"What Ought to Be Seen"', 323–25.

82. Brian H. Murray, 'Introduction: Forms of Travel, Modes of Transport', in Henes and Murray, *Travel Writing, Visual Culture*, 9–12.

83. Irina V. Popova-Novak, 'The Odyssey of National Discovery: Hungarians in Hungary and Abroad, 1750–1850', in Bracewell and Drace-Francis, *Under Eastern Eyes*, 198–99.

84. Luminita Gatejel, 'Overcoming the Iron Gates: Austrian Transport and River Regulation on the Lower Danube, 1830s–1840s', *Central European History* 49 (2016): 162–80.

85. William Beattie, *The Danube: Its History, Scenery, and Topography . . . Splendidly Illustrated from Sketches Taken on the Spot, by Abresch, and Drawn by W.H. Bartlett* (London: George Virtue, 1844).

86. Ralf Roth and Henry Jacolin, eds, *Eastern European Railways in Transition: Nineteenth to Twenty-First Centuries* (Farnham: Ashgate, 2013).

87. John Paget, *Hungary and Transylvania, With Remarks on Their Condition, Social, Political and Economical*, 2 vols (London: John Murray, 1839). See also Borbála Bökös, 'Representations of Hungary and Transylvania in John Paget's Travelogue', *Acta Universitatis Sapientiae, Philologica* 9, no. 1 (2017): 87–98.

88. Henry Miller Madden, 'The Diary of John Paget', *The Slavonic and East European Review* 19, nos 53/54 (1939): 237–64.

89. Paget, *Hungary and Transylvania*, vol. 1, x–xi.

90. Paget, *Hungary and Transylvania*, vol. 1, vii.

91. Paget, *Hungary and Transylvania*, frontispieces to vol. 1, and vol. 2.

92. Judit Brody, 'The Széchenyi Chain Bridge at Budapest', *Technology and Culture* 29, no. 1 (January 1988): 104–17.

93. William Tierney Clark, *An Account, With Illustrations, of the Suspension Bridge Across the River Danube, Uniting Pesth and Buda and the Adjacent Country, in the Kingdom of Hungary* (London: John Weale, 1852–53).

94. Paget, *Hungary and Transylvania*, vol. 1, 228.

95. Paget, *Hungary and Transylvania*, vol. 1, 254.

96. See Angela Jianu, *A Circle of Friends: Romanian Revolutionaries and Political Exile, 1840–1859* (Leiden: Brill, 2011).

97. Bram Stoker, *Dracula* (Westminster: Archibald Constable and Company, 1897), 1.

98. On Dracula and Transylvania, see among others, Duncan Light, 'Imaginative Geographies, Dracula and the Transylvania "Place Myth"', *Human Geographies: Journal of Studies and Research in Human Geography* 2, no. 2 (November 2008): 6–17; Isabel Ermida, ed., *Dracula and the Gothic in Literature, Pop Culture and the Arts* (Leiden: Brill, 2015).

99. John Paget, *Hungary and Transylvania, With Remarks on Their Condition, Social, Political and Economical*, 2 vols (London: John Murray, 1855), feature *New Road on the Danube Bellow Panezover* as frontispiece to vol. 2.

100. Joseph Heinbucher Edlen von Bikkessy, *Panoniens Bewohner in ihrem volksthümlichen Trachten* (Vienna, 1820), 59, which in turn borrowed the plates from Karl Timlich, *Sammlung merkwürdiger Nationalkostüme des Königreichs Ungarn und Kroatien, nach der Natur gezeichnet in 60 Blättern* (Vienna: Schaumburg, 1816). In his ethnographic explanation to the plates, von Bikkessy described the dress of the Wallacks and supplied other details, such as their reputed longevity, but did not pay attention to Wallack women's craft.

101. Charles Boner's *Transylvania; Its Products and Its People* (London: Longmans, Green, Reader, and Dyer, 1865).

102. Boner, *Transylvania*, 231. The term 'Wallack' is a derivate of the term 'Vlach' which by the nineteenth century acquired negative connotations of savagery. See, Eliana Ionoaia, 'Othering the Wallachian National Identity: British Victorian Travellers Voyaging Down the Danube', in Iulian Boldea and Târgu Mureş, eds, *Globalization and Intercultural Dialogue: Multidisciplinary Perspectives – Literature* (Bucharest: Arhipelag, 2014), 915–24. Paget's ambitions for impartiality had also failed when it came to his description of the Wallacks: Paget, *Hungary and Transylvania*, vol. 2, 196–229. Boner provides also his own explanation of the distinction between the 'Wallachian', which denotes 'an inhabitant of Wallachia, in contradistinction to the descendants of the original dwellers on Transylvania, whom I designate Wallacks, or, as they now call themselves Romanen (Roumains)'. Boner, *Transylvania*, 66.

103. Boner, 'Preface', *Transylvania*, v–vii.

104. Etchings and lithographs by Thédore Valério, Dieudonné Auguste Lancelot, as well as Denis Auguste Raffet, working in Romania, Wallachia, Hungary, provide a broad comparative material.

105. Boner, *Transylvania*, 22. On the eroticised description of Romani women costumes, see Sacha E. Davis, '"A Most Picturesque Mass of Rags": Romani Costume and Undress in Nineteenth-century Travel Descriptions of Hungary', *Patterns of Prejudice* 53, no. 5 (2019): 464–86.

106. Boner, *Transylvania*, 239.

107. Paget, *Hungary and Transylvania*, vol. 2, 210.

108. Boner, *Transylvania*, 240.

109. Boner, *Transylvania*, 240–41.

110. Boner, *Transylvania*, 241.

111. In the German translation of the book, Boner's portrait in the frontispiece replaced the image of the 'Wallack Woman' which was moved into the first chapter, re-engraved in black and white. Charles Boner, *Siebenbürgen. Land und Leute* (Leipzig: J.J. Weber, 1868), 38. The woman with a distaff, spinning while walking, would become a trope repeated in travel books on Transylvania, see [Nina Elizabeth Mazuchelli], *'Magyarland;' Being the Narrative of our Travels Through the Highlands and Lowlands of Hungary by a Fellow of the Carpathian Society, Author of 'The Indian Alps' . . . with Illustrations*, 2 vols (London: Sampson Low, Marston, Searle & Rivington, 1881), vol. 2, 35; Emily Gerard, *The Land Beyond the Forest: Facts, Figures and Fancies from Transylvania* (New York: Harper and Brothers, 1888), 142, 144.

112. For the role of the 'ethnographic turn' in the art-theoretical discourse, see Matthew Rampley, 'Anthropology and the Origins of Art History', in Alex Coles, ed., *Site Specificity: The Ethnographic Turn* (London: Black Dog, 2000), 138–63. For the preoccupation with folk art in Austria-Hungary, see Rebecca Houze, *Textiles, Fashion, and Design Reform in Austria-Hungary Before the First World War: Principle of Dress* (Farnham and Burlington, VT: Ashgate, 2015).

113. 'Our grandmothers were indeed not members of the academy of fine arts . . . but they knew what to do when it came to designing an embroidery' – Gottfried Semper, *Der Stil in den technischen und tektonischen Künsten, oder Praktische Aesthetik. Ein Handbuch für Techniker, Künstler und Kunstfreunde*, 2 vols (Frankfurt am Main: Verlag für Kunst und Wissenschaft, 1860–63). English translation: 'Style in the Technical and Tectonic Arts or Practical Aesthetics' (1860–1863), in *The Four Elements of Architecture and Other Writings*, trans. Harry Francis Mallgrave and Wolfgang Herrmann (Cambridge: Cambridge University Press, 1989), 234. See David Crowley, 'The Peasant in the City: Embroidery in Writings on Architecture in Austria-Hungary Around 1900', in Katarzyna Murawska-Muthesius, ed., *Borders in Art: Revisiting 'Kunstgeographie'* (Warsaw: Institute of Art, 2000), 127–37.

114. Mathew Rampley, 'Peasants in Vienna: Ethnographic Display and the 1873 World's Fair', *History Yearbook* 42 (2011): 110–32; Rebecca Houze, 'At the Forefront of a Newly Emerging Profession? Ethnography, Education, and the Exhibition of Women's Needlework in Austria-Hungary in the Late Nineteenth Century', *Journal of Design History* 21, no. 1 (2008): 19–40.

115. See, among others, David Crowley, *National Style and Nation-State: Design in Poland From the Vernacular Revival to the International Style* (Manchester: Manchester University Press, 1992); Nicola Gordon Bowe, *Art and the National Dream: The Search for Vernacular Expression in Turn of the Century Design* (London and Dublin: Irish Academic Press, 1993); Jacek Purchla and Wolf Tegethoff, eds, *Nation, Style, Modernism* (Cracow: International Cultural Centre, 2006).

116. Rampley, 'Peasants in Vienna'; Purchla and Tegethoff, *Nation, Style, Modernism*.

117. Todorova, *Imagining the Balkans*, 63.

118. Harry De Windt, *Through Savage Europe: Being the Narrative of a Journey (Undertaken as Special Correspondent of the "Westminster Gazette"), throughout the Balkan States and European Russia* (London: T. Fischer Unwin, 1907). On twentieth-century travel reports from Eastern Europe, see among others, Larry Wolff, 'The Traveller's View of Central Europe: Gradual Transitions and Degree of Differences in European Borderlands', in Omer Bartow and Eric D. Weitz, eds, *Shatterzone of Empires: Coexistence and Violence in the German, Habsburg, Russian and Ottoman Borderlands* (Bloomington, IN: Indiana University Press, 2013), 23–71.

119. De Windt, *Through Savage Europe*, 300.

120. De Windt, *Through Savage Europe*, 15.

121. The book was published in the publisher's series Books on the Balkans and Russia.

122. Anonymous Reviewer, 'Harry De Windt, *Through Savage Europe*', *The Spectator*, 11 May 1907: 765.

123. De Windt, 'City of Pleasure', in De Windt, *Through Savage Europe*, 247–60, includes one small photo of a car-less street in Bucharest, with silhouettes of people reduced to dots.

124. Katarina Gephardt, '"The Enchanted Garden" or "The Red Flag": Eastern Europe in Late Nineteenth-Century British Travel Writing', *Journal of Narrative Theory* 35, no. 3 (Fall 2005): 292–306, in part. 300; Marija Krivokapić and Neil Diamond, *Images of Montenegro in Anglo-American Creative Writing and Film* (Newcastle upon Tyne: Cambridge Scholars Publishing, 2017), 83–100.

125. Gilbert H. Grosvenor (1899–1954), his son Melville Bell (1957–1967), and grandson Gilbert Melville (1970–2014). *National Geographic Magazine* changed its name to *National Geographic* in December 1959, with the introduction of photo covers. I will be using the abbreviated term throughout.

126. Catherine A. Lutz and Jane L. Collins, *Reading National Geographic* (Chicago and London: The University of Chicago Press, 1993), 36–37.

127. Lutz and Collins, *Reading National Geographic*, 26–27.

128. Ron Johnston, 'Popular Geographies and Geographical Imaginations: Contemporary English-language Geographical Magazines', *GeoJournal* 79 (2009): 348; A. Bonnett, 'Geography as the World Discipline: Connecting Popular and Academic Geographical Imaginations', *Area* 35 (2003): 55–63.

129. Courtland Dixon Barnes Bryan, *The National Geographic Society: 100 Years of Adventure and Discovery* (London: Harry N. Abrams, 1997).

130. Lutz and Collins, *Reading National Geographic*. Also Jessamyn Neuhaus, 'Colonizing the Coffee Table: The Erasure of Difference in the Representation of Women in National Geographic Magazine', *American Periodicals* 7 (1997): 1–26.

131. Tamar Y. Rothenberg, *Presenting America's World: Strategies of Innocence in 'National Geographic Magazine'* (Aldershot and Burlington, VT: Ashgate, 2007); Stephanie Hawkins, *American Iconographic: 'National Geographic', Global Culture, and the Visual Imagination* (Charlottesville: University of Virginia Press, 2010).

132. Jacobo García-Álvarez, Paloma Puente-Lozano and Juna-Manuel Trillo-Santamaria, 'Representing Spain: Cultural Image and Geographic Knowledge in *National Geographic*'s Articles on Spain (1888–1936)', *GeoJournal* 79, no. 5 (2014): 539–56.

133. Nemanja Radonjić, '"Not Exactly Out of Europe, Yet Somehow on the Fringes of the Orient": Image of the Balkans in the *National Geographic Magazine* (1888–2013)' (in Serbo-Croatian), *Godišnjak za društvenu istoriju* 3 (2013): 73–97. It does not include images.

134. Map 'New Balkans States and Central Europe', *National Geographic* 26 (August 1914), supplement.

135. Tad Szulc, 'Dispatches from Eastern Europe', *National Geographic* 179 (March 1991): 2–3.

136. Lutz and Collins, *Reading National Geographic*, 26–27.

137. Lutz and Collins, *Reading National Geographic*, 36.

138. Hon. Gardiner G. Hubbard (President of National Geographic Society), 'Russia in Europe', *National Geographic* 7, no. 1 (January 1896): 1–26; Edwin A. Grosvenor, 'Siberia', *National Geographic* 12, no. 9 (September 1901): 317–24; Gilbert H. Grosvenor, 'Young Russia: The Land of Unlimited Possibilities', *National Geographic* 26, no. 5 (November 1914): 423–520 (with first colour photographs).

139. William E. Curtis, 'The Great Turk and His Lost Provinces', *National Geographic* 14, no. 2 (February 1903): 45–61; Frederic Moore, 'The Changing Map of the Balkans', *National Geographic* 24, no. 2 (February 1913): 199–226; William Joseph Showalter, 'The Kingdom of Servia', *National Geographic* 27, no. 4 (April 1915): 417–32.

140. Marian Cruger Coffin, 'Where East Meets West: A Visit to Picturesque Dalmatia, Montenegro, and Herzegovina', *National Geographic* 9, no. 5 (May 1908): 309–44.

141. Felix J. Koch, 'In Quaint, Curious Croatia', *National Geographic* 19, no. 12 (December 1908): 809–32.

142. Moore, 'The Changing Map of the Balkans', 201. On ethnic clothing as resistance, see Mary Neuburger 'Veils, *Shalvari*, and Matters of Dress: Unravelling the Fabric of Women's Lives in Communist Bulgaria', in Susan E. Reid and David Crowley, eds, *Style and Socialism: Modernity and Material Culture in Post-War Eastern Europe* (Oxford and New York: Berg, 2000), 169–88.

143. Vesna Goldsworthy, *Inventing Ruritania: The Imperialism of the Imagination* (New Haven and London: Yale University Press, 1998), 31.

144. Anonymous, 'The Notes on Macedonia', *National Geographic* 19, no. 11 (November 1908), 796.

145. Showalter, 'The Kingdom of Servia', 422.

146. Frederic Moore, 'Wallachians', in 'The Changing Map of the Balkans', 221.

147. Frederic Moore, *The Balkan Trail* (London: Smith, Elder & Co, 1906), 266.

148. The expression used in relation to the Albanians by Cruger Coffin, 'Where East Meets West', 328.

149. Roland Barthes, 'The Photographic Message', in *Image, Music, Text*. Essays selected and translated by Stephen Heath (London: Fontana Press, 1977), 25. And, in the same collection, Roland Barthes, 'The Rhetoric of the Image', in *Image, Music, Text*. Essays selected and translated by Stephen Heath (London: Fontana Press, 1977), 37–41.

150. After WWII, a special department was established to write suggestive captions. Lutz and Collins, *Reading National Geographic*, 76–81.

151. *National Geographic* Image Collection is today largely available online on the magazine website, www.natgeoimagecollection.com.

152. C. Townley-Fullam, 'Hungary: A Land of Shepherd Kings', *National Geographic* 26, no. 4 (October 1914): 310–93. This article is illustrated with 89 photographs.

153. Townley-Fullam, 'Hungary', 361. The caption is written in the first person, but it is unclear whether it is the author of the text, or the photographer, who speaks.

154. Albert Kain, ed., *Ungarn. Im Auftrage des kön. ungarischen Handelsministers herausgegeben von der Direction der kön. ung. Staatsbahnen* (Budapest: Erdéleyi, 1909). I want to thank Eszter Molnar and Zsuzsanna Demeter for identifying Photo Erdélyi at the National Geographic Society with Mór Erdélyi.

155. In J. Theodore Mariner, 'Transylvania and its Seven Castles: A Motor Circuit through Rumania's New Province of Racial Complexity and Architectural Charm', *National Geographic* 49, no. 3 (March 1926): 348.

156. Rampley, 'Peasants in Vienna', 123–29.

157. Isaiah Bowman, 'Constantinople and the Balkans', in Edward Mandell House and Charles Seymour, eds, *What Really Happened at Paris; the Story of the Peace Conference, 1918–1919* (New York: C. Scribner's sons, 1912), 142.

158. Edwin A. Grosvenor, 'The Races of Europe', *National Geographic* 34, no. 5 (December 1918): 441–536, taking the whole issue), in part. 474, 487–88, 505, 508, 532. See also, William Joseph Showalter, 'Partitioned Poland', *National Geographic* 27, no. 1 (January 1915): 88–106; Aleš Hrdlička, 'Bohemia and the Czechs', *National Geographic* 31, no. 5 (May 1917): 163–87; Maynard Owen Williams, 'When Czechoslovakia Puts a Falcon Feather in Its Cap', *National Geographic* 63, no. 3 (March 1933): 40–49.

159. *Hans Hildenbrand, Hofphotograph und Pionier der frühen Farbfotografie* (Ubstadt-Weiher: Verlag Regionalkultur, 2018).

160. Hans Hildenbrand, *Costumes of Czechoslovakia*, in Worth E. Shoults's 'Hospitality of the Czechs', *National Geographic* 51, vol. 6 (June 1927): 723–42. Hildenbrand's *In the Land of the White Eagle*, in Melville B. Grosvenor, 'Poland, Land of the White Eagle', *National Geographic* 61, no. 4 (April 1932): 43–45. His *Rainbow Costumes of Poland Peasants*, accompanied Maynard Owen Williams's text 'The Poland of the Present', *National Geographic* 63, no. 3 (March 1933): 319–44.

161. Lutz and Collins, *Reading National Geographic*, 94.

162. Crowley, *National Style and Nation-State*, 64–72.

163. Władysław Stanisław Reymont, *The Peasants*, trans. Michael Henry Dziewicki, 4 vols (London: Jarrolds, 1925–26).

164. For exhibitions presenting the vernacular arts as the essential expression of national cultures, see Miklós Székely, ed., *Ephemeral Architecture in Central and Eastern Europe in the 19th and 20th Centuries* (Paris: L'Harmattan, 2015); Marta Filipová, ed., *Cultures of International Exhibitions 1840–1940: Great Exhibitions in the Margins* (Abingdon and New York: Ashgate, 2015).

165. Ryszard Kantor, *Ubiór – strój – kostium* (Cracow: Uniwersytet Jagielloński), 1982.

166. Michael Cohen, *Sisters: Relation and Rescue in Nineteenth-Century British Novels and Paintings* (Madison and Teaneck: Fairleigh Dickinson University Press, 1995), 9.

167. Christoph von Fürer-Haimendorf, 'A Wedding in the Bulgarian Mountains', *Geographical Magazine* 4, no. 3 (January 1937): 203–14; 'Balkan Nomads on the March', photographic supplement by W.O. von Riedemann, *Geographical Magazine* 5, no. 6 (October 1937): 435–39; Sacheverell Sitwell, 'Rumanian Wedding', *Geographical Magazine* 6, no. 6 (April 1938): 427–40; John Lehmann, 'Outside the Fold': I. Among the "Swabians" of Hungary', *Geographical Magazine* 8, no. 4 (February 1939): 225–32; John Lehmann, 'A Balkan Sequence. I: The Strangest Journey', *Geographical Magazine* 10, no. 3 (January 1940): 148–53.

168. A.T. Lutosławski, 'Poland's Window on the World', *Geographical Magazine* 1, no. 2 (June 1935): 98–106; Naděžda Melniková-Papoušková, 'The Changing Face of Prague', *Geographical Magazine* 2, no. 4 (February 1936): 295–310; Władysław Szafer, 'The National Parks in Poland', *Geographical Magazine* 7, no. 2 (June 1938): 129–40; The Countess of Listowel, 'The Indigestible Magyar', *Geographical Magazine* 7, no. 6 (October 1938): 361–76; Louise Llewellyn Jarecka, 'Popular Art in Poland', *Geographical Magazine* 8, no. 5 (March 1939): 345–62.

169. John Lehmann, 'Change in Slovakia', *Geographical Magazine* 4, no. 5 (March 1937): 313–28.

170. Karol Plicka, 'Among Slovakian Mountains', Photogravure supplement, *Geographical Magazine* 4, no. 5 (March 1937). Plicka supplied his photographs of Slovakian peasants

to Rochowanski's cultural guide *Columbus in der Slovakia*, 1936, another instance of the perception of affinity between the lands of eastern Europe to the 'wilds of America'. See Julia Secklehner, 'Artwork of the Month, April 2020: *Columbus in der Slovakei* by Leopold Wolfgang Rochowanski', https://craace.com/2020/04/28/artwork-of-the-month-april-2020-columbus-in-der-slovakei-by-leopold-wolfgang-rochowanski.

171. Karel Plicka, *Slovensko* (Martin: Matica slovenská, 1937).
172. *Geographical Magazine*'s eastern European covers include: W.O. Riedemann's photo of the Balkan mountains with shepherds, *Geographical Magazine* 5, no. 6 (February 1937), A. Costa, 'Rumanian Wedding', *Geographical Magazine* 6, no. 6 (April 1938); Oscar Marcus, 'A Hungarian Shepherd', *Geographical Magazine* 7, no. 6 (October 1938); The only non-ethnic cover presented a Rodchenko-like picture of a quasi-military youth camp in Romania, from the article written by the Balkan correspondent Derek Patmore: Herbert List, 'The Band Plays a Great Part in Camp's Life', *Geographical Magazine* 9, no. 2 (June 1939).
173. Maynard Owen Williams, 'The Poland of the Present', *National Geographic* 63, no. 3 (March 1933): 319–43; John Patric, 'Czechoslovaks, Yankees of Europe', *National Geographic* 74, no. 2 (August 1938): 173–225.
174. W. Robert Moore, 'Gaiety and Business in Praha Centre', photograph in Patric, 'Czechoslovaks, Yankees of Europe', 179.
175. Featuring also in later *National Geographic's* reports from Prague, photographed as double spread by James P. Blair, in Edward J. Linehan's 'Czechoslovakia: The Dream and the Reality', *National Geographic* 133, no. 2 (February 1968): 156–57.
176. W. Robert Moore, *The Czechoslovakian Cyclorama*, *National Geographic* 74, no. 2 (August 1938): 181–88, 197–204, 213–20.
177. Lutz and Collins, *Reading National Geographic*, 203–14; and Hawkins, *American Iconographic*, 159–65.
178. 'A Study in Skirts – And Centuries Lie Between', photograph in Dorothy Hosmer, 'An American Girl Cycles Across Romania: Two-Wheel Pilgrim Pedals the Land of Castles and Gypsies, Where Roman Empire Traces Mingle with Remnants of Oriental Migration', *National Geographic* 75, no. 5 (November 1938), 558.
179. W. Robert Moore, 'Pottery Reflects a Nation's Love of Colour', in *The Czechoslovakian Cyclorama*, 185, Plate V/ I.
180. Johnston, 'Popular Geographies', 348. David Matless, Jonathan Oldfield and Adam Swain, 'Geographically Touring the Eastern Bloc: British Geography, Travel Cultures and the Cold War', *Transaction of the Institute of British Geographers*, New Series 33, no. 3 (July 2008): 354–75.
181. From Arthur Calder-Marshall, 'Reconstruction in Yugoslavia', *Geographical Magazine* 19, no. 1 (May 1946): 40–54; Lovett F. Edwards, 'The New Albania', *Geographical Magazine* 19, no. 3 (July 1946): 104–15; Paul Tabori, 'The Endurance of Hungary', *Geographical Magazine* 29, no. 19 (February 1957): 505–16; F.E. Ian Hamilton, 'Bulgaria: Land of Change', *Geographical Magazine* 38, no. 4 (August 1965); David Williamson, 'The New Warsaw: Rebuilding the Old and New City', *Geographical Magazine* 38, no. 8 (December 1965): 596–607; F.W. Carter and R.A. French, 'New Era in Slovenia: Success Story of a Yugoslav Republic', *Geographical Magazine* 57, no. 9 (June 1975): 556–60; Anonymous photo supplement, 'Capital of Latvia: A Look at Modern Riga', *Geographical Magazine* 40, no. 10 (February 1968): 876–79; F.W. Carter, 'Four Countries Develop Their Own Energy: Resources in Albania, Bulgaria, Romania and Yugoslavia', *Geographical Magazine* 69, no. 1 (October 1976): 13–17.
182. F.E. Ian Hamilton, 'The East European and Soviet City', in a feature 'What Is the City but the People', *Geographical Magazine* 50, no. 8 (May 1978): 511–15.
183. Cover image: *Papercut from a Polish Village*, from Pearl Binder, 'Popular Art in Poland', *Geographical Magazine* 33, no. 3 (July 1960): 159–72.
184. Piotr Korduba, *Ludowość na sprzedaż: Towarzystwo Popierania Przemysłu Ludowego, Cepelia, Instytut Wzornictwa Przemysłowego* (Warsaw: Fundacja Bęc Zmiana, 2013); Joanna Kordjak, ed., *Polska – Kraj Folkloru?* (Warsaw: Zachęta – Narodowa Galeria Sztuki, 2016).
185. 'Country Visitors to Sofia', cover of *Geographical Magazine* 38, no. 4 (August 1965).
186. Hamilton, 'Bulgaria: Land of Change', 278–79.

187. Cover image: J. Allan Cash, 'Bulgarian Women', *Geographical Magazine* 22, no. 4 (August 1949).

188. Mary Neuburger, 'Veils, *Shalvari*, and Matters of Dress: Unravelling the Fabric of Women's Lives in Communist Bulgaria', in Reid and Crowley, *Style and Socialism*, 169–87.

189. Pablo Picasso who, during his visit to Poland to attend the Congress of Intellectuals in Defence of Peace in 1948, sketched a face of a woman in head kerchief, called it *La Polonaise*. Katarzyna Murawska-Muthesius, 'Paris From Behind the Iron Curtain', in *Paris: Capital of the Arts* (London: Royal Academy of Arts, 2002), 250–61, esp. 255.

190. Antony Lambert, 'Return of the Vampire', *Geographical* 61, no. 2 (February 1989): 16–21.

191. 'Airlift to Berlin', *National Geographic Magazine* 95, no. 5 (May 1949); Frederick C. Vosburgh, photos by staff photographer Volkmar Wentzel, 'Berlin, Island in a Soviet Sea', *National Geographic* 100, no. 5 (November 1951): 689–704; Robert Sisson, photos by the author, 'Freedom Flight from Hungary: A Story in Photographs', *National Geographic* 111, no. 3 (March 1957): 424–36; Delia and Ferdinand Kuhn, photos by Erich Lessing, Magnum, 'Poland Opens Her Door', *National Geographic* 114, no. 3 (September 1958): 354–98; Gilbert Melville Grosvenor, photos by the author, 'Yugoslavia's Window on the Adriatic', *National Geographic* 121, no. 2 (February 1962): 218–47.

192. Cover image: Bruno Barbey, 'Polish Coal Miner', *National Geographic* 161, no. 4 (April 1982). The caption in the Contents page, says: 'The strength of Poland's character shines in the face of a coal miner, who wears a photograph of the Pope and the emblem of the Solidarity worker' movement'. The first 'eastern European' cover featured the Parliament building in Budapest on the bank of the Danube, referring to William Slade Backer's text, with photos by Richard S. Durrance, 'Down the Danube', *National Geographic* 123, no. 2 (July 1965): 35–79. The cover testified to the adventure of a group of American students who went down the Danube in their canoes, from Ulm to the Black Sea, repeating the experience of traversing west and east. *National Geographic*'s policy does not allow for reproducing its covers.

193. It is accessible on archive.org https://archive.org/details/nationalgeograph161nati/page/n542. The editorial, signed by Wilbur E. Garrett, *National Geographic* 161, no. 4 (April 1982).

194. Yva Momatiuk and John Eastcott, 'Slovakia's Spirit of Survival', *National Geographic* 171, no. 1 (January 1987): 120–46; Małgorzata Niezabitowska, photos by Tomasz Tomaszewski, 'Discovering America', *National Geographic* 173, no. 1 (January 1988, Centenary Issue): 44–79; Tad Szulc, photos by staff photographer James L. Stanfield, 'Poland: The Hope That Never Dies', *National Geographic* 173, no. 1 (January 1988, Centenary Issue): 80–121; Priit J. Vesilind, 'The Baltic: Arena od Power', *National Geographic* 175, no. 5 (May 1989): 602–36.

195. Gilbert M. Grosvenor, 'From the President: Window on the Soviet Union', *National Geographic* 177, no. 3 (March 1990), nonpaginated.

196. Szulc, 'Dispatches from Eastern Europe', 2–3.

197. Cover images: Steve McCurry, 'An Ethnic Albanian Farm Woman . . . [and] Her Daughter', *National Geographic* 178, no. 2 (August 1990); Larry C. Price, 'Joseph Stalin Gets the Brush-Off', *National Geographic* 178, no. 5 (November 1990); James Nachtwey, 'Carbon-blackened Boys Play Near a Factory in Copşa Mică, Romania', *National Geographic* 179, no. 6 (June 1991). The first two covers are accessible on Internet Library of Free and Borrowable Books archive.org: https://archive.org/details/nationalgeograph178nati/page/n206; https://archive.org/details/nationalgeograph178nati/page/n742.

198. Alexandra Boulat, 'Eyewitness Kosovo', *National Geographic* 197, no. 2 (February 2000): 92–93. It was the cover of *Time*, 17 August 1992, showing the emaciated bodies of Bosnian prisoners, which exposed the scale of the atrocities in the Balkans.

199. Derek Hall, 'Eastern Europe Opens Its Doors', *Geographical* 62, no. 4 (April 1990): 10–14.

200. Adam Nicolson, photo by Rena Effendi, 'Hay Beautiful', *National Geographic* 224, no. 1 (June 2013): 114–15.

201. As confirmed by a booklet listing all the traditional skills still performed in the region – Teofil Invanciuc, photo Radu Lazar, *Meşteşuguri tradiţionale din Ţara Maramureşului* (Baia Mare: Proema, 2016).

202. Ann Hetzel Gunkel, 'Global Górale and Postmodern Polskość: Polish Roots Music and the Post-Communist Recovery of Folk', *The Polish Review* 57, no. 4 (2012): 63–74; Joseph Grim Feinberg, *The Paradox of Authenticity: Folklore Performance in Post-Communist Slovakia* (Madison, WI and London: The University of Wisconsin Press, 2018).
203. 'There Is No Shame in Being Eastern European', Roma Piotrowska in discussion with Katarzyna Perlak, *Contemporary Lynx*, 7 April 2018, https://contemporarylynx.co.uk/there-is-no-shame-in-being-eastern-european.

4   Mr Punch Draws Eastern Europe

The visual analysis of eastern Europe's maps and travel images in Chapters 2 and 3 generated diverse results. If maps kept confirming the area's instability and temporariness, images in travelogues, by contrast, implied a sense of uniformity and permanence conveyed by the 'timeless' body of the peasant woman in her white embroidered chemise. The disparity between the visual messages sent by maps and travelogues was bridged when post-Versailles eastern Europe entered the political sphere and was promptly targeted by cartoonists. And it was the cartoonists who, borrowing from both mapmakers and travellers, had arrived at a catchy visual formula to conceptualise the region's spatial discomfort and its ethnic apparel in one pregnant image. Since the 1920s and for many decades to come, a cartoon with a bunch of children in ethnic costumes, squeezed together in a narrow space of a classroom or a playground and disciplined by Dame Europa, Hitler, or Stalin, was to be instantly recognisable as a metaphorical 'group portrait' of the region (Figure 4.1).[1]

The affinity between representational strategies of mapmaking and cartoon-making has already been raised above. This chapter focuses on cartoons, the most rhetorical among the images disseminated by the press. It examines the ways in which cartoonists, both west and east, defined the eastern European 'group person',[2] constructing one of the most persistent images identified with the region. Unlike the previous chapters on maps and travelogues, covering several hundred years and many countries, this section narrows down the field of investigation to the twentieth century and it focuses on Britain. After an introductory inquiry into the operational mechanisms of 'cartoonwork', it looks at cartoons published in *Punch* in the interwar era and in the Cold War period. If the book so far has focused mostly on the mechanisms of representation, on maps and images of the region produced from outside, this chapter will also pay attention to the tropes of self-fashioning, to the ways in which the transnational communist space and body was constructed from within, by cartoonists confined inside the Iron Curtain area. A post-scriptum on representational codes applied to eastern Europe by post-1989 cartoons and their disappearance from newspaper pages in recent decades will round up this chapter.

Cartoonwork

An established technique of both the 'overloaded' and the 'liberated' image, of an 'evil eye' or a 'keyhole gaze', cartoons constitute an especially relevant medium for the studies of visuality and its imbrication with language, space, and bodies, deserving as much serious attention as that given to film, photography, or cartography.[3]

THE GOOD BOY OF THE EAST.

Turkey (*from the corner in which Europa has put him*). "I FEAR, MADAM, THAT OUR YOUNG FRIENDS ARE CAUSING YOU SOME EMBARRASSMENT. BUT, WHILE GREATLY DEPLORING THEIR INSUBORDINATION, I REGRET THAT I AM NOT IN A POSITION TO RENDER ANY APPRECIABLE ASSISTANCE TO YOUR AUTHORITY."

Figure 4.1 Leonard Raven-Hill, 'The Good Boy of the East', *Punch*, 4 June 1913. By permission of Topfoto.

Responding to current events with the speed of a newspaper report, cartoons form part of the news and, often positioned next to the editorial, provide the daily critical commentary, turned ingeniously into a humorous, or an overtly denunciatory drawing. The topicality and wit are the defining features, but the type of humour and the tenor of critique varies widely from newspaper to newspaper. Their lifespan also varies since most of the cartoons are space- and time-specific, and when the memory of personalities, events, and verbal battles fade, the deciphering of their meaning – let alone getting the joke – requires expert historical knowledge and an intense research of the local media.[4] Because of their intrinsic topicality, cartoons are often treated as 'ancillary evidence' for studying historical events and opinions.[5]

The cartoon's power is fuelled by the fundamental strategies of the medium which produces meaning by deformation and metaphorical substitution. By emphasising bodily deformities and by adopting well-known literary tropes, figures of speech and metaphor-prone images, such as 'Snow White' or the 'imperialist warmonger', cartoons boast their striking capacity to 'explain' the current political events in an easy visual formula. Moreover, by clinging to the same visual 'phrase', they elevate it to the rank of a critical commentary, to an insight which reveals the 'real' nature of things.[6] Manoeuvring between a piercing insightfulness and a worn-out cliché, blatantly subjective and yet parading as a more 'truthful' or 'rebellious' vision of reality than an 'unmediated' camera image or a cartographic record, they have been perceived as instruments of subversion, but also as tools of myth-making, preserving the status quo.[7] During times of conflict cartoons drawn for the illustrated press, from *Le Charivari* and *Punch* to *Simplicissimus*, *L'Assiette au beurre*, *The Masses*, *Krokodil* and *Der Stürmer*, as well as to *Private Eye* and *The Daily Mail*, have played major roles in identifying the enemy on both sides of the barricade. By deriding the vices of the despised Other, to include both capitalists and revolting masses, Jews and Catholics, Irish and Blacks, suffragettes and gays, Eastern Europeans and Muslims, cartoons have been contributing to the articulation and strengthening of the values of the majority, be it Catholic, Protestant, white, western European, patriarchal, heterosexual, or militantly secular.[8]

A transdisciplinary medium *per se*, cartoons are a 'no man's land', providing an open playground for representatives of various disciplines: history, politics, social sciences, media studies, art history, and visual culture.[9] There is no shortage of books, histories, and studies of cartoons which range from various types of monographs to popular albums, as well as to theoretical inquiries into the strategies of the medium. They are approached either as a visual source for studying public opinion, or, as *explicanda* demanding attention for themselves.[10] By embracing the visual and the verbal, the topical and the timeless, the complexity of the signified and the alleged simplicity of the signifiers, and indeed thriving on the logic of binary oppositions – cartoons have provided an ideal material for semioticians. The communication scholars Martin J. Medhurst and Michael A. DeSousa classified them as the forms of 'non-oratorical discourse', of graphic persuasion which follows the rules of classical rhetoric.[11] The cultural historian Peter Wagner renamed cartoons 'iconotexts', stressing that it is the combination of visual and verbal messages which stands for the specificity of cartoons as a 'signifying system'.[12] As argued by the art historian Alex Potts, cartoons, in contrast to the high art of the twentieth century, operate 'a publicly recognised and explicitly coded system', and are 'the closest that contemporary visual culture comes to the elaborate iconographical codings of traditional allegory and religious imagery'.[13]

Another strand of cartoon studies has been inspired by Freudian psychoanalysis and his study of caricature, alongside dreams and jokes, as the product of the unconscious.[14] The major contribution was provided by Ernst Gombrich, for whom psychology and strategies of visual representation, including those of pictorial satire, was a life-time preoccupation. After his early inquiry into the principles of caricature published jointly with Ernst Kris in 1938,[15] he went on to apply Freud's analysis of dreamwork – the process of the formation of dreams out of the repressed desires drawn from the unconscious – to the composition of cartoons. As claimed by Gombrich, cartoons involve the same or similar techniques, such as 'condensation of a complex idea in one striking and memorable image', displacement, degradation, the use of absurdity, as well as the representation by the opposite.[16] Even if Gombrich never used the term 'cartoonwork', the latter fits directly the medium's operational principles outlined in his seminal essay 'The Cartoonist's Armoury'. At the core of it is the 'conscious use of unconscious material'[17] and the borrowing from a multitude of texts, clichés and images that circulate in people's minds, whether innocent or indecent. As if lifted up from the unconscious, cartoons are being adapted as the vehicles of new visual metaphors, suitable for the cartoon's topic. And just as in dreams and jokes, the norms and hierarchies are turned upside down, adults and rulers turned into children or animals, and vice-versa. Almost every cartoon activates a memory of an image which has already been seen, but has been changed and fused with another, its meaning altered and unsettled. As Freud insisted, pleasure comes from the 'rediscovery of what is familiar', when the seemingly unrelated scenes and events are suddenly joined into a new single phrase, be it verbal or visual.[18] The momentary recognition of both the absurdity as well as the ingenuity of this reconfiguration produces satisfaction and understanding. Explaining the ways in which metaphorical condensation works and is trusted by the reader, Gombrich concluded: 'Any comparison that will make the unfamiliar clearer in terms of something more familiar will give us the satisfaction of pretended insight, whatever else it may stir up in us'.[19]

In his last text on the subject, however, published 30 years later, in 1992, Gombrich came up with an entirely new approach to cartoons, closer to cultural studies rather than psychoanalysis. He de-emphasised their standard identification with 'weapons', comparing them instead to 'sermons' which preach to the converted.[20] He now stressed the psychological mechanism of constituting the Self through degrading the Other: 'What is described nowadays as a sense of identity is always buttressed by an assumption of superiority over those who do not belong. It is this function satire has always served, whether we think of images, songs, or merely anecdotes and jokes at the expense of the neighbours'.[21] Gombrich's radical shift reflected the current debates within the interdisciplinary field of caricature and cartoon studies, concerned with their social roles. Whether investigated from the perspective of sociological, historical, media or literary studies, the newspaper cartoon has now been theorised as a constitutive part of a coercive press ritual, the tool of social exclusion which, in the words of Martha Banta, upholds the 'civilised modes of conduct', capable of hiding the defence of the status quo behind the 'etiquettes for anger'.[22]

The 'Danish cartoon war' of 2006 and even more so, the brutal assassination of the journalists of the satirical magazine *Charlie Hebdo* in Paris in 2015 in retaliation for mocking Islam, gave a special urgency to the re-evaluation of the power of the cartoon, its ethics, and its impact in the age of the World Wide Web. A seemingly irresolvable dilemma of incitement to religious hatred versus the right to offend, or, in another guise, cultural racism versus freedom of speech, emerged as the dominant pairs of opposites.[23] From hindsight, it is difficult to deny that, regardless of their essentially critical drive, the 'racism versus freedom' binary is built into the very structure of the political cartoon as a visual medium.[24] Even if cartoons of eastern Europe have never produced a comparable outcry or violence, my approach is informed by this latter perspective, positioning them as statements of consensus, and as visual metaphors 'buttressed by an assumption of superiority over those who do not belong'.[25]

Mr Punch and the Eastern European Group Person

Several journals and newspapers in Europe and America, to include *Simplicissimus*, *L'Assiette au beurre*, *Le cri de Paris*, *Judge* or *Puck*, commented on political conundrums in post-Versailles successor states and in the Balkan countries in the interwar years.[26] It was *Punch*, however, which approached the region as a whole, representing it consistently as an assembly of immature states, best imagined as children in ethnic costumes, troublesome and unruly, or bullied and lectured to, or, at particularly chaotic times, identifiable with untamed animals.[27] The magazine remained faithful to the formula for over 30 years, turning it into the iconic image of the region, applicable both to the small states of the interwar era and, with no changes required, to the Communist Bloc. When picked up by other western European cartoonists during the Cold War (Figure 4.24), it seemed as if the image grasped the 'essence' of this part of Europe, offering the 'timeless' portrayal of the eastern European group person, underdeveloped, multifarious and hence powerless – the sheer anti-thesis of John Bull or Uncle Sam.

One of the longest running satirical magazines, and the inventor of the term 'cartoon', *Punch* belongs also to the most studied journals.[28] The vast majority of *Punch* studies has focused on the wealth of the visual material it contains, examining the magazine's views on the limitless range of issues tackled by its cartoons over 150 years, from wars and family life, art and music, housing and education, to anti-semitism, racism, and gender.[29] The Large Cut, the 'editorial' cartoon signed by the magazine's Principal Cartoonist, was the collaborative product par excellence. It was conceptualised down to the minutest detail, including the title and the caption, by the members of staff and guests invited to the weekly Wednesday dinner in the publishers' office in Bouverie Street. Cartoonists would contribute to the discussion as well but, by and large, their task was reduced to execute the idea which had been approved by the *Punch* Table.[30] Addressing the reader, who was not very likely to desire anything subversive, rebellious, or vulgar,[31] *Punch* appealed to the gentlemanly consensus, mindful of the status quo which should be defended rather than subverted. Distortion, the fundamental strategy of the cartoon, promising critique and hence an insight into a hidden truth, was not *Punch's* preferred *modus operandi*. It was the witty concept, the ingenuity of the translation of a complex topical judgement into an easily legible image, which really mattered. And the subtlety of the invention was not to be compromised by a draftsman's overly aggressive pencil stroke. As a result, all the Large Cuts, from John Tenniel of mid-Victorian times down to Leslie G. Illingworth in the 1950s, look as if they were drawn by the same artist. A Victorian diary of Table-talks confirms the extent to which the cartoons were build up in many arguments concerning their intelligibility and respectability, often in direct reference to earlier Large Cuts.[32] Although no such diary was kept for later periods, the uniformity of draftsmanship as well as the recurring set of visual formulas suggest that similar methods were upheld at least until the 1950s.

Punch provides also an astonishingly fertile ground for examining the ways of drawing eastern Europe. Its volumes from 1841 to 1992 allow for an overview of the changing attitudes towards individual nations of the region during the Victorian era, followed by the region's formation as a community and a political entity during the interwar years, to its 'naturalisation' in the early Cold War period. Significantly, *Punch* cartoons prove that the notion of 'eastern Europe' had not existed before the realignment of powers during the First World War. While the Balkans emerged in *Punch* as a region at the time of the Great Eastern Crisis of the 1870s (Figure 4.2), no 'group portraits' of 'eastern Europeans' occurred in its pages before 1916.[33]

It is difficult to pin down the reasons for *Punch's* 'leadership' in devising the iconic image of eastern Europe, but what must have played a role was a peculiar conflation of academic expertise with the pronounced indifference towards the region on the part of British foreign policy. The relationship between Britain and the Balkans, and between Britain and central Europe, have been the topic of many studies.[34] On the one hand, the very constitution of the New Europe as an assembly of small states had

THE DOGS OF WAR.

Bull A 1. "TAKE CARE, MY MAN! IT MIGHT BE AWK'ARD IF YOU WAS TO LET 'EM LOOSE!"

Figure 4.2 John Tenniel, 'The Dogs of War', *Punch*, 17 June 1876. By permission of Topfoto.

been facilitated by putting them on the map by British academics, geographers, and historians, such as Robert Seton-Watson, discussed in Chapter 2. On the other hand, as has been widely documented, the project had been disavowed by the most prominent British politicians, including Winston Churchill, who kept associating 'the belt of little states we are now calling into being' with gloomy prophecies of extravagant territorial claims, misconduct, and chaos.[35] A senior member of the Foreign Office, Sir George Clerk, responsible for the successor states, went as far as to suggest that 'the whole lot, Czechs, Magyars, Poles, Jugos, Roumanians should be put in a bag and shaken up and handed over to a decent Briton to administer'.[36] For the chief British economist John Maynard Keynes the new nations were a mass of 'greedy, jealous, immature, and economically incomplete, nationalist States', in need to be managed by the League of Nations.[37] A bewildering range of condescending metaphors, such as the 'monstrous' children of Versailles, or the 'mad dog[s] . . . which have to be chained up', used by Churchill, Lloyd George, and other cabinet members, as well as freely disseminated by the daily press, set up the terms and tunes of the discourse.[38] Their persuasiveness affected even Eric Hobsbawm's comparison of 'the national conflicts tearing the continent apart in the 1990s' to 'the 'old chickens of Versailles once again coming home to roost'.[39]

Considering the mechanism of cartoonwork, those tenacious figures of speech provided an ideal material for *Punch* cartoonists. Some of those metaphors had already been explored by the magazine in the past. Since the Victorian era, both the 'mad dogs' and truculent children had been used by *Punch* to explain international conflicts,[40] and had already been applied to the Balkans. In John Tenniel's cartoon of June 1876 (Figure 4.2), drawn during the Great Eastern Crisis, 'the dogs of war' stood for the resurgent nations of the Balkans, Herzegovina, Serbia, Montenegro, and Bosnia, which took up arms against the Ottoman Empire. Pulling forward aggressively to attack the Turkish figure, they could hardly be kept on a leash by a Russian. The latter, always meddling in the affairs of the Orthodox populations in the Balkans, is being advised over the fence by Kaiser Wilhelm I that 'it might be awkward if you was to let 'em loose'.[41] This evaluation of the state of affairs in the Balkans, achieved by means of the dog-walking metaphor, juxtaposed cunningly the vigilance of the western leader to the uncontrollable pugnacity of the 'mad dogs', ready to fight, regardless of the consequences.

The alternative to the dog-walking formula was a somewhat milder scene with a group of misbehaving school boys in a classroom, disciplined by Dame Europa.[42] Turning the politician into a child has been a standard strategy of cartooning to attack the figure of authority and was sometimes applied also to a group of nations.[43] It was introduced to represent the Balkans in Leonard Raven-Hill's cartoon 'The Good Boy of the East' of June 1913. Commenting on the outbreak of the Second Balkan War (Figure 4.1), it shows a fight which erupts between three schoolboys sitting on a bench under a wall-map: a Serbian and a Bulgarian are attacking a Greek minor.[44] Dame Europa, in the role of a headmistress with a cane, is telling them off, while a Turkish child – as 'the good boy of the East', who had already been 'put in the corner' by the Treaty of London which ended the First Balkan War – delivers an articulate statement on his enforced non-involvement: 'I regret that I am not in a position to render any appreciable assistance to your authority'. As in other media, the visual codes manufacturing the regimes of truth about immaturity and violence defining the whole region of eastern Europe were formulated first in relation to the Balkans. According to Patrick Leary, 'some Large Cuts struck the public mind with such force that the events or issues they depicted remained . . . framed by those cartoons for years, or even decades, afterward'.[45] And indeed, 'The Good Boy of the East' initiated a whole series of *Punch* commentaries on conflicts in the larger territory of eastern Europe in the late 1930s, presented under the guise of the classroom formula. By evoking the memory of disciplined children, abundant in Victorian book illustrations as well as cartoons, the classroom formula often demonstratively alluded to its own visual ancestry, reinforcing in this way the 'naturalness' of the didactic message about the hierarchy of identities and ethnicities.[46] The rhetorical language of the politicians was seamlessly interwoven with the evocative metaphors propounded by cartoons, both of them drawing from the multitude of other texts and images, including fairy tales and nursery rhymes,[47] and later, photography and film, inciting each other in a constant process of exchange. The classroom formula formed the kernel of the 'iconographical bubble', which could be blown endlessly at the *Punch* Table while commenting on good and bad boys 'from the East'. Unlike travelogue imagery from Europe's east which was chasing peasant women, in the *Punch* school for eastern European children girls might have entered the classroom occasionally, but would not play any major roles.

'The Göblins Will Get You If You Don't Watch Out!'

The dominant issue was immaturity. Even before the adoption of the classroom formula, the eastern European group person seems to have been born in Bernard Partridge's nesting eggs' cartoon from the time of the Great War. Published in *Punch* in April 1916, it was clearly underpinned by the rising threat of Pangermanism, borrowing Masarýk's successful metaphor, discussed in Chapter 2. A colossal elephant, 'the champion of the smaller nations', was shown as ready to smash the nesting eggs on the ground while declaring its desire to protect them, as explained by the caption (Figure 4.3). The image of 'unprotected' nesting eggs constitutes one of the visual signifiers of the uniform assembly of 'small nations' which are about to hatch, developed in parallel with new cartographic conceptualisations of the New Europe and shared much of its rhetoric. Nominating a foster parent for the eggs which 'want mothering' was to become one of the important topics and would stick to the emerging image of the region, fixing its purportedly submissive nature.

In the world created on the pages of *Punch*, the eastern European group person, once emerged from its nest, turned into a bunch of children, and was to remain a child forever. The rule did not apply to the representation of developments in

THE CHAMPION OF THE SMALLER NATIONS.

Imperial Pachyderm. "OUR HEART GOES OUT TO THESE POOR LITTLE UNPROTECTED EGGS. THEY WANT MOTHERING. WE WILL SIT ON THEM." [*Does so.*]

[With Mr. Punch's apologies to a noble animal.]

Figure 4.3 Bernard Partridge, 'The Champion of the Smaller Nations', *Punch*, 26 April 1916. By permission of Topfoto.

individual countries, such as the Polish-Bolshevik war of 1920 or events during the Second World War.[48] But, when it would come to representing a group of states of the region, the 'pedocratic' regime reigned supreme. Variations were possible as long as the hierarchy between the mature and the immature was maintained. Frank Reynolds's 'The Benevolent Debtor' of 1924 reimagined the immaturity of the new states, their poverty, and dependency on the elder European brothers, representing them as a gang of underage beggars. Dressed in peasant costumes and fur caps, they surround their benefactor Raymond Poincaré who is throwing money into the crowd (Figure 4.4).[49] As explained in a note under the caption, the cartoon targeted the irresponsibility of France which, in spite of its war-debt to England, was lending money to Poland, Romania, and Yugoslavia to support their armament.[50] The boys' squinted eyes as they look up to their patron, elevated on a plinth, add to the sense of disparity between the sun-like west and the backward east, not without an ironic stab at French self-aggrandisement.

Towards the end of the 1930s, the threat of another war which could be ignited in the region, already alluded to in the caption of 'The Benevolent Debtor', was intensified by Germany's claims to *Lebensraum* in the east, and the policy of appeasement adopted by Neville Chamberlain.[51] 'Whose Turn Next?', drawn by Ernest H. Shepard,

THE BENEVOLENT DEBTOR.

M. Poincaré (*distributing largesse to the Little Entente and other new friends*). "THERE YOU ARE, MY BOYS. NOW GO AND BUY YOURSELVES SOME SOLDIERS AND GUNS."

[France has recently lent some eight hundred millions of francs to Poland, Roumania and Yugo-Slavia, to be expended in war-material. The French war-debt to this country, including accrued interest, now amounts to about six hundred millions sterling.]

Figure 4.4 Frank Reynolds, 'The Benevolent Debtor', *Punch*, 9 January 1924. By permission of Topfoto.

WHOSE TURN NEXT?

Dame Europa. "The Göblins will get you if you don't watch out!"

Figure 4.5 Ernest H. Shepard, 'Whose Turn Next?', *Punch*, 18 May 1938. By permission of Topfoto.

the illustrator of *Winnie the Pooh* [1926], on 18 May 1938, responds to the Nazi threat rising after the Anschluss of Austria in March, the first violent breach of the Versailles Treaty (Figure 4.5).[52] It adopts, almost point by point, the composition of 'The Good Boy of the East', copying the class interior with a row of children on a school bench, a map on the wall, and the figure of the headmistress. The school moved from the Balkans to central Europe and is attended collectively by Czechoslovakian, Hungarian, Romanian and Polish children. This time the boys do not fight among themselves but, visibly scared, hold tightly onto each other, their small bodies not unlike that given by Shepard to Christopher Robbin. All of them, however, are dressed in their peasant costumes, their nationality inscribed at the bottom of their aprons. A tablet left on the bench signifies the disappearance of the Austrian boy, and the Czechoslovakian boy is gawking anxiously at the empty space next to him. Instead of the cane, the elderly headmistress Dame Europa brandishes the Treaty of Versailles under her arm, warning the boys: 'The Göblins will get you if you don't watch out!' Referring to the virulent propaganda of Goebbels's and reminding the reader of the decrees of the Versailles agreement, the cartoon addresses the joint statement by Britain and France on the rights of German minorities, issued to Czechoslovakia on the

7th of May 1938.[53] Ironically, the cartoon had directly preceded the May Crisis, when Hitler's troop concentration along the Czechoslovakian border, between 19 and 22 May, made the danger of war imminent. The much maligned map of central Europe which hangs on the classroom wall seems to correspond to the placement of children on the school bench. Their uneasiness and fear strengthen the message of the cartoon which, according to the indictments of the Versailles treaty in the late 1930s, undermines the very legality of their existence and sustains the irrevocability of their subjection to one power or another.

The confrontation between the small bodies of children and a big body of their teacher visualises the same asymmetry of power which had been professed and naturalised by the *Mitteleuropa* or the 'Middle Tier' generations of maps. By giving a prominent role to the map, the cartoon discloses the mechanism of signification, common both to cartography and cartoon-making, which identifies geographical territories with bodies that stand for them, present in virtually all the images discussed in this chapter. Both maps and cartoons metaphorise the relations of power by reverting, ultimately, to the image of the body. The hierarchy of bodies was implied by the sketchy meta-maps of Mackinder, hiding the images of the heroic seamen, the subdued Slavs, and the steppe-loving Asians. The closed configuration of children's bodies standing in *Punch* cartoons for the New Europe was brought up by the same mechanism of metaphorical substitution, which had moulded the map of Europe into the body of the Queen. The class they attend marks their shared territory, and the position of their 'cartographic bodies' approximate their location on the map. As argued earlier, the boundaries between cartography and cartooning blur and disappear as both of them are controlled by the same hierarchy of unequal bodies, imposing a 'natural' obedience of the subjugated and the 'natural' hegemony of a main single player, whose identity could be claimed by various contenders.

Already at that time, the role of the 'natural leader' of the region was given by *Punch* to Hitler, as articulated by two cartoons signed by Partridge. In 'The New Protector', published in December 1938, two urchins, standing for Poland and Hungary, bully a smaller child representing Ruthenia (https://punch.photoshelter.com/image/I00000fwKnrQWj70).[54] The cartoon refers to the events of the so-called Vienna Arbitration, when Czechoslovakia lost the Sudetenland to the Third Reich, and other parts of its territory to Poland and Hungary. The image warns of the pernicious results of violent nationalisms which were said to characterise the unruly successor states, constantly squabbling amongst themselves about their ethnic rights to territories granted to them at Versailles. It also makes clear that those eastern European minors are not ready to settle the matters by themselves, their boisterous behaviour not only encouraging, but indeed calling for the intervention of a new peacemaker, the New Protector, as had already been suggested by Sir George Clerk in 1923.[55] The second cartoon on Hitler's advances in the region appeared just two weeks later, in the Christmas 1938 issue, this time casting the relationship between the self-declared protector and the small states in a novel fashion, under the guise of a scene from *Snow White and the Seven Dwarfs*, Disney's much-loved animated film (Figure 4.6).[56] The latter had been released in London earlier in the same year, beating all records of popularity.[57] The headmistress was now displaced by Snow White, with Hitler's moustache and a swastika lollypop, and the children turned into Disney's dwarfs, identified by names on their funny hats as 'Poly', 'Hungry', 'Juggy', 'Bulgy', 'Roumy', 'Lithy' and 'Czechy'. Their small bodies and a sundry of mimic expressions on their clownish faces, from

—— —— AND THE SEVEN DWARFS

Figure 4.6 Bernard Partridge, '. . . And the Seven Dwarfs', *Punch*, 21 December 1938. By permission of Topfoto.

incapacitation and subordination to fear, grumpiness, or anger, marked the diversity of responses of the eastern European states to Nazi politics. And if the tone of the Snow White fairy tale could not have been further away from the political scene in eastern Europe, the cartoonwork strategy of borrowing from popular cultural texts to drive the argument home worked very well indeed. The critical comment was uttered, the satisfaction from grasping the joke achieved, and laughter, or, at least a knowing smile, was duly induced, but the principles of propriety and ironic detachment did not suffer.

Shepard proved particularly adept in finding alternative sources to reimagine the classroom formula. In his cartoon from August 1940, 'The Balkan Imbroglio' (Figure 4.7), commenting on Hitler's search for allies in south-eastern Europe, he used the much reproduced illustration to Victorian children's book *The Great Panjandrum Himself* by Randolph Caldecott.[58] Caldecott's sequence of illustrations to the classic nonsense poem, a disorderly string of phrases, was an attempt to create sense by reverting to the classic templates of a garden, a street, children, and the schoolmaster. Often reprinted, they provided an ideal breeding ground for cartoonists.[59] 'The Balkan Imbroglio' condensed two of Caldecott's illustrations in the book: that of

THE BALKAN IMBROGLIO

". . . and they all fell to playing the game of catch-as-catch-can, till the gunpowder ran out at the heels of their boots."

Figure 4.7 Ernest H. Shepard, 'The Balkan Imbroglio', *Punch*, 14 August 1940. By permission of Topfoto.

the headmaster falling on the floor while 'playing the game of catch as catch can' with children (https://ufdc.ufl.edu/UF00053691/00001/25j) and that of 'a great she-bear coming up the street, [which] pops its head into the shop' (https://ufdc.ufl.edu/UF00053691/00001/8).[60] By turning the headmaster into Hitler who is about to grab a Romanian boy and by replacing flowers on she-bear's dress by the pattern made of hammer and sickle, Shepard turned well-known Victorian images for children into a dark assessment of the unlikely alliances and shifting relations of power in the Balkans at this stage of WWII.

The smokes of fire emanating from the figures' shoes to match the poem's final line 'till the gunpowder ran out at the heels of their boots' confirm Shepard's willingness to explore all the incongruities of the text and image, outdoing Caldecott. As said earlier, the politics of the region itself encouraged the limitless application of the grotesque as one of the ways of dealing with its complex geography, history, and languages.[61] *Punch* joined the fashion, including satirical texts on 'Blurbia' and 'Boshonia', the dictatorships popping up on the remote peripheries of Europe, where the Latin alphabet produces unpronounceable words, composed of consonants and unintelligible diacritical marks, and where the boundary between the familiar and unfamiliar, between reality and dream, wavers and vanishes.[62] Eastern Europe as drawn by Mr Punch on the eve of WWII was a bunch of unruly boys standing for a map of the faraway countries 'of which we know nothing',[63] the land of the absurd and of nightmares, where borders are in a state of flux, where Snow White is bound to turn into a dictator, and where 'the Göblins will get you if you don't watch out!'

Drawing the Iron Curtain

The Cold War realigned the field substantially. It set up the new protector and it radically enlarged the boundaries of eastern Europe. Translated into an image with a fresh vigour derived from the newly coined figures of speech, this new Eastern Europe, spelled with two upper key 'E's, was reinvented as a constellation of 'satellites' confined behind the 'Iron Curtain'. It was largely in this typically Cold War guise of victimised satellites in which the region entered classroom atlases, history books, and newspapers. If in the interwar period, it had lived its life mostly on the pages of *Punch*, Cold War turned Eastern Europe into a 'universal topic'. Feeding easily into the universal theme of the battle between 'good and evil', it was drawn by an army of cartoonists all over the western world, from David Low in London to Herblock in Washington. While American cartoons tended to focus on the confrontation between the two superpowers, captured Europe attracted much attention in Germany, the Netherlands, France, and Britain. The cartoons of the region by the Dutch journalist Leo Jordaan, working for *Vrij Nederland* and *Het Parool* in the early 1950s, rehearsed a whole range of images suitable for the topics of political subjugation and resistance – from puppetry and satellite planets to over-boiling pots and dissonant orchestras.[64]

David Low, the New Zealand cartoonist active in Britain and author of the memorable visual commentary on the Molotov-Ribbentrop pact and Stalin's invasion of Poland,[65] was particularly alert to issues concerning Eastern Europe, coming up with new visual metaphors. One of the most striking was his 'Look Things in the Face', published as early as October 1945, which used the long-established metaphor of the mirror to comment on the affinities and differences between western and eastern views of democracy (Figure 4.8). While the attribute of the first is a ballot box, the second relies on a heavy volume of Marxist-Leninist doctrine.[66] As argued by David Elliott, who began one of his texts on art in Western and Eastern Europe from discussing this cartoon, 'there is something tentative, even benign, about Low's characterisation of the East – the mirror reflection of ourselves. There are none of the broad cheek bones, slit eyes and low foreheads which became stereotypes of anti-Soviet propaganda. The face and body of the man are the same on both sides; there is only the black patch over the eye'.[67] This was one of the few attempts to personify Eastern Europe just by one body instead of many, giving up on folk dress, and going for the 'generic' male, even if it meant identifying him with *homo sovieticus*. While picking the *Punch* group portrait formula, Low revised it in a number of his cartoons, including a series on Eastern European countries missing out on the Marshall Plan, a big topic in itself in the late 1940s.[68] In September 1945, he came up with an intriguing visualisation of Soviet expansionism, in which the Foreign Minister Molotov, standing in front of a thick curtain, raises it only as much as to show just the dirty boots of people hidden behind it, labelled as Hungary, Romania, and Bulgaria (Figure 4.9).[69] The cartoon, entitled 'Behind the Curtain', comments on the Big Four meeting of foreign secretaries in London, during which Molotov

LOOK THINGS IN THE FACE

Figure 4.8 David Low, 'Look Things in the Face', *London Evening Standard*, 24 October 1945.
 By permission of Solo Syndication.

tried to persuade Ernest Bevin and Joseph Byrnes that the pro-Soviet governments
established in the former Axis states, enjoyed the support of the 'overwhelming
majority of the people of these countries'. The bodies and faces of 'the people' confined behind the curtain are unknown however, and their overwhelming support is
nowhere to be seen. Built on notions of concealment and division associated with
the curtain, Low's cartoon seems to anticipate the gist of Churchill's Iron Curtain
metaphor, providing a pattern to be used by a number of other cartoonists after the
Fulton speech had been delivered in March 1946.[70]

Punch, clearly, had now its competitors, but it retained its leadership in the early
years of the Cold War as one of the most consistent suppliers of images of the region,
while drawing from its existing repertory. This was helped by the continuity of its staff
from between the interwar era down to the 1950s, with Shepard made the Chief Cartoonist in 1945. Due to the unprecedented boom in newspaper sales in Britain during
the 1940s, *Punch* reached the peak of its popularity, selling 175,000 copies in 1948,
which was the highest figure during the long period of its run.[71] It joined the British
press in manufacturing what Tony Shaw has named the 'Cold War consensus'.[72] Its

BEHIND THE CURTAIN

Figure 4.9 David Low, 'Behind the Curtain', *London Evening Standard*, 25 September 1945. By permission of Solo Syndication.

anti-communism was hardly driven by a particular concern for Eastern Europe, but by the deepening apprehension over security in Europe.

The first *Punch* cartoon representing the Iron Curtain, published as late as October 1946, might have been devised in a direct reference to Low's image. In Shepard's cartoon 'In Front of the Curtain', reasserting *Punch*'s high-finish drawing style, Stalin is immaculately dressed. Turned into a show presenter, he assures the invisible audience that 'there's no danger', as if the alarming clouds of smoke were coming not from behind the safety curtain, but from his pipe (Figure 4.10).[73] A piece of paper in front refers to the report by Alexander Werth, the *Sunday Times* correspondent in Moscow, on the possibility of a new war.[74] The cartoon sends a contradictory message, inherent in the Iron Curtain discourse as a whole, uttering both critique as well as endorsement of the division of Europe. The blame for drawing the curtain, marked by the two crossed hammers logo on the top, is put on the Soviets. But what really distresses the western audience is not the question whether it should have been drawn at all, but rather whether it is tight enough. As visualised by *Punch*, the Iron Curtain was an

IN FRONT OF THE CURTAIN
" Please keep your seats—there's no danger."

Figure 4.10 Ernest H. Shepard, 'In Front of the Curtain', *Punch*, 2 February 1946. By permission
of Topfoto.

extension of Mackinder's *cordon sanitaire* policy, a protection against communism, this time provided conveniently by Stalin himself. What mattered was the security of the audience rather than the fate of those locked in behind. A similar rhetoric prevails in other *Punch* cartoons from the end of the 1940s which, almost totally deprived of critical drive, adopt an exalted celebratory mode to derive comfort from the assurance of safety and prosperity guaranteed by the fortress of the 'Western Union', the Truman doctrine of containment, and the Marshall Plan. In 'The Truman Line', published in May 1947, the Cold War border is presented directly as a western-made economic boundary, built from the solid signs of American dollars. Dug into the soil by Truman himself, they are to protect western Europe from any calamity coming from the dark lands behind the forest (Figure 4.11).[75] The desire for the boundary was so strong that Illingworth's cartoon, commenting on the anti-communist riots in Berlin in 1953, drew an imaginary wall between Western and Eastern Germany, built of iron and personified as a policeman with the face of Georgy Malenkov, Stalin's successor at the time (Figure 4.13). *Punch* had designed the Berlin Wall long before it was built.[76]

THE TRUMAN LINE

Figure 4.11 William Sillince, 'The Truman Line', *Punch*, 28 May 1947. By permission of Topfoto.

An urban scenery is the location of another one of Shepard's cartoons, entitled the 'Iron Door', which comments on the communist coup in Czechoslovakia (Figure 4.12).[77] Highly intertextual, it mimics and develops the rhetoric of the Iron Curtain, drawing from a well-established stockpile of anti-bolshevism, as well as from fairy tales, horror stories, and films.[78] A woman in folk dress as the vernacularised personification of Czechoslovakia is being abducted by a Soviet bear. Its presence is signified by voracious paws which grab the victim from behind the open door in the otherwise firmly closed shutter. This is the moment when the female body, in her obligatory ethnic dress, enters the *Punch* imaginarium of Eastern Europe. The persuasiveness of this cartoon stems from the ways in which it metaphorises the act of political assault on the democratically elected socialist government in Czechoslovakia by representing it through the narrative pattern of 'beauty and the beast', present in the Red Riding Hood or the *Murder in the Rue Morgue* scenarios. Masculinist signifying economy reduces the personification of Czechoslovakia to a defenceless victim of sexual abuse, and will resonate in Milan Kundera's much later identification of East Central Europe with the 'kidnapped west'.[79] As in an overdetermined dream, in which its latent elements 'are combined and fused into a single unity',[80] the door pushed ajar in the

THE IRON DOOR

Figure 4.12 Ernest H. Shepard, 'The Iron Door', *Punch*, 3 March 1948. By permission of Topfoto.

middle of the closed shutter, opens the road to the unconscious, to the land behind the forest, to the house of horror, the uncanny world behind the Iron Curtain, which could accommodate socially unacceptable desires. And, as before the war, this world is mostly inhabited by children.

'Believe It or Knout': Mr Punch as Cold Warrior

The classroom and the playground formulas, which were suspended by the *Punch* Table in relation to eastern Europe for the duration of WWII, required just one major change on their return: Hitler and Dame Europa had to be replaced by Stalin and his ministers. The playground metaphor, however, was reworked into a complex cartoon drawn by Shepard in August of 1948 (Figure 4.14).[81] A team of children in ethnic costumes, labelled as Hungary, Czechoslovakia, Yugoslavia, Romania, Bulgaria, and Ukraine, are dancing to the tune of the Soviet Deputy Foreign Minister Andrei Vyshinskii in a walled-up space, with a swing. Entitled 'One Man River', the cartoon comments on the international conference, held in Belgrade in the summer of 1948, which accepted the new Danubian Treaty brought by Vyshinskii from Moscow and

WALLSCAPE WITH FIGURES

A Midsummer Night's Dream.

Figure 4.13 Leslie G. Illingworth, 'Wallscape with Figures', *Punch*, 8 July 1953. By permission
of Topfoto.

was signed without the participation of western delegates.[82] The cartoon's title is a
warning. It paraphrases 'Ol' Man River', a popular American song about the toil
of African-American workers on the Mississippi, which was made famous by the
athlete, singer, and defender of African-American human rights Paul Robeson.[83]
The image poses Vyshinskii, mesmerising the Danubians by playing the balalaika to
the accompaniment of his one-man-band, as 'another Robeson'. Excluded from the
game, Marianne, John Bull, and Uncle Sam are watching the subjugated children
pensively from the top of a high brick wall surrounding the playground, a clear reference to the Iron Curtain. As suggested by Alex Drace-Francis, the setting bears also
a reference to the 'Wall Game', a form of rugby played at Eton College, in which the
spectators watch the ground from the top of a wall. Explaining the topical events in
terms of the familiar, the cartoon invites the viewer on a wit-teasing tour through
the net of floating signifiers just to solicit him or her to the approval of the existing
regimes of truth.

The eastern European school returns with minimal updates, modelled on 'Whose
Turn Next?', borrowing again from Caldecott's *Panjandrum* (https://ufdc.ufl.edu/
UF00053691/00001/1), as well as from David Low.[84] In 'Believe it or knout', drawn

ONE MAN RIVER

Figure 4.14 Ernest H. Shepard, 'One Man River', *Punch*, 25 August 1948. By permission of
Topfoto.

by Shepard's successor Leslie G. Illingworth, a group of schoolboys is being taught
by their new teacher, Stalin, about the origins of the Korean War (Figure 4.15). The
map of central Europe gives way to that of Korea and the book about the rules of
Versailles to a blackboard with a new lesson to be learned. Instead of comprehend-
ing the doctrine of self-determination, they have to internalise a much simpler truth,
namely that 'The warmonger Truman has launched a brutal and unprovoked attack
upon the defenceless peoples of North Korea'. The threat posed by the 'Göblins' is
gone, but the children are now exposed to a new educational practice that relies on the
threat of corporal punishment, the 'Believe it or Knout' rule. The 'threat of the knout'
has functioned as an old signifier of Russia's barbarism,[85] and the boys' hunched
bodies suggest defeat and compliance. They have lost their ethnic dress, having been
put into school uniforms, like prisoners, and they differ from each other only by
hair colour and ethnic labels at the back. A newcomer to the pack, the East German
boy, is already indistinguishable from his peers. Their protruding heads and half-open
mouths connote blank incomprehension.

  Nothing could show better the difference between the imputed submissiveness of
the eastern European group person and the assertiveness of the individual western

BELIEVE IT OR KNOUT

Figure 4.15 Leslie G. Illingworth, 'Believe it or Knout', *Punch*, 12 July 1950. By permission of
Topfoto.

European subject, inscribed in bodily terms, than the comparison between the terri-
fied adolescents on school benches in 'Believe it or Knout' and an image of a boy from
'Western Europe' in another cartoon about the Korean war, titled 'Urgent Request'
(Figure 4.16). The boy is sitting comfortably at home, by a fireplace decorated for
Christmas with holly leaves, while writing a letter to Santa, in which 'Western Europe'
features as the senders' address.[86] He is also seen from the back, almost exactly like
his Eastern European contemporaries, but every detail of his body and dress is marked
as utterly different, testifying to his safe upbringing in a middle-class family, generating his self-assurance and enabling him to take on the agency over his own fate. His
dreams seem to be exclusively motivated by Cold War threats and desires, as he asks
Santa for 'lots of soldiers, airplanes, tanks, ships, and guns', adding in a Post Scriptum
with a chilling sobriety: 'I would like some German soldiers too'. This prematurely
grown-up boy stands for the generic western European subject, as much as the pack of
doleful schoolboys signify the imputed community of passive Eastern Europeans. The
persuasiveness of the cartoon, addressing British homes preparing for Christmas, is
strengthened by the deployment of the master metaphor of the threatened family, the
most effective justification for war. Western Europe is identified with domestic bliss,

URGENT REQUEST

Figure 4.16 Leslie G. Illingworth, 'Urgent Request', *Punch*, 20 December 1950. By permission
        of Topfoto.

material comfort, privilege, and safety, which could be irretrievably lost if it does not
face the forces of evil from outside.[87]

   The policy looking at the world from the perspective of the middle-class lounge
was soon to be radically questioned by a new editor of *Punch*, appointed in 1953 to
improve the already falling subscription numbers. Malcolm Muggeridge became the
first editor of the magazine who grew up in a lower middle-class household and did
not have access to the bound volumes of *Punch* in the family library.[88] In the belief
that humour should 'hurt in order to amuse', instead of convincing the 'English middle
and upper classes . . . that their world remained intact', his goal became the resur-
rection of the early *Punch* radicalism by purifying the magazine from jokes about
'strayed revellers and children with tousled heads saying their prayers'.[89] Not satis-
fied with the formula of polite satire and identifying himself with Mr Punch, whose
'crooked back and enormous nose and minute stature' must induce his 'cantankerous
disposition, with a natural propensity towards disrespect rather than consideration',
Muggeridge injected a large dose of vitriol into *Punch*. He even tried to change the
stale formula of narrative drawings by commissioning more aggressively modern cartoons from Ronald Searle and Norman Mansbridge. Not infrequently, he employed

also artists from Eastern Europe who, like Feliks Topolski, would share the impetus of their strokes with Searle rather than with Illingworth.[90]

Muggeridge differed also from his predecessors by his open involvement in politics. An agent of MI6 and a founder member of the British Society for Cultural Freedom, Muggeridge was closely linked to the *Encounter* and to the activities of the Information Research Department of the British Foreign Office.[91] His passionate anti-communism stemmed from his youthful infatuation with the communist utopia followed by a deep disillusion on his visit to Russia in the 1930s.[92] His anti-Soviet crusade brought special issues of *Punch*, parodying the satirical magazine *Krokodil*,[93] and opposing the official visit of Bulganin and Khrushchev to England in 1956.[94] Muggeridge's support for resistance in Eastern Europe resulted in publishing a cartoon unmasking the Polish leader Gomułka's hypocrisy towards Cardinal Stefan Wyszyński, a unique representation of an Eastern European leader on his own, rather than in a jumble of satellites.[95] As well as chasing Khrushchev, Muggeridge would not hesitate to publish an unflattering portrait of Churchill with a caption calling for his retirement which resulted in the massive cancellations of subscriptions, ending his career at *Punch* in 1957.[96]

Muggeridge wished to get rid of 'cartoons of comic schoolmasters' and replaced children with animals, as in the cartoons in reaction to the Hungarian revolution in the autumn of 1956, drawn by Illingworth. None of these cartoons have titles or captions, thus reducing the means of encoding a message to almost purely visual terms. A novelty was the introduction of the notion of resistance, as in the cartoon which used the metaphor of bear-training by Khrushchev to illustrate the acts of disobedience on the parts of some of the 'satellites'.[97] A month later, another cartoon by Illingworth proposed a more complex comment on the defeat of the Hungarian revolution, when the attention of the world was stolen by the Suez Crisis (Figure 4.17).[98] The cartoon attempts to equate those almost contemporary events unfolding in the autumn of 1956 by returning to the well-worn framework of the school metaphor. It characterises Khrushchev as the 'playground bully' who assaults a Hungarian boy at the back of a classroom. The schoolmistress, however – the role given to the Secretary-General of the United Nations, Dag Hammarskjöld – is totally oblivious of what is going on behind her, as she is fully preoccupied with the task of punishing the three western leaders for their misbehaviour during the Suez Canal affair. David Ben-Gurion of Israel, Guy Mollet, Prime Minister of France, and John Selwyn Lloyd, Foreign Secretary of the United Kingdom are shown as schoolboys ordered to copy the line 'I must not bully'. Egyptian President Gamal Abdul-Nasser watches his fellow pupils with an obvious satisfaction, and the wide grin on his face, as well as his Teddy boy outfit, unmask him as a real bully, who, like Khrushchev, has just got away with it. The cartoon, obviously, blames the United Nations (and Nasser) for the lack of support for Hungary. Alas, the representation of Hungary as a bullied child merely confirmed the old truth about its liability to be bullied, just on the basis of being Eastern European. The cartoon thus asserts, rather than subverts, the post-war security status quo in Europe, based on the principle of limited involvement in the internal affairs of the 'Soviet playground'.

The whole generation of playground and school cartoons discussed in this chapter contributed to maintaining the principle of 'appeasement'.[99] What they helped to generate over the decades, from the 1910s to the 1950s, was the aforementioned 'playground consensus', which justified the existing relations of power. From the late 1950s, Eastern Europe as a topic disappeared from the *Punch* Table. The very last

Figure 4.17 Leslie G. Illingworth, no caption, *Punch*, 28 November 1956. By permission of Topfoto.

playground cartoon, which associated communism with colonialism, '"Now let one of yours go – I dare you!"', was discussed in Chapter 1. By the late 1980s, *Punch* was already unable to compete with a new kind of humour introduced by *Private Eye*, attracting the viewers with its photos of politicians turned into memes, nor with the immediacy of editorial cartoons in daily newspapers. Having helped to invent and defend British identity for more than 150 years, *Punch* closed in April 1992, and it is perhaps just a coincidence that the demise of the magazine was announced soon after the end of the Cold War.[100]

Eastern Europe Strikes Back: Imaging the 'Imperialist Warmonger'

The Cold War was the 'golden age' of the political cartoon industry in Eastern Europe, which was generously supported by the state as one of its major propaganda tools. The dominant visual regimes were imported from Moscow, favouring aggressive deformation over witty comparisons, and, not unlike Muggeridge, following the 'punitive' rather than the 'laughing' type of caricature.[101] The most widespread formula was that of the imperialist warmonger, which served as the image of the western Other. Although often represented as a part of the warmongers' crowd, it did not aim to sum up the truth about a 'western European group person', essentialising *en bloc* the whole of western society. It targeted solely specific individuals, the western politicians deemed responsible for pushing the world onto the brink of war. But, in the same way in which the concept of the 'immature' east confirmed the superiority of the 'civilised' west, the warmonger imagery was a declaration of the moral victory of communism over capitalism. The representation of 'the west' in the eyes of 'the east', or, in other words, the imaging of the western Other in the visual culture of Stalinism, has attracted only limited critical attention.[102] Revisiting the Iron Curtain imagery, this section draws examples from Eastern European satirical journals, while the following one focuses on Poland where, as I want to argue, the overproduction of warmonger cartoons generated a new mode of ironical resistance.

Today virtually extinct, the warmongers discourse marked itself strongly in the new signification system established by the Cold War, among the web of the new terms and tropes of the bipolarised world, such as the Iron Curtain, the Communist Bloc, Soviet Satellites, and so on.[103] Skimming through the headlines and cartoons of the daily press around 1950, glancing over the coffee-table books of political caricatures, or watching old newsreels, confirms the ubiquitous presence of the warmongers in the popular culture of Stalinism. Identified with the 'dragons of our time' to be consumed in the rituals of collective derision, large papier-mâché figures of warmongers were exposed to crowds during the First of May Parades, or were turned into puppets in the communist variation of Punch and Judy shows, screened on television.[104] Nearly every title page of the satirical magazines, from Soviet *Krokodil* to Bulgarian *Starshel*, would include their familiar figures, a rich array of the deformed and contorted bodies and grim faces, individualised through their military attributes.[105] Their caricatures would be instantly denotable as referring to particular politicians, such as the warmonger number one, Sir Winston Churchill (Figure 4.19), as well as Ernest Bevin, George Marshall, Harry Truman, General Douglas MacArthur, Konrad Adenauer, or Marshal Tito and Chiang Kai-Shek.

The term warmonger appears with a prominent lexical differentiation in many European languages, such as *Kriegstreiber* in German or *podzhigatel' voiny* in Russian. In English, it signifies the 'one who traffics in war'; in Slavonic languages, the particle 'monger' is replaced, as in Russian, by a separate word *podzhigatel*, denoting an arsonist. The term became frequent during the interwar years and, even in English, it came to be associated with Winston Churchill, otherwise known for the militancy of his anti-Bolshevik and anti-appeasement campaigns.[106] The origins of the specific post-WWII imagery of the 'warmongering west', however, is linked to Churchill's Iron Curtain speech of March 1946, discussed earlier, which invoked a new Manichean world order based on the confrontation of the two superpowers.[107] It was in Stalin's venomous riposte to the Fulton speech, when Churchill was overtly called a warmonger, a 'follower of Hitler' and a racist who advocates the supremacy of 'English speaking countries'.[108] Stalin's response was reprinted in the people's democracies press, establishing a new paradigm of addressing the former allies in revenge to the new vocabulary launched by Churchill. As commented in *The New York Times*, on March 13, 'the entire Russian propaganda apparatus has opened up a barrage on Mr. Churchill as warmonger'.[109]

Stalin's exegesis of Churchill's prophecy initiated also the new visual regime of looking at Churchill 'and his friends' in such a way as to see them as warmongers. Stalin's words were duly translated from the figurative language into the language of figures by Soviet cartoonists which, from this time onwards, would not represent Churchill in any other way than as warmonger. In Boris Efimov's cartoon 'Performance in Fulton', Stalin's comparison linking Churchill to 'Hitler and his friends' was visualised by the shadows of Hitler and Goebbels cast on the wall behind him, an old cartoonist trick to reveal the real nature of the person (Figure 4.18). The approving grimaces on their faces watching Churchill's performance in front of the microphone suggest the master-pupil relationship, emphasised by the caption 'Churchill and his predecessors'. Churchill's calls for the 'Anglo-Saxon rule of the world' and his accusation of the 'Iron Curtain over Europe' are represented as nothing but war slogans, printed on banners attached to hand grenades, brandished by the warmongering

Figure 4.18 Boris Efimov, 'Performance in Fulton', in B. Efimov, *For the Lasting Peace, Against Warmongers: Drawings by Efimov*, Moscow: Iskusstvo, 1950.

Ofensywa pokoju   Наступление мира

L'offensive de la paix   Peace Offensive

Figure 4.19 Jerzy Zaruba, 'Peace Offensive', 1950, in Jan Lenica, Antoni Marianowicz, and Jan Szeląg, *Polska Karykatura Polityczna*, Warsaw: Czytelnik, 1951. By permission of the Museum of Caricature in Warsaw.

leader. His cigar emitting considerable puffs of smoke characterises Churchill as an arsonist. Apart from the visual wit, it was bodily deformation which was used to its full potential. There was no room for immaculate dress, so diligently observed by *Punch* in cartoons of Stalin. Churchill's heavy body, with a pistol and an outmoded sabre around his waist, is dressed as a child who wants to play war. The sheer obesity of Churchill's body, to cite Efimov's own description, 'like a leather sack filled up to the rim with anger and alcohol', is combined with exasperated and ludicrous movements, improper for a man of his age and posture, who hops on the stage like an old bear dancing in a circus, straddling his legs obnoxiously, and is hardly able to balance his torso on the top of his foot. 'It seems that this massive, inflated toad will burst out of the excessive pressure any second', to quote Efimov again.[110] His head plunged into his torso, the baggy double chin and cheeks over his ridiculous polka dot bow-tie, the furrows on his forehead, the open mouth with a giant cigar and the hardly visible downcast eyes, as well as hair on his hands – the man could hardly have been more repulsive.[111]

Efimov's cartoon of Churchill provided a master image of the western warmonger, a paradigmatic example of a 'punitive' type of caricature practiced in Russia. Maxim Gorki's comparison of caricature to the eye that has ability to spot those twists on the faces of figures of authority, which are difficult to be noticed, and revealing them to the masses of the ordinary 'unarmed' eyes, was habitually quoted in Soviet texts on caricature.[112] This was very much in tune with Freudian analysis of caricature as a technique, which 'brings about degradation, by emphasising in the general impression given by the exalted object a single trait that is comic in itself but was bound to be overlooked . . . By isolating this, a comic effect can be attained which extends in our memory over the whole object'.[113] In the Soviet world, cartoons identified as weapons were meant to be the acts of outright aggression, in other words, the visualisation of the Orwellian 'hate-speech'.

Soviet political caricature as the model of political interpellation was widely disseminated across Eastern Europe by way of travelling exhibitions, as well as luxurious albums of Soviet masters of political cartooning. Efimov's *Za proch'nyi mir, protiv podzhigateley voiny* (For the lasting peace, against warmongers), 1950 and *Kukryniksy's Bredovye Anglo-amerikanizatory* (Mad Anglo-Amerikanisators), 1951 were reprinted with translations in Eastern Germany, Poland, and Romania.[114] Large shows of caricatures of individual peoples' democracies, articles in professional art journals, as well as congresses devoted to political satire, organised in Warsaw, Berlin, Bucharest, and other East European capitals were the means to reproduce the official patterns of the 'vigilant eye', as the caricature was labelled in those years, as well as to enrich the central gaze with novel insights.[115] Every country of the Bloc had at least one major satirical magazine, generously supported by the state. Their long list includes Polish *Szpilki* (Pins), East German *Frischer Wind* (A fresh breeze), Czech *Dikobraz* (Porcupine), Hungarian *Lúdas Matyi* (Goose Boy), Romanian *Urzica* (Nettles), and Bulgarian *Starshel* (Hornet). Except for *Szpilki*, the left-wing journal appearing in Poland since the 1930s, all were established shortly after WWII, some of them reconnecting with the older periodicals of the same names.[116] In all of those journals, a special section was devoted to caricatures produced in the Soviet Union as well as in the brotherly countries, so as to disseminate new catchy concepts.

Warmongers occupied the privileged space, featuring on the magazines' front pages (Figures 4.20 and 4.21), almost invariably represented as being defeated by

Figure 4.20 Jerzy Zaruba, 'Peace Will Win! . . .', *Szpilki*, 19 November 1950. By permission of the Museum of Caricature in Warsaw.

Figure 4.21 Josef Novák, 'Good Morning, Comrade Krokodil!', *Dikobraz*, 23 November 1952.

the defenders of peace, as in medieval battle of virtues and vices. The dialectic of the new communist Self required the image of the Other, and every cartoon of the beastly warmonger implied the image of the 'peace-loving communist Self'. Warmonger and Peace-defender constituted two parts of the same body, always represented through each other. Indeed, peace versus war constituted the dominant binary in Stalinism's signification codes. While the capitalist west was fighting for 'freedom', the communist east would opt for 'peace' as the main slogan of its politics, as in the Polish cartoonist Jerzy Zaruba's 'Peace Offensive', which juxtaposed the international march of peace defenders to the crowd of warmongers fleeing in panic (Figure 4.19).[117] Numerous international congresses, organised on both sides of the Iron Curtain by the World Council for the Defence of Peace, adopted the image of Picasso's famous dove which, designed by the artist as an emblem for the First International Peace Congress in Paris in 1949, was reproduced in millions of copies.[118] On the cover of *Szpilki*, published to celebrate the II World Congress for the Defence of Peace, which had moved in November 1950 from Sheffield to Warsaw, a white dove is chasing down a pack of warmongers so successfully that they are falling off the globe, together with their bombs and top hats (Figure 4.21).[119] By representing warmongers as a group of small and amusing figures, this and other similar cartoons came close to the *Punch* group body formula of Eastern European children in folk dress. The difference was in social classification: while *Punch* children stood for the homogenised Eastern European subject, with social diversification not applicable, the warmongers were associated exclusively with the western political and financial establishment. Ordinary inhabitants of the west, if featured at all, were given the role of fellow travellers, marching in defence of peace.

Satirical journals, fully aware of their agency in the communist propaganda, often represented themselves as fighting against warmongers. The front page of *Dikobraz* celebrated the anniversary of the Soviet Revolution by assembling the logos of the major Eastern European journals as supporting their big brother *Krokodil* in the act of cleansing the world from the warmongers (Figure 4.21).[120] The image provides a chronicle of *Krokodil's* battling with the evils of the world, from its establishment in 1922 at the end of the Civil War in Russia, its contribution to overcoming Hitler, as well as General MacArthur in Korea. Both of the *Dikobraz's* cover, by Josef Novák and that of *Szpilki*, designed by Jerzy Zaruba, are conceptually based on the poster by Victor N. Deni, *Comrade Lenin Cleanses the Earth of Impurities*, of 1920, which supplied the visual matrix for innumerable cartoons and for propaganda imagery over the decades.[121]

The Ketman of the Cartoonist: 'How to Draw and Gain Fame'

The Polish contribution to the warmonger discourse involved many major graphic artists. Their cartoons contain numerous clues pointing to the principle of ironical detachment from the propaganda battles. The toy-like figures of the warmongers and the equal attention given to their shiny top hats and to the bombs in the *Szpilki* cover, already pointed in that direction. Lipiński, equally adroit in the matter of drawing and writing, was the first editor of the journal, the co-author of the first history of Polish caricature, as well as the founder and director of one of the first museums of caricature, established in Warsaw in 1978. Lipiński's memoirs, focussed on the history of his journal, offer a captivating insight into the cartoon industry in Poland and suggest a great deal of subversion towards the dominant visual regimes.[122] And indeed, some of his cartoons could easily be charged for the lack of pathos and ambiguity, undermining the ideological efficiency of caricature. A particularly blatant example of Lipiński's evasive cartooning was his warmongers' puzzle 'Cut and Hang' in the Christmas issue of *Szpilki* of 1950. A double-page drawing, containing 12 images of the leading warmongers whose heads and bodies have been mixed up, challenged the reader to match the heads with the rest of the figures, promising 'valuable book prizes' to the lucky winners.[123]

Unsurprisingly, a number of critics expressed anxiety regarding the sincerity of Lipiński's ideological commitment. The novelist Tadeusz Borowski, the author of a long text on Polish caricature, unmasked him as the 'political humourist' par excellence:

> He cannot dare express the unrelenting hatred against the class enemy. Apart from that, as almost all Polish cartoonists – Lipiński has a contempt for detail, he likes to stylise his figures: hence they are flat, unconvincing. A keen realist . . . for the false aesthetic concepts and the insufficient political discernment – Lipiński frequently slips into formalism and harms his own beautiful talent. Not conducting

his own political studies, the artist is dependable on topics from newspapers, he operates mainly within foreign subjects. . . . The artist stands in the position of the people's revolution, but his aesthetic taste is far away from it. This can lead to the degeneration of his artistic workshop. A pity'.[124]

Borowski was well qualified to unmask Lipiński's double game. He was the tragic character Beta described in Miłosz's *Captive Mind*, a detailed analysis of the Stalinist interpellation of intellectuals. *The Captive Mind*, brought out first in English by the publisher of Bradbury's books on Slaka, Secker & Warburg in 1953,[125] introduced two metaphors which provided a frame to understand the mechanism of domination, obedience, and the strategies of resistance available for the intellectuals of the people's democracies: the Pill of Murti-Bing and the practice of Ketman. The first worked like a tranquiliser; it stood for the Stalinist version of dialectical materialism and was capable of curing intellectuals from their chronic anxieties, bringing serenity as well as oblivion. In effect, it was turning them into loudspeakers of the new society. 'Instead of writing the dissonant music of former days, they composed marches and odes. Instead of painting abstraction as before, they turned out socially useful pictures'.[126]

The method of Ketman, in turn, made it possible to resist the effects of the Pill. Not of Miłosz's invention either, it originated in Persia and was made known in Europe during the nineteenth century through the writings of the otherwise infamous Count de Gobineau, the French diplomat in Persia, promoter of the inequality of races and the concept of white supremacy.[127] While categorically distancing himself from those views, Miłosz quoted at length de Gobineau's writings, finding the Persian practice of Ketman (*Kitman*) strikingly similar to the 'customs cultivated in the countries of the New Faith'. The method consisted of permanent acting and of pretending to preach the New Faith by reciting its various articles in public, while preserving in secrecy one's own beliefs. 'To say something is white when one thinks it black, to smile inwardly when one is outwardly solemn, to hate when one manifests love, to know when one pretends not to know [. . .]. Acting on a comparable scale has not occurred often in the history of the human race'.[128]

Miłosz presented the practice of Ketman as the solely available method of resistance, allowing for the preservation of 'one's own' Self by its denial and by strategic entering the skin of the 'prescribed Self'. While stressing the dangers of Ketman which leads to the traumatic split of the subject and to the confusion between the true and simulated Self, Miłosz also pointed to its advantages. Paradoxically, they are most apparent in comparison with what he described – under the influence of Jean Paul Sartre – as the paralysing freedom of the intellectual in the west, leading to a dispersal of ideas and a continuous malaise. In contrast, the very existence of the 'enclosing fence' helped to generate resistance necessary in the process of finding the core of one's Self.

> In short, Ketman means self-realization *against* something. He who practices Ketman suffers because of the obstacles he meets; but if these obstacles were suddenly to be removed, he would find himself in a void which might perhaps prove much more painful. Internal revolt is sometimes essential to spiritual health, and can create a particular form of happiness. . . . Who knows whether it is not in

man's lack of an internal *core* that the mysterious success of the New Faith and its charm for the intellectual lie?[129]

Miłosz listed many different varieties of Ketman, corresponding to various issues proclaimed by the 'Center', such as the National Ketman, the Ketman of the Revolutionary Purity, or the Aesthetic Ketman. Although Miłosz wrote mainly about poets and writers, his observations could easily be extended to the omnipresent visual propaganda, and with that, to the tropes and tricks of the Ketman of the Cartoonist.

Lipiński mastered the Ketman strategy to the extent that he outlined it openly in his satirical text 'How to Draw and Gain Fame', which appeared unillustrated in the magazine *Prasa Polska* [Polish Press] in March 1954, published by the Association of Polish Journalists. Significantly, the spring 1954 witnessed the first signs of both political and cultural thaw. Addressing his fellow professionals, Lipiński's text was entirely devoted to the satirical 'deconstruction' of the regimes guiding satirical representation of the Self and the Other in Poland, and was targeting in particular the patented ways used by cartoonists in their countless images of warmongers. Although highly self-referential, suspended between ritualistic Stalinist self-critique and ironic dissidence, the text fits in seamlessly with an approved line of criticism, condemning 'schematism' as one of the errors to be overcome in the process of building a truly socialist society. Even while debunking the rules, it pretended to command his fellow cartoonists to obey them:

> Thinking is a difficult thing and sometimes also effort-consuming. Apart from anything else, why should we think about things that have already been thought about. This being so, we look through the yearbooks of satirical magazines, Polish and foreign. We keep browsing as long as we find the concept we have been looking for. What we have to do is only to update the figures. The figures are as follows: warmongers, inner enemies and positive characters. For the drawing of warmongers, there are established rules and practices – in this way we get a double effect: disgust towards warmongers and towards the drawing. . . . If the warmonger has his mouth open – one ought to insert in it a minimal number of teeth, it is highly desirable that the particular teeth would be sharp, as fangs. It is also a good effect if saliva drools from the corner of the mouth. A dollar sign, absolutely, should be inserted into a composition. . . . In some situations a swastika should be added.[130]

Surely, the text was meant to be read *au rebours*, as a parody of 'all the clichés which [were] still lingering here and there' amongst Polish cartoonists. Its Ketman premises were plainly obvious for his fellow journalists in Poland, used to the double-speak of the communist satire. Alas, Lipiński's text was entirely misunderstood by western correspondents who took it literally as an official instruction for Polish cartoonists how to represent the west. Indignant commentaries appeared in the Vienna edition of *New York Herald Tribune* ('Poles Told Cartoons on west must Arouse More Loathing') and in *Le Monde*.[131] For Lipiński all this was too good to be ignored. Not only did he reprint his article in *Szpilki*, but he also devised a new cartoon entitled 'How to Draw and Gain Fame', which now provided a visual comment both to this text and to the inability of the west to read witticism of the east (Figure 4.22).[132]

Figure 4.22 Eryk Lipiński, 'How to Draw and Gain Fame', *Szpilki*, 27 June 1954. By permission of Zuzanna Lipińska and the Museum of Caricature in Warsaw.

Put on top of the page, above his reproduced article and the cut-out from *The New York Herald Tribune*, the cartoon translated into visual terms what has been expressed verbally on the issue of political cartooning. It can be read as a visual commentary not only on the notorious misunderstanding on the east-west axis, but also on the ambiguity of the regimes of representation of Self and Other in the popular culture of Stalinism. Lipiński shows himself in a prison cell, hand-cuffed to his table, with an iron ball fastened to his legs. He is mass producing cartoons of warmongers under surveillance of an armed militiaman behind his back. Although it might seem that by stressing the formulaic nature of the cartoons produced under state command, the image follows exactly Lipiński's misunderstood article and provides the hands-on evidence of state censorship, the cartoon clearly evades such a literal reading. By exaggerating the worn-out signifiers of captivity, such as the figure of an unconvincing militiaman, the ridiculous iron ball and chain, as well as by multiplying the images of warmongers, all of them amusing rather than detestable, the cartoon clearly opts for the Ketman-like derision. Moreover, while underplaying the seriousness of the police state, it pokes fun at the western misinterpretation of the article which had targeted 'schematism' rather than providing schematic formulas.

Importantly, Lipiński's cartoon remained faithful to the principle of intertextual borrowing which he himself advocated. His image provides an obvious reference to Thomas Theodor Heine's self-caricature 'How I Will Be Making My Next Drawing', published on the cover of *Simplicissimus* in 1898 (Figure 4.23).[133] Heine had been sentenced to six months in prison for lampooning the agenda of Kaiser Wilhelm II's visit to Palestine.[134] The cartoon represents the artist himself in prison chained to his working table, surrounded by soldiers with bayonet guns and a priest who embraces him closely from behind while spying on the image he is drawing. Lipiński incorporated almost all the elements of Heine's composition, either repeated verbatim or through equivalents, but there is one major difference which sets the tenor of both caricatures wide apart. While Lipiński's representation of himself obeying the commands of the police state to draw warmongers is ironic, Heine's caricature is heroic. The image Heine is drawing is that of the angry bulldog, the icon of *Simplicissimus*, which reasserts the critical mission of the cartoonist and the political radicalism of the Munich satirical magazine. The seriousness of the drawing which

Figure 4.23 Thomas Theodor Heine, 'How I Will Be Making My Next Drawing', *Simplicissimus*, 2 November 1898.

denunciates the intervention of censorship and the apparatus of prosecution was cryptically challenged by the quotation from Schiller 'Ernst is das Leben, heiter die Kunst' [Life is earnest, art is cheerful].[135] By declaring the unwavering commitment to freedom, Heine's cartoon joined the already established tradition of caricature which declares openly its struggle against censorship, aligning itself with the militant praxis of Daumier and Philipon, the latter also serving prison sentences under the July Monarchy.[136]

Lipiński's cartoon, however, could not have been further from the declaration of heroism and martyrdom. 'How to Draw and Gain Fame' says something entirely opposite. By subscribing to what Nicholas Mirzoeff calls 'a new mantra of visual subjectivity: "I am seen and I see that I am seen"',[137] it pokes fun on prison sentencing and persecution, and withdraws from any outward gestures of political resistance, favouring other forms of satirical persuasion: irony, ambiguity, paradox, and detachment, obliterating the difference between truth and lie. Any truths and solemn declarations were to be put in quotation marks, any existing visual tropes were there to be subverted; any image of the Other contained the projection of the Self. This and many other of Lipiński's cartoons were a mastery of deception, evading both hate speech and didacticism, as well as any instruction, under the multiple veils of irony. 'How to Draw and Gain Fame' summed up the condition of the political cartoonist in the Communist Bloc. Perhaps even more than that. It turned into a meta-image, a visual reflection on the general status of the cartoonist and on the medium of the political caricature which, since James Gillray, had always already been inalienably allied with power.

Of course, Lipiński was not the only cartoonist practising Ketman behind the Iron Curtain. By 1954, irony, deception, and the Aesopian language, blurring the boundaries between enemies and allies, were becoming part and parcel of political satire in Poland and in other countries of the Communist Bloc. It led to the reinvention of the body of the Other but, above all, to a manifest denial of the identification with a collective Eastern European/Internationalist/communist Self.[138]

1989 and Beyond

Since its rise in 1961, the Berlin Wall turned the Iron Curtain discourse into reality, rising to a new signifier of Eastern Europe. It functioned as a peculiar optical device which enabled both to see and un-see the world on the other side, according to the prescribed scopic regimes.[139] It dominated the attention of the media, novelists, filmmakers, and cartoonists, both east and west, long after its destruction and as such deserves a separate comparative study.[140] Apart from the wall, other major political developments within the region, such as the expulsion of Jews from Poland in 1968, the Soviet invasion of Czechoslovakia, the debate on central Europe as 'kidnapped west', or the rise of the Solidarity movement in Poland, most of them making headlines in the western media, did not produce any memorable visual commentaries. The worn-out *Punch* formula of a group of the subjugated individuals in ethnic dress kept returning right until 1989, as in Fritz Behrendt's cartoons in *Frankfurter Allgemeine Zeitung* (Figure 4.24).[141] But the absence of the Sartrean 'fence' also wrought a crisis in the political cartoon world in the former Communist Bloc. The 'return to Europe' project required not only the identification of new enemies, new visual metaphors,

Geburtstagswünsche

Figure 4.24 Fritz Behrendt, 'Birthday Wishes', *Frankfurter Allgemeine Zeitung*, 22 December 1976. By permission of Wolfgang Baaske.

and a new type of humour, but also a total reset of the cartoon industry. Cutting off state subsidies led to massive closures of satirical journals all over eastern Europe. The Romanian *Urzica* ceased its existence in 1989, *Dikobraz* and *Szpilki* in 1990, *Ludás Matyi* in 1993; even *Krokodil*, after ten years of struggle and reduction of the number of issues, closed down eventually in 2008.[142]

The years after 1989 might have put eastern Europe into the limelight in the west, rewriting its histories, reinventing its maps, reassessing its record of human rights, as well as paying unprecedented attention to its contemporary art. But all this attention did not translate into a construction of a new memorable image of the region from the hands of cartoonists.

At the very beginning of the period after the Fall of the Wall, the *Punch* formula was the only one available. It was adopted on the cover of *The Economist* on 25 November 1989, in which a crowd of rowdy figures, drunk and uncouth, celebrating their newly gained freedom with bottles in their hands, in ethnic furs and headgears, storm into a room where the major European leaders are having dinner. The caption 'Gatecrashers' Europe', the topic of the editorial, did not leave any doubt as to whether or not they had been invited (Figure 4.25).[143] Although no longer children, they are immature, unruly, and unpredictable; the peasant dress, as before, confirming their lack of civility. The playground rhetoric had also been lingering for quite a while, reappearing in the tabloid press, as well as in pronouncements of major political players, espousing 'newness', 'smallness', and disloyalty of the new entrants to the old institutions defending European safety and prosperity. This attitude was particularly pronounced during the 1990s secessionist and political conflicts in the post-multicultural society of the former Yugoslavia, when the notion of political immaturity and moral baseness were fixed and historicised as an essential feature of the Balkans. The long debates about the access of East European countries to the international bodies, such as NATO and the European Union, were underpinned by much the same rhetoric, as captured by Steve Bell's cartoon in *The Guardian*, representing Poland, Czech Republic, and Hungary as three cute little bears which are enthusiastically soaring into the air to follow their new protector, the old warmongering eagle, with a distinctly Churchillian grin, cigar-smoking, and blasé (Figure 4.26).[144]

The week preceding the enlargement of the European Union on 1 May 2004, when three East Central European countries were accepted, generated a jumble of rather gloomy cartoons, both combing through the repertory of the established signifiers of eastern European difference and searching for new ones. A twisted bottle of vodka dreaming of the European Union did not incite followers.[145] Another issue was the language difference, difficult to express in visual terms. On the cover of the *Guardian Two*, on 23 April 2004, it was turned into a job advertisement for translators from Slovak, Hungarian, and Lithuanian languages, with an ominous caption warning against the 'multilingual nightmare of the new Europe'.[146] Pocket cartoons by Jonathan Pugh in *The Times*, invariably staged as a conversation of two British persons, prophesised Queen Speech to be delivered in Polish and requiring English subtitles.[147] Scott Clissold's image in the *Sunday Express* (Figure 4.27), showing a bunch of new-born multiples, sweetly asleep and nursed by the Union, while still based on the old *Punch* formula, raised the issue which was to dominate the political controversies of the new millennium, including the infamous Brexit visual propaganda. The Union mother nurse is being warned that the little ones will start teething soon and will join the older babies, already crying uncontrollably, 'Asylum & Migration' and 'Crime'.[148] Predictably, migration from eastern Europe was represented differently by the left- and right-wing press. Austin's pocket cartoon in *The Guardian* saw the 1 May as an opportunity to fill in labour shortages, presenting a crowd of employers seeking plumbers, electricians, and computer programmers among the arrivals from eastern Europe.[149] When Romania and Bulgaria joined the European Union in 2007, both Pugh and Matt in the *Daily Telegraph* let their characters claim that they do not want Romanians and Bulgarians 'coming here and taking Polish jobs'. This was announced both by a British elderly couple by their breakfast table and, in Pugh's cartoon, by two Poles walking in a street (Figure 4.28).[150] In the new millennium, the eastern Europeans can no longer be recognised in the crowd; what matters is their function in the job market hierarchies; their bodies and dress cannot serve as markers of difference any more.

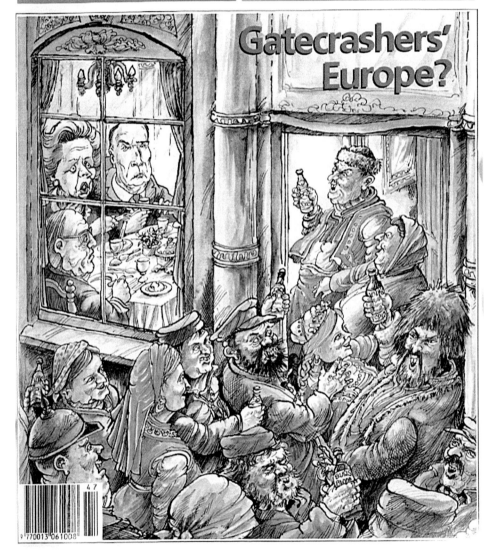

Figure 4.25 'Gatecrashers' Europe', *The Economist*, 25 November–1 December 1989. By permission of *The Economist*.

Figure 4.26 Steve Bell, no caption, *The Guardian*, 9 July 1997. By permission of Steve Bell.

Figure 4.27 Scott Clissold, 'It Might Seem Easy Now, but Wait until They Start Teething', *Sunday Express*, 2 February 2004. By permission of Scott Clissold.

Within the next 15 years, there were plenty of new maps and new books on East Central Europe and the Balkans, as well as plenty of novels, films, and TV documentaries on immigrants from Poland, Ukraine, and Romania,[151] but cartoonists, as it seems, lost their interest. Neither the eastern European fruit pickers, nor even the blatant encroachment on human rights in some of the post-communist countries, their governments' unwillingness to accommodate refugees, the criminalisation of sexual minorities in Hungary and Poland, and the undermining of judicial independence in Poland, have activated the cartoonists' armoury. It seems that as a group person with a set of defining characteristics, 'eastern Europe' is no longer representable in the world of political cartoons: it has vanished as an image. The argument in this book is led by the agency of visual representation. In the past, the travelogues produced the 'timeless' image of the eastern European difference as signified by the ethnic body long before the emergence of the region and, arguably, it has retained its validity until the present. Clearly, the worlds of travel and politics overlap, but they produce different sets of images. Does the disappearance of the visual signifier of the eastern European group person from the political cartoon columns in the contemporary press foreshadow its demise as a political entity? The final chapter focusing on recent book covers will return to this question.

Figure 4.28 Jonathan Pugh, 'You Can't Have Them Coming Here Taking All Our Polish Jobs', drawing, 2007. By permission of Jonathan Pugh.

Notes

1. Katarzyna Murawska-Muthesius, 'On Small Nations and Bullied Children: Mr Punch Draws Eastern Europe', *The Slavonic and East European Review* 84, no. 2 (2006): 279–305.
2. The term 'group person' is a paraphrase of the famous concept of Hobbes's *Leviathan* (1651), visualised in the frontispiece of the book with a torso of a giant sovereign emerging from the landscape, his body composed of tiny figures of his subjects. The term features in discussion of Hobbes's and the strategies and ethics of political representation. Hobbes stressed that 'it is the Unity of the Representer, not the Unity of the Represented, that maketh the Person One'. Thomas Hobbes, *Leviathan* [1651] (Oxford: Clarendon Press, 1929), 126. For 'group person', see David Runciman, 'Hobbes's Theory of Representation: Anti-democratic or Proto-democratic', in Ian Shapiro, Susan C. Stokes, Elisabeth Jean Wood and Alexander S. Kirshner, eds, *Political Representation* (Cambridge and New York: Cambridge University Press, 2009), 15–34.
3. Among recent literature, see especially Martha Banta, *Barbaric Intercourse: Caricature and the Culture of Conduct, 1841–1936* (Chicago and London: Chicago University Press, 2003).
4. Roy Douglas's books are particularly instructive in this approach. Roy Douglas, *Great Nations Still Enchained: The Cartoonists' Vision of Europe 1848–1914* (London: Routledge, 1993) and Roy Douglas, *The Great War 1914–1918: The Cartoonists' Vision* (London and New York: Routledge, 1995).
5. Douglas, *Great Nations Still Enchained*, vii.

6. Ernst H. Gombrich, 'The Cartoonist's Armoury', in *Meditations on a Hobby Horse and Other Essays on the Theory of Art* (London: Phaidon, 1963), 127–42.

7. Martin J. Medhurst and Michael A. DeSousa, 'Political Cartoons as Rhetorical Form: A Taxonomy of Graphic Discourse', *Communication Monographs* 48, no. 3 (1981): 197–236; Janis L. Edwards, *Political Cartoons in the 1988 Presidential Campaign: Image, Metaphor, and Narrative* (New York and London: Garland, 1997).

8. See, among others, Lewis Perry Curtis, *Apes and Angels: The Irishman in Victorian Caricature* (Newton Abbott: David and Charles, 1971); Matthew Baigell, *The Implacable Urge to Defame: Cartoon Jews in the American Press, 1877–1935* (New York: Syracuse University Press, 2017).

9. W.A. Coupe, 'Observations on a Theory of Political Caricature', *Comparative Studies on Society and History* 11, no. 1 (1969): 79–95.

10. On the stylistic radicalism of cartoons and their close relationship to the aesthetics of the avant-garde, see Patricia Leighten, 'The World Turned Upside Down: Modernism and Anarchist Strategies of Inversion in *L'Assiette au beurre*', *The Journal of Modern Periodical Studies* 4, no. 2 (2013): 133–70.

11. Medhurst and DeSousa, 'Political Cartoons as Rhetorical Form'; John Fiske, *Introduction to Communication Studies* [1982] (London and New York: Routledge, 1990), 48–51, 60–63.

12. Peter Wagner, *Reading Iconotexts: From Swift to the French Revolution* (London: Reaktion, 1995).

13. Alex Potts, 'Sign', in Robert S. Nelson and Richard Shiff, eds, *Critical Terms for Art History* (Chicago and London: The University of Chicago Press, 1996), 23. Mieke Bal, 'Basic Instincts and Their Discontents', in Martin Heusser et al., eds, *Text and Visuality* (Amsterdam: Rodopi, 1999) has foregrounded her defence of semiotics in approaching high art with the analysis of a cartoon.

14. Sigmund Freud, *Jokes and Their Relations to the Unconscious* [1905], trans. and ed. by James Strachey, The Penguin Freud Library, vol. 6, ed. Angela Richards (Harmondsworth: Penguin Books, 1991).

15. Ernst Kris and Ernst H. Gombrich, 'The Principles of Caricature', *British Journal of Medical Psychology* 17 (1938): 319–42.

16. Ernst H. Gombrich, 'The Cartoonist's Armoury', in *Meditations on a Hobby Horse and Other Essays on the Theory of Art* (London: Phaidon, 1963), 130.

17. James Sherry, 'Four Modes of Caricature: Reflections Upon a Genre', *Bulletin of Research in the Humanities* 87, no. 1 (1986–87): 59.

18. Freud, *Jokes*, 300; Sherry, 'Four Modes', 43.

19. Gombrich, 'The Cartoonist's Armoury', 131.

20. Ernst H. Gombrich, 'Magic, Myth and Metaphor: Reflections on Pictorial Satire', in *The Uses of Images: Studies in the Social Function of Art and Visual Communication* (London: Phaidon, 1999), 195.

21. Gombrich, 'Magic, Myth and Metaphor', 195.

22. Edwards, *Political Cartoons*, 3–18; Banta, *Barbaric Intercourse*, 231–93.

23. For the Danish cartoon war, see Jytte Klausen, *The Cartoons That Shook the World* (New Haven and London: Yale University Press, 2009); Zygmunt Bauman, 'The Charlie Hebdo Attack and What It Reveals about Society', *Social Europe*, 13 January 2015, www.socialeurope.eu/2015/01/charlie-hebdo/ (accessed 20 January 2015).

24. Katarzyna Murawska-Muthesius, 'The Jyllands Posten Muhammad Cartoons Controversy: Racism and "Cartoonwork" in the Age of the World Wide Web', in Graham Huggan and Ian Law, eds, *Racism, Postcolonialism, Europe* (Liverpool: Liverpool University Press, 2009), 148–61.

25. Gombrich, 'Magic, Myth and Metaphor', 195.

26. It must be noted that an early cartoon representing European states during the Peace conference in Paris as fighting schoolchildren and entitled '*Les enfants terribles*' was published by *Le Cri de Paris* (2 February 1919). Woodrow Wilson, disguised as a teacher, is informed by a French girl in the liberty cap that 'they have already joined the League of Nations', the organisation just approved by the conference. The crowd of children includes a Polish boy in his typical four-pointed *rogatywka* cap beating a German girl with long plaits.

27. Murawska-Muthesius, 'On Small Nations'.
28. It has been the topic of numberless books and articles, focusing on its history: Marion H. Spielmann, *The History of 'Punch'* (London: Cassell and Co., 1895), Richard G.G. Price, *A History of 'Punch'* (London: Collins, 1957), on its role in British social reforms: Richard D. Altick, *Punch: The Lively Youth of a British Institution, 1841–1851* (Columbus: Ohio State University Press, 1997), as well as on its modes of operation: Patrick Leary, *The Punch Brotherhood: Table Talk and Print Culture in Mid-Victorian London* (London: The British Library, 2010); Henry Miller, 'The Problem with *Punch*', *Historical Research* 82 (2009): 285–302. On the origins of the term cartoon, see, Altick, *Punch*, 674–75.
29. This demand was largely generated by *Punch* itself, initiated by the Punch Library of Humour in 1907, and make possible today on the *Punch* archive website *Punch.co.uk*. See, among others, R.F. Foster, *Paddy and Mr. Punch: Connections in Irish and English History* (London: Allen Lane, 1993); Julie Codell, 'Imperial Differences and Culture Clashes in Victorian Periodicals' Visuals: The Case of *Punch*', *Victorian Periodicals Review* 39, no. 4 (2006): 410–28; Tracy J.R. Collins, 'Athletic Fashion, *Punch*, and the Creation of the New Woman', *Victorian Periodicals Review* 43, no. 3 (Fall 2010): 309–35; Dominic Williams, '*Punch* and the Pogroms: Eastern Atrocities in John Tenniel's Political Cartoons, 1876–1896', *RACAR: Revue d'art canadienne / Canadian Art Review* 42, no. 1 (2017): 32–47.
30. Leary, *The 'Punch' Brotherhood*, 35–56.
31. Mark Lemon's remark of the 1850s that 'Punch keeps up by its keeping to the gentlemanly view of things and its being known that Bohemians don't write for it' sounds equally valid for the 1950s – Price, *A History of 'Punch'*, 101; see also Henry J. Miller, 'John Leech and the Shaping of the Victorian Cartoon: The Context of Respectability', *Victorian Periodicals Review* 42, no. 3 (2009): 267–91.
32. Leary, *The 'Punch' Brotherhood*, 35–56.
33. John Tenniel, 'The Dogs of War', *Punch*, 17 June 1876; John Tenniel, 'The New Leg', *Punch*, 6 July 1878. The 'first' cartoon of the successor states, Bernard Partridge, 'The Champion of the Smaller Nations', *Punch*, 26 April 1916. See fig. 4.3.
34. Gábor Bátonyi, *Britain and Central Europe 1918–1933* (Oxford and New York: Oxford University Press, 1999); Eugene Michail, *The British and the Balkans: Forming Images of Foreign Lands 1900–1950* (London and New York: Continuum, 2011).
35. Draft letter of Winston Churchill to Lloyd George, after Bátonyi, 'The "Monstrous Child" of the New Europe', in G. Bátonyi, *Britain and Central Europe*, 10.
36. After Bátonyi, 'The "Monstrous Child"', 13.
37. John Maynard Kenyes, *The Economic Consequences of the Peace* (London: Macmillan, 1920), 248–50.
38. Bátonyi, 'The "Monstrous Child"', 9–17.
39. Eric Hobsbawm, *Age of Extremes: The Short Twentieth Century 1914–1991* (London: Abacus, 1995), 31.
40. Leonard Raven-Hill, 'Discipline', *Punch*, 24 April 1918 (on Alsace-Lorraine, Carl von Habsburg and Kaiser Wilhelm II).
41. Indeed, the Russo-Turkish War (1877–78) was the effect of this conflict.
42. Bernard Partridge, 'Settled', *Punch*, 2 April 1913, in which a Turkish boy is put in the corner of a classroom by Dame Europa.
43. Such as the much quoted cartoon on Lord John Russell condemning the establishment of a Catholic hierarchy in Britain: John Leach, 'This Is the Boy Who Chalked Up "No Popery" and then Ran Away', *Punch* 20 (1851, no date): 119.
44. Leonard Raven-Hill, 'The Good Boy of the East', 4 June 1913, which refers directly to Partridge's 'Settled', see note 42.
45. Leary, *The 'Punch' Brotherhood*, 36.
46. Such as David Low's 'Economy Lesson', *The Star*, 12 January 1926, in the British Cartoons Archive, University of Kent, https://archive.cartoons.ac.uk/GetMultimedia.ashx?db=Catalog&type=default&fname=LSE7355.jpg.
47. On nursery as the source of popular imagination, see Banta, 'War in the Nursery', in *Barbaric Intercourse*, 295–338.
48. Cf. Leonard Raven-Hill, 'The Polish Hug', *Punch*, 13 October 1920.

49. Frank Reynolds, 'The Benevolent Debtor', *Punch*, 9 January 1924.

50. Its caption explains: 'M. Poincaré (distributing largesse to the Little Entente and other new friends). 'There you are, my boys. Now go and buy yourselves some soldiers and guns'. [France has recently lent some eight hundred millions of francs to Poland, Roumania and Yugoslavia, to be expended in war-material. The French war-debt to this country, including accrued interest, now amounts to about six hundred millions sterling.]". See Dragan Bakić, *Britain and Interwar Danubian Europe: Foreign Policy and Security Challenged, 1919–1936* (London and New York: Bloomsbury, 2017), 64.

51. Peter Mellini, '*Not the Guilty Men? Punch* and Appeasement', *History Today* 46 (May 1996): 38–44. See note 63.

52. Ernest H. Shepard, 'Whose Turn Next?', *Punch*, 18 May 1938.

53. Anita J. Prażmowska, *Eastern Europe and the Origins of the Second World War* (Basingstoke: Palgrave Macmillan, 2000), 92–99.

54. Bernard Partridge, 'The New Protector', *Punch*, 7 December 1938.

55. Bátonyi, 'The "Monstrous Child"', 12–13.

56. Bernard Partridge, '. . . and the Seven Dwarfs', *Punch*, 21 December 1938.

57. Annette Kuhn, 'Snow White in 1930s Britain', *Journal of British Cinema and Television* 7, no. 2 (2010): 183–99.

58. Ernest H. Shepard, 'The Balkan Imbroglio', *Punch*, 14 August 1940. Randolph Caldecott, *The Great Panjandrum Himself* (London: George Routledge & Sons, 1885), had responded in turn to the line of eighteenth-century gibberish written by the playwright Samuel Foote, reputedly to test the actor's memory. Wim Tigges, *An Anatomy of Literary Nonsense* (Amsterdam: Rodopi, 1988), 127.

59. David Low, 'The Economy Lesson'.

60. Images available on University of Florida George A. Smalthers Libraries website: https://uflib.ufl.edu/.

61. Wolff, *Inventing Eastern Europe*, 106–15.

62. *Punch*, 4 November 1936 and 23 December 1936.

63. 'How horrible, fantastic, incredible it is that we should be digging trenches and trying on gas-masks here because of a quarrel in a far-away country between people of whom we know nothing'. Neville Chamberlain, BBC radio broadcast, 27 September 1938, in Neville Chamberlain, *In Search of Peace: Speeches, 1937–1938* (London: Hutchinson & Co., 1939), 274–76.

64. Leo Jordaan's cartoons from this period were available on a website, now defunct. A separate study on the image of Eastern Europe in the Cold War press is needed.

65. David Low, 'Rendezvous', *Evening Standard*, 20 September 1939.

66. David Low, 'Look Things in the Face', *Evening Standard*, 24 October 1945. The cartoon of course relies on the formula which had been used by Low in his interwar cartoons.

67. David Elliott, 'Looking Things in the Face', in Bojana Pejić and David Elliott, eds, *After the Wall: Art and Culture in Post-Communist Europe* (Stockholm: Moderna Museet, 1999), 029.

68. David Low, 'Noses Left', *Evening Standard*, 8 July 1947, also Leslie G. Illingworth, no title, *Daily Mail*, 7 January 1947; 23 March 1948.

69. David Low, 'Behind the Curtain', *Evening Standard*, 25 September 1945.

70. Leslie G. Illingworth, no title, *Daily Mail*, 6 March 1946. On cartoons of the Iron Curtain, see Katarzyna Murawska-Muthesius, 'Who Drew the Iron Curtain? Images East and West', in K. Murawska-Muthesius, ed., *Borders in Art: Revisiting 'Kunstgeographie'* (Warsaw: Instytut Sztuki PAN, 2000), 241–48.

71. Archives of *Punch* Cartoon Library (in its former seat in Harrods' Department Store, Knightsbridge, London).

72. Tony Shaw, 'The British Popular Press and the Early Cold War', *History* 83 (1998): 66–85. Alan J. Foster, 'The British Press and the Coming of the Cold War', in Ann Deighton, ed., *Britain and the First Cold War* (Basingstoke and London: Palgrave Macmillan, 1990), 11–31.

73. Ernest H. Shepard, 'In Front of the Curtain', *Punch*, 2 October 1946.

74. J.V. Stalin, 'Replies to Questions Put by Mr. Alexander Werth, Moscow, Correspondent of the *Sunday Times*, 24 September 1946', *Soviet News*, 1947. Quoted after Marxist International Archive, www.marxists.org/reference/archive/stalin/works/1946/09/24.htm.

75. Ernest H. Shepard, 'The Truman Line', *Punch*, 28 May 1947; Ernest H. Shepard, 'The Tower of Safety', 17 March 1948.
76. L.G. Illingworth, 'Wallscape with Figures', *Punch*, 8 July 1953. This cartoon belonged to a long series of *Punch* cartoons, by Partridge, Shepard and Illingworth which, since 1929 have been using Shakespearean wall between two lovers from *A Midsummer Night's Dream* to visualise political separation.
77. Ernest H. Shepard, 'The Iron Door', 3 March 1948.
78. In film-noir of the late 1930s and the 1940s, the door marked the boundary between normality and insanity, such as *The Double Door* (1934); *The Door with Seven Locks* (1940), *Secret Beyond the Door* (1948). A distinctly Cold War genre of spy films, from the late 1940s onwards, identified the world behind the Iron Curtain with deprivation of individual rights: *Iron Curtain* (1948), or, Hitchcock's *Torn Curtain* (1966).
79. Milan Kundera, 'A Kidnapped West or Culture Bows Out', *Granta*, no. 11 (1984): 95–118.
80. Sigmund Freud, 'The Dream-Work', in *The Interpretation of Dreams* [1900, trans. and ed. James Strachey. The Penguin Freud Library, vol. 4. Harmondsworth: Penguin, 1991, 381-651.
81. Ernest H. Shepard, 'One Man River', *Punch*, 25 August 1948.
82. Stanley M. Max, 'Cold War on the Danube: The Belgrade Conference of 1948 and Anglo-American Efforts to Reinternationalize the River', *Diplomatic History* 7, no. 1 (Winter 1983): 57–77.
83. I owe the solving of the cartoon's title to Michał Murawski. On Paul Robeson and 'Ol' Man River', see, J.C. Stewart, ed., *Paul Robeson: Artist and Citizen* (New Brunswick, NJ: Rutgers University Press, 1998).
84. Leslie G. Illingworth, 'Believe It or Knout', *Punch*, 12 July 1950. It is modelled on David Low's cartoon of Churchill giving a lecture on economy to public school boys (see note 46), which in turn had borrowed the scene from the title-page of Caldecott's *Panjandrum*.
85. David Kunzle, 'Gustave Doré's *History of Holy Russia*: Anti-Russian Propaganda from the Crimean War to the Cold War', *The Russian Review* 42, no. 3 (1983): 271–99.
86. Leslie G. Illingworth, 'Urgent Request', *Punch*, 20 December 1950.
87. The cartoon follows a policy of the Information Research Department which was actively engaged in generating the public consensus for a massive rearmament programme during the Korean War, including the remilitarisation of Germany, see Tony Shaw, 'The Information Research Department of the British Foreign Office and the Korean War, 1950–1953', *Journal of Contemporary History* 34 (1999): 263–81.
88. Malcolm Muggeridge, 'Tread Softly, for You Tread on My Jokes', in *Tread Softly, for You Tread on My Jokes* (London: Collins, 1966), 14–15.
89. Muggeridge, 'Tread Softly', 13–22.
90. John Bright-Holmes, ed., *Like It Was: The Diaries of Malcolm Muggeridge* (London: Collins, 1981), 449–81.
91. Frances Stonor Saunders, ed., *The Cultural Cold War: The CIA and the World of Art and Letters* (New York: The New Press, 1990), 174–75.
92. Malcolm Muggeridge, 'America Needs a *Punch*', *Esquire* 49 (April 1958): 59–61.
93. *Punch*, 6 April 1955.
94. *Punch*, 18 April 1956.
95. Leslie G. Illingworth, no title, *Punch*, 19 June 1957. See also Muggeridge's foreword to *A Freedom Within: The Prison Notes of Stefan Cardinal Wyszyński*, trans. Barbara Krzywicki-Herbert and Walter J. Ziemba (London: Hodder and Stoughton, 1985).
96. On the Churchill cartoon by Illingworth, see Ian Hunter, *Malcolm Muggeridge. A Life* (London: Hamilton, 1980), 187–88.
97. Leslie G. Illingworth, no title, *Punch*, 31 October 1956; also L.G. Illingworth, 'Mush!', *Punch*, 20 March 1968.
98. Leslie G. Illingworth, no title, *Punch*, 28 November 1956.
99. Csaba Békés, 'The 1956 Hungarian Revolution and World Politics', Working Paper no. 16, *Cold War International History Project* (Washington, DC: Woodrow Wilson International Center for Scholars, 1996).
100. Re-launched in 1996 by Mohammed Al Fayed, it closed once again in 2002.
101. Coupe, 'Observations on a Theory of Political Caricature'.

102. An exception is György Petéri, ed., *Imagining the West in Eastern Europe and the Soviet Union* (Pittsburgh, PA: University of Pittsburgh Press, 2010). See also, Dagnosław Demski and Kamila Baraniecka-Olszewska, eds, *Images of the Other in Ethnic Caricatures of Central and Eastern Europe* (Warsaw: Institute of Archaeology and Ethnology, 2010).

103. This section is a shortened and updated version of my article 'How to Look at a Warmonger, 'How to See the Self? Imaging the West in Stalinist Cartoons, 1946–1954', in Elwira Grossmann, ed., *Studies in Language, Literature, and Cultural Mythology in Poland: Investigating 'the Other'* (Lewiston-Lampeter, Wales: The Edwin Meller Press, 2002), 227–57.

104. Cf. Polish newsreels registering the 'Trumanillo circus' during the May Day parades – Archives of Wytwórnia Filmów Dokumentalnych i Fabularnych, Kr21/50; Kr 22/51; the warmongers puppets shows by Jerzy Zaruba and Antoni Marianowicz were reproduced in *Świat*, a Polish magazine based on *Life*, throughout 1951.

105. See, John Etty, *Graphic Satire in the Soviet Union: Krokodil's Political Cartoons* (Jackson: University Press of Mississippi, 2019); Eryk Lipiński, *Drzewo szpilkowe* (Warsaw: Czytelnik, 1976).

106. *The Oxford English Dictionary*, ed. John Simpson, 20 vols (Oxford: Clarendon Press, 1989), vol. 19, 918; *Slovar' sovremennogo russkogo iazika*, ed. Vaslili I. Chernyshev, 17 vols (Moscow-Leningrad: Izdatel'stvo Akademii Nauk SSSR, 1948–65), vol. 10 (1963), 358–59. Manfred Werdhorn, 'A Contrarian's Approach to Peace', in James W. Muller, ed., *Churchill as Peacemaker* (Cambridge and New York: Woodrow Wilson Centre Press and Cambridge University Press, 2002), 24–53.

107. Hostetler, 'The Enigmatic Ends of Rhetoric', 1997.

108. Joseph V. Stalin, 'Otvet korrespondentu *Pravdy*', in Robert H. McNeal, ed., *Sochinenia*, 3 vols. (Stanford, CA: The Hoover Institute on War, Revolution and Peace, Stanford University, 1967), vol. 3 (1946–1953), 35–36. English translation of Stalin's answer in *Keesing's Contemporary Archives* (London: Keesing's Publications Limited, 1931– c.1986.), vol. 6, 7793 A.

109. Harbutt, *The Iron Curtain*, 325, n.10.

110. Boris Efimov, *Za prochnyi mir, protiv podzhigatelei voiny. Risunki Bor. Efimova* (Moscow: Gosudarstvennoe Izdatel'stvo Iskusstvo, 1950); Boris Efimov, *Osnovy ponimania karikatury* (Moscow: Izdatel'stvo Akademi Khudozhestv SSSR, 1961), 49–54. On Efimov, see Stephen M. Norris, 'Two Worlds: Boris Efimov, Soviet Political Caricature and the Construction of the Long Cold War', in Aga Skrodzka at al., eds, *The Oxford Handbook of Communist Visual Cultures* (Oxford: Oxford University Press, 2018), 520–41.

111. The cartoon was reproduced in Germany, with German translation of the slogans on the flag, see Winifred Ranke, Katharina Klotz and Wilfried Rogasch, eds, *Deutschland im kalten Krieg 1945 bis 1963* (Berlin: Deutsches Historisches Museum, 1992), 193.

112. Coupe, 'Observations on a Theory of Political Caricature', 89–95. See also L. Shakina, 'Politicheskaia satira', *Iskusstvo*, no. 3 (1950): 29–34.

113. Freud, *Jokes*, 262.

114. Efimov's Za proch'nyi mir was translated into German: Boris Jefimov, *Für einen dauerhaften Frieden – gegen Kriegsbrandstifter: Zeichnungen von Boris Jefimov* (Dresden: Sachsenverlag, 1951), while Kukryniksy's *Bredovye anglo-amerikanizatory* into Polish: Kukryniksy, *Opętani anglo-amerykanizatorzy* (Warsaw: Wydawnictwo MON, 1951). For a Polish edition of contemporary Romanian political caricatures see, S. Collillieux, ed., *Karykatura oręż walki o pokój: Zbiór prac karykaturzystów rumuńskich* (Warsaw: Wydawnictwo MON, 1951). See also Frank Althaus and Mark Sutcliffe, eds, *Drawing the Curtain: The Cold War in Cartoons* (London: Fontanka, 2010).

115. Caricature was called the art of the 'vigilant eye' by Jan Lenica, Antoni Marianowicz and Jan Szeląg, *Polska karykatura polityczna* (Warsaw: Czytelnik, 1951), 5. On the congresses of political satire, see Lipiński, *Drzewo szpilkowe*, 137–49.

116. Etty, *Graphic Satire in the Soviet Union*; Lipiński, *Drzewo szpilkowe*, 10–11.

117. Lenica, Marianowicz, Szeląg, *Polska karykatura polityczna*, non-paginated. 'In the struggle for peace . . . Soviet satirists, as snipers, keep a vigilant eye on imperialist camp. With the unerring shots of their dangerous weapon they strike the warmongers canvassing for a new war.' – Ł. Povolotskaia, 'Politicheskaia satira Kukryniksov', *Iskusstvo*, no. 6 (1949): 35.

118. The Councils' periodical Pour *la Paix*, later *Defense de la Paix* [Polish ed.: *W Obronie Pokoju*, English ed., published in Australia: *Peace*], was published in twelve languages all over the world. Katarzyna Murawska-Muthesius, 'Modernism between Peace and Freedom: Picasso and Others at the Congress of Intellectuals in Wrocław', in David Crowley and Jane Pavitt, eds, *Cold War Modern: Design 1945–1970* (London: V&A Publishing, 2008), 33–41.

119. Jerzy Zaruba, 'Peace Will Win! . . .', *Szpilki* 16, no. 47 (1950). On Sheffield congress, John Jenks, 'Making Peace a Fighting Word', in *British Propaganda and News Media in the Cold War* (Edinburgh: Edinburgh University Press, 2006), 114–31.

120. Josef Novák, 'Good Morning, Comrade Krokodil!', *Dikobraz* 8, no. 47 (1952).

121. Katarzyna Murawska-Muthesius, 'Socialist Realism's Self-Reference? Cartoons on Art, c. 1950', in Susan E. Reid and David Crowley, eds, *Style and Socialism: Modernity and Material Culture in Post-War Eastern Europe* (New York and London: Berg, 2000), 149–67.

122. Lipiński, *Drzewo szpilkowe*; Eryk Lipiński, *Pamiętniki* (Warsaw: Fakt, 1990).

123. Eryk Lipiński, '*Wytnij i powieś*' (Cut and hang), *Szpilki* 16, no. 52 (1950): 4–5, 8.

124. Tadeusz Borowski, 'O postępowych i wstecznych tradycjach karykatury politycznej', *Przegląd Artystyczny*, nos 10–12 (1950): 55–56.

125. Czesław Miłosz, *The Captive Mind*, trans. Jane Zielonko (London: Secker & Warburg, 1953), 111–34. Borowski took his own life in 1951, soon after the publication of his text on caricature. On Borowski, see Tadeusz Drewnowski, ed., *Postal Indiscretions: The Correspondence of Tadeusz Borowski*, trans. by Alicia Nitecki (Evanston, IL: Northwestern University Press, 2007).

126. Miłosz, *Captive Mind*, 5.

127. De Gobineau described the practice of 'kitman' in his *Religions and Philosophies of Central Asia* [1865]. Large parts of the text are translated in Geoffrey Nash, ed., *Comte de Gobineau and Orientalism: Selected Eastern Writings*, trans. Daniel O'Donoghue (New York and London: Routledge, 2009), 111–211, esp. 119–21, 135.

128. Miłosz, *Captive Mind*, 56.

129. Miłosz, *Captive Mind*, 80.

130. Eryk Lipiński, '*Jak rysować i zdobyć sławę*', *Prasa Polska* 8, no. 1 (1954).

131. 'Comment les dessinateurs polonais doivent représenter les hommes d'état occidentaux', *Le Monde*, 28 May 1954; 'À propos des "Consignes" des dessinateurs polonais', *Le Monde*, 5 June 1954. I was not able to locate the text in the *New York Herald Tribune*.

132. Eryk Lipiński, '*Jak rysować i zdobyć sławę*', *Szpilki* 20, no. 26 (1954).

133. Thomas Thedor Heine, 'Wie Ich meine nächste Zeichnung machen werde', *Simplicissimus* 3, no. 34 (1898).

134. According to Hiles, Heine began his six-month sentence in March 1899 – Timothy W. Hiles, *Fin-de-Siècle Munich and the Origins of Simplicissimus* (New York: Peter Lang, 1996), 67.

135. On the interpretation of Schiller's phrase by Theodor Adorno, see Ulrich Plass, *Language and History in Theodor W. Adorno's Notes to Literature* (New York: Routledge, 2007), 175–78.

136. Robert Justin Goldstein, *Censorship of Political Caricature in Nineteenth-Century France* (Kent, OH and London: Kent State University Press, 1989), 27–29. The satirist's heroic commitment to freedom acquires new dimension in the aftermath of the Danish cartoon war and the *Charlie Hebdo* murder. See the website run by the American cartoonist Daryl Cagle, www.cagle.com/news/Muhammad, and http://charliehebdo.fr/en (accessed 20 January 2020).

137. Nicholas Mirzoeff, 'The Subject of Visual Culture', in Mirzoeff, *The Visual Culture Reader* (New York and London: Routledge, 2002), 10.

138. I elaborated on this topic in two articles: '1956 in the Cartoonist's Gaze: Fixing the Eastern European Other and Denying the Eastern European Self', *Third Text* 20, no. 2 (2006): 189–99; 'The Cold-War Traveller's Gaze: Jan Lenica's 1954 Sketchbook of London', in Wendy Bracewell and Alex Drace-Francis, eds, *Under Eastern Eyes: A Comparative Introduction to East European Travel Writing on Europe* (Budapest and New York: CEU Press, 2008), 325–54.

139. I raised this issue in my unpublished paper at the 2009 CAA conference in Los Angeles, 'Techniques of the Cold-War Observer'.

140. Sunil Manghani's *Image Critique and the Fall of the Berlin Wall* (Chicago and London: University of Chicago Press, 2009) covers the post-1989 period.

141. '*Geburtstagwünsche*', and, no caption, *Frankfurter Allgemeine Zeitung* (22 December 1976, 4 January 1990).

142. The exception is the Bulgarian *Starshel* which boasts uninterrupted existence until today.

143. 'Gatecrashers' Europe', *The Economist* 313, no. 7630 (November 1989). I was unable to establish the authorship of this cartoon.

144. Steve Bell, no caption, *The Guardian*, 9 July 1997.

145. *The Guardian*, 29 April 2004.

146. 'The Multilingual Nightmare of Europe', *Guardian Two*, 23 April 2004.

147. Jonathan Pugh, 'I Didn't Catch It All – It Was in Polish with English Subtitles', *The Times*, 7 November 2007.

148. Scott Clissold, 'It Might Seem Easy Now, But Wait Until They Start Teething', *Sunday Express*, 2 May 2004.

149. David Austin, no caption, *The Guardian*, 29 April 2004.

150. Pugh's original caption for this cartoon was revised by *The Times* into 'You Can't Have Romanians and Bulgarians Coming Here and Taking Polish Jobs', *The Times*, 2 January 2007, and was followed by Matt (when Romania and Bulgaria joined the EU), 'I Don't Want Bulgarians and Romanians Coming Over Here Taking Jobs Away from the Poles', *Daily Telegraph*, 26 November 2013.

151. Andaluna Borcila, *American Representations of Post-Communism: Television, Travel Sites, and Post-Cold War Narratives* (London and New York: Routledge, 2014).

5   The Battle of the Dust Jackets

A rare guest in the titles of books before 1910, eastern Europe emerged as the topic of academic studies in the interwar period and grew rapidly at the time of the Cold War. By the 1960s, when covers of political and social studies were greatly emboldened with the work of graphic designers, the vertical cartographical 'portrait' of the region, discussed in Chapter 2, was turned into a veritable logo of the 'lands between' (Figure 5.1). Minimalist and clearly recognisable, not only did it do the job by identifying the book's topic as eastern Europe, but it conveyed, through purely visual means, the message about the separateness of the region. It also confirmed one of the major truth regimes, namely that it is eastern European geography which determines its politics, history, and identity. The ubiquity of the cartographical logo, alongside the red star, and hammer and sickle, ran its course throughout the 1990s, when a novel range of images came to be associated with the region, including now bodies and cities. Throughout the new millennium, when books on eastern Europe are flooding the market, their dust jackets and front covers have emerged as an entirely novel terrain for any studies of the iconosphere of eastern Europe. The previous chapters claimed that the region, as a recognisable image, has been vanishing from maps and newspaper cartoons. This final section argues that the process of reimaging the area shows no signs of winding down, with book covers playing now a major role.

In the 1990s, eastern Europe has risen to one of the most speedily evolving subject areas of academic studies within a great number of disciplines, including history, anthropology, politics, economics, human geography, social and urban studies, literature, art history, and visual culture. New periodicals and new book series, set up by virtually all academic publishers, trace the region's radical makeover from the time of its transition after the Fall of the Wall to the rise of nationalism, ethnic violence, migration to western Europe and, more recently, hostility towards sexual and ethnic minorities. The sheer volume of the publications led bookshops to create shelves dedicated specifically to 'Eastern European History', set apart both from 'European History' and from 'Russian History'. While the vast majority of those new books on East Central Europe are strictly academic and unillustrated, many of them feature images on their covers.

Clearly, many of those books opt for abstract designs, but images, especially those photography-based, are on the rise. This chapter covers the shortest time span in this book, examining the images which are addressed to the narrowest circle of readers, to the fellow authors and their students, who constitute a more clearly defined social strata than the consumers of maps, travel images and cartoons. The significant rise of authors and editors from among eastern European scholars, many of them in diaspora, widens this 'inner dialogue'. It problematises further the distinction between the

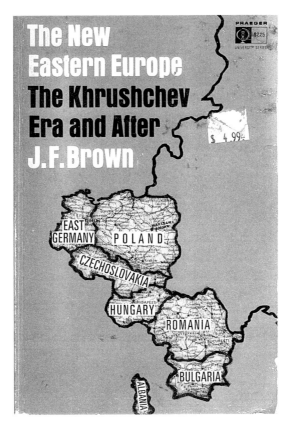

Figure 5.1 Cartographic logo of Eastern Europe, dust jacket. J.F. Brown, *The New Eastern Europe: The Khrushchev Era and After*, New York: Praeger, 1966.

patterns of representation and self-representation, the boundary which had already been entangled and blurred at various times by travel images, cartoons, and media photographs. The collaborative production of the books has also diversified the range of images, breaching the hegemony of photographic agencies, such as Keystone, Hulton, and Getty, and bringing over lesser known pictures from eastern European archives, public and private. By identifying the visual themes which, negotiated by teams of authors, publishers and designers, migrate freely between disciplines, this chapter looks at the continuity of the established tropes, but also at the emergence of the new bodies and spaces, new emphases, and new silences.

Book Covers as Paratexts

Recent research on the materiality of the book draws from the writings of the French literary theorist Gérard Genette. His book *Paratexts* focused on diverse structuring devices, such as 'a title, preface, illustrations' which enable the text to 'become a book and to be offered as such to readers'. Genette compared them to 'thresholds', or, to vestibules 'that offer the world at large the possibility of either stepping inside or turning back'.[1] Both of those metaphors fit particularly well the book cover and the dust jacket, discussed by Genette as the 'publisher's peritext', and defined as the zone 'that exists merely by the fact that a book is published and possibly republished and offered to the public in one or several more or less varied presentations'.[2]

A book's cover has its own history, and the twentieth century brought diverse forms of interaction between it and the dust jacket, which led to the migration of the 'marketing' substance of the latter onto the book's paperback cover and often its hardback cover as well. When discussing the dust jacket, Genette could hardly hide his condescension. 'The most obvious function of the jacket is to attract attention using means even more dramatic than those a cover can or should be permitted', he wrote, and when spelling out those means, he began from 'a garish illustration, a reminder of a film or television adaptation, or simply a graphic presentation more flattering than the cover standards . . . would allow'.[3] The ambiguous status of the detachable dust jacket as an 'advertising space', habitually removed by libraries, has been addressed in several recent studies.[4] Whether looked down upon for its attention-seeking predisposition, or cut off because of its aesthetic autonomy, as a 'part of the story of graphic design rather than the story of the book', the dust jacket is perceived as an alien formation, 'confusing boundaries and muddying the issue what is inside and outside'.[5]

The separateness of the dust jacket is related to its inclusion of images, whether figurative or abstract. While admitting that illustrations constitute 'an immense continent' among paratexts, Genette excluded them from his analysis.[6] He explained that the study of visual paratexts requires special 'technical and iconological skill (think of the illustrations and frontispieces of the classical period)', and thus 'exceeds the means of a plain "literary person"'.[7] By separating the 'classical' illustrations that require interpretive skills from the 'garish' contemporary dust jacket imagery, Genette inadvertently stepped into the shoes of the narrator of Jonathan Swifts's *Battle of the Books*, privileging the ancients over the modern.[8] In response to Genette's inattention to illustrations, a growing community of authors, from early modern scholars to contemporary writers, have stressed the paratextual agency of images, their power to invite or even impel its readers by suggesting 'the modus legendi', as well as helping them to remember the text.[9]

One of the very few examinations of academic book covers has been offered by Corinne Kratz's article 'Telling/Selling the book by its cover'.[10] Reflecting on the increase of the photographic covers in the field of cultural studies, Kratz stressed that 'despite the text-oriented nature of most academic writing', the image functions as 'a diagrammatic representation or summary of the book' in the eyes of both the publishers and the readers.[11] She also compared book covers to 'allegories about power inequalities' and 'moral narratives' which 'promote certain values and a certain vision of the world'.[12] As she argued, the potentially loose relationship between the cover, designed by graphic artists employed by the publishers and the arguments of the author, does not diminish its ability to be interpreted in relation to 'issues urgently relevant in the wider political context of our times'.[13] For the reader of the book, the image on the cover might function as 'motto'. At the same time, it might be dismissed as an alien body, added to the book by the designer and the publisher just in order to attract the buyer. By promising what the book does not offer, as in the case of the *Why Come to Slaka?*, the cover could also mislead the reader. And yet, the slippage between the cover and the text is a record of the first reception of the book, articulated in visual terms by the designer, who searches for the best match within the available stock of images. A figurative book cover constitutes the space in which writing and imaging collide, and in which the first conversation about the book takes place between the author, the publisher, and the designer, and eventually, the reader. To a considerable degree, the image of eastern Europe today is the product of multiple conversations of this kind.

The Battle of the Dust Jackets

The rise of the photography-based covers in cultural studies books in the last decade of the twentieth century coincided with the boom for books on East Central Europe. Functioning in several public spheres, including bookshops, libraries, and internet, they enter the battle for signification and can be subjected, in the same way as the other images in this book, to visual discourse analysis. What follows is an introductory survey of dust jackets and covers, selected from circa 500 academic books about history, politics, economic, society, as well as art in eastern Europe. As in previous chapters, I am focusing first and foremost on the images themselves, rather than on the arguments of the books, but I do consider the latter in order to try and assess the

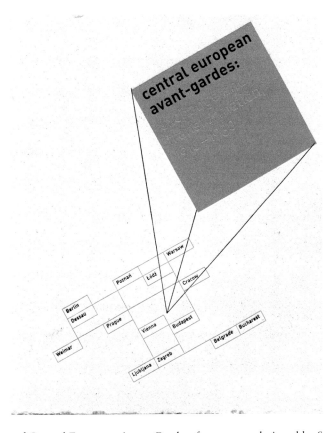

Figure 5.2 Map of Central European Avant-Gardes, front cover, designed by Scott Taylor with Katherine Go. Timothy O. Benson, ed., *Central European Avant-Gardes: Exchange and Transformation*, Los Angeles County Museum of Art/The MIT, 2002. By permission of LACMA.

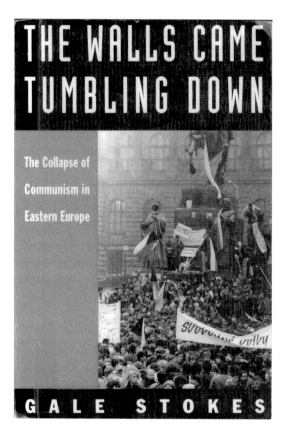

Figure 5.3 Velvet Revolution, 1989, Prague, Václavské Náměstí, dust jacket, photo AP/Wide
World Photos, cover design by David Tran. Gale Stokes, *The Walls Came Tumbling
Down: The Collapse of Communism in Eastern Europe*, Oxford: Oxford University
Press, 1993. By permission of Oxford University Press.

relationship between image and word. Taking clues from Kratz, I approach the covers
as particular kinds of political allegories which, just like cartoons, are intertextual,
borrowing from a plethora of sources. Importantly, they transcend the repertory of
visual themes discussed so far, drawing from the stock of images related to news items
and political iconography, such as protesting crowds and toppled statues, emphasising dissent rather than subordination. When they use the older signifiers of the area
they tend to modify or contradict their meanings, exposing them to a multiplicity of
further readings.

The map has kept its hold as the most obvious signifier of the region. However, the
cheerless cartographic logo of the Cold War period, so effective in disseminating the
notion that eastern Europe was identical with the Communist Bloc, has since been
displaced by very diverse maps of the area, drawn from its cartographic history, reaching back to Ptomely's Sarmatia Europea and Münster's *Cosmography*.[14] An entirely
new generation of the cartographic reconceptualisations of the region emerged in art
books. The cover of the exhibition catalogue *Central European Avant-Gardes* in Los

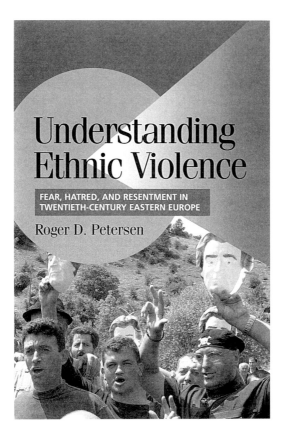

Figure 5.4 Rally of Radovan Karadžić's Supporters, Montenegro, Yugoslavia, front cover, photo
by Milos Bicanski. Roger D. Petersen, *Understanding Ethnic Violence: Fear, Hatred
and Resentment in Twentieth-Century Eastern Europe*, Cambridge: Cambridge
University Press, 2002. By permission of Cambridge University Press.

Angeles County Museum of Art in 2002 literarily reinvented the map, replacing the
cluster of small states with a geometrical grid of East Central European capitals and
art centres, interacting with Russian Constructivism (Figure 5.2).[15] The map expands
horizontally, to include German and Austrian capitals of the avant-garde, as well the
Balkan cities, turning the region into a network of transnational, multicultural, and
cosmopolitan communities, connected with, rather than detached from, the rest of the
continent. United under the shadow-less red square, eastern Europe acquires a new
strong identity, turning into a space of construction and social transformation.

An intense confrontation between old and new takes place when it comes to the use
of the tropes and signifiers of communism, one of the dominant topics of academic
books. After 1989, the old *Punch* formula of eastern Europe as a bunch of children
bullied by dictators is gone entirely, ousted by its opposite, the now ubiquitous image
of protesting bodies in the street and of toppled statues. A typical cover of a book
about the collapse of communism includes a press photograph of an anonymous
crowd with banners over their heads, and a few figures of new leaders, standing on

Figure 5.5 Removal of the Statue of Lenin in Bucharest, front cover, photo by Alfred Yagosladeh, cover design by Leigh Hurlock. *The Revolutions of 1989: Rewriting Histories*, ed. Vladimir Tismaneanu, New York and London: Routledge, 1999. By permission of Routledge.

a pedestal, as in Gale Stokes's *The Walls Came Tumbling Down* of 1993, with the Velvet Revolution protesters which now take hold of Václavské Náměstí in Prague (Figure 5.3), at the same spot which had been captured by *National Geographic* in 1938 (Figure 3.17).[16] The same formula, standing now for the universal allegory of dissent in the region, has also been used to represent the Hungarian Revolution of 1956, as in Ben Fowkes's *The Rise and Fall of Communism in Eastern Europe*.[17] Its ubiquity as a 'master image' of eastern European history has been confirmed by the dust jacket of John Connelly's recent book *From Peoples Into Nations: A History of Eastern Europe*, of 2020.[18]

But the marching crowds are not just the property of the 1956 or the 1989 fighters for democracy. Indeed, as it was briefly signalled in Chapter 4, when discussing eastern European cartoons presenting the communist Self (Figure 4.19), the theme was one of the brand images of the Communist Bloc, in which the street parade with banners was the most recognisable performative formula of the International Communist Movement. However, soon after the collapse of communism, the medium of

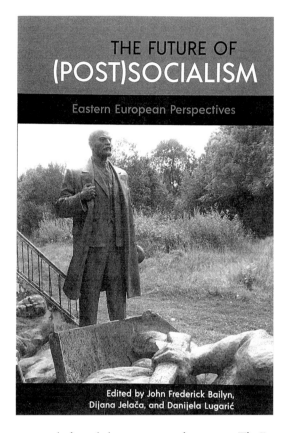

Figure 5.6 Lenin in a graveyard of toppled mounuments, front cover. *The Future of (Post)Socialism: Eastern European Perspectives*, eds John Frederick Bailyn, Dijana Jelača and Danijela Lugarić, State University of New York Press, 2018. By permission of SUNY.

the street parade was now also adopted by far-right groups across eastern Europe to proclaim their nationalist, xenophobic and homophobic agendas. The photo on the cover of Roger D. Petersen's *Understanding Ethnic Violence: Fear, Hatred, and Resentment in Twentieth-Century Eastern Europe*, of 2002, which records a march of the supporters of Radovan Karadžić in Montengro, testifies to the process of this multistage semiosis of the 'protesting bodies' trope (Figure 5.4).[19] It did not stop with the displacement of the notion of political subjugation by that of resistance, but was also associated with ethnic violence and hatred. Whether marked in positive or negative terms, the image of protesting bodies still functions as a fitting signifier of the region and it could be selected for the cover even if a particular photo has nothing to do with the book's contents, as in the case of the storming of the National Assembly building in Sofia on the cover of David King's *Extreme Politics: Nationalism, Violence, and the End of Eastern Europe*, of 2010, which focuses on nationalist riots in Moldova and the Caucasus.[20]

The toppled statues of the communist leaders constitute another common theme on dust jackets, and it, too, has undergone a radical change.[21] The act of their destruction was once unreservedly attached to the notion of historical justice and revenge. An important collection of essays *The Revolutions of 1989: Rewriting Histories* was announced by a photo of the removal of Lenin's statue in Bucharest, zooming onto his head with a rope tied round his neck, aligning the act of 'rewriting histories' with execution (Figure 5.5).[22] Twenty years later, the toppled statue of Lenin no longer serves as a motive for rewriting history but for rethinking it. The cover of *The Future of (Post) Socialism: Eastern European Perspectives*, of 2018, which shows the same variant of Lenin's figure, now photographed among the rubble of other monuments, scattered on the ground and surrounded by weeds, connotes a reflection on the unfinished project of the communist revolution, as suggested by the title of the book, and the telling use of brackets around the prefix 'post' (Figure 5.6).[23]

The landscapes of communism, including architecture, urban planning, fashion, photography, posters, and design, received a new lease of life on the covers of academic books published in the new millennium.[24] Stalinist buildings which, like the Palace of Culture in Warsaw, had been threatened with demolition after 1989, not only became the object of an intense anthropological scrutiny but acquired an aura of stardom.[25] Even blocks of flats, roundly condemned as an epitome of the uniformity of Eastern European cityscapes, are examined as rightful components of the socialist city. Moreover, they are re-evaluated as vehicles of modernity, the latter spelled out on the cover of Nicolas Grospierre's photo reportage on 'modern forms' in twentieth-century architecture (Figure 5.7).[26] Using informal photos from popular magazines and private albums has been a recent strategy for books that focus on socialist commodities and on material culture of people's democracies, marked by nostalgia. This trend has produced many beguiling covers, with socialist cars, shops, fashion, and holiday resorts. They offer a glimpse into the everyday life behind the Iron Curtain, but also show the 'eastern European' body and dress, missing from the images discussed in previous chapters. To quote the review on the back cover of the *Socialist Escapes*, which shows the audience of rock concerts on its front, those kinds of photos testify to 'the possibility of pleasure and fun of living in the socialist world . . . [providing] a much-needed antidote to stereotyped representations of socialism as monotonous, dreary, and dull'.[27]

The rhetoric of the everyday is also a frame which suits the task of the portrayal of the heroes of the democratic opposition. The iconic photograph of a clandestine meetings between the Václav Havel, Adam Michnik, Jacek Kuroń, in the Karkonosze (Krkonoše) Mountains, on the border between Poland and Czechoslovakia in August 1978, has been chosen recently as the cover of the volume *Intellectual Horizons*, in the Routledge *History Handbook of Central and Eastern Europe in the Twentieth Century*, 2020 (Figure 5.8).[28] The photo records a group in their holiday clothes, squeezed together by a narrow picnic table. Havel is speaking while making notes, Michnik with a cigarette in his mouth looks directly to the camera, while Kuroń, in reaction to something that has been said, is pursing his lips. A profile of Antoni Macierewicz, who swerved to the right after 1989, is caught at the end of the table, while the singer of the Czechoslovak Spring, Marta Kubišová, in front of Havel leans towards him, hiding her face from the camera. The original photo was larger, included other figures, and the way in which it has been cropped for the cover coincidentally evokes the famous trio of Marxist ideologues: Marx, Engels, and Lenin. Such a reference is not entirely out of tune, considering the leftist turn of some of the former

Figure 5.7 Nicolas Grospierre, photo of the House of Soviets, Kaliningrad, Russia, 2011, front cover. Nicolas Grospierre, *Modern Forms: A Subjective Atlas of 20th-Century Architecture*, Prestel, 2018. © Nicolas Grospierre. By permission of Prestel.

anti-communist activists, such as Michnik and Kuroń. Notwithstanding the presence of Kubišová, the photo also acts as an index of the conspicuously masculinised makeup of the opposition.

The issue of gender has been another underlying theme of eastern European studies and of the corresponding dust jackets. A collection of articles on *Gender Politics and Everyday Life in State Socialist Eastern and Central Europe*, of 2009, features a photograph of a group of joyful female workers of a Hungarian hosiery factory, taken in front of the factory building, with a star above the cornice (Figure 5.9). The photo was included in the chapter of the book by Eszter Zsófia Tóth, analysing memories of women forming part of the 'Liberation brigade', which won a state prize in 1970.[29] It allowed them to purchase consumer goods otherwise not affordable for low-paid female workers, and the photo was a record of their achievement. While stressing the economic advantages of entering the labour force and acquiring professional identities by women, the book brings attention also to systemic inequality, whether at home or work, shared by women under Socialism. As informal and enlivened by the community spirit as the photo of the opposition leaders in the mountains,

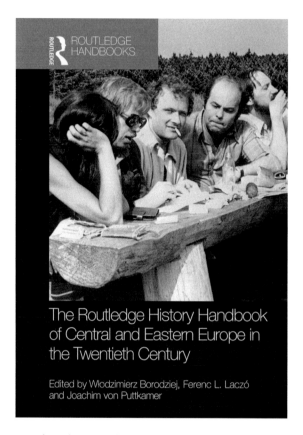

Figure 5.8 A Meeting of Václav Havel, Adam Michnik, Jacek Kuroń, in the Karkonosze
Mountains, front cover, photo by Jiří Bednař. Włodzimierz Borodziej et al., *The
Routledge History Handbook of Central and Eastern Europe in the Twentieth
Century, Vol. 3: Intellectual Horizons*, New York and London: Routledge, 2020. By
permission of Routledge.

the cover belongs to the novel representation of happy people under communism,
not supplied by the political propaganda apparatus, even if undoubtedly informed by
it. The selection of this picture for the cover invites an inquiry into the conditions of
women's emancipation under socialism and has been followed by even more challenging cover designs. The winner among them should be Kristine Ghodsee's book *Why
Women Had Better Sex Under Socialism,* in which the provocative title, spelled in huge
letters across the cover, has been accompanied by a figure of a female javelin thrower,
taken from a Soviet poster of 1947 promoting sport education (www.penguin.co.uk/
books/111/1117204/why-women-have-better-sex-under-socialism/9781529110579.
html).[30] The strength of this iconotext derives from a victorious female body. Interestingly, the choice of a woman athlete is as arbitrary as the Bulgarian Assembly in
relation to the Caucasus, since Ghodsee's book does not discuss sport as an emancipation strategy. Unexpectedly, this gives credit to socialist realist conventions of the
triumphant body, for decades dismissed as laughable by armies of critics.

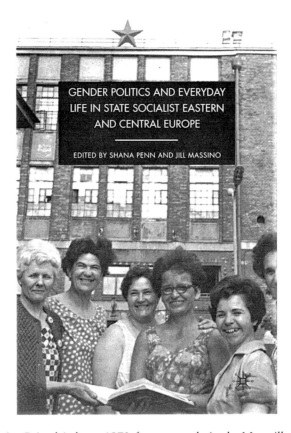

Figure 5.9 'Liberation Brigade' photo, 1970, front cover, design by Macmillan Design Solutions. *Gender Politics and Everyday Life in State Socialist Eastern and Central Europe*, eds Shana Penn and Jill Massino, New York: Palgrave, 2009. Photograph courtesy of Eszter Zsofia Tóth. By permission of Palgrave.

When it comes to books on art in eastern Europe, the scenery and props change dramatically. In art publications and especially in exhibition catalogues, the cover is selected from the list of images which make up the book. In spite of the abundance of images of socialist cities and commodities in history books, socialist realism as the signifier of Eastern European art has not made it to the covers. When it did, on the occasion of exhibitions which focused on socialist realism in individual countries, it featured almost exclusively like a burden of proof in a criminal investigation – framed or drowned by an ominous red, never as evidence of the transnational 'ism'. The absence of studies inquiring into the vicissitudes or the social impact of socialist realism in Eastern Europe speaks of the wholesale refusal to acknowledge it for what it once was, a common denominator of art and visual culture in Eastern Europe. It is difficult not to read this gap as a symptom of what Piotr Piotrowski called 'traumaphobia', the unpreparedness to work through the trauma of the Stalinist experience which affected the art world of the whole of the region.[31]

More recent art book covers are dominated by the body of the artist. The catalogue of the exhibition of eastern European art post-1945, staged at the Centre Pompidou in 2010, shows a frame from a video performance by the Serbian conceptual artist Neša Paripović, which is an image of a jump (Figure 5.10).[32] One may be tempted to compare Paripović's jump to the jump on the cover of *Why Come to Slaka?* Clearly, there is a world of difference between those two books and the jumps themselves, in terms of the category of publications and their dates, the socio-political circumstances of the jumps, their artness, audiences, and the identity of the jumping subjects. They belong to opposing sides of high versus low, mainstream art versus folk binaries, and they differ in terms of class and gender, as well as in the directionality of the jump itself. The jump chosen for the cover of the Centre Pompidou exhibition is a frame from Paripović's experimental film of 1977, *N77*. Even if the viewer does not know the artist, his velvet suit and formal shoes, as well as the townscape around him, stand for professionalism and the middle class.

What these jumps share, however, is the performativity of the act. Also, their selection for the cover made them stand for eastern Europe. As said earlier, the folk jump from the postcard absolutises eastern European culture as folk culture, and promotes

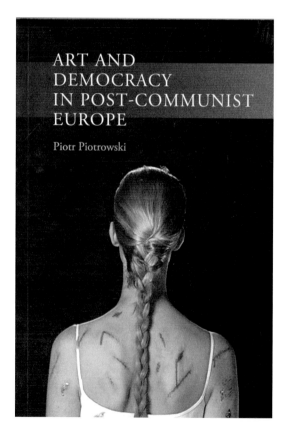

Figure 5.10 Milica Tomić, *I'm Milica Tomić*, 1998, front cover. Piotr Piotrowski, *Art and Democracy in Post-Communist Europe*, London: Reaktion, 2009. © Milica Tomić. By permission of Reaktion.

competitive masculinity as the criterion of excellence. Its placement on a satire of the region makes it hilarious, adequate for the 1980s perception of 'eastern European' culture as the Other. The balcony jump, by contrast, extends horizontally, aiming for an unknown surface ahead, and even if performed by a man, it has nothing excessively masculine about it. Its position on the catalogue of the mainstream exhibition in a major museum forecloses any possibility to read it as a satire. Instead, it connotes anxiety and rebellion. Although it might well have been a purely 'conceptual jump', or it might have been provoked by an unknown existential trauma, its position between two parts of the exhibition title, between the metaphorical 'Promises of the Past' and the subtitle 'A Discontinuous History of Art in Former Eastern Europe', almost automatically turns it into an allegory of a 'political jump', a jump to freedom. Inadvertently, the jumper becomes the figure of the 'eastern European' Self.

The issue of identity and performance is also posed by the cover of Piotr Piotrowski's book *Art and Democracy in Post-Communist Europe*, of 2012 (Figure 5.11).[33] It shows a frame from the 1998 video installation *I am Milica Tomić*, by another Serbian artist who, dressed only in a white petticoat, is observed from the back, her body covered with wounds. Her beauty evokes voyeurism and tempts the reader of any gender

Figure 5.11 Neša Paripović, *NP 77*, front cover. *Promises of the Past: A Discontinuous History of Art in Former Eastern Europe*, eds Christine Macel, Joanna Mytkowska, Zurich: JRP/Ringier/Centre Pompidou, 2010. By permission of JRP/Ringier.

to watch the performance, easily available online.[34] It lasts ten minutes, during which the artist keeps introducing herself in various languages, each time adopting different national and ethnic identity: '*Ich bin Milica Tomić, Ich bin Deutsche; Sono Milica Tomić, sono Italiana; Jestem Milica Tomić, jestem Polką*'. Her imagined identities range widely from European, East European to American, African, and Asian. Young, beautiful, and perfectly composed, she turns round while she speaks, as if not noticing that every time she declares her new identity, her model-like body acquires a new bleeding wound, administered by an invisible hand. At the end, the artist's body is covered in blood, her white gown soiled. The performance declares that not just the imposition of a collective identity, but also its voluntary adoption is an act of violence. Piotrowski grapples with the national and political context of the work. Although Tomić addresses the issue of violence associated with identity in general terms, the viewer is 'trapped', he writes, by an awareness that she is Serbian and that her other works comment on the atrocities of the Yugoslav wars of the 1990s. Referring to Ernesto Laclau, he concedes to a dialectic between the particular as the prerequisite of the universal, both to be found in Tomić's performance.[35] But, by selecting this image of a wounded female body with a long ethnic plait for the cover of the book on art of post-communist Europe, Piotrowski has nominated yet another signifier of the whole region, well-tuned to the discourses on violence, political subjection, and gender oppression.

It is almost impossible to draw conclusions from this exceedingly brief survey of the iconosphere of eastern Europe as created by book covers of last two decades. When juxtaposed to the material discussed in previous chapters of this book, it serves as a test for omissions and exclusions at both ends. It reveals both the themes missed in the book and some absences among the dust jackets. The covers that draw from the media imagery and political iconography devote substantial space to political dissidence which, largely absent in cartography and travelogues', was hardly accounted for in cartoons. Likewise, minorities, ethnic, religious and sexual, constitute another powerful cluster of images which were given an increasing visibility on book covers, but only cursory attention in previous chapters of this book. Representation and self-representation of the LGBTQ communities has indeed become a burning issue at the time of preparing the final version of the manuscript in the summer of 2020, with an unprecedented escalation of violence and harassment targeting non-heterosexual activists and individuals.

There are also significant gaps on the other side, some of them generated by the 'traumaphobic attitude' towards mainstream communist art, to use again Piotrowski's expression, coined in relation to the museum world.[36] But the most notable absentee on book covers in the new millennium is the image of the peasant woman in ethnic dress.[37] And yet, her image has always been one the most recognisable signifiers of the region, and the meaning-making tool at the same time, capable of expressing multiple values, aesthetic, social, national, or regional, as well as transgressing the boundary between the codes of representation and self-representation. She would make a fitting cover for a book on othering eastern Europe, an equivalent of the nineteenth-century orientalist paintings reproduced on paperback editions of Said' *Orientalism*. And, with equal ease, she could announce a book on the eastern European Self. This is the reason for which I have chosen her for the cover of this book. I am using the frame from Katarzyna Perlak's video *I Once Had a Lover* (2016), which I discussed at the end of Chapter 3. *I Once Had a Lover*, which refers to the same sex lover, queers the image of the ethnic body, exploding the notion of folk as the guardian of public decency and status quo, and using it as the tool in the struggle for equal rights and love, liberated from heteronormativity. At first sight, the image does not differ substantially from Hilden-brand's photos in *National Geographic*, or from the media footage accompanying political campaigns. All the major ingredients are there: the young female bodies, the folk dress, and the air of festivity. It is the balaclava masks on the girls' faces which destabilise the image. They identify it as performance and enforce rethinking, that is queering the values associated with it. In Perlak's art, as if taking further the principle of Šafařík's collection of Slavic folk songs and his map of Slavdom, folk culture is the point of departure. However, no longer does it serve the struggle against external domi-nation, but turns into a medium of struggle for equality within, the sheer medium of dissent. It both stands for eastern Europe as an entity, and it queers it, unveiling not just the repressed wants and feelings of fellow individuals, but also multiple mechanisms of repression, inseparable from any adoption and performance of identities.

Notes

1. Gérard Genette, *Paratexts: Thresholds of Interpretation* [1987], trans. Jane E. Lewin (Cam-bridge: Cambridge University Press, 1997), 1–2.
2. Genette, *Paratexts*, 16.
3. Genette, *Paratexts*, 28.
4. Gill Partington, 'Dust Jackets', in Dennis Duncan and Adam Smyth, eds, *Book Parts* (Oxford: Oxford University Press, 2019), 20–22; Thomas Tanselle, *Book-Jackets: Their History, Forms and Use* (Charlottesville: VAL Bibliographical Society of the University of Virginia, 2011); Martin Salisbury, *The Illustrated History of the Dust-Jacket: 1920–1970* (London: Thames and Hudson, 2017).
5. Partington, 'Dust Jackets', 22–23.
6. Genette, *Paratexts*, 406.
7. Genette, *Paratexts*, 406.
8. Jonathan Swift, 'An Account of a Battle Between the Ancient and Modern Books in St. James's Library', in *A Tale of a Tub* (London: John Nutt, 1704).
9. Hester Lees-Jeffries, 'Pictures, Places, and Spaces: Sidney, Wroth, Wilton House, and the *Songe de Poliphile*', in Helen Smith and Louise Wilson, eds, *Renaissance Paratexts* (Cam-bridge: Cambridge University Press, 2011), 197.
10. Corinne Kratz, 'On Telling/Selling a Book by Its Cover', *Cultural Anthropology* 9, no. 2 (May 1994): 179–200.
11. Kratz, 'On Telling/Selling', 179, 187.
12. Kratz, 'On Telling/Selling', 181–82.
13. Kratz, 'On Telling/Selling', 181.
14. Tomasz Zarycki, *Ideologies of Eastness in Central and Eastern Europe* (New York and London: Routledge, 2014); Gerhard Jaritz and Katalin Szende, eds, *Medieval East Central Europe in a Comparative Perspective: From Frontier Zones to Lands in Focus* (London: Routledge, 2016).
15. Timothy O. Benson, ed., *Central European Avant-Gardes: Exchange and Transformation, 1910–1930* (Los Angeles: LACMA, 2002). Cover design by Scott Taylor with Katherine Go.
16. Gale Stokes, *The Walls Came Tumbling Down: The Collapse of Communism in Eastern Europe* (Oxford and New York: Oxford University Press, 1993). Photo came from AP/Wide World Photos agency, cover design by David Tran.
17. Ben Fowkes, *The Rise and Fall of Communism in Eastern Europe* (Basingstoke: Macmil-lan, 1993).
18. John Connelly, *From Peoples Into Nations: A History of Eastern Europe* (Princeton, NJ: Princeton University Press, 2020).
19. Roger D. Petersen, *Understanding Ethnic Violence: Fear, Hatred, and Resentment in Twentieth-Century Eastern Europe* (Cambridge: Cambridge University Press, 2002). AFP photo by Milos Bicanski. Cover design Alice Soloway.

20. David King, *Extreme Politics: Nationalism, Violence, and the End of Eastern Europe* (Oxford: Oxford University Press, 2010).
21. Interestingly, the protests against the public monuments to individuals engaged in the Atlantic slave trade, triggered by the murder of George Floyd in June 2020, as well as the public discussion on the fate of those toppled monuments, point to yet another complex parallel between postcolonialism and post-communism.
22. Vladimir Tismaneanu, ed., *The Revolutions of 1989: Rewriting Histories* (London: Routledge, 1999). Cover photo by Alfred Yagosladeh; cover design by Leigh Hurlock.
23. John Frederick Bailyn, Dijan Jelača, and Danijela Lugarić, eds, *The Future of (Post)Socialism: Eastern European Perspectives* (New York: SUNY, 2018). Date and location of the cover photo unknown.
24. I borrow the phrase from Owen Hatherley's *he Landscapes of Communism* (London: Allen Lane, 2015).
25. Michał Murawski, *The Palace Complex: A Stalinist Skyscraper, Capitalist Warsaw, and a City Transfixed* (Bloomington: Indiana University Press, 2019).
26. Nicolas Grospierre, eds Alona Pardo and Elias Redstone, introduction by Adam Mazur, *Modern Forms: A Subjective Atlas of 20th-Century Architecture* (Munich: Prestel, 2018).
27. Cathleen M. Giustino, Catherine J. Plum and Alexander Vari, eds, *Socialist Escapes: Breaking Away From Ideology and Everyday Routine in Eastern Europe, 1945–1989* (New York: Berghahn, 2013). Photo FORTEPAN.
28. Włodzimierz Borodziej, Ferenc L. Laczó and Joachim von Puttkamer, eds, *The Routledge History Handbook of Central and Eastern Europe in the Twentieth Century, Volume 3: Intellectual Horizons* (London: Routledge, 2020). For the context, see Václav Havel, *An Uncanny Era: Conversations between Václav Havel and Adam Michnik*, edited and translated, and with an introduction by Elżbieta Matynia (New Haven and London: Yale University Press, 2014).
29. Eszter Zsófia Tóth, '"My Work, My Family, and My Car": Women's Memories of Work, Consumerism, and Leisure in Socialist Hungary', in Shana Penn and Jill Massino, eds, *Gender Politics and Everyday Life in State Socialist Eastern and Central Europe* (New York: Palgrave, 2009), 33–44.
30. Kristen R. Ghodsee, *Why Women Had Better Sex Under Socialism* (New York: Nation Books, 2018). Cover design based on the poster by Leonid Golovanov, *Youth – to the stadiums!* 1947.
31. Piotr Piotrowski, 'New Museums in New Europe', in *Art and Democracy in Post-Communist Europe*, trans. Anna Brzyski (London: Reaktion, 2012), 209.
32. Christine Macel and Nataša Petrešin-Bachelez, eds, *Promises of the Past: A Discontinuous History of Art in Former Eastern Europe* (Paris: Centre Georges Pompidou/ Zurich: JRP/ Ringier, 2010).
33. Piotrowski, *Art and Democracy*.
34. Milica Tomić, *I am Milica* Tomić, 1998/99, https://www.youtube.com/watch?v=b1kag FMbQ5k.
35. Piotrowski, 'Between Real Socialism and Nationalism', in *Art and Democracy*, 191.
36. Piotrowski, 'New Museums in New Europe'.
37. An exception is the cover of Bracewell and Drace-Francis, eds, *Under Eastern Eyes*, which includes a Romanian photograph of the 1930s showing a peasant exploring stereoscope viewers frame a fair stall.

6   Farewell to Slaka

Eastern Europe has been defined and redefined many times, and much ink has been spilled on discussing its multiple transformations. In this book, I have argued that the central role in the construction of the region as an entity, political, social, and cultural has been played by images, and in particular by maps, travel illustrations, press cartoons, as well as more recently, by the covers of academic publications. The book gathered in one long and uneven stretch many diverse acts of representing the 'eastern European space' and the 'eastern European body', drawn at different times and by different hands, as well as addressing different audiences.

One of my claims was that the absence of the term 'eastern Europe' did not obstruct the discontinuous process of the formation of its image. It commenced in the early modern era with the rise of cartography, positioning Ptolemy's Sarmatia Europea on the maps of the continent, between Magna Germania, Muscovy, and Tartary, its lands in a state of flux, conquering, and being conquered by neighbouring sovereignties. At that time, the primary role in assembling the iconosphere of Europe's east was played by travellers, followed by ethnographers, and representations of country folk in ethnic dress, originating in the Balkans, were to dominate illustrated reports from the whole region. The production of visual knowledges intensified in the modern period, when new modes of transport and techniques of reproduction led not only to the discovery of the remotest parts of Europe's east, but also to the diversification of its images. The interaction between codes of representation with those of self-fashioning invested the ethnic body with new meanings, turning it into an icon of vernacular craftsmanship as well as of national identities. The radical change came with the collapse of the mighty empires, when the region acquired a name and a new political 'sameness'. Reinstalled on the map as a cluster of the small states of the New Europe, it reached the newspaper pages, inspired novelists, and became the target of cartoonists. Immaturity was now posed as the common denominator, and it was the cartoonists, I have argued, who created a catchy formula of a bunch of children in ethnic dress bullied by the dictators, which has served as a metaphorical portrayal of eastern Europe well until the end of the Cold War. The re-emergence of the region after the Fall of the Berlin Wall meant another shake-up in the repertory of visual signifiers of the region, now represented on the covers of academic books by images of protesting crowds, of modern bodies and, increasingly, by its historical as well as its socialist visual heritage.

Postcolonial theory as well an 'ideologically aware iconology' provided the methodological frame of the book, and the diverse visual codes of the eastern European alterity were clearly among the recurrent themes. At the same time, the issue of the region's otherness, widely debated already, was not the only research agenda of the book, which was also preoccupied with shifts in the range of images standing for eastern Europe at various periods, with their audiences, with the borrowings from nonvisual media, with repetitions, emphases and absences, and with the pliability of the mechanisms of imaging specific to maps, travel imagery, cartoons and book covers.

A major recurring issue was the power of visual technologies, which determined the dissemination of maps and body images. The manuscript maps of Sarmatia Europea could have been known to only a handful of humanists and their patrons; by contrast, Šafařík's counter-map of Slavic Europe of 1842, etched and sold together with his book, gave hope and power to the hundreds of writers and intellectuals across the region at the time when all eastern European nations were deprived of their statehood. Similarly, while the prints of the country woman in Fortis's *Travels Into Dalmatia* responded to the passion for the noble savage cherished by the eighteenth-century European elite, it was *National Geographic's* photographs of peasant women in South-Eastern Europe, Poland, and Czechoslovakia, landing on the coffee tables of millions of its subscribers, which turned the ethnic body into the widely recognised signifier of the region. The atlases of the Cold War period, addressing multinational academic readers, as well as the cartographic cartoons of the Iron Curtain in the daily press, seen by mass audiences, legitimised the binary division of post-1945 Europe. If *Punch* cartoons succeeded in identifying the eastern European group person with the bodies of children, history book covers, addressing a different reader, responded after 1989 with the counter-image of protesting crowds.

What this study has also shown was the interaction between modes of production specific to a variety of mediums, leading to an inquiry into the very mechanisms of imaging. Maps, travel images, cartoons, and book covers make different claims for their cognitive status, and more often than not they abandon their disciplinary boundaries. Maps, such as those of Sarmatia Europea, following the Ptolemaic trapezoidal projection to adjust the three-dimensional space to the flatness of the page, belong to science, but they also tend to deform, exaggerate, and simplify the space in order to make a point, by adopting a mode specific to allegory and caricature, such as Münster's Europe or Chapin's 'Europe from Moscow'. Travel images oscillate between the exercise in primary visualisation, a record of 'rarely or not at all to be met with', to use the words of the scientist Edward Brown, but they also subscribe to well-established visual discourses, repeating the same trope again and again, as in the case of Hildenbrand's photographs of eastern European peasantry for the *National Geographic*. Cartoons cannot exist without visual metaphors that amalgamate a variety of other representations and texts, including maps and travel images, and the borderline between cartoons showing maps and the maps themselves is often impossible to define. The book covers draw from the whole spectrum of images, adopting all kinds of modes, celebratory, critical, satirical, and their separateness from the texts inside confirms the unceasing process of semiosis and strengthens the value of the image as the prime bearer of meaning.

My final claim returns to the question of the autonomy of the image. As repeated many times, this book was preoccupied primarily with the images themselves. Emphatically, it did not aim to 'illustrate' the truths that had already been established by politicians, historians, geographers, and anthropologists. Overlaps were inevitable, of course. In parallel with texts, maps and images of eastern Europe both commented on, and contributed to, the major concerns troubling the region, such as geographical determinism, subordination, instability, underdevelopment, otherness, and epistemic violence. But, they were also an ideal medium not just to record, but to valorise hybridity and encourage resistance. Did the images communicate those issues better or faster, or did they reveal something more about eastern Europe, something which had not been conveyed by texts? The notorious semantic volatility of the iconic sign makes this question difficult to answer, as every image reproduced in the book could be approached in many different ways, depending on the research agenda of the one who asks. What I consider the major result of this study, however, is the realisation of the sheer centrality of the map and the body as the major sites of the production of knowledge about eastern Europe, past and present. Maps not only confined but also spread, they imposed the status quo as well as resisting it; they were at once controlling and counterhegemonic. Most eagerly, they have been used as the 'truthful' portrayal of the region, testifying to its problematic relationship with the rest of Europe. The human body proved to be equally volatile, evolving from the statuesque peasant body in ethnic dress to the homogenised 'group person', to the dissident body, the ethnic minority body, as well as the everyday body.

While noting the recent disappearance of the image of eastern Europe from maps and cartoons, this book does not proclaim the end of the region as such. New images of spaces and bodies are bound to be produced, even if they were going to appear in entirely new spatial configurations of a 'former west' and a new 'global east'. As for now, at the time of finalising this book, it is resistance which, practiced in eastern Europe for centuries, whether against the occupier, or against bouts of social phobias, constitutes the major mode of addressing the region, both from within and without. Even the familiar formula of the ethnic body, or indeed the traditional embroidery pattern, could become the medium of dissidence, of realigning the field rather than reproducing it.

Bibliography

Adamovsky, Ezequiel. *Euro-Orientalism: Liberal Ideology and the Image of Russia in France (c.1740-1880)*. Oxford: Peter Lang, 2006.

'Airlift to Berlin'. Photo Essay. *National Geographic* 95, no. 5 (May 1949): 595–614.

Alloula, Malek. *The Colonial Harem*. Trans. Myrna Godzich and Vlad Godzich. Minneapolis and London: University of Minnesota Press, 1986.

Althaus, Frank and Mark Sutcliffe, eds. *Drawing the Curtain: The Cold War in Cartoons*. London: Fontanka, 2010.

Altick, Richard D. *Punch: The Lively Youth of a British Institution, 1841–1851*. Columbus: Ohio State University Press, 1997.

Alù, Giorgia and Sarah Patricia Hills. 'The Travelling Eye: Reading the Visual in Travel Narratives'. *Studies in Travel Writing* 22, no. 1 (2018): 1–15.

Alù, Giorgia and Sarah Patricia Hill, eds. *Travel Writing and the Visual*. Special issue of *Studies in Travel* Writing 22, no. 1 (2018).

Andrews, J.H. 'Introduction: Meaning, Knowledge and Power in the Map Philosophy of J.B. Harley'. In *Harley, The New Nature of Maps: Essays in the History of Cartography*, ed. Paul Laxton, introduction by J.H. Andrews, 1–32. Baltimore, MD: The John Hopkins University Press, 2001.

Anonymous, 'The Notes on Macedonia'. *National Geographic* 19, no. 11 (November 1908): 790–802

Araeen, Rasheed. 'A New Beginning. Beyond Postcolonial Cultural Theory and Identity Politics'. In *The "Third Text" Reader*, eds Rasheed Araeen, Sean Cubitt and Ziauddin Sardar, 333–45. London: Continuum, 2002.

Aulich, James and Marta Sylvestrová. *Political Posters in Central and Eastern Europe 1945–95*. Manchester and New York: Manchester University Press, 1999.

Babiracki, Patryk and Kenyon Zimmer, eds. *Cold War Crossings: International Travel and Exchange Across the Soviet Bloc, 1940s–1960s*. College Station: Texas A&M University Press, 2014.

Baigell, Matthew. *The Implacable Urge to Defame: Cartoon Jews in the American Press, 1877–1935*. New York: Syracuse University Press, 2017.

Bailyn, John Frederick, Dijan Jelača and Danijela Lugarić, eds. *The Future of (Post)Socialism: Eastern European Perspectives*. New York: SUNY, 2018.

Bakić, Dragan. *Britain and Interwar Danubian Europe: Foreign Policy and Security Challenged, 1919–1936*. London and New York: Bloomsbury, 2017.

Bakić-Hayden, Milica. 'Nesting Orientalisms: The Case of Former Yugoslavia'. *Slavic Review* 54, no. 4 (1995): 917–31.

Bal, Mieke. 'Basic Instincts and Their Discontents'. In *Text and Visuality: Word and Image Interaction*, eds Martin Heusser et al., 13–32. Amsterdam: Rodopi, 1999.

Bałus, Wojciech. 'Mieczysław Porębski: Man and Architecture in the Iconosphere'. In *Re-Humanizing Architecture: New Forms of Community, 1950–1970*, Vol. 1, *East West Central*

Re-Building Europe 1950–1970, eds Ákos Moravánszky and Judith Hopfengärtner, 85–98. Basel: Birkhäuser, 2017.

Banta, Martha. *Barbaric Intercourse: Caricature and the Culture of Conduct, 1841–1936*. Chicago and London: Chicago University Press, 2003.

Barnley, Timothy. *Mapping The Cold War: Cartography and the Framing of America's International Power*. Chapel Hill: The University of North Carolina Press, 2015.

Barron, Roderick M. 'Bringing the Map to Life: European Satirical Maps 1845–1945'. *Belgeo: Revue belge de géographie* 3–4 (2008): 445–64. https://doi.org/10.4000/belgeo.11935.

Bartetzky, Arnold, Marina Dmitrieva and Stefan Troebst, eds. *Neue Staaten – neue Bilder? Visuelle Kultur im Dienst staatlicher Selbstdarstellung in Zentral und Osteuropa seit 1918*. Cologne, Weimar and Vienna: Böhlau Verlag, 2005.

Barthes, Roland. 'The *Blue Guide*'. In *Mythologies*. Essays selected and translated by Anette Lavers, 74–77. London: Vintage, 1993.

Barthes, Roland. 'The Photographic Message'. In *Image, Music, Text*. Essays selected and translated by Stephen Heath, 15–31. London: Fontana Press, 1977.

Barthes, Roland. 'The Rhetoric of the Image'. In *Image, Music, Text*. Essays selected and translated by Stephen Heath, 32–51. London: Fontana Press, 1977.

Bartlett, Djurdja and Pamela Smith, eds. *The Berg Encyclopedia of World Dress and Fashion, Volume 9: East Europe, Russia and the Caucasus*. Oxford: Berg, 2010.

Bartlett, Djurdja. 'Introduction to Dress and Fashion in East Europe, and the Caucasus'. In *The Berg Encyclopedia of World Dress and Fashion, Volume 9: East Europe, Russia and the Caucasus*, eds D. Bartlett and P. Smith, 3–14. Oxford: Berg, 2010.

Bassin, Mark. 'Imperialism and the Nation State in Friedrich Ratzel's Political Geography'. *Progress in Human Geography* 11 (1987): 473–95.

Bátonyi, Gábor. *Britain and Central Europe 1918–1933*. Oxford and New York: Oxford University Press, 1999.

Bauman, Zygmunt. 'The Charlie Hebdo Attack and What It Reveals About Society'. *Social Europe*, 13 January 2015, www.socialeurope.eu/2015/01/charlie-hebdo/.

Beattie, William. *The Danube: Its History, Scenery, and Topography . . . Splendidly Illustrated From Sketches Taken on the Spot, by Abresch, and Drawn by W.H. Bartlett*. London: George Virtue, 1844.

Bechmann Pedersen, Sune and Christian Noack, eds. *Tourism and Travel During the Cold War: Negotiating Tourist Experiences Across the Iron Curtain*. New York and London: Routledge, 2019.

Beck, Paul, Edward Mast and Perry Tapper. *The History of Eastern Europe for Beginners*. New York and London: Writers and Readers Publishing, 1997.

Békés, Csaba. 'The 1956 Hungarian Revolution and World Politics'. Working Paper no. 16. *Cold War International History Project*. Washington, DC: Woodrow Wilson International Center for Scholars, 1996.

Benson, Timothy O., ed. *Central European Avant-Gardes: Exchange and Transformation, 1910–1930*. Los Angeles: LACMA, 2002.

Berghaus, Heinrich. *Physikalischer Atlas*. Gotha: J. Peters, 1848.

Berghaus, Heinrich, ed. *Physikalischer Atlas: 75 Karten in sieben Abteilungen: enthaltend 514 Darstellungen über Geologie, Hydrographie, Meteorologie . . . begründet 1836 durch Heinrich Berghaus vollständig neu bearbeitet und unter Mitwirkung von Oscar Drude [et al.]*. Gotha: Justus Perthes, 1892.

Białostocki, Jan. *The Messsage of Images: Studies in the History of Art*. Vienna: IRSA, 1988.

Bideleux, Robert and Ian Jeffries. *A History of Eastern Europe: Crisis and Change*. London and New York: Routledge, 1998.

Bill, Stanley. 'Seeking the Authentic: Polish Culture and the Nature of Postcolonial'. *Nonsite.org* (Online Journal in the Humanities), no. 12 (August 2014).

Binder, Pearl. 'Popular Art in Poland'. *Geographical Magazine* 33, no. 3 (July 1960): 159–72.

Bjelić, Dušan I. and Obrad Savić, eds. *Balkan as Metaphor: Between Globalization and Fragmentation*. Cambridge, MA: The MIT Press, 2002.

Black, Jeremy. *Maps and History: Constructing the Image of the Past*. New Haven and London: Yale University Press, 1997.

Black, Jeremy. *Maps and Politics*. London: Reaktion, 2000.

Blakemore, Michael J. and J.B. Harley. 'Concepts in the History of Cartography: A Review and Perspective', ed. Edward H. Dahl. *Cartographica* 17, no. 4 (1980): 76–86.

Bohlen, Charles E. *Witness to History, 1929–1969*. New York: Norton, 1973.

Bökös, Borbála. 'Representations of Hungary and Transylvania in John Paget's Travelogue'. *Acta Universitatis Sapientiae, Philologica* 9, no. 1 (2017): 87–98.

Boner, Charles. *Siebenbürgen. Land und Leute*. Leipzig: J.J. Weber, 1868.

Boner, Charles. *Transylvania; Its Products and Its People*. London: Longmans, Green, Reader, and Dyer, 1865.

Bonnett, A. 'Geography as the World Discipline: Connecting Popular and Academic Geographical Imaginations'. *Area* 35 (2003): 55–63.

Borcila, Andaluna. *American Representations of Post-Communism: Television, Travel Sites, and Post-Cold War Narratives*. London and New York: Routledge, 2014.

Borodziej, Włodzimierz, Ferenc L. Laczó and Joachim von Puttkamer, eds. *The Routledge History Handbook of Central and Eastern Europe in the Twentieth Century, Volume 3: Intellectual Horizons*. New York and London: Routledge, 2020.

Borowski, Tadeusz. 'O postępowych i wstecznych tradycjach karykatury politycznej'. *Przegląd Artystyczny*, nos 10–12 (1950): 47–59.

Bosworth, C. Edmund. *An Intrepid Scot: William Lithgow of Lanark's Travels in the Ottoman Lands, North Africa, and Central Europe, 1609–21*. Aldershot: Ashgate, 2006.

Boulat, Alexandra. 'Eyewitness Kosovo'. *National Geographic* 197, no. 2 (February 2000): 72–97.

Bowe, Nicola Gordon. *Art and the National Dream: The Search for Vernacular Expression in Turn of the Century Design*. London and Dublin: Irish Academic Press, 1993.

Bowman, Isaiah. 'Constantinople and the Balkans'. In *What Really Happened at Paris: the Story of the Peace Conference, 1918–1919*, eds Edward Mandell House and Charles Seymour, 140–75. London: Hodder & Stoughton, 1921.

Bracewell, Wendy and Alex Drace-Francis, eds. *A Bibliography of East European Travel Writing in Europe*. Budapest: CEU Press, 2007.

Bracewell, Wendy. 'Travels through the Slav World'. In *Under Eastern Eyes: A Comparative Introduction to East European Travel Writing on Europe*, eds Wendy Bracewell and Alex Drace-Francis, 147–94. Budapest and New York: Central European University Press, 2008.

Bracewell, Wendy and Alex Drace-Francis, eds. *Under Eastern Eyes: A Comparative Introduction to East European Travel Writing on Europe*. Budapest: CEU Press, 2008.

Bracewell, Wendy. 'Lovrich's Joke: Authority, Laughter and Savage Breasts in an 18th-C. Travel Polemic'. *Études Balkaniques* 2, no. 3 (2011): 224–49.

Bracewell, Wendy. 'Europe'. In *The Routledge Companion to Travel Writing*, ed. Carl Thompson, 341–50. London and New York: Routledge, 2015.

Bradbury, Malcolm. 'New Rates of Exchange: British Fiction and Britain Today'. In *Britain and Europe*, eds Ludmilla Kostova, Margaret Dobbing and Nick Wadham-Smith. Sofia: Petrikov, 1994.

Bradbury, Malcolm. *Rates of Exchange*. Harmondsworth: Penguin Books, 1985.

Bradbury, Malcolm. *Why Come to Slaka?* Harmondsworth: Penguin Books, 1991.

Bright-Holmes, John, ed. *Like It Was: The Diaries of Malcolm Muggeridge*. London: Collins, 1981.

Brody, Judit. 'The Széchenyi Chain Bridge at Budapest'. *Technology and Culture* 29, no. 1 (1988): 104–17.

Brown, Edward. *A Brief Account of Some Travels in Divers Parts of Europe: viz. Hungaria, Servia, Bulgaria, Macedonia, Thessaly, Austria, Styria, Carinthia, Carniola, and Friuli: as*

Also Some Observations on the Gold, Silver, Copper, Quick-Silver Mines, Baths and Mineral Waters in Those Parts: With the Figures of some Habits and Remarkable Places. London: Printed for Benj. Tooke, 1763.

Brown, Edward. *M. D. auf genehmgehaltenes Gutachten und Veranlassung der Kön. Engell. Medicinischen Gesellschaft in Londen Durch Niederland, Teutschland, Hungarn, Servien, Bulgarien, Macedonien, Thessalien, Oesterreich, Steurmarck, Kärnthen, Carniolen, Friaul, etc*. Nürnberg: Johann Ziege, 1711.

Brown, Edward. *Naauwkeurige en Gedenkwaardige Reysen van Edward Brown . . . Door Nederland, Duytsland, Hongaryen, Serbien, Bulgarien, Macedonien, Thessalien, Oostenr., Stierm., Carinthien, Carniole en Friuli, enz*. Amsterdam: Jan ten Hoorn, 1696.

Bryan, Courtland Dixon Barnes. *The National Geographic Society: 100 Years of Adventure and Discovery*. London: Harry N. Abrams, 1997.

Bugge, Peter. '"Shatter Zones": The Creation and Recreation of Europe's East'. In *Ideas of Europe Since 1914: The Legacy of the First World War*, eds Menno Spiering and Michael Wintle, 47–68. Basingstoke and New York: Palgrave Macmillan, 2002.

'Bulgaria, the Peasant State'. *National Geographic* 19, no. 11 (November 1908): 760–63.

Burchfield, R.W. *A Supplement to the Oxford English Dictionary*, 4 vols. Oxford: Clarendon Press, 1972–86.

Burke, Edmund. *A Philosophical Enquiry Into the Origin of Our Ideas of the Sublime and Beautiful*. London: R. and J. Dodsley, 1757.

Burke, Peter. *Eyewitnessing: The Uses of Images as Historical Evidence*. London: Reaktion, 2001.

Buyantueva, Radzhana and Maryna Shevtsova, eds. *LGBT+ Activism in Central and Eastern Europe: Resistance, Representation and Identity*. Cham: Palgrave Macmillan, 2019.

Byron, Lord [George Gordon]. *Child Harold's Pilgrimage: Romaunt and Other Poems*, 3rd ed. London: John Murray, 1812.

Cairns, David and Shaun Richards. *Writing Ireland: Colonialism, Nationalism and Culture*. Manchester: Manchester University Press, 1988.

Caldecott, Randolph. *The Great Panjandrum Himself*. London: George Routledge & Sons, 1885.

Calder-Marshall, Arthur. 'Reconstruction in Yugoslavia'. *Geographical Magazine* 19, no. 1 (May 1946): 40–54.

'Capital of Latvia: A Look at Modern Riga'. Photo supplement. *Geographical Magazine* 40, no. 10 (February 1968): 876–79.

Caquard, Sébastien and Claire Dormann. 'Humorous Maps: Explorations of an Alternative Cartography'. *Cartography and Geographic Information Science* 35, no. 1 (2008): 51–64.

Carrara, Francesco. *La Dalmazia Descritta . . . con 48 tavole minate rappresentanti i principali costumi nazionali*. Zara: Fratelli Battara, 1846–48.

Carter, F.W. 'Four Countries Develop Their Own Energy: Resources in Albania, Bulgaria, Romania and Yugoslavia'. *Geographical Magazine* 69, no. 1 (October 1976): 13–17.

Carter, F.W. and R.A. French. 'New Era in Slovenia: Success Story of a Yugoslav Republic'. *Geographical Magazine* 57, no. 9 (June 1975): 556–60.

Casas-Cortes, Maribel, Sebastian Cobarrubias and John Pickles. 'Riding Routes and Itinerant Borders: Autonomy of Migration and Border Externalization'. *Antipode* 47, no. 4 (2015): 894–914.

Chalk, Aidan. 'Childe Harold's Pilgrimage: A Romaunt and the Influence of Local Attachment'. *Texas Studies in Literature and Language* 40, no. 1 (Spring 1998): 48–77.

Chamberlain, Neville. *In Search of Peace: Speeches, 1937–1938*. London: Hutchinson & Co., 1939.

Chappe d'Auteroche, Jean-Baptiste. *Voyage en Sibérie fait par ordre du Roi en 1761, . . . enrichi de cartes géographiques, de plans, de profils du terrain, de gravures. . . .* Paris: Debure, Père, 1768.

Chmielewska, Ella. 'Logos or the Resonance of Branding: A Close Reading of the Iconosphere of Warsaw'. *Space and Culture* 8, no. 4 (2005): 349–80.

Chowaniec, Czesław. 'The First Geographical Map of Bernard Wapowski'. *Imago Mundi* 12 (1955): 59–64.

Christie, Agatha. *The Secret of Chimneys* [1925]. London: HarperCollins, 2010.

Churchill, Winston. 'The Sinews of Peace' [1946]. In *Winston S. Churchill: His Complete Speeches, 1897–1963*, ed. Robert Rhodes James, vol. VII, 7285–93. New York and London: Chelsea House, 1974.

Cilauro, Santo, Tom Gleisner and Rob Sitch. *Molvania: A Land Untouched by Modern Dentistry*. Jetlag Travel Guide. London: Atlantic Books, 2004.

Clark, William Tierney. *An Account, With Illustrations, of the Suspension Bridge across the River Danube, Uniting Pesth and Buda and the Adjacent Country, in the Kingdom of Hungary*. London: John Weale, 1852–53.

Codell, Julie. 'Imperial Differences and Culture Clashes in Victorian Periodicals' Visuals: The Case of *Punch*'. *Victorian Periodicals Review* 39, no. 4 (2006): 410–28.

Cohen, Michael. *Sisters: Relation and Rescue in Nineteenth-Century British Novels and Paintings*. Madison and Teaneck: Fairleigh Dickinson University Press, 1995.

Collillieux, S., ed. *Karykatura oręż walki o pokój: Zbiór prac karykaturzystów rumuńskich*. Warsaw: Wydawnictwo MON, 1951.

Collins, Tracy J.R. 'Athletic Fashion, *Punch*, and the Creation of the New Woman'. *Victorian Periodicals Review* 43, no. 3 (Fall 2010): 309–35.

Connelly, John. *From Peoples Into Nations: A History of Eastern Europe*. Princeton, NJ: Princeton University Press, 2020.

Cosgrove, Denis. 'Introduction: Landscape, Map and Vision'. In *Geography and Vision: Seeing, Imagining and Representing the World*, ed. D. Cosgrove, 1–12. London: I.B. Tauris, 2008.

Cosgrove, Denis. 'Maps, Mapping, Modernity: Art and Cartography in the Twentieth Century'. *Imago Mundi* 57, no. 1 (2005): 35–54.

Coupe, William Arthur. 'Observations on a Theory of Political Caricature'. *Comparative Studies on Society and History* 11, no. 1 (1969): 79–95.

Crampton, R.J. *Bulgaria*. Oxford: Oxford University Press, 2009.

Crampton, R.J. and Benjamin Crampton. *Atlas of Eastern Europe in the Twentieth Century*. London: Routledge, 1996.

Crang, Mike. 'Visual Methods and Methodologies'. In *The SAGE Handbook of Qualitative Geography*, eds Dydia DeLyser, Steve Herbert, Stuart Aitken, Mike Crang and Linda McDowell, 208–25. London: Sage, 2009.

Crowley, David. *National Style and Nation-State: Design in Poland From the Vernacular Revival to the International Style*. Manchester: Manchester University Press, 1992.

Crowley, David. 'The Peasant in the City: Embroidery in Writings on Architecture in Austria-Hungary Around 1900'. In *Borders in Art: Revisiting 'Kunstgeographie'*, ed. Katarzyna Murawska-Muthesius, 127–37. Warsaw: Institute of Art, 2000.

Cruger Coffin, Marian. 'Where East Meets West: A Visit to Picturesque Dalmatia, Montenegro, and Herzegovina'. *National Geographic* 9, no. 5 (May 1908): 309–44.

Curta, Florin. *The Making of the Slavs: History and Archaeology of the Lower Danube Region, c. 500-700*. Cambridge and New York: Cambridge University Press, 2007.

Curtis, Lewis Perry. *Apes and Angels: The Irishman in Victorian Caricature*. Newton Abbott: David and Charles, 1971.

Curtis, William E. 'The Great Turk and His Lost Provinces'. *National Geographic* 14, no. 2 (February 1903): 45–61.

Dalché, Patrick Gautier. 'The Reception of Ptolemy's *Geography* (End of the Fourteenth to Beginning of the Sixteenth Century)'. In *The History of Cartography, Volume 3, Cartography in the European Renaissance*, ed. David Woodward, 285–364. Chicago and London: University of Chicago Press, 2007.

Das, Nandi and Tim Youngs, eds. *The Cambridge History of Travel Writing*. Cambridge: Cambridge University Press, 2019.

Davies, Norman. *Europe: A History*. Oxford: Oxford University Press, 1996.

Davis, Lynn Etheridge. *The Cold War Begins: Soviet-American Conflict over Eastern Europe*. Princeton, NJ: Princeton University Press, 1974.

Davis, Sacha E. '"A Most Picturesque Mass of Rags": Romani Costume and Undress in Nineteenth-Century Travel Descriptions of Hungary'. *Patterns of Prejudice* 53, vol. 5 (2019): 464–86.

Demski, Dagnosław and Kamila Baraniecka-Olszewska, eds. *Images of the Other on Ethnic Caricatures of Central and Eastern Europe*. Warsaw: Institute of Archaeology and Ethnology, 2010.

Destani, Bejtullah D. and Robert Elsie, eds. *Edward Lear in Albania: Journals of a Landscape Painter in the Balkans*. London: I.B. Tauris, 2008.

De Windt, Harry. 'Through Savage Europe'. Review. *The Spectator*, 11 May 1907: 765.

Dodge, Martin, Rob Kitchin and Chris Perkins, eds. *The Map Reader: Theories of Mapping Practice and Cartographic Representation*. London: John Willey & Sons, Ltd., 2011.

Dormeier, Heinrich. 'Humoristisch-satirische Europakarten von 1848 bis zum ersten Weltkrieg. Bestand und Besonderheiten'. In *Geschichtsbilder. Festschrift für Michael Salewski*, eds Thomas Stamm-Kuhlmann, Jürgen Elvert, Birgit Aschmann and Jens Hohensee, 525–42. Wiesbaden: Franz Steiner Verlag, 2003.

Douglas, Roy. *Great Nations Still Enchained: The Cartoonists' Vision of Europe 1848–1914*. London: Routledge, 1993.

Douglas, Roy. *The Great War 1914–1918: The Cartoonists' Vision*. London and New York: Routledge, 1995.

Drace-Francis, Alex. 'Towards a Natural History of East European Travel Writing'. In *Under Eastern Eyes: A Comparative Introduction to East European Travel Writing on Europe*, eds Wendy Bracewell and Alex Drace-Francis, 1–26. Budapest: CEU Press, 2008.

Drace-Francis, Alex. 'The Traditions of Invention. Representations of the Romanian Peasant from Ancient Stereotype to Modern Symbol'. In *The Traditions of Invention: Romanian Ethnic and Social Stereotypes in Historical Context*, 1–59. Leiden and Boston: Brill, 2018.

Drace-Francis, Alex. 'Travel Writing From Eastern Europe'. In *The Cambridge History of Travel Writing*, eds Nandi Das and Tim Youngs, 191–205. Cambridge: Cambridge University Press, 2019.

Drewnowski, Tadeusz, ed. *Postal Indiscretions: The Correspondence of Tadeusz Borowski*. Trans. Alicia Nitecki. Evanston, IL: Northwestern University Press, 2007.

Dzenovska, Dace. 'Eastern Europe, the Moral Subject of the Migration/Refugee Crisis and Political Futures'. *Near Futures Online*, www.academia.edu/22938312/Eastern_Europe_the_Moral_Subject_of_the_Migration_Refugee_Crisis_and_Political_Futures.

East, Gordon. 'The Concept and Political Status of the Shatter Zone'. In *Geographical Essays on Eastern Europe*, ed. Norman J.G. Pounds, 1–27. Bloomington, IN: Indiana University Press, 1963.

Edney, Matthew H. *The Origins and Development of J.B. Harley's Cartographic Theories*. Toronto: Toronto University Press, 2005.

Edwards, Janis L. *Political Cartoons in the 1988 Presidential Campaign: Image, Metaphor, and Narrative*. New York and London: Garland, 1997.

Edwards, Lovett F. 'The New Albania'. *Geographical Magazine* 19, no. 3 (July 1946): 104–15.

Efimov, Boris. *Osnovy ponimania karikatury*. Moscow: Izdatel'stvo Akademi Khudozhestv SSSR, 1961.

Efimov, Boris. *Za prochnyi mir, protiv podzhigatelei voiny. Risunki Bor. Efimova*. Moscow: Gosudarstvennoe Izdatel'stvo Iskusstvo, 1950.

Elkins, James. *The Domain of Images*. Ithaca and London: Cornell University Press, 1999.

Elliott, David. 'Looking Things in the Face'. In *After the Wall: Art and Culture in Post-Communist Europe*, eds Bojana Pejić and David Elliott, 29–33. Stockholm: Moderna Museet, 1999.

Erickson, Peter and Clark Hulse. *Early Modern Visual Culture: Representation, Race, Empire in Renaissance England*. Philadelphia: University of Pennsylvania Press, 2000.

Ermida, Isabel, ed. *Dracula and the Gothic in Literature, Pop Culture and the Arts*. Leiden: Brill, 2015.

Esipova, Neli and Julie Ray. 'Syrian Refugees Not Welcome in Eastern Europe'. *World*, 5 May 2017, https://news.gallup.com/poll/209828/syrian-refugees-not-welcome-eastern-europe.aspx.

Etty, John. *Graphic Satire in the Soviet Union: Krokodil's Political Cartoons*. Jackson: University Press of Mississippi, 2019.

Farago, Clare. 'Silent Moves: On Excluding the Ethnographic Subject From the Discourse of Art History'. In *Art of Art History: A Critical Anthology*, ed. Donald Preziosi, 195–214. Oxford and New York: Oxford University Press, 2009.

Feinberg, Joseph Grim. *The Paradox of Authenticity: Folklore Performance in Post-Communist Slovakia*. Madison, Wisconsin and London: The University of Wisconsin Press, 2018.

Fernie, Eric. *Art History and Its Methods*. London: Phaidon, 1995.

Filipová, Marta, ed. *Cultures of International Exhibitions 1840–1940: Great Exhibitions in the Margins*. Abingdon and New York: Ashgate, 2015.

Fisher-Galati, Stephen. *Eastern Europe and the Cold War: Perceptions and Perspectives*. New York: Boulder, 1994.

Fiske, John. *Introduction to Communication Studies* [1982]. London and New York: Routledge, 1990.

Fortis, Alberto. *Viaggio in Dalmazia*. Venice: Alvise Milocco, 1774.

Fortis, Alberto. *Reisen in Dalmatien*. Bern: Typographische Gesellschaft, 1776.

[Fortis, Alberto]. *Die Sitten der Morlacken*. Bern: Typographische Gesellschaft, 1775.

Fortis, Alberto. *Travels into Dalmatia*. London: J. Robson, 1778.

Foster, Alan J. 'The British Press and the Coming of the Cold War'. In *Britain and the First Cold War*, ed. Ann Deighton, 11–31. Basingstoke and London: Palgrave Macmillan, 1990.

Foster, R.F. *Paddy and Mr. Punch: Connections in Irish and English History*. London: Allen Lane, 1993.

Fowkes, Ben. *The Rise and Fall of Communism in Eastern Europe*. Basingstoke: Macmillan, 1993.

Freud, Sigmund. 'The Dream-Work'. In *The Interpretation of Dreams* [1900]. Trans. and ed. James Strachey, 381-651. The Penguin Freud Library, vol. 4. Harmondsworth: Penguin, 1991.

Freud, Sigmund. *Jokes and Their Relations to the Unconscious* [1905]. Trans. and ed. James Strachey. The Penguin Freud Library, vol. 6. Ed. Angela Richards. Harmondsworth: Penguin, 1991.

Frucht, Richard, ed. *Encyclopedia of Eastern Europe: From the Congress of Vienna to the Fall of Communism*. New York and London: Garland, 2000.

Fürer-Haimendorf, Christoph von. 'A Wedding in the Bulgarian Mountains'. *Geographical Magazine* 4, no. 3 (January 1937): 203–14.

Gandhi, Leela. *Postcolonial Theory: A Critical Introduction*. New York: Columbia University Press, 2019.

García-Álvarez, Jacobo, Paloma Puente-Lozano and Juna-Manuel Trillo-Santamaria. 'Representing Spain: Cultural Image and Geographic Knowledge in *National Geographic*'s Articles on Spain (1888–1936)'. *GeoJournal* 79, no. 5 (2014): 539–56.

Garrett, Wilbur E. 'The Editorial'. *National Geographic* 161, no. 4 (April 1982).

Garton Ash, Timothy. 'Does Central Europe Exist? [1986]'. In *The Uses of Adversity: Essays on the Fate of Central Europe*, 95–108. Cambridge: Granta Books, 1989.

Gatejel, Luminita. 'Overcoming the Iron Gates: Austrian Transport and River Regulation on the Lower Danube, 1830s–1840s'. *Central European History* 49 (2016): 162–80.

Genette, Gérard. *Paratexts: Thresholds of Interpretation*. Trans. Jane E. Lewin. Cambridge: Cambridge University Press, 1997.

Gephardt, Katarina. '"The Enchanted Garden" or "The Red Flag": Eastern Europe in Late Nineteenth-Century British Travel Writing'. *Journal of Narrative Theory* 35, no. 3 (Fall 2005): 292–306.

Gerard, Emily. *The Land Beyond the Forest: Facts, Figures and Fancies From Transylvania*. New York: Harper and Brothers, 1888.

Ghodsee, Kristen R. *Why Women Had Better Sex Under Socialism*. New York: Nation Books, 2018.

Gibbon, Edward. *The History of the Decline and Fall of the Roman Empire*, vol. 4. London: A. Strahan and T. Cadell, 1788.

Gilpin, William. *Three Essays on Picturesque Beauty; on Picturesque Travel; and on Sketching Landscape: To Which Is Added a Poem, on Landscape Painting*. London: R. Blamire, 1792.

Ginsburger, Nicolas. 'André Chéradame et l'émergence d'une cartographie géopolitique de guerre en 1916'. *Cartes & géomatique, Comité français de cartographie*, no. 223 (March 2015): 79–90.

Giustino, Cathleen M., Catherine J. Plum and Alexander Vari, eds. *Socialist Escapes: Breaking Away From Ideology and Everyday Routine in Eastern Europe, 1945–1989*. New York: Berghahn, 2013.

Goffart, Walter. *Historical Atlases: The First Three Hundred Years 1570-1870*. Chicago and London: The University of Chicago Press, 2003.

Goldstein, Robert Justin. *Censorship of Political Caricature in Nineteenth-Century France*. Kent, OH and London: Kent State University Press, 1989.

Goldsworthy, Vesna. *Inventing Ruritania: The Imperialism of the Imagination*. New Haven and London: Yale University Press, 1998.

Gombrich, Ernst H. 'The Cartoonist's Armoury'. In *Meditations on a Hobby Horse and Other Essays on the Theory of Art*, 127–42. London: Phaidon, 1963.

Gombrich, Ernst H. 'Magic, Myth and Metaphor: Reflections on Pictorial Satire'. In *The Uses of Images: Studies in the Social Function of Art and Visual Communication*, 184–211. London: Phaidon, 1999.

Górny, Maciej. *Kreślarze Ojczyzn: Geografowie i granice międzywojennej Europy*. Warsaw: Instytut Historii PAN, 2017.

Gorsuch, Anne E. and Diane P. Koenker, eds. *Turism: The Russian and East European Tourist Under Capitalism and Socialism*. Ithaca: Cornell University Press, 2006.

Götz, Norbert and Janne Holmén, eds. 'Mental Maps: Geographical and Historical Perspectives'. Special issue of *Journal of Cultural Geography* 35, no. 2 (2018).

Grospierre, Nicolas. *Modern Forms: A Subjective Atlas of 20th-Century Architecture*. Eds Alona Pardo and Elias Redstone, introduction by Adam Mazur. Munich: Prestel, 2018.

Grossen, Michiel van. *The Representations of the Overseas World in the De Bry Collection of Voyages (1590–1634)*. Leiden and Boston: Brill, 2008.

Grosvenor, Edwin A. 'The Races of Europe'. *National Geographic* 34, no. 5 (December 1918): 441–536.

Grosvenor, Edwin A. 'Siberia'. *National Geographic* 12, no. 9 (September 1901): 317–24.

Grosvenor, Gilbert H. 'Young Russia: The Land of Unlimited Possibilities'. *National Geographic* 26, no. 5 (November 1914): 423–520.

Grosvenor, Gilbert Melville. 'From the President: Window on the Soviet Union'. *National Geographic* 177, no. 3 (March 1990).

Grosvenor, Gilbert Melville. 'Yugoslavia's Window on the Adriatic'. *National Geographic* 121, no. 2 (February 1962): 218–47.

Grosvenor, Melville Bell. 'Poland, Land of the White Eagle'. *National Geographic* 61, no. 4 (April 1932): 435–36.

Hagen, Joshua. 'Redrawing the Imagined Map of Europe: The Rise and Fall of the "Center"'. *Political Geography* 22 (2003): 489–517.

Hall, Derek. 'Eastern Europe Opens Its Doors'. *Geographical* 62, no. 4 (April 1990): 10–14.

Hamilton, F.E. Ian. 'Bulgaria: Land of Change'. *Geographical Magazine* 38, no. 4 (August 1965). 276–89.

Hamilton, F.E. Ian. 'The East European and Soviet City'. In a feature 'What Is the City but the People?'. *Geographical Magazine* 50, no. 8 (May 1978): 511–15.

Hammond, Andrew. 'Through Savage Europe: The Gothic Strain in British Balkanism'. *Third Text* 21, no. 2 (March 2007): 117–27.

Hans Hildenbrand. Hofphotograph und Pionier der frühen Farbfotografie. Ubstadt-Weiher: Verlag Regionalkultur, 2018.

Happel, Jörn and Christophe von Werdt, with assistance of Mira Jovanović. *Osteuropa kartiert–Mapping Eastern Europe.* Berlin: LIT Verlag, 2010.

Harbutt, Fraser J. *The Iron Curtain: Churchill, America and the Origins of the Cold War.* Oxford and New York: Oxford University Press, 1986.

Harley, J. Brian. 'The Iconology of Early Maps'. In *Imago et Mensura Mundi: Atti del IX Congresso Internazionale di Storia della Cartografia*, ed. Carla C. Marzoli, vol. 1, 29–38. Rome: Istituto della Enciclopedia Italiana, 1985, 2 vols.

Harley, J. Brian. 'Maps, Knowledge and Power'. In *The Iconography of Landscape*, eds Daniel Cosgrove and Stephen Daniels, 277–312. Cambridge: Cambridge University Press, 1988.

Harley, J. Brian. 'Deconstructing the Map'. *Cartographica* 26, no. 2 (1989): 1–20.

Harley, J. Brian. 'Introduction: Texts and Contexts in the Interpretation of Early Maps'. In *From Sea Charts to Satellite Images: Interpreting North American History Through Maps*, ed. David Buisseret, 3–15. Chicago and London: University of Chicago Press, 1990.

Harley, J. Brian. *The New Nature of Maps: Essays in the History of Cartography*, ed. Paul Laxton, introduction by J.H. Andrews. Baltimore, MD: The John Hopkins University Press, 2001.

Hatherley, Owen. *The Landscapes of Communism.* London: Allen Lane, 2015.

Havel, Václav. *An Uncanny Era: Conversations Between Václav Havel and Adam Michnik*, edited and translated, and with an introduction by Elżbieta Matynia. New Haven and London: Yale University Press, 2014.

Hawkins, Stephanie. *American Iconographic: 'National Geographic', Global Culture, and the Visual Imagination.* Charlotesville: University of Virginia Press, 2010.

Heffernan, Mike. 'Fin de siècle? Fin du monde? On the Origins of European Geopolitics, 1890–1920'. In *Geopolitical Traditions*, eds Klaus Dodds and David Atkinson, 27–51. London: Routledge, 2000.

Heinbucher Edlen von Bikkessy, Joseph. *Panoniens Bewohner in ihrem volksthümlichen Trachten.* Vienna, 1820.

Henes, Mary and Brian H. Murray, eds. *Travel Writing, Visual Culture and Form, 1760–1900.* Basingstoke and New York: Palgrave MacMillan, 2016.

Henningsen, Charles Frederic. *Eastern Europe and the Emperor Nicholas.* London: T.C. Newby, 1846.

Henrikson, Alan K. 'Maps, Globes and the "Cold War"'. *Special Libraries* 65 (1974): 445–54.

Herb, Guntram Henrik. *Under the Map of Germany: Nationalism and Propaganda 1918–1945.* London: Routledge, 1997.

Herbert, Francis. 'The Royal Geographical Society's Membership, the Map Trade, and Geographical Publishing in Britain 1830 to ca 1930: An Introductory Essay with Listing of Some 250 Fellows in Related Professions'. *Imago Mundi* 35 (1983): 67–95.

Herder, Johann Gottfried. 'Slawische Völker'. In *Ideen zur Philosophie der Geschichte der Menschheit (1774–1791)*, ed. J.G. Herder, vol. 4, 37–43. Riga and Leipzig: Johann Friedrich Hartnoch, 1792.

Herder, Johann Gottfried. 'On Slav Nations: Johann Gottfried Herder (1774–1803)'. Trans. Ernest A. Menze with Michael Palma. In *The Czech Reader: History, Culture, Politics*, eds Jan Bažant, Nina Bažantová and Frances Starn, 123–25. Durham, NC: Duke University Press, 2010.

Hetzel Gunkel, Ann. 'Global Górale and Postmodern Polskość: Polish Roots Music and the Post-Communist Recovery of Folk'. *The Polish Review* 57, no. 4 (2012): 63–74.

Hildenbrand, Hans. *Costumes of Czechoslovakia*. In Worth E. Shoults. 'Hospitality of the Czechs'. *National Geographic* 51, no. 6 (June 1927): 723–42.

Hildenbrand, Hans. *In the Land of the White Eagle*. In Melville Bell Grosvenor. 'Poland, Land of the White Eagle'. *National Geographic* 61, no. 4 (April 1932): 43–45.

Hildenbrand, Hans. *Rainbow Costumes of Poland Peasants*. In Maynard Owen Williams. 'The Poland of the Present'. *National Geographic* 63, no. 3 (March 1933): 319–44.

Hiles, Timothy W. *Fin-de-Siècle Munich and the Origins of Simplicissimus*. New York: Peter Lang, 1996.

Hill, Gillian. *Cartographical Curiosities*. London: British Library, 1978.

Hinds, Lynn Boyd and Theodore Otto Windt, Jr. *The Cold War as Rhetoric: The Beginnings*. New York: Praeger, 1991.

Hobbes, Thomas. *Leviathan* [1651]. Oxford: Clarendon Press, 1929.

Hobhouse, J.C. *A Journey Through Albania and Other Provinces of Turkey in Europe and Asia to Constantinople During the Years 1809 and 1810*. London: James Cawthorn, 1813.

Hobsbawm, Eric. *Age of Extremes: The Short Twentieth Century 1914–1991*. London: Abacus, 1995.

Hoelscher, Steven. 'Landscape Iconography'. In *International Encyclopedia of Human Geography*, editors-in-chief Rob Kitchin and Nigel Thrift, vol. 6, 132–39. Chicago and London: Elsevier, 2009.

Hosmer, Dorothy. 'An American Girl Cycles Across Romania: Two-Wheel Pilgrim Pedals the Land of Castles and Gypsies, Where Roman Empire Traces Mingle With Remnants of Oriental Migration'. *National Geographic* 75, no. 5 (November 1938): 557–88.

Hostetler, Michael J. 'The Enigmatic Ends of Rhetoric: Churchill's Fulton Address as Great Art and Failed Persuasion'. *Quarterly Journal of Speech* 83 (1997): 426–28.

House, Edward Mandell and Charles Seymour, eds. *What Really Happened at Paris: the Story of the Peace Conference, 1918–1919*. London: Hodder & Stoughton, 1921.

Houze, Rebecca. 'At the Forefront of a Newly Emerging Profession? Ethnography, Education, and the Exhibition of Women's Needlework in Austria-Hungary in the Late Nineteenth Century'. *Journal of Design History* 21, no. 1 (2008): 19–40.

Houze, Rebecca. *Textiles, Fashion, and Design Reform in Austria-Hungary before the First World War: Principle of Dress*. Farnham and Burlington, VT: Ashgate, 2015.

Hubbard, Hon. Gardiner G. 'Russia in Europe'. *National Geographic* 7, no. 1 (January 1896): 1–26.

Hughes, Rev. Thomas Smart. *Travels in Sicily, Greece and Albania*, 2 vols. London: J. Mawman, 1820.

Hulme, Peter and Tim Youngs, eds. *The Cambridge Companion to Travel Writing*. Cambridge: Cambridge University Press, 2002.

Hunter, Ian. *Malcolm Muggeridge: A Life*. London: Hamilton, 1980.

Hůrský, Josef. 'Vznik a poslání Šafaříkova Slovanského Zeměvidu'. In *Slovanský Národopis*, eds Hana Hynková, with Josef Hůrský and Luboš Reháček, 218–88. Prague: Československé Akademie Věd, 1955.

Imre, Anikó. 'White Man, White Mask: Mephisto Meets Venus'. *Screen* 40 (Winter 1999): 405–22.

Invanciuc, Teofil. *Meșteșuguri tradiționale din Țara Maramureșului*. Photo Radu Lazar. Baia Mare: Proema, 2016.

Ionoaia, Eliana. 'Othering the Wallachian National Identity: British Victorian Travellers Voyaging Down the Danube'. In *Globalization and Intercultural Dialogue: Multidisciplinary Perspectives – Literature*, ed. Iulian Boldea, 915–24. Târgu Mureș, Bucharest: Arhipelag, 2014.

Jaritz, Gerhard and Katalin Szende, eds. *Medieval East Central Europe in a Comparative Perspective: From Frontier Zones to Lands in Focus*. London: Routledge, 2016.

Jefimov, Boris. *Für einen dauerhaften Frieden – gegen Kriegsbrandstifter: Zeichnungen von Boris Jefimov*. Dresden: Sachsenverlag, 1951.

Jenks, John. 'Making Peace a Fighting Word'. In *British Propaganda and News Media in the Cold War*, 114–27. Edinburgh: Edinburgh University Press, 2006.

Jezernik, Božidar. *Wild Europe: The Balkans in the Gaze of Western Travellers*. London: SAQI/ The Bosnian Institute, 2004.

Jianu, Angela. *A Circle of Friends: Romanian Revolutionaries and Political Exile, 1840–1859*. Leiden: Brill, 2011.

Johnston, Ron. 'Popular Geographies and Geographical Imaginations: Contemporary English-language Geographical Magazines'. *GeoJournal* 79 (2009): 347–62.

Jones, Stephen. 'Global Strategic Views'. In *Military Aspects of World Political Geography*, 39–67. Air University, Maxwell Air Force Base. Alabama: Air Force Reserve Training Corps, 1959.

Kain, Albert, ed. *Ungarn. Im Auftrage des kön. ungarischen Handelsministers herausgegeben von der Direction der kön. ung. Staatsbahnen*. Budapest: Erdélyi, 1909.

Kamusella, Tomasz. 'School Historical Atlases and Ethnolinguistic Nationalism'. In *Osteuropa kartiert*, eds Happel and von Werdt, 215–33. Berlin: LIT Verlag, 2010.

Kantor, Ryszard. *Ubiór – strój – kostium*. Cracow: Uniwersytet Jagielloński, 1982.

Kaufmann, Thomas DaCosta. *Court, Cloister & City: The Art and Culture of Central Europe, 1450–1800*. London: Weidenfeld & Nicolson, 1995.

Kaufmann, Thomas DaCosta. *Toward a Geography of Art*. Chicago: University of Chicago Press, 2004.

King, David. *Extreme Politics: Nationalism, Violence, and the End of Eastern Europe*. Oxford: Oxford University Press, 2010.

Kirschbaum, Stanislav J. *Historical Dictionary of Slovakia*. Lanham, MD, Toronto and Plymouth: The Scarecrow Press, 2007.

Klausen, Jytte. *The Cartoons That Shook the World*. New Haven and London: Yale University Press, 2009.

Koch, Felix J. 'In Quaint, Curious Croatia'. *National Geographic* 19, no. 12 (December 1908): 809–32.

Kohn, Hans. *Panslavism, Its History and Ideology*. Notre Dame: Notre Dame University Press, 1956.

Kołodziejczyk, Dorota. 'Post-Colonial Transfer to Central-and-Eastern Europe'. *Teksty Drugie* 1 (2014): 124–42, http://rcin.org.pl/Content/51837/WA248_71048_P-I-2524_kolodz-post-colon.pdf.

Kołodziejczyk, Dorota and Cristina Șandru, eds. *Postcolonial Perspectives on Postcommunism in Central and Eastern Europe*. London: Routledge, 2016.

Kombst, Gustaf. [Explanation to] 'Ethnographic map of Europe, or the Different Nations of Europe, Traced According to Race, Language, Religion, and Form of Government'. In *National Atlas of Historical, Commercial and Political Geography*, ed. Alexander Keith Johnston. Edinburgh [1843] 1856.

Komska, Yuliya. 'Introduction: A Discontigious Eastern Europe'. In *Eastern Europe Unmapped: Beyond Borders and Peripheries*, eds Irene Kacandes and Yuliya Komska, 1–28. New York and Oxford: Berghahn Books, 2018.

Kordjak, Joanna, ed. *Polska – Kraj Folkloru?* Warsaw: Zachęta – Narodowa Galeria Sztuki, 2016.

Korduba, Piotr. *Ludowość Na Sprzedaż: Towarzystwo Popierania Przemysłu Ludowego, Cepelia, Instytut Wzornictwa Przemysłowego*. Warsaw: Fundacja Bęc Zmiana, 2013.

Korte, Barbara, Eva Ulrike Pirker and Sissy Helff, eds. *Facing the East in the West: Images of Eastern Europe in British Literature*. Amsterdam and New York: Rodopi, 2010.

Kósa, László. *A Cultural History of Hungary: From the Beginnings to the Eighteenth Century*. Budapest: Corvina, 1999.

Koshar, Rudy. '"What Ought to Be Seen": Tourists' Guidebooks and National Identities in Modern Germany and Europe'. *Journal of Contemporary History* 33, no. 4 (July 1998): 323–40.

Kostova, Ludmilla, Margaret Dobbing and Nick Wadham-Smith, eds. *Britain and Europe*. Sofia: Petrikov, 1994.

Kratz, Corinne. 'On Telling/Selling a Book by Its Cover'. *Cultural Anthropology* 9, no. 2 (May 1994): 179–200.

Kris, Ernst and Ernst H. Gombrich. 'The *Principles of Caricature*'. *British Journal of Medical Psychology* 17 (1938): 319–42.

Krivokapić, Marija and Neil Diamond. *Images of Montenegro in Anglo-American Creative Writing and Film*. Newcastle upon Tyne: Cambridge Scholars Publishing, 2017.

Kuhn, Annette. 'Snow White in 1930s Britain'. *Journal of British Cinema and Television* 7, no. 2 (2010): 183–99.

Kuhn, Delia and Ferdinand. 'Poland Opens Her Door'. Photos by Erich Lessing, Magnum. *National Geographic* 114, no. 3 (September 1958): 354–98.

Kukryniksy. *Opętani anglo-amerykanizatorzy*. Warsaw: Wydawnictwo MON, 1951.

Kundera, Milan. 'A Kidnapped West or Culture Bows Out'. *Granta*, no. 11 (1984): 95–118.

Kundera, Milan. 'The Tragedy of Central Europe'. *The New York Review of Books* (26 April 1984): 33–38.

Kunzle, David. 'Gustave Doré's *History of Holy Russia*: Anti-Russian Propaganda from the Crimean War to the Cold War'. *The Russian Review* 42, no. 3 (1983): 271–99.

Kutscheit, John Valerius. *Hand Atlas zur Geographie und Geschichte des Mittelalters*. Berlin: E.H. Schröder, 1843.

Labberton, Robert Henlopen. *An Historical Atlas: A Chronological Series of One Hundred and Twelve Maps at Successive Periods*. New York: T. Mac Coun, 1884.

Lambert, Antony. 'Return of the Vampire'. *Geographical* 61, no. 2 (February 1989): 16–21.

Langsam, Walter Consuelo. *The World Since 1919*. New York: Macmillan [1933], 1954.

Lavallée, Joseph. *Voyage Pittoresque et Historique de L'Istrie et la Dalmatie*. Paris: Louis François Cassas, 1802.

Lear, Edward. *Journals of a Landscape Painter in Albania, &c*. London: Richard Bentley, 1851.

Leary, Patrick. *The 'Punch' Brotherhood: Table Talk and Print Culture in Mid-Victorian London*. London: The British Library, 2010.

Lees-Jeffries, Hester. 'Pictures, Places, and Spaces: Sidney, Wroth, Wilton House, and the *Songe de Poliphile*'. In *Renaissance Paratexts*, eds Helen Smith and Louise Wilson, 185–203. Cambridge: Cambridge University Press, 2011.

Lehmann, John. 'Change in Slovakia'. *Geographical Magazine* 4, no. 5 (March 1937): 313–28.

Lehmann, John. 'Outside the Fold': I. Among the "Swabians" of Hungary'. *Geographical Magazine* 8, no. 4 (February 1939): 225–32.

Lehmann, John. 'A Balkan Sequence. I: The Strangest Journey'. *Geographical Magazine* 10, no. 3 (January 1940): 148–53.

Leighten, Patricia. 'The World Turned Upside Down: Modernism and Anarchist Strategies of Inversion in *L'Assiette au beurre*'. *The Journal of Modern Periodical Studies* 4, no. 2 (2013): 133–70.

Leitch, Stephanie. 'Visual Images in Travel Writing'. In *The Cambridge History of Travel Writing*, eds Nandi Das and Tim Youngs, 456–73. Cambridge: Cambridge University Press, 2019.

Lenica, Jan, Antoni Marianowicz and Jan Szeląg. *Polska karykatura polityczna*. Warsaw: Czytelnik, 1951.

Light, Duncan. 'Imaginative Geographies, Dracula and the Transylvania "Place Myth"'. *Human Geographies: Journal of Studies and Research in Human Geography* 2, no. 2 (November 2008): 6–17.

Linehan, Edward J. 'Czechoslovakia: The Dream and the Reality'. *National Geographic* 133, no. 2 (February 1968): 156–57.

Lipiński, Eryk. 'Wytnij i powieś'. *Szpilki* 16, no. 52 (1950): 4–5, 8.

Lipiński, Eryk. 'Jak rysować i zdobyć sławę'. *Prasa Polska* 8, no. 1 (1954).

Lipiński, Eryk. 'Jak rysować i zdobyć sławę'. *Szpilki* 20, no. 26 (1954).

Lipiński, Eryk. *Drzewo szpilkowe*. Warsaw: Czytelnik, 1976.

Lipiński, Eryk. *Pamiętniki*. Warsaw: Fakt, 1990.

Listowel, The Countess of. 'The Indigestible Magyar'. *Geographical Magazine* 7, no. 6 (October 1938): 361–76.

Lithgow, William. *The Total Discourse of the Rare Adventures and Painefull Peregrinations of Long Nineteene Yeares Travailes From Scotland, to the Most Famous Kingdomes in Europe, Asia and Africa*. London: I. Okes, 1640.

Lithgow, William. *Willem Lithgouws 19 jaarige lant-reyse, uyt Schotlant nae de vermaerde deelen des werelts Europa, Asia en Africa*. Amsterdam: Jacob Benjamin, 1653.

Livezeanu, Irina and Árpád von Klimó, eds. *The Routledge History of East Central Europe Since 1700*. London: Routledge, 2017.

Llewellyn Jarecka, Louise. 'Popular Art in Poland'. *Geographical Magazine* 8, no. 5 (March 1939): 345–62.

Long, Jonathan James. *W.G. Sebald – Image, Archive, Modernity*. Edinburgh: Edinburgh University Press, 2007.

Lovrich, Giovanni. *Osservazioni di Giovanni Lovrich: sopra diversi pezzi del Viaggio in Dalmazia del Signor Abate Alberto Fortis: coll'aggiunta della vita di Sociviza*. Venice: Francesco Sansoni, 1776.

Łuczyński, Jarosław. 'Ziemie Rzeczpospolitej w kartografii europejskiej XVI wieku'. *Polski Przegląd Kartograficzny* 41, no. 2 (2009): 128–44.

Lutosławski, A.T. 'Poland's Window on the World'. *Geographical Magazine* 1, no. 2 (June 1935): 98–106.

Lutz, Catherine A. and Jane L. Collins. *Reading National Geographic*. Chicago and London: The University of Chicago Press, 1993.

McCallam, David. '(Ac)claiming Illyria: Eighteenth-Century Istria and Dalmatia in Fortis, Cassas, and Lavallée'. *Central Europe* 9, no. 2 (November 2011): 125–41.

MacDonald, Fraser. 'Visuality'. In *International Encyclopedia of Human Geography*, editors-in-chief Rob Kitchin and Nigel Thrift, vol. 12, 151–56. Chicago and London: Elsevier, 2009.

McLean, Matthew. *The 'Cosmographia' of Sebastian Münster: Describing the World in the Reformation*. Aldershot: Ashgate, 2007.

Macel, Christine and Nataša Petrešin-Bachelez, eds. *Promises of the Past: A Discontinuous History of Art in Former Eastern Europe*. Paris: Centre Georges Pompidou/ Zurich: JRP/Ringier, 2010.

Mackinder, Halford. 'The Geographical Pivot of History'. *The Geographical Journal* 23, no. 4 (1904): 421–37.

Mackinder, Halford. 'The Teaching of Geography from an Imperial Point of View, and the Use Which Could and Should Be Made of Visual Instruction'. *The Geographical Teacher* 6, no. 2 (1911): 79–86.

Mackinder, Halford. *Democratic Ideals and Reality*. London: Constable & Co., 1919.

Madden, Henry Miller. 'The Diary of John Paget'. *The Slavonic and East European Review* 19, no. 53/54 (1939): 237–64.

Magocsi, Paul Robert, cartographic design by Geoffrey J. Matthews. *Historical Atlas of East Central Europe*. Seattle and London: University of Washington Press, 1993.

Magocsi, Paul Robert. *Historical Atlas of Central Europe: From the Early Fifth Century to the Present*. London: Thames and Hudson, 2002.

Manesson-Mallet, Alain. *Description de l'univers, contenant les différents systèmes du Monde, les Cartes générales & particulières de la Géographie Ancienne & Moderne: Les Plans & les Profils des principales Villes & des autres lieux considérables de la Terre*. Paris: Denys Thierry, 1683.

Manghani, Sunil. *Image Critique and the Fall of the Berlin Wall*. Chicago and London: University of Chicago Press, 2009.

Mariner, J. Theodore. 'Transylvania and Its Seven Castles: A Motor Circuit Through Rumania's New Province of Racial Complexity and Architectural Charm'. *National Geographic* 49, no. 3 (March 1926): 319–52.

Martin, Geoffrey J. 'Paris Peace Conference'. In *The History of Cartography, Volume 6: Cartography of the Twentieth Century*, ed. Mark Monmonier, 1049–53. Chicago: University of Chicago Press, 2015.

Masarýk, Thomas G. *The Problems of Small Nations in the European Crisis*. Inaugural lecture at the University of London, King's College. [London]: Council of International Relations, [1916].

Masarýk, Thomas G. 'Why Germany Wants Peace Now'. *The New Europe* 1 (1916).

Masarýk, Thomas G. *The New Europe* (The Slav Standpoint). London: Eyre & Spottiswoode, 1918.

Matless, David Jonathan Oldfield and Adam Swain. 'Geographically Touring the Eastern Bloc: British Geography, Travel Cultures and the Cold War'. *Transaction of the Institute of British Geographers*, New Series 33, no. 3 (July 2008): 354–75.

Max, Stanley M. 'Cold War on the Danube: The Belgrade Conference of 1948 and Anglo-American Efforts to Reinternationalize the River'. *Diplomatic History* 7, no. 1 (Winter 1983): 57–77.

Mazierska, Ewa Lars Kristensen and Eva Naripea, eds. *Postcolonial Approaches to Eastern European Cinema: Portraying Neighbours on Screen*. London: I.B. Tauris, 2013.

[Mazuchelli, Nina Elizabeth]. *"Magyarland;" Being the Narrative of Our Travels Through the Highlands and Lowlands of Hungary by a Fellow of the Carpathian Society, Author of "The Indian Alps"* . . . *with Illustrations*, 2 vols. London: Sampson Low, Marston, Searle & Rivington, 1881.

Medhurst, Martin J. and Michael A. DeSousa. 'Political Cartoons as Rhetorical Form: A Taxonomy of Graphic Discourse'. *Communication Monographs* 48, no. 3 (1981): 197–236.

Mellini, Peter. 'Not the Guilty Men? *Punch* and Appeasement'. *History Today* 46 (May 1996): 38–44.

Mellini, Peter. 'Not the Guilty Men? *Punch* and Appeasement'. *History Today* 46 (May 1996): 38–44.

Mellish, Liz. 'Bulgarian Ethnic Dress'. In *East Europe, Russia, and the Caucasus*, eds Djurdja Bartlett and Pamela Smith, 412–18. *The Berg Encyclopedia of World Dress and Fashion*, vol. 9. Oxford: Berg, 2010.

Melniková-Papoušková, Naděžda. 'The Changing Face of Prague'. *Geographical Magazine* 2, no. 4 (February 1936): 295–310.

Meurer, Peter H. 'Cartography in the German Lands, 1450–1650'. In *The History of Cartography, Volume 3: Cartography in the European Renaissance*, ed. David Woodward, 1172–245. Chicago and London: The University of Chicago Press, 2007.

Meurer, Peter H. 'Europa Regina. 16th Century Maps of Europe in the Form of a Queen'. *Belgeo: Revue belge de géographie* 3–4 (2008): 1–12, http://journals.openedition.org/belgeo/7711.

Michail, Eugene. *The British and the Balkans: Forming Images of Foreign Lands 1900–1950*. London and New York: Continuum, 2011.

Milanesi, Marica. 'A Forgotten Ptolemy: Harley Codex 3686 in the British Library'. *Imago Mundi* 48 (1996): 43–64.

Milanesi, Marica. *Vincenzo Coronelli, Cosmographer (1650–1718)*. Turnhout: Brepols, 2016.

Miller, Henry J. 'John Leech and the Shaping of the Victorian Cartoon: The Context of Respectability'. *Victorian Periodicals Review* 42, no. 3 (2009): 267–91.

Miller, Henry J. 'The Problem with *Punch*'. *Historical Research* 82 (2009): 285–302.

Miłosz, Czesław. *The Captive Mind*. Trans. Jane Zielonko. London: Secker and Warburg, 1953.

Mirzoeff, Nicholas. 'The Subject of Visual Culture'. In *The Visual Culture Reader*, ed. N. Mirzoeff, 3–23. New York and London: Routledge, 2002.

Mishkova, Diana and Balázs Trencsényi, eds. *European Regions and Boundaries: A Conceptual History*. New York and Oxford: Berghahn, 2017.

Mitchell, W.J.T. *Iconology: Image, Text, Ideology*. Chicago and London: The University of Chicago Press, 1986.

Mitchell, W.J.T. *Picture Theory: Essays on Verbal and Visual Representation*. Chicago and London: The University of Chicago Press, 1994.

Mitchell, W.J.T. 'Word and Image'. In *Critical Terms for Art History*, eds Robert S. Nelson and Richard Shiff, 47–57. Chicago and London: The University of Chicago Press, 1996.

Mitchell, W.J.T. 'Showing Seeing: A Critique of Visual Culture'. *Journal of Visual Culture* 1, no. 2 (2002): 165–81.

Momatiuk, Yva and John Eastcott. 'Slovakia's Spirit of Survival'. *National Geographic* 171, no. 1 (January 1987): 120–46.

Monmonier, Mark. *Maps With the News*. Chicago and London: University of Chicago Press, 1989.

Moore, David Chioni. 'Is the Post- in Postcolonial the Post- in Post-Soviet? Toward a Global Postcolonial Critique'. *PMLA* 116, no. 1 (January 2001): 111–28.

Moore, Frederic. *The Balkan Trail*. London: Smith, Elder & Co., 1906.

Moore, Frederic. 'The Changing Map of the Balkans'. *National Geographic* 24, no. 2 (February 1913): 199–226.

Moore, Norman. 'Edward Browne (1644–1708)'. In *Dictionary of National Biography*, ed. Stephen Leslie, vol. 7, 42–43. London: Smith, Elder & Co, 1886.

Moore, W. Robert. *The Czechoslovakian Cyclorama. National Geographic* 74, no. 2. (August 1938).

Muggeridge, Malcolm. 'America Needs a *Punch*'. *Esquire* 49 (April 1958): 59–61.

Muggeridge, Malcolm. 'Tread Softly, for You Tread on My Jokes'. In *Tread Softly, for You Tread on My Jokes*. London: Collins, 1966.

Muir, Ramsay. *A New School Atlas of Modern History*. London: George Philip & Son, 1911.

Muljačić, Žarko. *Fortisološke studije*. Split: Književni krug, 2011.

Muljačić, Žarko. *Putovanja Alberta Fortisa po Hrvatskoj i Sloveniji (1765–1791)*. Split: Književni krug, 1996.

Münster, Sebastian. *Cosmographey: das ist Beschreibung aller Länder, Herrschafften und für nemesten Stetten des gantzen Erdbodens: sampt ihren Gelegenheiten, Eygenschafften, Religion, Gebräuchen, Geschichten und Handtierungen* [et]c. Basel: Heinrich Petri [1588].

Murawska-Muthesius, Katarzyna. 'Socialist Realism's Self-reference? Cartoons on Art, c. 1950'. In *Style and Socialism: Modernity and Material Culture in Post-War Eastern Europe*, eds Susan E. Reid and David Crowley, 149–67. New York and London: Berg, 2000.

Murawska-Muthesius, Katarzyna. 'Who Drew the Iron Curtain? Images East and West'. In *Borders in Art: Revisiting 'Kunstgeographie'*, ed. K. Murawska-Muthesius, 241–48. Warsaw: Instytut Sztuki PAN, 2000.

Murawska-Muthesius, Katarzyna. 'How to Look at a Warmonger, 'How to See the Self?' Imaging the West in Stalinist Cartoons, 1946–1954'. In *Studies in Language, Literature, and Cultural Mythology in Poland: Investigating 'the Other'*, ed. Elwira Grossmann, 227–57. Lewiston-Lampeter, Wales: The Edwin Meller Press, 2002.

Murawska-Muthesius, Katarzyna. 'Paris From Behind the Iron Curtain'. In *Paris: Capital of the Arts*, ed. Sarah Wilson, 250–61. London: Royal Academy of Arts, 2002.

Murawska-Muthesius, Katarzyna. 'Mapping the New Europe: Cartography, Cartoons and Regimes of Representation'. *Centropa* 4, no. 1 (2004): 4–18.

Murawska-Muthesius, Katarzyna. '1956 in the Cartoonist's Gaze: Fixing the Eastern European Other and Denying the Eastern European Self'. *Third Text* 20, no. 2 (2006): 189–99.

Murawska-Muthesius, Katarzyna. 'Iconotext of Eastern Europe: The "Iron Curtain" Cartography'. In *Grenzen überwindend: Festschrift für Adam S. Labuda zum 60. Geburtstag*, eds Katja Bernhardt and Piotr Piotrowski, 57–70. Berlin: Lukas Verlag, 2006.

Murawska-Muthesius, Katarzyna. 'On Small Nations and Bullied Children: Mr Punch Draws Eastern Europe'. *The Slavonic and East European Review* 84, no. 2 (2006): 279–305.

Murawska-Muthesius, Katarzyna. 'Modernism between Peace and Freedom: Picasso and Others at the Congress of Intellectuals in Wrocław'. In *Cold War Modern: Design 1945–1970*, eds David Crowley and Jane Pavitt, 33–41. London: V&A Publishing, 2008.

Murawska-Muthesius, Katarzyna. 'The Cold-War Traveller's Gaze: Jan Lenica's 1954 Sketchbook of London'. In *Under Eastern Eyes: A Comparative Introduction to East European Travel Writing on Europe*, eds Wendy Bracewell and Alex Drace-Francis, 325–54. Budapest and New York: CEU Press, 2008.

Murawska-Muthesius, Katarzyna. 'The Jyllands Posten Muhammad Cartoons Controversy: Racism and "Cartoon Work" in the Age of the World Wide Web'. In *Racism, Postcolonialism, Europe*, eds Graham Huggan and Ian Law, 148–61. Liverpool: Liverpool University Press, 2009.

Murawska-Muthesius, Katarzyna. 'Mapping Eastern Europe: Cartography and Art History'. *Artl@s Bulletin* 2, no. 2 (Fall 2013): 14–25.

Murawska-Muthesius, Katarzyna. 'Mapmaking as Image-making: The Case of East central Europe'. In *Anti-Atlas: Towards a Critical Area Studies*, eds Wendy Bracewell, Tim Beasley-Murray and Michal Murawski. London: UCL Press, forthcoming.

Murawski, Michał. *The Palace Complex: A Stalinist Skyscraper, Capitalist Warsaw, and a City Transfixed*. Bloomington: IN, 2019.

Murphy, David Thomas. *The Heroic Earth: Geopolitical Thought in Weimar Germany, 1918–1933*. Kent, OH and London: The Kent State University Press, 1997.

Murray, Brian H. 'Introduction: Forms of Travel, Modes of Transport'. In *Travel Writing, Visual Culture and Form, 1760–1900*, eds Mary Henes and Brian H. Murray, 1–18. Basingstoke and New York: Palgrave MacMillan, 2016.

Nash, Geoffrey, ed. *Comte de Gobineau and Orientalism: Selected Eastern Writings*. Trans. Daniel O'Donoghue. New York and London: Routledge. 2009.

Naumann, Friedrich. *Mitteleuropa*. Berlin: Georg Reimer, 1915.

Neuburger, Mary. 'Veils, *Shalvari*, and Matters of Dress: Unravelling the Fabric of Women's Lives in Communist Bulgaria'. In *Style and Socialism: Modernity and Material Culture in Post-War Eastern Europe*, eds Susan E. Reid and David Crowley, 169–88. Oxford and New York: Berg, 2000.

Neuhaus, Jessamyn. 'Colonizing the Coffee Table: The Erasure of Difference in the Representation of Women in National Geographic Magazine'. *American Periodicals* 7 (1997): 1–26.

Neumann, Iver B. *Uses of the Other: "The East" in European Identity Formation*. Manchester: Manchester University Press, 1999.

Nicolson, Adam. 'Hay Beautiful'. Photographs by Rena Effendi. *National Geographic* 224, no. 1 (June 2013): 106–25.

Niezabitowska, Małgorzata. 'Discovering America'. Photos by Tomasz Tomaszewski. *National Geographic* 173, no. 1 (January 1988, Centenary Issue): 44–79.

Nisbet, H. Barry. 'Herder's Conception of Nationhood and Its Influence in Eastern Europe'. In *The German Lands and Eastern Europe: Essays on the History of Their Social, Cultural and Political Relations*, eds Roger Bartlett and Karen Schönwälder, 115–35. Basingstoke: Macmillan, 1999.

Nixon, Paul G. 'A Never Closer Union? The Idea of the European Union in Selected Works of Malcolm Bradbury'. In *The Idea of Europe in Literature*, eds Susanne Fendler and Ruth Wittlinger, 138–55. New York: St Martin's Press, 1999.

Norris, Stephen M. 'Two Worlds: Boris Efimov, Soviet Political Caricature and the Construction of the Long Cold War'. In *The Oxford Handbook of Communist Visual Cultures*, eds Aga Skrodzka, Xiaoning Lu and Katarzyna Marciniak, 520–41. Oxford: Oxford University Press, 2018.

Nycz, Ryszard. 'Forewod'. In *Post-Colonial or Post-Dependence Studies*. Special issue of *Teksty Drugie* 1 (2014): 5–11, http://tekstydrugie.pl/wp- content/uploads/2016/06/t2en_2014_1webCOMB.pdf.

O'Dwyer, Conor. *Coming Out of Communism: The Emergence of LGBT Activism in Eastern Europe*. New York: New York University Press, 2018.

Ó Tuathail, Gearóid. *Critical Geopolitics: The Politics of Writing Global Space*. London: Routledge, 1996.

The Oxford English Dictionary, ed. John Simpson, 20 vols. Oxford: Clarendon Press, 1989.

Paget, John. *Hungary and Transylvania: With Remarks on Their Condition, Social, Political and Economical*. London: John Murray, 1839.

Palmer, Adam. *The Lands Between: A History of East-Central Europe Since the Congress of Vienna*. London: Weidenfeld and Nicolson, 1970.

Palsky, Gilles. 'Emmanuel de Martonne and the Ethnographical Cartography of Central Europe (1917–1920)'. *Imago Mundi* 54, no. 1 (2002): 111–19.

Partington, Gill. 'Dust Jackets'. In *Book Parts*, eds Dennis Duncan and Adam Smyth, 11–21. Oxford: Oxford University Press Roger D., 2019.

Patric, John. 'Czechoslovaks, Yankees of Europe'. *National Geographic* 74, no. 2 (August 1938): 173–225.

Pelizza, Simone. 'The Geopolitics of International Reconstruction: Halford Mackinder and Eastern Europe, 1919–20'. *The International History Review* 38, no. 1 (2016): 174–95.

Petéri, György, ed. *Imagining the West in Eastern Europe and the Soviet Union*. Pittsburgh, Pennsylvania: University of Pittsburgh Press, 2010.

Petersen, Roger D. *Resistance and Rebellion: Lessons From Eastern Europe*. Cambridge and New York: Cambridge University Press, 2001.

Petersen, Roger D. *Understanding Ethnic Violence: Fear, Hatred, and Resentment in Twentieth-Century Eastern Europe*. Cambridge: Cambridge University Press, 2002.

Petronis, Vytautas. *Constructing Lithuania: Ethnic Mapping in Tsarist Russia, ca. 1800–1914*. Stockholm: Acta Universitatis Stockholmiensis, 2007.

The Philosophical Transactions of the Royal Society in London, 1669–1774, accessible online on The Royal Society website, royalsocietypublishing.org/action/doSearch?AllField=edward+brown.

Pickles, John. *A History of Spaces: Cartographic Reason, Mapping and the Geo-coded World*. London and New York: Routledge, 2004.

Piechocki, Katharina N. *Cartographic Humanism: The Making of Modern Europe*. Chicago and London: The University of Chicago Press, 2019.

Piechocki, Katharina N. 'Erroneous Mappings: Ptolemy and the Visualization of Europe's East'. In *Early Modern Cultures of Translation*, eds Jane Tylus and Karen Newman, 76–96. Philadelphia: University of Pennsylvania Press, 2015.

Pinault Sørenesen, Madeleine. 'Étude sur Le Prince et les dessinateurs et graveurs du *Voyage en Sibérie*'. In *Voyage en Sibérie*, ed. Michel Mervaud, vol. 1, 123–226. Oxford: Voltaire Foundation, 2004, 2 vols.

Piotrowska, Roma. 'There Is No Shame in Being Eastern European'. Roma Piotrowska in discussion with Katarzyna Perlak, *Contemporary Lynx*, 7 April 2018, https://contemporarylynx.co.uk/there-is-no-shame-in-being-eastern-european.

Piotrowski, Piotr. *Art and Democracy in Post-Communist Europe*. Trans. Anna Brzyski. London: Reaktion, 2012.

Piotrowski, Piotr. 'Between Real Socialism and Nationalism'. In *Art and Democracy in Post-Communist Europe*. Trans. Anna Brzyski, 155–201. London: Reaktion, 2012.

Piotrowski, Piotr. 'New Museums in New Europe'. In *Art and Democracy in Post-Communist Europe*. Trans. Anna Brzyski, 202–11. London: Reaktion, 2012.

Piotrowski, Piotr. 'East European Art Peripheries Facing Post-Colonial Theory'. *Nonsite.org* (Online Journal in the Humanities), no. 12 (August 2014).

Plass, Ulrich. *Language and History in Theodor W. Adorno's Notes to Literature*. New York: Routledge, 2007.

Plicka, Karol. 'Among Slovakian Mountains'. Photogravure Supplement. *Geographical Magazine* 4, no. 5 (March 1937).

Plicka, Karol. *Slovensko*. Martin: Matica slovenská, 1937.

Popova-Novak, Irina V. 'The Odyssey of National Discovery: Hungarians in Hungary and Abroad, 1750–1850'. In *Under Eastern Eyes: A Comparative Introduction to East European*

Travel Writing on Europe, eds Wendy Bracewell and Alex Drace-Francis, 195–222. Budapest: CEU Press, 2008.

Potts, Alex. 'Sign'. In *Critical Terms for Art History*, eds Robert S. Nelson and Richard Shiff, 17–30. Chicago and London: The University of Chicago Press, 1996.

Povolotskaia, E. 'Politicheskaia satira Kukryniksov'. *Iskusstvo* no. 6 (1949): 35–39.

Pratt, Mary Louise. *Imperial Eyes: Travel Writings and Transculturation*. New York and London: Routledge, 2008.

Prażmowska, Anita J. *Eastern Europe and the Origins of the Second World War*. Basingstoke: Palgrave Macmillan, 2000.

Price, Richard G.G. *A History of 'Punch'*. London: Collins, 1957.

Ptolemy, Claudius. *Cosmographia*. Trans. Jacopo Angeli da Scarpia. Rome: Arnoldus Buckink, 1478.

Ptolemy, Claudius. *Geography*. Trans. Edward Luther Stevenson. New York: Dover Publications, 1991.

Purchla, Jacek and Wolf Tegethoff, eds. *Nation, Style, Modernism*. Cracow: International Cultural Centre, 2006.

Rácz, Istvan. '"A Writer Is Sceptical, Questioning, Dialogic" (And Interview with Malcolm Bradbury)'. *Angol Filológial Tanulmányok/ Hungarian Studies in English* 21 (1990): 99–102.

Radonjić, Nemanja. '"Not Exactly Out of Europe, Yet Somehow on the Fringes of the Orient": Image of the Balkans in the *National Geographic* (1888–2013)'. [In Serbo-Croatian]. *Godišnjak za društvenu istoriju* 3 (2013): 73–97.

Rampley, Matthew. 'Anthropology and the Origins of Art History'. In *Site Specificity: The Ethnographic Turn*, ed. Alex Coles, 138–63. London: Black Dog, 2000.

Rampley, Mathew. 'Peasants in Vienna: Ethnographic Display and the 1873 World's Fair'. *History Yearbook* 42 (2011): 110–32.

Ranke, Winifred, Katharina Klotz and Wilfried Rogasch, eds. *Deutschland im kalten Krieg 1945 bis 1963*. Berlin: Deutsches Historisches Museum, 1992.

Reid, Susan E. and David Crowley, eds. *Style and Socialism: Modernity and Material Culture in Post-War Eastern Europe*. Oxford and New York: Berg, 2000.

Reilly, Maura. '*Ars Homoerotica* / The National Museum in Warsaw (Poland), Curated by Paweł Leszkowicz'. In *Curatorial Activism: Towards an Ethics of Curating*, 196–201. London: Thames and Hudson, 2018.

Reymont, Władysław Stanisław. *The Peasants*. Trans. Michael Henry Dziewicki, 4 vols. London: Jarrolds, 1925–26.

Riedemann, W.O. von. 'Balkan Nomads on the March'. Photographic Supplement. *Geographical Magazine* 5, no. 6 (October 1937): 435–39.

Rose, Gillian. *Feminism and Geography: The Limits of Geographical Knowledge*. Cambridge: Polity, 1993.

Rose, Gillian. 'On the Need to Ask How, Exactly, Is Geography "Visual"?'. *Antipode* 35, no. 2 (March 2003): 212–21.

Roth, Ralf and Henry Jacolin, eds. *Eastern European Railways in Transition: Nineteenth to Twenty-First Centuries*. Farnham: Ashgate, 2013.

Rothenberg, Tamar Y. *Presenting America's World: Strategies of Innocence in 'National Geographic Magazine'*. Aldershot and Burlington, VT: Ashgate, 2007.

Runciman, David. 'Hobbes's Theory of Representation: Anti-Democratic or Proto-Democratic'. In *Political Representation*, eds Ian Shapiro, Susan C. Stokes, Elisabeth Jean Wood and Alexander S. Kirshner, 15–34. Cambridge and New York: Cambridge University Press, 2009.

Ryan, James R. 'Visualizing Imperial Geography: Halford Mackinder and the Colonial Office Visual Instruction Committee, 1902–1911'. *Ecumene* 1, no. 2 (1994): 157–76.

Šafařík, Pawel Josef. *Slovanský Národopis, s mappau*. Prague: Wydawatele, 1842.

Salisbury, Martin. *The Illustrated History of the Dust-Jacket: 1920–1970*. London: Thames and Hudson, 2017.

Şandru, Cristina. *Worlds Apart: A Postcolonial Reading of Post-1945 East-Central European Culture*. Newcastle: Cambridge Scholars Publishing, 2012.

Saunders, Frances Stonor, ed. *The Cultural Cold War: The CIA and the World of Art and Letters*. New York: The New Press, 1999.

Schenk, Frithjof Benjamin. 'Eastern Europe'. In *European Regions and Boundaries: A Conceptual History*, eds Diana Mishkova and Balázs Trencsényi, 188–209. New York and Oxford: Berghahn, 2017.

Schenk, Frithjof Benjamin. 'Mental Maps: the Cognitive Mapping of the Continent as an Object of Research of European History'. *European History Online (EGO)*, 2013, http://ieg-ego.eu/en/threads/theories-and-methods/mental-maps/frithjof-benjamin-schenk-mental-maps-the-cognitive-mapping-of-the-continent-as-an-object-of-research-of-european-history.

Schlager, Carly. *Cold War*, https://coldwarproject2013.weebly.com/index.html.

Schulten, Susan. 'Richard Edes Harrison and the Challenge to American Cartography'. *Imago Mundi* 50 (1998): 174–88.

Schulten, Susan. *The Geographical Imagination in America, 1880–1950*. Chicago and London: The University of Chicago Press, 2001.

Secklehner, Julia. *Artwork of the Month, April 2020: Columbus in der Slovakei by Leopold Wolfgang Rochowanski*, https://craace.com/2020/04/28/artwork-of-the-month-april-2020-columbus-in-der-slovakei-by-leopold-wolfgang-rochowanski.

Seegel, Steven. *Mapping Europe's Borderlands: Russian Cartography in the Age of Empire*. Chicago and London: The University of Chicago Press, 2012.

Seegel, Steven. *Map Men: Transnational Lives and Deaths of Geographers in the Making of East Central Europe*. Chicago and London: The University of Chicago Press, 2018.

Semper, Gottfried. *Der Stil in den technischen und tektonischen Künsten, oder Praktische Aesthetik. Ein Handbuch für Techniker, Künstler und Kunstfreunde*. 2 vols. Frankfurt am Main: Verlag *für* Kunst und Wissenschaft, 1860–63.

Semper, Gottfried. 'Style in the Technical and Tectonic Arts or Practical Aesthetics' (1860–1863). In *The Four Elements of Architecture and Other Writings*, trans. Harry Francis Mallgrave and Wolfgang Herrmann, 181–263. Cambridge: Cambridge University Press, 1989.

'Servia and Montenegro'. *National Geographic* 19, no. 11 (November 1908): 774–89.

Seton-Watson, Hugh and Seton-Watson, Christopher. *The Making of a New Europe: R.W. Seton-Watson and the Last Years of Austria-Hungary*. London: Methuen, 1981.

Seton-Watson, Robert William. *German, Slav, and Magyar: A Study in the Origins of the Great War*. London: Williams & Norgate, 1916.

Seton-Watson, Robert William. *History of the Czechs and Slovaks*. London: Hutchinson and Co, 1943.

Seymour, Charles. 'The End of an Empire: Remnants of Austria-Hungary'. In *What Really Happened at Paris: The Story of the Peace Conference, 1918–1919. By American Delegates*, eds Edward Mandell House and Charles Seymour, 87–111. London: Hodder & Stoughton, 1921.

Shakina, l. 'Politicheskaia satira'. *Iskusstvo* no. 3 (1950): 29–34.

Shaw, Tony. 'The British Popular Press and the Early Cold War'. *History* 83 (1998): 66–85.

Shaw, Tony. 'The Information Research Department of the British Foreign Office and the Korean War, 1950–1953'. *Journal of Contemporary History* 34 (1999): 263–81.

Sherry, James. 'Four Modes of Caricature: Reflections upon a Genre'. *Bulletin of Research in the Humanities* 87, no. 1 (1986–87): 29–62.

Showalter, William Joseph. 'Partitioned Poland'. *National Geographic* 27, no. 1 (January 1915): 88–106.

Showalter, William Joseph. 'The Kingdom of Servia'. *National Geographic* 27, no. 4 (April 1915): 417–32.

Sieger, Robert and Albrecht Penck. 'Zwischeneuropa?'. *Zeitschrift der Gesellschaft für Erdkunde zu Berlin* (1916): 177–80.

Sisson, Robert. 'Freedom Flight from Hungary: A Story in Photographs'. *National Geographic* 111, no. 3 (March 1957): 424–36.

Sitwell, Sacheverell. 'Rumanian Wedding'. *Geographical Magazine* 6, no. 6 (April 1938): 427–40.

Slade Backer, William. 'Down the Danube'. Photos by Richard S. Durrance. *National Geographic* 123, no. 2 (July 1965): 35–79.

Slovar' sovremennogo russkogo iazika, 17 vols. Ed. Vasili, I. Chernyshev Moscow-Leningrad: Izdatel'stvo Akademii Nauk SSSR, 1948–65.

Sowa, Jan. 'Forget Postcolonialism, There's a Class War Ahead'. *Nonsite.org* (Online Journal in the Humanities), no. 12 (August 2014).

Spielmann, Marion H. *The History of 'Punch'*. London: Cassell and Co., 1895.

Spivak, Gayatri Chakravorty. *Outside in the Teaching Machine*. New York: Routledge, 1993.

Spruner, Karl. *Spruners Historisch-Geographischen Hand-Atlas zur Geschichte der Staaten Europa's von Anfang des Mittelalters bis auf die neueste Zeit*. Gotha: J. Peters, 1846.

Stafford, Barbara Maria. *Voyage Into Substance: Art, Science, Nature, and the Illustrated Travel Account, 1760–1840*. Cambridge, MA: MIT Press, 1984.

Stafford, Barbara Maria. *Good Looking: Essays on the Virtue of Images*. Cambridge, MA and London: The MIT Press, 1996.

Stalin, Joseph V. 'Otvet korrespondentu *Pravdy*'. In *Sochinenia*, ed. Robert H. McNeal, 3 vols. Stanford, CA: The Hoover Institute on War, Revolution and Peace, Stanford University, 1967.

Stalin, Joseph V. 'Replies to Questions Put by Mr. Alexander Werth, Moscow, Correspondent of the *Sunday Times*, 24 September 1946'. *Soviet News*, 1947. Quoted after Marxist International Archive, www.marxists.org/reference/archive/stalin/works/1946/09/24.htm.

Starosta, Anita. *Form and Instability: Eastern Europe, Literature, Postimperial Difference*. Evanston, IL: Northwestern University Press, 2016.

Stewart, J.C., ed. *Paul Robeson: Artist and Citizen*. New Brunswick, NJ: Rutgers University Press, 1998.

Stieler, Adolf. *Hand-Atlas über alle Theile der Erde und über das Weltgebäude*. Gotha: Justus Perthes, 1882.

Stoicheva, Tatyana. 'Rates of Exchange: Rates of Constituting Eastern Europe'. In *Britain and Europe*, eds Ludmilla Kostova, Margaret Dobbing and Nick Wadham-Smith, 126–29. Sofia: Petrikov, 1994.

Stoker, Bram. *Dracula*. Westminster: Archibald Constable and Company, 1897.

Stokes, Gale. *The Walls Came Tumbling Down: The Collapse of Communism in Eastern Europe*. Oxford and New York: Oxford University Press, 1993.

Stone, Jeffrey P. *British and American News Maps in the Early Cold War Period, 1945–1955*. Cham, Switzerland: Palgrave Macmillan, 2019.

Surić, Maša, Robert Lončarić, Anica Čuka and Josip Faričić. 'Geological Issues in Alberto Fortis' *Viaggio in Dalmazia* (1774)'. *C.R. Geoscience* 339 (2007): 640–50.

Swift, Jonathan. 'An Account of a Battle Between the Ancient and Modern Books in St. James's Library'. In *A Tale of a Tub*. London: John Nutt, 1704.

Szafarik, P.J. *Slavianskoe narodopisan'e, z kartou*. Trans. O. Bodianski. Moscow: Universitetskaia Tipografia, 1843.

Szafarzyk, P.J. *Słowiański Narodopis*. Trans. Piotr Dahlman. Wrocław: P. Schletter, 1843.

Szafer, Władysław. 'The National Parks in Poland'. *Geographical Magazine* 7, no. 2 (June 1938): 129–40.

Székely, Miklós, ed. *Ephemeral Architecture in Central and Eastern Europe in the 19th and 20th Centuries*. Paris: L'Harmattan, 2015.

Szulc, Tad. 'Poland: The Hope That Never Dies'. Photos by James L. Stanfield. *National Geographic* 173, no. 1 (January 1988, Centenary Issue): 80–121.

Szulc, Tad. 'Dispatches from Eastern Europe'. *National Geographic* 179 (March 1991): 2–59.

Tabori, Paul. 'The Endurance of Hungary'. *Geographical Magazine* 29, no. 19 (February 1957): 505–16.

Tanselle, G. Thomas. *Book-Jackets: Their History, Forms and Use*. Charlottesville: VAL Bibliographical Society of the University of Virginia, 2011.

Thompson, Carl, ed. *The Routledge Companion to Travel Writing*. London: Routledge, 2015.

Thompson, Ewa M. *Imperial Knowledge: Russian Literature and Colonialism*. Wespost, CT, and London: Greenwood Press, 2000.

Tibenský, Ján. *Pavol Jozef Šafárik: život a dielo: hviezda prvej veľkosti v slovanskej vede*. Bratislava: Osvetový ústav, 1975.

Tigges, Wim. *An Anatomy of Literary Nonsense*. Amsterdam: Rodopi, 1988.

Timlich, Karl. *Sammlung merkwürdiger Nationalkostüme des Königreichs Ungarn und Kroatien, nach der Natur gezeichnet in 60 Blättern*. Vienna: Schaumburg, 1816.

Tismaneanu, Vladimir, ed. *The Revolutions of 1989: Rewriting Histories*. London: Routledge, 1999.

Todorova, Maria. *Imagining the Balkans*. New York and Oxford: Oxford University Press, 1997.

Todorova, Maria and Zsuzsa Gille, eds. *Post-Communist Nostalgia*. New York: Berghahn Books, 2010.

Tomić, Milica. *I am Milica Tomić*, 1998/99, https://www.youtube.com/watch?v=b1kagFMbQ5k.

Topping, Margaret. 'Travel Writing and Visual Culture'. In *The Routledge Companion of Travel Writing*, ed. Carl Thompson, 78–88. London: Routledge, 2015.

Tóth, Eszter Zsófia. '"My Work, My Family, and My Car": Women's Memories of Work, Consumerism, and Leisure in Socialist Hungary'. In *Gender Politics and Everyday Life in State Socialist Eastern and Central Europe*, eds Shana Penn and Jill Massino, 33–44. New York: Palgrave, 2009.

Townley-Fullam, C. 'Hungary: A Land of Shepherd Kings'. *National Geographic* 26, no. 4 (October 1914): 310–93.

Traub, Valerie. 'Mapping the Global Body'. In *Early Modern Visual Culture: Representation, Race and Empire in Renaissance England*, eds Peter Erickson and Clark Hulse, 44–97. Philadelphia: Pennsylvania University Press, 2000.

'Travels into Dalmatia. In a Series of Letters from Abbé Alberto Fortis, &c.'. *Gentleman's Magazine* 43 (April 1778): 181.

Tudeer, Lauri O. Th. 'On the Origins of the Maps Attached to Ptolemy's Geography'. *The Journal of Hellenic Studies* 27 (1917): 62–76.

Turnau, Irena. *History of Dress in Central and Eastern Europe From the Sixteenth to the Eighteenth Century*. Warsaw: Institute of the History of Material Cultures, Polish Academy of Sciences, 1991.

Ugrešić, Dubravka. *The Museum of Unconditional Surrender*. London: Phoenix, 1999.

Unstead, J.F. 'The Belt of Political Change in Europe'. *The Scottish Geographical Magazine* 39 (1923): 183–92.

Vecellio, Cesare. *Habiti antichi et moderni di tutto il mondo; di nuovo accresciuti di molte figure. Vestitus antiquorum recentiorumque totius orbis*. Venice: Gio. Bernardo Sessa, 1598.

Veličković, Vedrana. *Eastern Europeans in Contemporary Literature and Culture: Imagining New Europe*. London: Palgrave Macmillan/ Springer Nature Ltd, 2019.

Vesilind, Priit J. 'The Baltic: Arena of Power'. *National Geographic* 175, no. 5 (May 1989): 602–36.

Vosburgh, Frederick C. 'Berlin, Island in a Soviet Sea'. Photos by Volkmar Wentzel. *National Geographic* 100, no. 5 (November 1951): 689–704.

Vujakovic, Peter. '"A New Map Is Unrolling Before Us": Cartography in News Media Representations of Post-Cold War Europe'. *The Cartographic Journal* 36, no. 1 (June 1999): 43–57.

Vujakovic, Peter. 'Maps as Political Cartoons'. In *The History of Cartography, Volume 6: Cartography in the Twentieth Century*, ed. Mark Monmonier, 1162–65. Chicago and London: University of Chicago Press, 2015.

Wagner, Peter. *Reading Iconotexts: From Swift to the French Revolution*. London: Reaktion, 1995.

Waldseemüller, Martin. *Geographia*. Strasbourg: Johann Schott, 1513.

Welters, Linda. 'Differences and Similarities in Ethnic Dress in East Europe, Russia, and the Caucasus'. In *East Europe, Russia, and the Caucasus*, ed. Djurdja Bartlett and Pamela Smith, 37–71. *The Berg Encyclopedia of World Dress and Fashion*, vol. 9. Oxford: Berg, 2010.

Werdhorn, Manfred. 'A Contrarian's Approach to Peace'. In *Churchill as Peacemaker*, ed. James W. Muller, 24–53. Cambridge and New York: Woodrow Wilson Centre Press and Cambridge University Press, 2002.

Werner, Elke Anna. 'Anthropomorphic Maps: On the Aesthetic Form and Political Function of Body Metaphors in the Early Modern Discourse'. In *The Anthropomorphic Lens. Anthropomorphism, Microcosmism and Analogy in Early Modern Thought and Visual Arts*, eds W.S. Melion, B. Rothstein, M. Weemans, 251–72. Leiden: Brill, 2015.

West, Shearer. *Portraiture*. Oxford and New York: Oxford University Press, 2004.

Western Europe. *Oxford Regional Economic Atlas*. Oxford: Clarendon Press, 1971.

White, Hayden. 'Historiography and Historiophoty'. *The American Historical Review* 93, no. 5 (1988): 1193–99.

Whiting Fox, Edward, ed., with the assistance of S. Deighton. *Atlas of European History*. New York: Oxford University Press, 1957.

Widawski, Krzysztof and Jerzy Widakowski, eds. *The Geography of Tourism of Central and Eastern European Countries*, 2nd ed. Cham, Switzerland: Springer, 2017.

Williams, Dominic. '*Punch* and the Pogroms: Eastern Atrocities in John Tenniel's Political Cartoons, 1876–1896'. *RACAR: revue d'art canadienne/Canadian Art Review* 42, no. 1 (2017): 32–47.

Williams, Maynard Owen. 'The Poland of the Present'. *National Geographic* 63, no. 3 (March 1933): 319–43.

Williams, Maynard Owen. 'When Czechoslovakia Puts a Falcon Feather in Its Cap'. *National Geographic* 63, no. 3 (March 1933): 40–49.

Williamson, David. 'The New Warsaw: Rebuilding the Old and New City'. *Geographical Magazine* 38, no. 8 (December 1965): 596–607.

Wilson, Joseph. *A History of Mountains, Geographical and Mineralogical . . . to Accompany a Picturesque View of the Principal Mountains of the World . . . Painted and Published by Robert Andrew Riddell*. London: T. Bensley, 1809.

Windt, Harry De. *Through Savage Europe: Being the Narrative of a Journey (Undertaken as Special Correspondent of the "Westminster Gazette"), Throughout the Balkan States and European Russia*. London: T. Fischer Unwin, 1907.

Wintle, Michael. *The Image of Europe: Visualizing Europe in Cartography and Iconography Throughout the Ages*. Cambridge: Cambridge University Press, 2009.

Wolff, Larry. *Inventing Eastern Europe: The Map of Civilization on the Mind of the Enlightenment*. Stanford, CA: Stanford University Press, 1994.

Wolff, Larry. *Venice and the Slavs: The Discovery of Dalmatia in the Age of the Enlightenment*. Stanford: Stanford University Press, 2001.

Wolff, Larry. 'The Global Perspective of Enlightened Travellers: Philosophic Geography from Siberia to the Pacific Ocean'. *European Review of History – Revue européene d'histoire* 13, no. 3 (2006): 437–53.

Wolff, Larry. 'The Traveller's View of Central Europe: Gradual Transitions and Degree of Differences in European Borderlands'. In *Shatterzone of Empires: Coexistence and Violence in the German, Habsburg, Russian and Ottoman Borderlands*, eds Omer Bartow and Eric D. Weitz, 23–71. Bloomington, IN: Indiana University Press, 2013.

Wolff, Larry. *Mental Mapping and Eastern Europe*, 12th Södertörn Lectures. Huddinge. Sweden: Södertörn University, 2016.

Wolff, Larry. *Woodrow Wilson and the Reimagining of Eastern Europe*. Stanford, CA: Stanford University Press, 2020.

Womack, Peter. 'The Writing of Travel'. In *A Companion to English Renaissance and Culture*, ed. Michael Hathaway, 148–60. Malden: Blackwell, 2000.

Woodward, David, ed. *Art and Cartography: Six Historical Essays*. Chicago and London: University of Chicago Press, 1987.

Woodward, David. 'Introduction'. In *Art and Cartography*, ed. David Woodward, 1–9. Chicago and London: University of Chicago Press, 1987.

The World Today and Yesterday: Europe as It Looks Today, Maps of the New Countries, What the New Treaties Mean. Chicago: Rand McNally & Co., c. 1919.

Youngs, Tim, ed. *The Cambridge Introduction to Travel Writing*. Cambridge: Cambridge University Press, 2013.

Zarycki, Tomasz. *Ideologies of Eastness in Central and Eastern Europe*. New York and London: Routledge, 2014.

Zeigler, Donald J. 'Post-Communist Eastern Europe and the Cartography of Independence'. *Political Geography* 21, no. 5 (2002): 671–86.

Zeissig, Hans, ed. *Neuer Geschichts- und Kulturatlas von der Urzeit zur Gegenwart*. Hamburg, Frankfurt and Munich: Atlantik Verlag, 1950.

Index

Note: Page numbers in *italics* indicate a figure on the corresponding page.

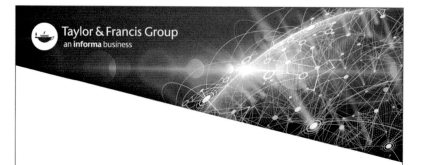